SING OF MARY

D0705908

Sing of Mary

Giving Voice to
Marian Theology and Devotion

Stephanie A. Budwey

A Michael Glazier Book

LITURGICAL PRESS
Collegeville, Minnesota

www.litpress.org

A Michael Glazier Book published by Liturgical Press

Cover design by Jodi Hendrickson. Cover photo: The Annunciation to the Blessed Virgin Mary, a stained-glass window in the Lady Chapel of the Society of St. John the Evangelist, Cambridge, Mass. Used by permission.

Excerpt from the English translation of *Rite of Funerals* © 1970 (superseded), International Commission on English in the Liturgy Corporation. All rights reserved.

Unless otherwise indicated, excerpts from documents of the Second Vatican Council are from *Vatican Council II: The Conciliar and Postconciliar Documents*, edited by Austin Flannery, OP, © 1996. Used with permission of Liturgical Press, Collegeville, Minnesota.

Unless otherwise indicated, Scripture texts in this work are taken from the *New Revised Standard Version Bible*, © 1989, Division of Christian Education of the National Council of the Churches of Christ in the United States of America. Used by permission. All rights reserved.

| 1 | 2 | 3 | 4 | 5 | 6 | 7 | 8 | 9 |

Library of Congress Cataloging-in-Publication Data

Budwey, Stephanie A.
   Sing of Mary : giving voice to Marian theology and devotion / By Stephanie A. Budwey.
       pages   cm
   "A Michael Glazier book."
   Includes bibliographical references.
   ISBN 978-0-8146-8268-5 — ISBN 978-0-8146-8293-7 (ebook)
   1. Mary, Blessed Virgin, Saint.   2. Mary, Blessed Virgin, Saint—Devotion to.
I. Title.

BT603.B83   2014
232.91—dc23
                                       2014020831

To my mother, Rita, and my grandmother, Effie, who have always supported me. They taught me how to pray the rosary and the importance of devotion to the Blessed Virgin Mary.

Contents

Figures

Acknowledgments

First and foremost, I want to thank Liturgical Press for supporting my work. Thank you to Hans Christoffersen for guiding me through this process and giving me this amazing opportunity to share my work on Mary. Thank you for your interest in my work from the very beginning and for your incredible kindness, support, and patience. I could not have asked for a better experience in working with an editor than in working with you, and I can't thank you enough for that. Thank you also to Bill Kauffmann, Colleen Stiller, and especially to Patrick McGowan for his tremendous work during the copyediting process. His outstanding attention to detail was a remarkable help in getting the manuscript ready.

I want to thank Dr. Sharon Elkins who introduced me to the study of Mary during my time at Wellesley College, which was further enriched by my study of Mariology with Dr. Margaret Guider during the first semester of coursework of my doctorate. It was the final presentation for Dr. Guider's class that began the work of my dissertation, which is the foundation of this work. I also want to thank the Boston University School of Theology community under the leadership of Dean Mary Elizabeth Moore, to Anastasia Kidd, and to all the members of my dissertation committee: Dr. Karen Westerfield Tucker, Dr. Andrew Shenton, Dr. Carl P. Daw, Jr., Dr. Phillis Sheppard, and Dr. Francine Cardman. I especially want to thank Dr. Westerfield Tucker and Dr. Daw for all of their helpful revisions and for their support and encouragement throughout this entire process; I cannot thank you enough for your continued advice and friendship that has continued past your roles as "advisor." It means the world to me.

xiii

Thanks to those who helped to shape this work along the way, offering helpful feedback. I would like to particularly thank the music seminar of the North American Academy of Liturgy, who heard a presentation on the early results of this study in January 2011. I would also like to thank the Hymn Society in the United States and Canada, which gave me the opportunity to present my work in various stages at their Research-in-Progress Posters Session in July 2010 and the Emerging Scholar Forum in July 2011. I would also like to thank them for the support of the McElrath-Eskew Research Fund which helped to fund this work. Special thanks to Dr. Deborah Carlton Loftis, Tina Schneider, and Dr. Robin Knowles Wallace for their helpful feedback and continued support.

I am most grateful to the library staffs at both Boston University and Boston College for all of their help in my quest to obtain so many hymnals. I would especially like to thank Justine Sundaram at the John J. Burns Library at Boston College. Her help was invaluable to having the opportunity to survey some of the rare hymnals in the Liturgy and Life Collection.

To all my friends and family—both in the United States and Germany—who are too numerous to name: thank you from the bottom of my heart for all of your support throughout this process. Special thanks to Dr. Peter Scagnelli and Chris Grady who helped me to crystallize the idea of the dissertation over dinner at La Cantina, and to Peter for always having the answer to whatever question I might throw his way. Many, many thanks to Dr. Ryan Danker, my dear friend through the doctoral process and now my dear colleague in the publication process. To Benjamin Mead for his words of encouragement, and to Sean Glenn for your constant support and late night conversations. And to Katja Lang for your constant friendship, encouragement, and support, which has been such a source of strength for me, especially at the end of the publication process. Ohne Dich hätte ich das nicht machen können. Thank you especially to my mother, Rita, my father, Michael (thank you for all of the scans along the way!), my brother, Mike, my grandmother, Effie, and also to my grandfather, Alvin, who passed away during my dissertation process and to whom my dissertation is dedicated. I cannot begin to thank you enough for all of your love and support, and for all the prayers, novenas, and rosaries.

Thank you to Lauren L. Murphy at Liturgical Press for her help in securing permissions, to all the authors and composers who personally corresponded with me about the use of their work, and to all the publishers who helped me in obtaining the proper permissions. Special thanks to Carl Daw, Adam Tice, Alan Hommerding, Mary Frances Fleischaker, Catherine Silvia (Ray Silvia's wife), John Dunn of the Boston Boy Choir, Bishop Shane B. Janzen, Wayne Leupold, Susan Gilbert at Hope Publishing Company, and Kyle Cothern at GIA Publications.

The following works are in the public domain:

"Amours, qui bien set enchanter"
"At the cross her station keeping"
"Ave Maria! thou Virgin and Mother"
"The clouds hang thick o'er Israel's camp"
Concordi lætitia
"Daily, daily sing to Mary"
"Daughter of a mighty Father"
"The God whom earth and sea and sky"
"Green are the leaves"
"Hail Queen of Heaven, the Ocean Star"
"Hail Queen of the Heavens: hail Mistress of earth"
"Hail! Thou first begotten daughter"
"Hail, Virgin dearest Mary!"
"How pure, how frail, and white"
"I'll sing a hymn to Mary"
"Immaculate Mary, our hearts"
"Look down, O Mother Mary"
"Maiden Mother, meek and mild"
"Mary Immaculate, Star of the Morning"
"Mary the dawn"
"Memorare"
"Most noble Queen of Victory"
"Mother dear, oh pray for me"
"Mother dearest, Mother fairest"
"Mother Mary at thine altar"
"Mother Mary, Queen most sweet"

"O Heart of Mary pure and fair"
"O Maiden, Mother mild!"
"O Mary, my Mother, most tender, most mild"
"O Mother blest! whom God bestows"
"O Mother! I could weep for mirth"
"O purest of creatures"
"O Queen of the Holy Rosary"
O sanctissima
"Oh! turn to Jesus, Mother, turn"
"On this day, O beautiful Mother"
"Queen and Mother! many hearts"
"Remember, holy Mary"
Salve, mater misericordiae, from *Cantate et Iubilate Deo*
"Sing, sing, ye angel bands"
Sub tuum praesidium ("We fly to your patronage"). The translation used in this work is in the public domain.
"This is the image of our Queen"
"What a sea of tears and sorrows"
"What mortal tongue can sing thy praise"
"Whither thus in holy rapture"
"Wilt thou look upon me, Mother"

The following works are used with the kind permission of the copyright holders:

Excerpts from Stephanie A. Budwey, "Mary, Star of Hope: Marian Congregational Song as an Expression of Devotion to the Blessed Virgin Mary in the United States from 1854 to 2010," *The Hymn* 63, no. 2 (Spring 2012): 7–17. Used by permission.

"By God kept pure," © 2007; "Come, sing a home and family," © 1994; "Sing 'Ave!,'" © 2002; "We sing with holy Mary," © 2008. All by Alan J. Hommerding. Used by permission of World Library Publications, wlpmusic.com. All rights reserved.

"Canticle of the Turning," Rory Cooney, #624 in *Worship* 4th ed., © 1990; "Come, join in Mary's prophet-song," Adam Tice, from *Woven into Harmony,* © 2009; "Mary, first among believers," Delores Dufner, #897 in *Worship* 4th ed., © 2011. GIA Publications, Inc. 7404 S. Mason Ave., Chicago, IL 60638 www.giamusic .com 800.442.1358. All rights reserved. Used by permission.

"Gentle Joseph heard a warning," Words: Carl P. Daw, Jr., © 1990 Hope Publishing Company, Carol Stream, IL 60188. All rights reserved. Used by permission.

"Hail Mary: Gentle Woman" (81283) © 1975, 1978, Carey Landry and OCP, 5536 NE Hassalo, Portland, OR 97213. All rights reserved. Used with permission.

"Mary, Mary, quite contrary," Words: Fred Kaan, © 1999 Hope Publishing Company, Carol Stream, IL 60188. All rights reserved. Used by permission.

"My soul proclaims with wonder," Words: Carl P. Daw, Jr., © 1989 Hope Publishing Company, Carol Stream, IL 60188. All rights reserved. Used by permission.

"Sing of Mary, pure and lowly," © Estate of Father Roland F. Palmer, SSJE. Courtesy of Bishop Shane B. Janzen, metropolitan and bishop ordinary, the Anglican Catholic Church of Canada.

"Sing we a song/Magnificat now," Words: Fred Kaan. © 1968 Hope Publishing Company, Carol Stream, IL 60188. All rights reserved. Used by permission.

Permission for the following was in process at the time of publication:

"We remember Mary," Edith Sinclair Downing, Courtesy Wayne Leupold. © 2009 by Wayne Leupold Editions, Inc.

Attempts to obtain permission have been made for the following:

"Lullaby of the Spirit," Ray Silvia-F.E.L./Lorenz Company.

"Mary, woman of the promise," Mary Frances Fleischaker, © 1988. Copyright held by Selah Publishing Co., Inc.

Preface

O Higher Than the Cherubim, More Glorious Than the Seraphim[1]

Mary was able to turn a stable into a home for Jesus, with poor swad-dling clothes and an abundance of love. She is the handmaid of the Father who sings his praises. She is the friend who is ever concerned that wine not be lacking in our lives. She is the woman whose heart was pierced by a sword and who understands all our pain. As mother of all, she is a sign of hope for peoples suffering the birth pangs of justice. She is the missionary who draws near to us and accompanies us throughout life, opening our hearts to faith by her maternal love. As a true mother, she walks at our side, she shares our struggles and she constantly surrounds us with God's love. . . . As she did with Juan Diego, Mary offers [her children] maternal comfort and love, and whispers in their ear: "Let your heart not be troubled. . . . Am I not here, who am your Mother?"[2]

—Pope Francis, *Evangelii Gaudium*

1. From the second stanza of #886, "Ye Watchers and Ye Holy Ones," in *Worship*, ed. Kelly Dobbs-Mickus, 4th ed. (Chicago: GIA Publications, 2011). This stanza is "a paraphrase of the *theotokion* 'Hymn to the Mother of God.'" See Marilyn Kay Stulken and Catherine Salika, *Hymnal Companion to Worship*, 3rd ed. (Chicago: GIA Publications, 1998), 417.

2. Francis, *Evangelii Gaudium* (On the Proclamation of the Gospel in Today's World), November 2013, 286, http://w2.vatican.va/content/francesco/en /apost_exhortations/documents/papa-francesco_esortazione-ap_20131124 _evangelii-gaudium.html, accessed June 2, 2014.

Introduction and Statement of the Problem

Throughout the history of Christianity, Mary has been a beacon of hope to many who look to her for help during difficult times, from a man dying of AIDS praying to her for a cure in Lourdes[3] to Christians in Algeria living under her gaze while working to live in peace with their Muslim sisters and brothers.[4] Today, Pope Francis writes of the importance of Mary in the Church, calling her "The Star of the New Evangelization."[5] He describes how in Mary, the "interplay of justice and tenderness, of contemplation and concern for others, is what makes the ecclesial community look to Mary as a model of evangelization."[6]

While Christians have always prayed to Mary, they have also sung to her in times of joy and sorrow. From the earliest hymn to Mary—the third-century *Sub tuum praesidium*—to hymns to Mary that are still being written today such as Adam Tice's 2005 text "Come, join in Mary's prophet-song," Christians find hope, solace, and inspiration in singing to the Blessed Mother. The "interplay of justice and tenderness, of contemplation and concern for others" that Francis speaks of is most clearly on display in Mary's *Magnificat*, which continues to challenge Christians to action today.

The notion of Mary serving as "a star of hope" and guiding pilgrims on the "often dark and stormy"[7] journey of life is reminiscent of a popular congregational song to Mary, "Mother dearest, Mother fairest":

1. Mother dearest, Mother fairest,
    Help of all who call on thee,
    Virgin purest, brightest, rarest,
    Help us, help, we cry to thee.

---

3. Randy Shilts, *And the Band Played On: Politics, People and the AIDS Epidemic* (New York: St. Martin's Griffin, 1987), 537–38.

4. John W. Kiser, *The Monks of Tibhirine: Faith, Love, and Terror in Algeria* (New York: St. Martin's Griffin, 2002), 82.

5. Francis, *Evangelii Gaudium*, 287.

6. Ibid., 288.

7. Benedict XVI, *Spe Salvi*, November 30, 2007, 49, The Holy See, http://www.vatican.va/holy_father/benedict_xvi/encyclicals/documents/hf_ben-xvi_enc_20071130_spe-salvi_en.html, accessed June 2014.

> **Refrain:** Mary, help us, help, we pray;
> Mary, help us, help, we pray;
> Help us in all care and sorrow, Mary, help us, help, we pray.[8]

First published in the *Wreath of Mary* in 1883 under the caption "Our Lady of Help," this text is paradigmatic of what Marian congregational song looked like in the late nineteenth and early twentieth centuries.[9] Although these Marian congregational songs were very popular to those who sang them, they have often been overlooked, criticized, or dismissed by academics as being too sentimental, lacking sound theological content, and focusing more on individualistic piety than corporate worship. While some of these criticisms may be true, in looking at the congregational songs of the late nineteenth and early twentieth centuries, liturgical scholar Bernard Botte wrote:

> In the meantime the faithful prayed as best they could, and on their own. The only times they prayed together was when the rosary was recited aloud or when hymns were sung. Much has been said mocking these hymns; and it's true that several were ridiculous. It would perhaps be amusing to compile an anthology of this literature, but to tear them apart is too easy, and, really, it's unjust. Thousands of simple people have found nourishment for their piety in those naïve stanzas. By singing them together they were able to experience a moment when they were a fraternal community of believers and not an anonymous crowd like travelers brought together by chance in the lobby of a train station. The scandal doesn't lie in Christians singing these hymns, but rather in their not having anything else to nourish their faith and piety. For we must admit that preaching was at its lowest level in those days.[10]

---

8. "Mother dearest, Mother fairest," Hymnary.org, http://www.hymnary.org /text/mother_dearest_mother_fairest, accessed April 2014. Taken from #152 in *American Catholic Hymnal: An Extensive Collection of Hymns, Latin Chants, and Sacred Songs for Church, School, and Home, Including Gregorian Masses, Vesper Psalms, Litanies*, ed. Marist Brothers (New York: P.J. Kenedy & Sons, 1913), 187.

9. J. Vincent Higginson, *Handbook for American Catholic Hymnals* (New York: The Hymn Society of America, 1976), 85. The text might have been suggested by the refrain of a text by Frederick Faber, "O flower of grace, divinest flower" printed in Police's *Parochial Hymn Book* in 1880 (ibid.).

10. Bernard Botte, *From Silence to Participation: An Insider's View of Liturgical Renewal*, trans. John Sullivan (Washington, DC: The Pastoral Press, 1988), 3–4.

This body of Marian congregational song was very dear to the hearts of the faithful, so it is important not to look at them as others have by taking them at face value but rather to look at the contexts out of which they came and what needs they fulfilled for those who sang them in order to understand why they were written. The purpose of this study is to see Marian theology and devotion through the hermeneutical lens of hymnody. This allows a unique perspective into Marian theology and devotion as these were the hymns that were actually being sung by the people in the pews. Looking at these texts alongside the "official" doctrines allows an insight into the corresponding lived theology and devotions at the time.

Definitions

First, a few definitions of the terminology that will be used throughout this study. In his definition, Edward Foley writes that sacred music is "(1) the preferred term in universal documents of the RC Church for music composed for 'the celebration of divine worship.' (2) Liturgical music. (3) A general term for religious music not necessarily intended for use in worship, especially that which is considered art music, e.g., the *Manzoni Requiem* by Verdi."[11] Since this study focuses on music that was sung by congregations during liturgical services, the first two definitions are used to clarify what is meant by "sacred music."

To focus on a more specific aspect of sacred music, St. Augustine defines a hymn as "a song of praise to God,"[12] which is extended to include the praise of Mary and/or the communion of saints who act as mediators to God. At the outset of the study, the decision had to be made whether to discuss "Marian hymnody" or "Marian congregational song." Dr. Carl P. Daw, Jr., was consulted, and he suggested that a decision needed to be made whether

11. Edward Foley, "Sacred music [Latin *musica sacra*]," in *Worship Music: A Concise Dictionary*, ed. Edward Foley (Collegeville, MN: Liturgical Press, 2000), 269.

12. Stephen A. Marini, *Sacred Song in America: Religion, Music, and Public Culture* (Urbana: University of Illinois Press, 2003), 7.

to focus on (a) what people are likely to have experienced in congregational singing and in songs for personal devotional practice or (b) the full range of what was created for their use (whether it was actually used or not). The experiential emphasis would make the "congregational song" terminology more pertinent, while "hymnody" would embrace a greater range of material (e.g., texts that might have been written to be sung but were encountered as devotional poetry rather than as part of the singing tradition). There is, of course, much overlap in how the terms are used.[13]

This study will for the most part use the term "congregational song" instead of "hymnody" as "Marian congregational song" includes hymns, chants, and contemporary songs.[14] Therefore, Marian congregational songs are defined as songs of praise where the majority of the texts are directed toward Mary, come from Mary or are attributed to Mary (e.g., the *Magnificat*, which is directed to God but was spoken by Mary), or are about Mary and are written in order to be sung in liturgical settings by a congregation, and not by a choir alone.[15]

While "Marian congregational song" will be used in chapters 4 through 8, in chapters 1 through 3 the term "Marian hymnody" will be used. The reason "Marian hymnody" will be used mostly before the nineteenth century and "Marian congregational song" afterward is to differentiate between what is sung by the laity and what was most likely sung by a choir or monks chanting the Divine Office. Since we are not entirely sure who sang what during the period covered in chapters 1 through 3, it seemed appropriate to use "Marian hymnody."[16]

13. Carl P. Daw, Jr., e-mail message to author, August 9, 2010.

14. In cases where other authors have used the word "hymn," their language will be maintained.

15. Thanks to Anthony Ruff, OSB, for his help in clarifying this definition.

16. Daw points out that making this distinction between Marian hymnody before the nineteenth century and Marian congregational song after "might help to communicate that the singers were not ordinarily laypersons attending Mass. The rub, of course, is that when a group of monks are singing their offices, these hymns are congregational, though a specialized sort of congregation. There is also the consideration that there existed what might be called 'popular Marian hymnody' sung by laypersons in extra-liturgical settings. In addition, Anthony Ruff has called attention to the congregational song of Austrian RC's during the

As noted above, the specific focus of this study is on songs that are sung in liturgical settings, and to define what classifies as "liturgy," James Empereur's definition is used:

> We use the word liturgy . . . in a somewhat equivocal manner, since it is impossible to do otherwise today. Our use is almost always broader than the Eucharist and is never limited to the juridical reality. It is not the same as private prayer. Our usual use of the term liturgy will refer to the rites of the church in the approved ordering. But our overarching definition of liturgy is more inclusive. Thus, we see no need to make use of the category, *paraliturgical*. We consider worship often so designated, e.g., a community's celebration of the Stations of the Cross, to be true liturgy. Such services may not have the same kind of approval as do the rites of baptism and marriage. But to the extent that they are instances of the church coming to an event of offering itself to God in an assembly, they are authentic acts of liturgy. In this sense, liturgy means for us the symbolic articulation of the Christian community's relationship with its God in communal ritual activity.[17]

This definition of the liturgy is extremely important to this study because the laity did not have much of an opportunity to sing during the Mass before Vatican II; rather, most of their singing was done at services outside of the Mass (what have in the past been termed "paraliturgical")—such as Benediction, novenas, and the Stations of the Cross—and this type of service is where many of the Marian congregational songs were sung.

Finally, for a definition of a hymnal, Donald Boccardi's designation is used that a hymnal is "a collection of hymns and service

---

Counter-reformation and before." While Daw describes this situation as "far from monolithic," this system seemed to do the best job of accurately describing what was sung by the laity or not. The quotes are taken from Carl P. Daw, Jr., e-mail message to author, October 26, 2011.

17. James Empereur and Christopher Kiesling, *The Liturgy That Does Justice* (Collegeville, MN: Liturgical Press, 1990), viii, as quoted in James Empereur, "Popular Piety and the Liturgy: Principles and Guidelines," in *Directory on Popular Piety and the Liturgy: Principles and Guidelines; A Commentary*, ed. Peter C. Phan (Collegeville, MN: Liturgical Press, 2005), 12. Thanks to Mary Frances Fleischaker for pointing to this source regarding what is considered "liturgy."

music written by a variety of composers for a variety of occasions meant for congregational singing."[18] This study, however, precludes looking at hymnals created exclusively for choirs that are not meant for congregational singing.

Significance of the Problem

The study of liturgical texts, and congregational songs in particular, allows a window into the thoughts and prayers of particular people at a certain place and time. To the question of why one should spend the time studying Marian congregational song, Joyce Ann Zimmerman provides an apt answer: "Unlike most other texts . . . liturgical texts hold meaning that has living and salvific implications. Thus the interpretation of liturgical texts is hardly a moot or simply academic exercise. A deeper grasp of the liturgical text affords us a greater insight into the very meaning of our lives. This is what is at stake."[19] Such a complex task requires a multifaceted approach; the case of Marian congregational song's mediation of theology and devotion is no exception. It is only in recent years that academicians such as Lawrence Hoffman have begun to apply such an approach to the liturgy; thus there is still the need to look at Marian theology and devotion with a holistic methodology.[20]

Dom Lambert Beauduin has said very clearly that the liturgy is the "theology of the people."[21] This means that the texts that are prayed and sung during a liturgy are what help to shape the theology of the faithful, therefore carrying great significance in their spiritual formation. With the understanding of the impact that congregational songs can have, the goal of this study is to do more than simply look

18. Donald Boccardi, *The History of American Catholic Hymnals Since Vatican II* (Chicago: GIA Publications, 2001), xiii.

19. Joyce Ann Zimmerman, *Liturgy and Hermeneutics*, American Essays in Liturgy (Collegeville, MN: Liturgical Press, 1999), 21.

20. Lawrence A. Hoffman, *Beyond the Text: A Holistic Approach to Liturgy* (Bloomington, IN: Indiana University Press, 1987). A further discussion of Hoffman's methodology will follow.

21. Lambert Beauduin, *Liturgy the Life of the Church*, trans. Virgil Michel (Collegeville, MN: Liturgical Press, 1926), 88.

at the texts, but rather, as Robert Orsi discusses, to look at religion "as a network of relationships between heaven and earth involving humans of all ages and many different sacred figures together. These relationships have all the complexities—all the hopes, evasions, love, fear, denial, projections, misunderstandings, and so on—of relationships between humans."[22] These relationships are forged through the communion of saints (of which Mary is a member), creating "bonds within families and between heaven and earth."[23] This study helps to show how Marian congregational song has acted as a mediator for these relationships between humans and Mary.

The singing of congregational songs is one such way to assist not only the creation of these bonds but also to facilitate sacred presence. Orsi describes how art may be used in such a way: "Encounters with images of the Virgin are encounters with presence. The whole range of emotion and behavior that is possible when persons are present to each other in one place characterizes these encounters too."[24] It seems possible, then, that much in the same way that visual art can serve as a point of encounter facilitating presence, so too can congregational song, leading to the notion of congregational song as being sacramental.[25] One can also apply Hans Urs von Balthasar's idea of seeing the "form," or Christ, the visible presence of the invisible God.[26] Music, which is finite, is a sacramental means to experience God, the infinite.

In looking at Marian congregational song in the United States after Vatican II, this study explores the possible correlation between

22. Robert A. Orsi, *Between Heaven and Earth: The Religious Worlds People Make and the Scholars Who Study Them* (Princeton and Oxford: Oxford University Press, 2005), 2.

23. Ibid., 13. This is a similar notion to what Ann Taves describes as a "Household of Faith." See Ann Taves, *The Household of Faith: Roman Catholic Devotions in Mid-Nineteenth Century America* (Notre Dame, IN: University of Notre Dame Press, 1986). Her work will be explored further in chap. 5.

24. Orsi, *Between Heaven and Earth*, 50.

25. Albert L. Blackwell, *The Sacred in Music* (Louisville, KY: Westminster John Knox Press, 1999).

26. Hans Urs von Balthasar, *The Glory of the Lord: A Theological Aesthetics*, vol. 1, *Seeing the Form*, ed. Joseph Fessio and John Riches, trans. Erasmo Leiva-Merikakis (San Francisco, CA: Ignatius Press, 1982).

the post–Vatican II decline in Marian congregational song and a perceived decline in the desire for the sacred presence of Mary from the hierarchy, who "did so little to prepare ordinary Catholics for the [post–Vatican II] changes" as described by Orsi: "One day the saints disappeared, the rosaries stopped, the novenas ended, just like that. This provoked resistance and confusion, and in turn this resistance in the parishes to the new agenda heightened the resolve of its advocates."[27] As Orsi points out, those who had already created a strong bond with the Virgin Mary were not going to give up that relationship without a fight. The hierarchy may be able to control a lot, but they cannot completely control anyone's personal piety.[28]

By using a holistic methodology, this study takes an interdisciplinary approach toward studying Marian theology and devotion through the lens of congregational song, drawing from anthropology, history, liturgy, musicology, psychology, sociology, and theology. This study consists of the following facets: a textual and musical analysis of the Marian congregational songs themselves;[29] an understanding of the place of Marian congregational song in the Catholic liturgy and devotional services; the impact of these congregational songs on Marian piety;[30] the historical and cultural contexts out of which the Marian congregational songs developed; and the issues raised by feminist and queer critiques of the texts. This interdisciplinary approach leads to contributions across a wide range of disciplines.

This project contributes to the study of Catholic congregational song in the United States during this period, showing firsthand the conflicts over different musical styles. Much judgment has been passed on Catholic sacred music of the late nineteenth and early twentieth centuries. Nicola A. Montani, a great critic of the *St. Basil's Hymnal*

27. Orsi, *Between Heaven and Earth*, 56.

28. Ibid., 62.

29. This study focuses more on the texts than the music as many of the texts of the nineteenth and twentieth centuries were often paired with multiple tunes. Where a text was usually paired with only one tune, that is made note of, and oftentimes the music and text are printed together.

30. While it is somewhat difficult to assess the impact of Marian congregational song on piety separately from other Marian prayers and devotions, this study tracks changes in the theology and emphases in the Marian congregational songs, thus showing trends in the texts that may have influenced piety.

(one of the most popular hymnals of that time period that contained many Marian congregational songs) and the compiler of the more "traditional" *St. Gregory Hymnal*, led the crusade against the "contemporary" music of the *St. Basil's Hymnal*, criticizing many of the tunes as being "inappropriate."[31] Montani was also the editor of the journal *The Catholic Choirmaster*, where his sentiments were also shared by his readers; one reviewer wrote the following: "As regards unchurchliness, musical incompetence, and the depravity of taste, the *St. Basil's Hymnal* is the saddest hymn book we have ever laid eyes on."[32]

The editors of the *St. Basil's Hymnal* attempted to make some changes in the 1925 edition and those printed after, but the most significant changes came in 1958, on the eve of Vatican II.[33] The preface to the *New St. Basil Hymnal* explains why some of the "good, old hymns" had been dropped, describing in detail many of the common criticisms of Marian congregational song in the United States up until that point, such as the sentimentality of the songs, their individualistic piety, their borrowing from secular music that was popular at the time, and their focus on Christ's humanity rather than divinity:

> Many who have used the *St. Basil's Hymnal* in the past will look in vain for some of the "good, old hymns." These have been passed over by the Committee because, as has been observed, they are really neither *good*, nor *old*. The majority of them reflect the sentimental, individualistic piety of the late Victorian period. Too frequently their melodies are poor copies of the secular music of that era, while their texts unduly emphasize the human nature of the Savior, tending to bring God to a purely human level rather than to lift man's thoughts to God. Such hymns are more than dated; they are positively harmful in that they attempt to express a religious emotion which is exaggerated, over-familiar and, eventually, false—since they teach the singer

---

31. J. Vincent Higginson, *History of American Catholic Hymnals* (Springfield, OH: The Hymn Society of America, 1982), 142. Montani wrote this criticism under the pseudonym "M. Colas." A member of the St. Gregory Society, Montani also helped to compile the "White List" of the 1920s, a list of "appropriate" music to be sung in church. See Higginson, *History of American Catholic Hymnals*, 177. The "banned" music of the corresponding "Black List" created by the Society of St. Gregory of America will be explored in chap. 5.

32. Ibid., 142.

33. Ibid., 143.

> to pray badly. In the present collection, then, they have yielded place
> to *better*, and in some cases *older* hymns of genuine piety and dignity.[34]

This quotation is extremely important; although it describes Catholic congregational songs from the late nineteenth and early twentieth centuries, it very well could be aimed at much of the "contemporary" music that has been produced in the United States following Vatican II. In studying Marian congregational song during this period, not only are we able to see the conflicting views over musical taste but we are also able to see the impact of congregational song on piety. Although the *New St. Basil Hymnal* attempted to quell the singing of "Bring flowers of the rarest," it failed—and the song is still used today. This shows the impact of congregational song and the "musical memories" associated with them.

It is easy to look at a congregational song at face value—particularly from an academic stance, taking a song out of its context—and judge it by the quality of its musicality or the theological value of its text. It is another thing to move beyond judgments of "good" and "bad" to recognize that for each individual person, there is a "musical memory" or special meaning attached to a song. Orsi notes that "the image on the wall is inevitably viewed through the lens of the image within."[35] This can be translated to the music and texts of Marian congregational song: the image of Mary created through congregational song is influenced by the lens of the image one contains within one's mind.[36]

One must be careful, however, to beware of "hidden normatives, implicit distinctions between 'good' and 'bad' religions."[37] Orsi advocates for the breaking of the normative paradigm in academia of "us vs. them" because Mary transcends the boundaries of popular/

---

34. The Basilian Fathers, ed., *The New Saint Basil Hymnal* (Cincinnati, OH: Ralph Jusco Publications / Willis Music Company, 1958), v (emphasis by the Basilian Fathers).

35. Orsi, *Between Heaven and Earth*, 69.

36. It seems the reverse could also be true; the image of Mary contained in congregational song influences the image one creates of Mary in one's mind.

37. Orsi, *Between Heaven and Earth*, 6. Orsi is drawing from the work of Danièle Hervieu-Léger, *Religion as a Chain of Memory*, trans. Simon Lee (New Brunswick, NJ: Rutgers University Press, 2000).

elite.[38] If relationships are viewed as contexts of understanding, it is possible to avoid labels of "good" or "bad" and rather see relationships between heaven and earth.[39] Orsi warns against falling into the normative paradigm of twentieth-century Catholicism as moving from a less mature, pre–Vatican II Catholicism to a more "mature," post–Vatican II Catholicism.[40]

Here the terrain becomes rocky; in the words of Albert Blackwell, "to judge music's sacramental value is to walk the razor's edge of many adjudications in religious matters: the edge between righteous indignation and self-righteousness."[41] Because of these difficulties, this study will be careful about judging a congregational song to be "good" or "bad." While it will point out where texts might be conveying unorthodox theologies as well as oppressive and/or dangerous theologies and cultural standards, it will not focus on judging the music associated with the texts. Compared to assessing texts, it is much more difficult to analyze a piece of music as "good" or "bad" using concrete criteria that does not venture into a judgment for or against a certain style of music. This study will, however, observe when debates occurred over different musical styles and explore how these debates affected Marian congregational song.

By understanding the impact a congregational song might have on someone's relationship with Mary, their experience of sacred presence, and their understanding of Mary in her role as mediator and/or mother, another facet on the judgment of the aesthetical and theological value of a congregational song is opened. There is, however, more to take into account than simply aesthetics. For example, one must look at how the music is joined to the rite or the occasion in which it is used. The authors of *The Milwaukee Symposia* choose to use the term "Christian ritual music" because it "underscores the interconnection between music and the other elements of the rite: distinguishable facets of a single event."[42]

38. Ibid., 64.
39. Ibid., 7.
40. Ibid., 9–10.
41. Blackwell, *The Sacred in Music*, 152.
42. Milwaukee Symposia for Church Composers, "The Milwaukee Symposia for Church Composers: A Ten-Year Report (July 9, 1992)," Archdiocese of Mil-

One must also look at the context out of which the music has arisen. What were the papal encyclicals advocating at the time? What language did they use? What styles of music were popular at the time? What was being said in regard to the use of different types of sacred music at the time a congregational song was written? It is not a coincidence that shortly after Pope Pius X issued *Tra le Sollecitudini* (a papal instruction on sacred music that made a clear distinction regarding what constituted "sacred" and "profane" music)[43] that we see people such as Montani criticizing some songs that seem to be taken from "popular" secular music and then creating a list of "appropriate" and "disapproved" music. Catholic congregational song in the United States was also influenced by developments in the liturgical movement—a movement led in the United States by Virgil Michel.[44] The effects that the liturgical movement's push for a greater focus on communal worship over private, individualistic devotions had on Marian congregational song and devotion will be explored in chapter 5.

By looking at these multiple facets rather than only using one criterion, this study provides not only a fuller understanding of Marian congregational song but also a picture of why certain congregational songs were more popular than others, and why some were favored by "traditional" hymnals and some by "contemporary" hymnals. This is a topic that is just as hotly debated today as it was almost one hundred years ago when Montani was criticizing the *St. Basil's Hymnal*. Therefore, this study is significant not only in its historical findings, but also in its application today in trying to determine why some congregational songs are more popular than others and why some, such as "Bring flowers of the rarest," while reviled by

waukee, 6, http://www.archmil.org/ArchMil/Resources/TheMilwaukeeStatement .pdf, accessed June 2014.

43. Pius X, Instruction on Sacred Music (*Tra le Sollecitudini*), November 22, 1903, Adoremus Society for the Renewal of the Sacred Liturgy, http://www .adoremus.org/MotuProprio.html, accessed June 2014.

44. Keith Pecklers, *The Unread Vision: The Liturgical Movement in the United States of America: 1926–1955* (Collegeville, MN: Liturgical Press, 1998). See especially chap. 5, which focuses on the twentieth-century liturgical movement and its attitudes toward sacred music.

some—in the words of the *New Saint Basil Hymnal*—as neither being "good" nor "old"—seem to withstand the test of time.

Another important factor in the study of any congregational song is how it was influenced by the culture out of which it came. This study contributes to the understanding of how Marian devotion and congregational song has changed in relation to theology and devotion, particularly over the past 150 years in relationship to cultures in the United States. Paul Bradshaw notes that liturgy is a "living literature" that is often revised "to reflect changing historical and cultural circumstances."[45] Throughout the study, it is important to see which congregational songs are kept, which ones are discarded, and why. It is also significant to note changes to texts over time.

One specific aspect of culture this study pays attention to is the influence of feminist issues on Marian congregational song. Marian devotion has had both positive and negative associations with women throughout the centuries. On the one hand, Mary has been shown as a strong woman and liberator,[46] while on the other hand she has also been portrayed as an unattainable woman who is both virgin and mother.[47] This study explores how Marian congregational songs have reflected both of these positions over time, and those in between.

There is also an exploration of trends in the appearance of Marian apparitions in nineteenth-century Europe to women, children, and the underprivileged, and how these apparitions were tied with what was happening culturally at the time. Robert Orsi also highlights this development:

---

45. Paul F. Bradshaw, *The Search for the Origins of Christian Worship: Sources and Methods for the Study of Early Liturgy* (New York: Oxford University Press, 2002), 5.

46. Ivone Gebara and Maria Clara Bingemar, *Mary: Mother of God, Mother of the Poor* (Maryknoll, NY: Orbis Books, 1989). See also Elizabeth Johnson, *Truly Our Sister: A Theology of Mary in the Communion of the Saints* (New York: Continuum, 2003).

47. Mary Daly, *The Church and the Second Sex* (Boston, MA: Beacon Press, 1985). See also Paula M. Kane, "Marian Devotion Since 1940: Continuity or Casualty?" in *Habits of Devotion: Catholic Religious Practice in Twentieth-Century America*, ed. James M. O'Toole (Ithaca, NY: Cornell University Press, 2004), 88–129.

Children, women, and "cripples" (as Catholics called persons with physical disabilities in the middle years of the last century) . . . were vulnerable and exposed to the fantasies of adults, of male church officials, and of persons without physical handicaps, and they were invited into relationships with holy figures—with the Virgin Mother of God, the angels and the saints—that endorsed and deepened these discrepancies of agency and power.[48]

While Mary and the saints "could be dangerous enforcers of cultural structures, norms, and expectations," they could also be used by women, children, and the disabled "to assist them to live against what others would make of them in this religious world, meaning that the very same figures who were called into play against them could become their allies in resistance and subversion."[49]

Orsi exposes here the tensions wrapped up in Mary and the saints in that, on the one hand, they were used to enforce cultural expectations against women, children, and the disabled, while, on the other hand, the same people who were supposed to be bound by them could also use them as liberating figures against these same oppressive expectations. This tension will be looked at in how it plays out in Marian congregational song.

Method of Investigation

In an attempt to move "beyond the text," and "integrate the entire act of worship into the study of liturgy," this study employs Lawrence Hoffman's methodology of what he terms "holistic."[50] Rather than focusing solely on the text, Hoffman advocates the importance of understanding the people who prayed the text, thus opening a "window onto the worshipers."[51] Hoffman points out the value of this type of study: "If we learn to see the liturgy as transcending words,

---

48. Orsi, *Between Heaven and Earth*, 4.
49. Ibid. This trend will be explored in chap. 8 through looking at liberation theology, in which Mary is seen as an aid in the uprising of women, the poor, and the oppressed. See Gebara and Bingemar, *Mary: Mother of God, Mother of the Poor*.
50. Hoffman, *Beyond the Text*, 15.
51. Ibid., 2–3.

even great words, we inherit a window on the past and present alike, in which the image on the other side of the glass may look remarkably like ourselves."[52] He advocates not only learning about the texts from the people but also the people from the texts, thus allowing a movement from beyond the material "to the worshipping community that lives beyond the text."[53]

In order to see through that window more clearly, Hoffman suggests using an interdisciplinary approach, similar to the use of multiple camera angles in order to create a more complete image.[54] This study utilizes Hoffman's interdisciplinary approach, employing methods from a variety of fields. Zimmerman describes the "sacred," or the "extra-textual reality" that is also involved in studying the liturgy which requires an interdisciplinary approach in order to fully appreciate the "divine/human encounter" that takes place during the liturgy.[55]

With this "holistic view" in mind, Marian congregational song is approached both diachronically and synchronically. Because this study is concerned with understanding the impact of what was occurring in the world at the time when the congregational songs were written, there is an emphasis on the relation of a text to its historical context. In looking at the actual Marian congregational songs, this study explores the theological composition of the texts. While the focus of this study is on the texts of the Marian congregational songs, at times musicological tools are also used to analyze the musical structures of the songs.

52. Ibid., 3.

53. Ibid., 8, 19. This approach could be seen as *lex orandi, lex credendi* rather than *lex credendi, lex orandi*. See Aidan Kavanagh, *On Liturgical Theology: The Hale Memorial Lectures of Seabury-Western Theological Seminary, 1981* (New York: Pueblo Pub. Co., 1984). See especially his discussion of *theologia prima* versus *theologia secunda*.

54. Hoffman, *Beyond the Text*, 15.

55. Zimmerman, *Liturgy and Hermeneutics*, 80–81. Zimmerman also cites Geoffrey Wainwright, who says language must be viewed as theological, historical, social, and aesthetic, as well as Kevin Irwin, who says liturgical theology should be based on both text and context, or data and use. See Zimmerman, *Liturgy and Hermeneutics*, 86, 88.

Sources of the Study and Limitations

The original study which is the basis for this book looked at Marian congregational songs in Latin and English from Catholic hymnals in the United States. It did not delve into texts in other languages, such as Spanish, which means it also did not focus on corresponding devotions associated with non-English speaking cultures. This was not done because the author does not deem these songs and devotions to be important; it was done solely to keep the scope of the study manageable. Our Lady of Guadalupe is a fascinating and extremely important devotion, and many books are written exclusively on this aspect of Marian devotion, which is why I had to deem it outside the scope of this study. I sincerely hope that others will take up the work of studying Marian congregational songs in different languages to show how they reflect Marian theologies and devotions from different cultures.

Marian Theology and Devotion through the Lens of Congregational Song, Past and Present

Chapter 1 examines the origins of Marian theology and devotion by exploring such important points as the place of Mary in the Bible, the discussion of Mary as *Theotokos* (Mother of God) at the Council of Ephesus in 431, and the early development of Marian liturgical feasts and hymnody. Chapter 2 focuses on medieval developments in Marian theology and devotion, particularly shifts that occurred in theology as a result of the millennium: devotion to Mary at the foot of the cross, Marian hymnody, and liturgical practices, to name a few. Chapter 3 looks at the place of Mary in the Reformation, the Council of Trent, and the Counter-Reformation, as well as early Marian devotion in the United States.

Chapter 4 investigates the beginning of "the so-called marian movement"[56] of the late nineteenth and early twentieth centuries, which saw a great surge of Marian devotion and congregational song under Popes Pius IX, Leo XIII, and Pius XII, among others. This includes an examination of papal declarations on Mary (beginning

56. Johnson, *Truly Our Sister*, 122.

with the Immaculate Conception in 1854), the influx of Marian apparitions in Europe, the personal piety of the popes, as well as social and cultural factors such as the fight over the Papal States (the "Roman Question") and the use of the rosary as a "weapon" against Communism. Chapter 5 continues by looking at factors in the United States, including the use of devotional books, the Victorian notion of "True Womanhood," and the influence of the liturgical movement. There is also a consideration of the influence of papal encyclicals and musical societies on the style of music used for congregational song, and how this in turn influenced Marian congregational song, as well as attention to when congregational song was allowed within the Catholic liturgy. Throughout both of these chapters, there is a reflection on how all of these factors were reflected in Marian congregational songs of the time with examples from the actual songs.

Chapter 6 begins by taking an in-depth look at the debate over whether or not the bishops would include Mary within *Lumen Gentium* (the Dogmatic Constitution on the Church) at Vatican II or deal with Mary in a separate document, as well as whether or not a new Marian definition would be proclaimed. The chapter includes a closer look at what Vatican II finally decided to say about Mary in *Lumen Gentium*. Chapter 7 continues by surveying other Marian developments in the Catholic Church. Following Vatican II, there were many significant changes both in Catholicism and in the world. The feminist movement, the continuing ecumenical movement, and an ever-changing society affected the Catholic Church as women asked for greater roles in the Church, dialogue was opened with both Christians and non-Christians, and the Church seemed to be more positive toward discussion of the cultural issues of the time. For some time it seemed as though Mary was lost to many in this shuffle, only to be reclaimed toward the end of the twentieth century through the Marian devotion of Pope John Paul II and the increase of Marian apparitions, some containing apocalyptic warnings. This chapter explores how these various factors, including official documents on sacred music, influenced Marian theology, devotion, and congregational song.

Chapter 8 looks at both the current state of Marian theology and devotion in US Catholicism and what the future might hold for Mary. As Robert Orsi writes, Mary "contributes to making and sustaining culture, and reinventing it, at the same time that she herself is made and sustained by culture, in dynamic exchanges with her devout."[57] This study concludes by trying to make sense of the seeming loss of Marian devotion after Vatican II by utilizing the lens of Marian congregational song, particularly the *Magnificat*. What is needed to reinvigorate Marian congregational song? What can be learned from cultures where Marian devotion is flourishing? How can Marian congregational song shed its former associations with anti-Communism and oppressive views toward women and be reinvented to speak to the post–Vatican II, twenty-first-century Catholic Church, and beyond? How can Marian congregational songs in the future proclaim Mary's prophetic—and dangerous—vision of a world in which the poor and oppressed are exalted and liberated?

57. Orsi, *Between Heaven and Earth*, 61.

Chapter One

We Fly to Your Patronage, O Holy Mother of God[1]

Sing of her, all singers,
and you will enchant the enchanter
who often enchants us.
If you sing of the mother of God,
every enchanter will be enchanted.
Fortunate is the one who sings of her.[2]

—Gautier de Coinci, "Amours, qui bien set enchanter"

Introduction

Gautier de Coinci (ca. 1177–1236), one of the "first important composer[s] of Old French songs to the Virgin," encourages his listeners to sing to Mary, who "occupies a liminal space between

---

1. *Sub tuum praesidium*, lines 1–2, as quoted in Anthony M. Buono, *The Greatest Marian Prayers: Their History, Meaning, and Usage* (New York: Alba House, 1999), 21.
2. Gautier de Coinci, "Amours, qui bien set enchanter," lines 7–12, as quoted in Daniel O'Sullivan, *Marian Devotion in Thirteenth-Century French Lyric* (Toronto: University of Toronto Press, 2005), 121.

humanity and divinity."[3] The Church has a long history of singing Mary's praises, beginning with such early prayers as the *Magnificat* (Luke 1:46-55) and the *Sub tuum praesidium*, the oldest prayer to Mary, dating from the third century.[4] The Council of Ephesus's (431) support for calling Mary *Theotokos* ("Mother of God") created a "flood of Marian devotions" in the Eastern Church, including the *Akathist*, a Greek alphabet acrostic hymn from the fifth or sixth century that eventually found its way to the West.[5] In addition, Marian feasts began to be celebrated in the West, leading to an outpouring of the creation of Marian texts, music, and prayers in the Middle Ages, including the *Ave maris stella*.

Devotion to Mary before the Council of Ephesus

Mary in the Bible and Apocryphal Literature

Biblical Foundations

For a woman about whom so much has been written throughout the ages, there are only a few references to Mary in the Bible. In fact, the gospels only mention Mary's name nineteen times, in contrast to the Qur'an where she is mentioned thirty-four times.[6] Jaroslav Pelikan notes that "the account of Mary in the New Testament is tantalizingly brief,"[7] so brief that while Mary is not mentioned among those to whom Christ appeared after the resurrection, by the time of Gregory of Nyssa (died ca. 394), it was a "widely accepted opinion that he appeared first to her."[8]

---

3. Ibid., 11.

4. Buono, *The Greatest Marian Prayers*, 21–22.

5. Joseph A. Jungmann, *Christian Prayer through the Centuries* (New York: Paulist Press, 1978), 102.

6. Miri Rubin, *Mother of God: A History of the Virgin Mary* (New Haven, CT, and London: Yale University Press, 2009), 83. In the Qur'an she is not referred to as the Virgin Mary. She is usually mentioned in the phrase "Isa son of Maryam."

7. Jaroslav Pelikan, *Mary through the Centuries: Her Place in the History of Culture* (New Haven, CT: Yale University Press, 1996), 8.

8. Hilda Graef, *The Devotion to Our Lady* (New York: Hawthorn Books, 1963), 15.

While Mary is not explicitly mentioned in Paul's letters and is only briefly mentioned in the Gospel of Mark, she does play a greater role in the infancy narrative in the Gospel of Matthew and particularly in the Gospel of Luke, "where she has an important role in the annunciation, the visitation, the birth at Bethlehem, the presentation in the Temple, and the finding of Jesus in the temple."[9] Luke's gospel contains the *Magnificat* (Luke 1:46-55), one of the most popular Marian texts of all time. In the Luke-Acts narrative, Mary is also described as being present in the Upper Room in Acts 1:14.[10]

Mary also plays an important role in the Gospel of John, where she is not named but is referred to only as the "mother of Jesus."[11] In regard to the story of the wedding feast at Cana (John 2:1-11, 12), some Catholics have interpreted John 2:5, where Mary tells the servants, "Do whatever he tells you," as "an example of Mary's power of intercession: the first miracle worked by Jesus was at the behest of his mother, and this is meant to teach us to pray to Jesus through Mary."[12] The notion of Mary's intercession for humankind will soon become important. Another concept that will take hold of the imagination of the faithful after the first millennium is the role of Mary at the foot of the cross (John 19:25-27), which is only described in the Gospel of John.[13]

The "woman clothed with the sun" in chapter 12 of the book of Revelation will later be interpreted by some as representing Mary.[14]

9. Raymond E. Brown, Karl P. Donfried, Joseph A. Fitzmyer, and John Reumann, eds., *Mary in the New Testament* (New York: Paulist Press, 1978), 105. Mary plays an important role in Luke's gospel, and as Carl Daw notes, "Luke is traditionally regarded as the first iconographer, with the icon naturally being of Mary, because he gives so much attention to her in his gospel." Carl P. Daw, Jr., e-mail message to author, February 4, 2012.

10. Brown et al., *Mary in the New Testament*, 173.

11. Ibid., 179.

12. Ibid., 193. The authors go on to note that this exegesis is "one extreme of the spectrum" and while "once popular among Roman Catholics," this notion is "scarcely held by any scholar today." Thanks to Peter Scagnelli for pointing to the idea that this passage may mark the beginning of Mary's intercession for humankind.

13. Rubin, *Mother of God*, 7.

14. Brown et al., *Mary in the New Testament*, 235–39.

During the first four centuries, the figure in Revelation 12 "was unanimously regarded as signifying the Church."[15] It seems that Quodvultdeus (died ca. 450), a student of Augustine, was the first to identify Mary with the woman in Revelation 12, and in the sixth century, the Greek author Oekumenius is the first to exegete Revelation 12 from a Marian perspective without mention of the Church at all.[16]

While the references to Mary in the New Testament are sparse, Ignazio Calabuig notes that these texts not only provide "the literary foundation for devotion to the Blessed Virgin in the liturgy" but they also tell us much about "the role of Mary in the history of salvation."[17] From these few descriptions of Mary will develop a great devotion to her, complete with feasts, prayers, music, and much more. As devotion to Mary grew, her devotees wanted to know more about her, and so by the end of the second century and beginning of the third century a growing body of apocryphal writings attempts to flesh out her life.

The Protoevangelium of James

Known by many names such as the *Protoevangelium of James*, the *Protogospel of James*, and also its oldest title, *Birth of Mary: Revelation of James*,[18] this Syrian text, dating from "the mid-second to early-third-century . . . is 'unusual in that it showed some interest in and development of Mary for her own sake.'"[19] Although condemned by the sixth century as an apocryphal text,[20] this narrative was extremely popular;

15. Graef, *The Devotion to Our Lady*, 15.

16. Ibid.

17. Ignazio M. Calabuig, "The Liturgical Cult of Mary in the East and West," in *Liturgical Time and Space*, vol. 5 of *Handbook for Liturgical Studies*, ed. Anscar J. Chupungco (Collegeville, MN: Liturgical Press, 2000), 220–21.

18. Brown et al., *Mary in the New Testament*, 248.

19. Robert Eno, "Mary and Her Role in Patristic Theology," in *The One Mediator, the Saints, and Mary,* ed. H. George Anderson et al., Lutherans and Catholics in Dialogue 8 (Minneapolis, MN: Augsburg Fortress, 1992), 164, as quoted in Maxwell E. Johnson, "*Sub Tuum Praesidium*," in *The Place of Christ in Liturgical Prayer: Trinity, Christology, and Liturgical Theology*, ed. Bryan D. Spinks (Collegeville, MN: Liturgical Press, 2008), 255.

20. Apocrypha refers to texts that are not part of the canon of the Bible.

many manuscripts survive in Greek, and it was translated into many languages, including Syriac and Armenian.[21] Maxwell Johnson points out that in addition to being unique in showing such interest in Mary, this document "provides several Marian elements that will develop and become, ultimately, the content of theological reflection, liturgical celebration, and popular devotion in the life of the church."[22]

First of all, the *Protoevangelium of James* provides the names of the parents of Mary, Anna and Joachim, who will later be honored with a memorial in the Catholic calendar on July 26.[23] Two other feasts will be subsequently based on the narratives found in the *Protoevangelium of James*: the Nativity of Mary (September 8) and the Presentation of Mary in the Temple (November 21).[24] This document also provided the sources for liturgical texts, Marian hymnody, and Marian iconography, including the iconography depicting Jesus being born in a cave near Jerusalem.[25]

The author of the *Protoevangelium of James* had a dogmatic motive; according to James Keith Elliott, the author of this text wanted to stress Jesus' virginal conception, Mary's maintaining of her virginity during Jesus' birth (*in partu*) and her virginity after Jesus' birth (her perpetual virginity).[26] Miri Rubin notes that the author of the *Protoevangelium of James* focused on Mary's purity, and that this might have been a result of the effort to convert Jews to Christianity. At the time, "there was no institution of celibacy and virginity in the Jewish

---

21. Rubin, *Mother of God*, 9; and James Keith Elliott, ed., "The Protoevangelium of James," in *The Apocryphal New Testament: A Collection of Apocryphal Christian Literature in an English Translation* (Oxford: Clarendon Press, 1993), 48.

22. Johnson, "*Sub Tuum Praesidium*," 267.

23. Calabuig, "The Liturgical Cult of Mary in the East and West," 233.

24. Johnson, "*Sub Tuum Praesidium*," 255.

25. Calabuig, "The Liturgical Cult of Mary in the East and West," 233–34, 259.

26. Elliott, "The Protoevangelium of James," 50. The part of the narrative that describes Mary's virginity *in partu* is rather graphic; in 19.I–20.I, Salome says that "unless I insert my finger and test her condition, I will not believe that a virgin has given birth." As she tests Mary's condition, her hand falls away and catches on fire until she professes belief in Mary's virginity *in partu*. See Elliott, "The Protoevangelium of James," 64–65. Daw points out that the withering hand motif "continues into some English medieval mystery plays (e.g., N-Town and Chester)." Carl P. Daw, Jr., e-mail message to author, February 4, 2012.

mainstream," so the author's focus on Jewish family life might have made Christianity seem more appealing to those they were trying to convert.[27] This text, which depicts Mary as "the honored model of the pure virginal life . . . as the will of God for his hearers" shows the growing desire in Christianity to uphold the virtue of virginity with Mary as the model for all to follow.[28]

Beginnings of a Theology of Mary

The Mary/Eve Parallel

Discussion of Mary's virginity is found fairly early in the history of the Church. As is often the case, Mariology serves as a foil to Christology. In the discussion of her virginity, Mary serves a "christological and soteriological purpose: Jesus' birth of the virgin is, on the one hand, proof of his messiahship and, on the other, the sign of a new time."[29] While Ignatius of Antioch (ca. 50–ca. 107) mentions the virginal conception in his writings, it is in Justin Martyr's (ca. 100–ca. 165) *Dialogue with Trypho* (ca. 135) where the "typological parallel between the virgin Eve and the virgin Mary" is found for the first time; while Eve's disobedience brought about sin, Mary's obedience brought Christ into the world who freed us from our sins.[30]

The Mary/Eve parallel was further expounded on by Irenaeus of Lyons (ca. 140/160–ca. 202) in his *Adversus haereses* (ca. 180). In this text, he draws from Paul's notion of recapitulation or second creation, saying that "the knot of Eve's disobedience was untied by Mary's obedience. What Eve bound through her unbelief, Mary loosed by her faith."[31] Just as Christ is the New Adam, so is Mary the New Eve. This

27. Rubin, *Mother of God*, 11–12.

28. Brown, et al., *Mary in the New Testament*, 253.

29. Ibid., 255.

30. Ibid. Many of the early discussions around Mary's virginity were polemical, as there were some who did not believe in the virginal conception or birth or in Christ's humanity and/or divinity. Justin Martyr's discussion was with Trypho, a Jew. Mary became somewhat of a dividing line between Christians and Jews from an early time in the Church's history, leading to some very unpleasant instances of anti-Semitism.

31. *Adversus haereses*, 3, 22, as quoted in Luigi Gambero, *Mary and the Fathers of the Church: The Blessed Virgin Mary in Patristic Thought* (San Francisco, CA:

parallel between Mary and Eve will become quite popular, particularly in the play on Mary's "Ave" as reversing what Eve, or "Eva" did (in Latin, "Ave" is "Eva" backward). This play on words will often appear in Marian hymnody from Hildegard of Bingen (1098–1179), to the medieval Carol "Nova, nova" which contains the Latin phrase "Ave fix ex Eva" ("'Hail' is made from 'Eve'"), to Marian congregational song in the mid-nineteenth to mid-twentieth centuries.[32]

Mary's Virginity

Luigi Gambero describes the notion of Mary's virginity as one of two prerogatives—the other being her divine motherhood—that is "directly suggested by the Eve-Mary parallel."[33] As seen in the *Protoevangelium of James*, there was belief in Mary's *virginitas ante partem* (the virginal conception), *virginitas in partu* (the virgin birth), and *virginitas post partum* (Mary remained a virgin after giving birth, often described as her "perpetual virginity").[34] While most accepted the idea of Jesus' virginal conception, others were not as inclined to believe in the virgin birth and Mary's perpetual virginity. Tertullian (ca. 160–ca. 225) argued that the concept of the virgin birth was Docetic and that Mary had children after Jesus because Jesus' brothers and sisters are referred to in passages in the New Testament.[35]

Mary's virginity also began to be upheld as a model for the growing number of people being drawn to consecrated virginity and asceticism.[36] Many writers began to praise Mary's virginity, including Ambrose (ca. 340–397), who compared Mary's virginity to "Ezekiel's image of a 'closed gate,'" and Jerome (ca. 340–420), who in

---

Ignatius Press, 1999), 54. Irenaeus also seems to be the first person to refer to Mary as *advocata*, another title that will become prominent in describing Mary. See Gambero, *Mary and the Fathers of the Church*, 56.

32. Thanks to Carl Daw for noting that this play on words can be found in "Nova, nova." The Latin translation of "Nova, nova" comes from Raymond F. Glover, ed., *Hymns 1 to 384*, vol. 3A of *The Hymnal 1982 Companion* (New York: The Church Hymnal Corporation, 1994), 518.

33. Gambero, *Mary and the Fathers of the Church*, 46–47.

34. Brown et al., *Mary in the New Testament*, 271–78.

35. Ibid., 273–78.

36. Gambero, *Mary and the Fathers of the Church*, 19.

translating Isaiah 7:14 rendered *alma* as "virgin" rather than "young woman."[37] This emphasis on Mary's virginity would soon be seen in Marian liturgies; many of these liturgies drew from the liturgy of the virgins.[38] There will also be a strong emphasis on Mary's virginity and purity in Marian congregational song in the mid-nineteenth to mid-twentieth centuries.

The Mary/Church Parallel

In addition to uplifting Mary's virginity, Ambrose was also the "first Christian author to call Mary the type and image of the Church."[39] Ambrose describes how Mary, a virgin, painlessly gave birth to Christ just as the Church, also a virgin, painlessly gives birth to its children in baptism.[40] Augustine (354–430) also heralded the parallel between Mary and the Church, describing Mary as the "physical Mother of the Redeemer" while the Church was the "spiritual Mother of the redeemed."[41] While the East was focused on more metaphysical issues, the West saw itself as a "visible institution," so it did much more to work out the Mary/Church parallel.[42]

In Augustine's focus on the motherhood of Mary and the Church, Hilda Graef sees "the beginnings of the later devotion to Mary as the mother of individual Christians, but still embedded in her near-identification with the Church."[43] The notion of Mary as the mother of each Christian, or as our "mother in heaven," is one that will become very popular and is prominent in Marian congregational song, particularly in texts before Vatican II. Another aspect of Mary's identification with the Church is the idea that both Mary and the

---

37. Rubin, *Mother of God*, 27, 30. The entire passage from Isaiah 7:14: "Behold a virgin shall conceive, and bear a son, and his name shall be called Emmanuel." See Rubin, *Mother of God*, 30.

38. Kilian McDonnell, "The Marian Liturgical Tradition," in *Between Memory and Hope: Readings on the Liturgical Year*, ed. Maxwell E. Johnson (Collegeville, MN: Liturgical Press, 2000), 396.

39. Gambero, *Mary and the Fathers of the Church*, 198.

40. Graef, *The Devotion to Our Lady*, 21.

41. Gambero, *Mary and the Fathers of the Church*, 223.

42. Graef, *The Devotion to Our Lady*, 21.

43. Ibid., 23.

Church act as bride and mother to Christ.[44] The bridal imagery surrounding Mary, particularly in connection with the Song of Songs, will become very prevalent, especially after the first millennium.

Early Prayers and Devotions to Mary

Marian Apparitions and Miracle Stories

From the third to the sixth century there was a growing devotion in the East to Mary as *Theotokos*, as she was now referred to. Graef notes that one aspect of this "intense personal devotion to the Theotokos" is the "earliest recorded Marian vision" given to Gregory the Wonderworker (ca. 213–ca. 270), which was recorded by Gregory of Nyssa (ca. 335–ca. 395).[45] In this apparition, Mary, along with John the apostle, appeared to Gregory the Wonderworker in a "blaze of light," and she instructed John "to make known to Gregory the true faith, which he was ready to do 'for the Mother of the Lord, since such was her wish.'" Another popular legend that comes to us from the East in the fifth century is the Theophilus legend. This story, which serves as the model for Christopher Marlowe's *Dr. Faustus* and other adaptations, tells of Theophilus, who sells his soul to the devil to get what he wants, and then repents and asks Mary for forgiveness. Mary wields her power and "compels the devil to give up the contract by which Theophilus had sold his soul to him." This story was important because it helped to solidify Mary's power in her role as intercessor. It also became extremely popular in the Middle Ages because it showed "evidence of Mary's power even over hell." The growing fear of judgment as well as a developing fear of purgatory and hell helped fuel the popularity of this story in the Middle Ages.

In the sixth century there is found the miracle story of the Jewish boy—this also shows the power of Mary's intercession. In Gregory of Tours's (ca. 538–ca. 594) *Libri Miraculorum*, he tells the story of a Jewish boy who went to Mass with his Christian classmates and received the Eucharist.[46] When he returned home, he told his father,

---

44. Ibid.
45. Ibid., 30. All quotations in this paragraph are taken from this reference.
46. Gambero, *Mary and the Fathers of the Church*, 355. The following account of the miracle story comes from Gambero, 355–56.

who became enraged and threw him in the furnace. The boy, however, was saved, similar to the three Hebrew boys in Daniel 3. In this case, the boy told how Mary covered him with her mantle and protected him from the fire, and he survived the incident unharmed. The father was thrown into the fire as a punishment while the boy and his mother converted to Christianity. This story exhibits the continued tensions between Christian and Jews and also provides an early example of how Mary was used as a weapon in polemical situations. The tensions between Christians and Jews often arose around the figure of Mary because the Jews could not believe that God would suffer the "indignity" of becoming flesh in Mary's womb; they also found the idea of the virgin birth "unreasonable."[47] Rubin explains that this story "asserted Mary's power against Jewish violence, it contrasted her mercy against the Jew's cruelty and offered the prospect of Jewish recognition in the boy's acknowledgment of Christian truth."[48] Mary was used as a weapon against those seen as heretics. Strangely, those sometimes deemed heretics suffered this fate due to a perceived worship of Mary.

Epiphanius and the Collyridians

By the fourth century, there is an account of anti-Marian and pro-Marian groups by Epiphanius of Salamis (315–403) in his *Panarion*, a book of heretical sects. The anti-Marian group was called the *Antidicomarianites*, and they denied Mary's perpetual virginity.[49] The pro-Marian group, the *Collyridians*, is described by Johnson as "a group comprised mostly of women who worshiped Mary as a 'goddess,' offered to her, and then themselves consumed, small cakes, and had a female priesthood."[50] In the words of Rubin, Epiphanius was "scandalized by the notion that a woman might be worshiped."[51]

Epiphanius's account is important because it shows that by the fourth century, "there was a popular veneration for the Virgin Mother

47. Rubin, *Mother of God*, 75.
48. Ibid.
49. Johnson, "*Sub Tuum Praesidium*," 260.
50. Ibid. This group was found in Arabia, Thrace, and Scythia. See Gambero, *Mary and the Fathers of the Church*, 122.
51. Rubin, *Mother of God*, 22.

which threatened to run extravagant lengths."[52] Elizabeth Johnson points out that this is an example of E. Ann Matter's maxim that "the practice of the pious often takes its own course."[53] There are many examples throughout the centuries where Marian devotion "took its own course" and needed to be corrected because it was seen as holding Mary in too high of esteem. The title of *Theotokos*, however, is one title for Mary that eventually received the stamp of orthodoxy, even though some felt it was heretical.

The Sub tuum praesidium *and Mary as* Theotokos

Maxwell Johnson writes that by the second century, "prayer to the martyrs, or at least asking for their intercession, even with regard to exercising the office of the keys, was becoming a common Christian practice."[54] There is also the possibility that third-century images of Mary can be found in the catacombs of S. Priscilla and the Cimitero Maggiore in Rome.[55] Origen (ca. 185–ca. 254) in his *De oratione* 14.6 wrote that it was proper to offer intercession and thanksgiving to both saints and others who had died, while supplication was only to be given to the saints who had the authority to forgive sins.[56] The *Sub tuum praesidium* is the earliest prayer to Mary, and is an example of an early Christian prayer asking for Mary's intercession. The prayer is dated by many as coming from third-century Egypt, but

> even if the text of the *Sub tuum praesidium* is no older than the early fourth century, it remains the earliest Marian prayer in existence— unless the greetings to Mary of the angel and Elizabeth (Luke 1) are already Christian hymn texts themselves—and testifies to some kind of Marian devotional piety well before Ephesus.[57]

52. H. Thurston, "Virgin Mary, Devotion to the Blessed—Down to the Council of Nicaea," in *The Catholic Encyclopedia* (New York: The Encyclopedia Press, 1913), 15:459–60, as quoted in Johnson, "*Sub Tuum Praesidium*," 260.

53. Elizabeth Johnson, *Truly Our Sister*, 119, as quoted in Maxwell Johnson, "*Sub Tuum Praesidium*," 260.

54. Johnson, "*Sub Tuum Praesidium*," 252.

55. Ibid., 256.

56. Ibid., 254.

57. Ibid., 255.

Johnson says that the only reason some argue against a third-century date is because of the use of the term *Theotokos*; since people believe the term came later, they do not believe the text can date from an earlier time.[58] The corrupted Greek version published by C.H. Roberts in 1938, however, is believed to be from the third century or earlier. This prayer was also "used liturgically in the Coptic, Greek, and Ambrosian Rites (for which the evidence is no earlier than the fifth and sixth centuries), and in the Roman Rite (for which evidence is no earlier than the seventh)."

The *Sub tuum praesidium* expresses what would become a familiar image of the supplicant flying to Mary for protection from danger:

> We fly to your patronage,
> O holy Mother of God,
> despise not our petitions
> in our necessities,
> but from all dangers,
> deliver us always,
> O glorious and blessed Virgin.[59]

Graef notes that this prayer "shows beyond doubt the complete trust with which Christians of the patristic age turned to the Theotokos in their needs."[60] The *Sub tuum praesidium* has been set to music throughout the ages, showing that Christians in the patristic age as well as today pray this "lived prayer" to Mary, having faith that she will protect them if they seek her intercession in the face of danger. Anthony Buono labels the *Sub tuum praesidium* a "lived prayer" because the "words were fashioned out of pressing need. When it was first used by Christians, the 'dangers' mentioned were a harsh reality for those who uttered the words—dangers that spelled fierce persecution and horrible death."[61] This prayer continues to be used in the Little Office

58. Ibid., 254. All information and quotations from this paragraph are taken from this reference.
59. James Socias and Christian F. Stepansky, eds., *Cantate et Iubilate Deo: A Devotional and Liturgical Hymnal* (Princeton, NJ: Scepter Publishers, 1999), 126.
60. Graef, *The Devotion to Our Lady*, 36.
61. Buono, *The Greatest Marian Prayers*, 22.

of Our Lady and at Compline,[62] and one can notice the similarities between the language of the prayer and the Vatican II document, *Lumen Gentium*: "Clearly from earliest times the Blessed Virgin has been honored under the title of *Mother of God*, and the faithful *have taken refuge under her protection in all their dangers and necessities.*"[63]

In addition to being the earliest prayer to Mary, the *Sub tuum praesidium* also offers an early example of the use of the title *Theotokos*, or Mother of God (see line two of the *Sub tuum praesidium*). Another reference to Mary as *Theotokos* comes from Alexander of Alexandria who "referred to Mary as Theotokos in his encyclical of circa 319 about the heresy of Arius."[64] Johnson points out that Alexander's use of *Theotokos* is not "to defend a particular Christological assertion about the unity of natures or personhood in Christ," as it was at the Council of Ephesus, but rather, here it is "used as little more than an honorific title for Mary."[65] Other instances that could be considered the "earliest" use of the term include: Luke 1:43 where Elizabeth says "mother of my Lord"; Ignatius of Antioch in *Ephesians* 18; and possible references by Origen.[66]

In 1989, Marek Starowieyski put together a list of authors from the fourth and fifth centuries who use the title *Theotokos*, including Ambrose of Milan, who was the first to use the title in Latin, "Mater Dei."[67] Because the list of authors in Starowieyski's study is so diverse and includes a range of Christologies, he concludes that the title *Theotokos* was used as a "simple appellation," allowing Johnson to conclude that by the fourth century this was a "common title for the Virgin Mary, one that cut across ecclesial lines as well as the boundaries of what might be called orthodoxy and heresy."[68] All this is to say, contrary to what has often been believed, that

---

62. Socias and Stepansky, *Cantate et Iubilate Deo*, 126.

63. *Lumen Gentium* 66, as quoted in Buono, *The Greatest Marian Prayers*, 28 (emphasis Buono).

64. Pelikan, *Mary through the Centuries*, 57, as quoted in Johnson, "*Sub Tuum Praesidium*," 244.

65. Johnson, "*Sub Tuum Praesidium*," 245.

66. Ibid., 246–50.

67. Ibid., 245–46.

68. Starowieyski, as quoted in Johnson, "*Sub Tuum Praesidium*," 246, 250.

devotion to Mary *Theotokos* did not spring up out of thin air, or merely fall out of heaven, at the Council of Ephesus. Nor did it simply "spread like wild fire" only after the Council of Ephesus. Rather, such devotion is rooted in piety and devotion from at least the third century.[69]

The developing Marian devotion before the Council of Ephesus was an "evolution," and not a "revolution," which received the stamp of orthodoxy at the Council of Ephesus, and thus in turn spurred the continued growth of Marian devotion.[70]

The Council of Ephesus up to the Millennium

Mary as Theotokos

The Council of Ephesus

The use of the title *Theotokos* for Mary was quite widespread by at least the fourth century. Gregory Nazianzen (ca. 329–ca. 390) was perhaps the first to call for the use of Mary's title *Theotokos* "as a criterion of orthodoxy."[71] However, by the mid-fourth century, Emperor Julian the Apostate is already "criticiz[ing] 'the superstition of the Christians for invoking the Theotokos'" in his work *Against the Galileans*.[72]

Another person who was not enthralled with such strong devotion to Mary was Nestorius (ca. 386–ca. 451), who was "scandalized" by the Marian devotion he found when he arrived as patriarch of Constantinople.[73] Nestorius was also outraged at the empress Pulcheria, who "had been permitted to receive communion within

---

69. Johnson, *"Sub Tuum Praesidium,"* 266.

70. Johnson sets out in his discussion of the use of *Theotokos* to explore how widespread its use was before the Council of Ephesus. His goal is to show whether the use of this title was a revolution brought on by the council, or simply an evolution that is continuous with Marian devotion practiced before the council. See Johnson, *"Sub Tuum Praesidium,"* 244, 267.

71. Gambero, *Mary and the Fathers of the Church*, 161.

72. Pelikan, *Mary through the Centuries*, 56, as quoted in Johnson, *"Sub Tuum Praesidium,"* 255.

73. Nicholas Constas, "Weaving the Body," 173–75, as quoted in Johnson, *"Sub Tuum Praesidium,"* 260.

the sanctuary of the Great Church."[74] When he told Pulcheria that only priests were to be in that space,

> she replied, "Why, have I not given birth to God?" "You?" he retorted, "have given birth to Satan," and proceeded to drive Pulcheria from the sanctuary. Not long after this confrontation, Nestorius publicly challenged the dignity of the Virgin Mary and began to preach against the propriety of calling her the Theotokos.[75]

Johnson points out that this conversation shows that what happened at the Council of Ephesus may not have only been about the "unitive personhood of Christ" but that it was "also the product of the *lex orandi* and of popular piety and devotion."[76]

The title of Mary as *Theotokos* was soon the subject of great debate between the two schools of thought in the East: the Alexandrian school, which taught the "unity of the subject of Christ," and the Antiochene school, which taught "differences between divinity and humanity."[77] This can be seen as a difference in emphasis, not doctrine.[78] The catalyst for this debate was a homily given by Proclus in 428 or 429, in the presence of Nestorius, in which Proclus called Mary *Theotokos*.[79] Nestorius preferred to call Mary *Christotokos*, believing that the title *Theotokos* "endangered the purity of the doctrine of the Incarnation."[80] Cyril of Alexandria joined in the attack against Nestorius, appealing to Pope Celestine I, while Nestorius appealed to Emperor Theodosius II, who called for an ecumenical council.[81]

---

74. Ibid.

75. Ibid.

76. Johnson, "*Sub Tuum Praesidium*," 261. Johnson also describes how Nestorius's predecessor, Atticus of Constantinople, told Pulcheria and her sisters "that if they imitated the virginity and chastity of Mary they would give birth to God mystically in their souls." Thus Pulcheria's response to Nestorius about giving birth to God "indicates that such a personal or popular devotion to the *Theotokos* could even become a kind of Marian mysticism." See ibid., 261.

77. Gambero, *Mary and the Fathers of the Church*, 233.

78. Graef, *The Devotion to Our Lady*, 26.

79. Gambero, *Mary and the Fathers of the Church*, 234.

80. Ibid., 235–36.

81. Ibid., 236.

In 431 the council was held in Ephesus, where tradition held that Mary lived with John in her later years and had died as well.[82] The council, which included many excommunications on both sides, ended with the proclamation "that it was an obligation binding on all believers to call Mary Theotokos, making dogmatically official what the piety of orthodox believers had already affirmed."[83] Elizabeth Johnson describes the outcome of the Council of Ephesus as allowing "the development of the marian cult to go public in the church. Although discourse about Mary had been in play to express Christological truths, it opened up the later trajectory where attention was focused on Mary herself."[84]

Marian Devotion Following the Council of Ephesus

Even though the West often lagged behind the East in Marian developments,[85] the effects of the Council of Ephesus were quickly seen with the construction of the first church in the West that was dedicated to Mary, the basilica of Santa Maria Maggiore (St. Mary Major) in Rome, by Pope Sixtus III (432–440).[86] Calabuig describes how Pope Sixtus III built this basilica to "perpetuate the memory of the Council of Ephesus and glorify the Mother of Jesus as Mother of God."[87]

---

82. Rubin, *Mother of God*, 46.

83. Pelikan, *Mary through the Centuries*, 56. Cyril of Alexandria stated against Nestorius: "If anyone does not confess that Emmanuel is God in truth, and therefore that the holy virgin is the mother of God [Theotokos] (for she bore in a fleshly way the Word of God become flesh), let him be anathema" (ibid.).

84. Johnson, *Truly Our Sister*, 117–18, as quoted in Johnson, "*Sub Tuum Praesidium*," 243.

85. While in the East, "the Marian cult reached its highest manifestations," in the West, they tended to repeat or amplify what had been worked out in the East. The West was dealing with barbarian invasions as well as being "concerned with different theological problems." See Gambero, *Mary and the Fathers of the Church*, 233, 323.

86. McDonnell, "The Marian Liturgical Tradition," 388; and Pierre Jounel, "The Veneration of Mary," in *Liturgy and Time*, vol. 4 of *The Church at Prayer: An Introduction to the Liturgy*, ed. Aimé Georges Martimort (Collegeville, MN: Liturgical Press, 1986), 133.

87. Calabuig, "The Liturgical Cult of Mary in the East and West," 244–45.

Mary's place continued to grow during the seasons of Advent and Christmas; she held an important role in the incarnation, and this was reflected in the liturgies. Seen as the "season of Mary's expectation" during the Ember days in Advent, the reading of the gospels of the annunciation and visitation fall on Wednesdays and Fridays.[88] Later on there will be a heightened emphasis on the use of the *Magnificat* in Vespers services with the use of the "O" antiphons from December 17 to December 23.[89]

An attempt to "relate the Marian cult to Christmas" led to the introduction of the *Natale sanctae Mariae* on January 1.[90] Celebrated since the seventh century, this feast has been described by Bernard Botte as "the first Marian feast of the Roman liturgy."[91] Known as the "Circumcision of the Lord," the feast would later be renamed "The Solemnity of Mary, Mother of God," in 1969.[92] Here is an example of where the focus on Mary's virginity is reflected in the use of the liturgy of the virgins for her feasts.[93]

Further evidence of a growing trust in Mary's intercession is reflected in the inclusion of Mary in the *Communicantes* of the Roman Canon. Dating from the end of the fifth century or early sixth century, this particular section of the Roman Canon says: "*Communicantes, / et memoriam venerantes, / in primis gloriosae semper Virginis Mariae, / Genetricis Dei et Domini nostri Iesu Christi.*"[94] Here Mary is described as "ever virgin" as well as "Mother of God and of our Lord Jesus Christ," two theological concepts that were debated in Christianity up to this point. It is also important to note that this insertion reflects the desire of the faithful to put their petitions and intercessions to Mary (and the saints) in the heart of the eucharistic prayer where they were believed to be most effective.[95] Calabuig writes that Mary

---

88. Jounel, "The Veneration of Mary," 134.

89. Ibid.

90. McDonnell, "The Marian Liturgical Tradition," 388–89.

91. Bernard Botte, as quoted in Jounel, "The Veneration of Mary," 133.

92. Christopher O'Donnell, *At Worship with Mary: A Pastoral and Theological Study* (Wilmington, DE: Michael Glazier, 1988), 13–14.

93. McDonnell, "The Marian Liturgical Tradition," 388–89.

94. Calabuig, "The Liturgical Cult of Mary in the East and West," 245.

95. See John F. Baldovin, *Bread of Life, Cup of Salvation: Understanding the Mass* (Lanham, MD: A Sheed & Ward Book/Rowman & Littlefield Publishers, 2003), 122.

is listed first "because of her unique dignity and . . . mission in salvation history."[96]

In addition to her inclusion in the *Communicantes*, the further growth of Marian devotion in the seventh century can be seen by the Western adaptation of four Eastern Marian feasts to the Roman Liturgy: February 2, March 25, August 15, and September 8.[97] Calabuig states that there are four factors that "worked together for the four Marian feasts: the participation of the bishop of Rome at the Eucharistic synaxis [gathering]; the place chosen for the celebration—the splendid Basilica of St. Mary Major; the stational procession; and the beauty of the Gregorian melodies."[98] Sergius I (687–701), an Eastern pope from Antioch in Syria, was the bishop of Rome who fostered the growth of these Marian feasts by participation in the stational procession to St. Mary Major (from St. Hadrian at the Forum).[99] John Baldovin notes that these Marian processions are some of the first examples in the Roman liturgy of *collectae* ("meetings at one church to go in procession to a *statio*").[100]

The Four Marian Feasts and Other Marian Liturgical Developments

The Four Marian Feasts

As has been previously noted, "the development of Marian piety in the East often preceded that in the West." This can be clearly seen in the history of the four Marian feasts.[101] The introduction of the Feast of the Presentation (February 2) to Rome is attributed to Theodorus I (642–649), who was born in Jerusalem.[102] It is in Jeru-

---

96. Calabuig, "The Liturgical Cult of Mary in the East and West," 246.

97. Ibid., 261–65. Jounel points out that "only two of these feasts had a strictly Marian title" and that "the feasts of March 25 and February 2 were originally feasts of the Lord, and in 1969 they became such once again." See Jounel, "The Veneration of Mary," 134–36. Some of these feasts that were originally christological were given a Marian emphasis and this was the case until the reforms of Vatican II.

98. Calabuig, "The Liturgical Cult of Mary in the East and West," 265.

99. Ibid., 264–65.

100. Baldovin, *The Urban Character of Christian Worship*, 122.

101. Calabuig, "The Liturgical Cult of Mary in the East and West," 238.

102. Ibid., 261. The feast falls forty days after Christmas. Before Christmas was set on December 25, the Presentation was celebrated forty days after Epiph-

salem that this feast is believed to have originated, as Egeria gives the "earliest account of the feast" from her travels there, most likely between 381 and 384.[103] The lighting of candles began in the fifth century, with the blessing of candles and *Nunc Dimittis* (Luke 2:29-32) added around the tenth century.[104]

The feast originally "had a predominantly Christological character" as it centered on the meeting of Simeon and Jesus, and was called by many names, including Candlemas and the Feast of the Meeting or *Hypapanti*.[105] Later, as the focus moved to Mary in both the location of the celebration (St. Mary Major) and the chants used in procession (*Ave gratia plena dei genetrix Virgo* and *Adorna thalamum tuum Sion*), it became known as the feast of the Purification of Mary.[106] It was known by this name until the reform of the calendar in 1969, when it returned to a more christological focus with the name "Presentation of the Lord."[107] The gospel reading from Luke 2:22-40, in which Mary is told that her soul will be pierced with a sword, would later lead to the devotion of Our Lady of Sorrows.[108] The meaning of this sword for Mary has received different interpretations. While Origen believed it was "a doubt that invaded Mary's heart when she saw her Son's sufferings," Ambrose believed it referred to Mary's suffering at the foot of the cross, which is the interpretation that Graef says "has never been questioned in the West."[109]

---

any (January 6) on February 13, the date it is still celebrated in the Armenian Church. See Paul F. Bradshaw and Maxwell E. Johnson, *The Origins of Feasts, Fasts and Seasons in Early Christianity* (London and Collegeville, MN: SPCK and Liturgical Press, 2011), 211.

103. O'Donnell, *At Worship with Mary*, 25.

104. Ibid., 26.

105. Calabuig, "The Liturgical Cult of Mary in the East and West," 261; and McDonnell, "The Marian Liturgical Tradition," 390.

106. Ibid., 261–62. The office for February 2 "lauded Mary as a model of humility and obedience to the Law for accepting the rite of purification." See Jounel, "The Veneration of Mary," 136.

107. O'Donnell, *At Worship with Mary*, 26.

108. Ibid., 31.

109. Graef, *The Devotion to Our Lady*, 13.

The Feast of the Annunciation (March 25)[110] celebrates the coming of the angel Gabriel to the Virgin Mary in which he addresses her with the salutation that would later become the first part of the Hail Mary (Luke 1:28). The evolution of this feast is somewhat unclear. According to Calabuig, since the third century March 25 "marked the beginning of spring prior to the Gregorian calendar reform."[111] Perhaps it is this early association between the Annunciation and springtime that led to the association of Mary and nature imagery that is found quite frequently in medieval French lyric poetry and also Marian congregational songs before Vatican II. Rubin notes that the coincidence of this date with springtime led to the joining of the "rebirth of humankind" with "that of nature" and that Germanus of Constantinople (631/649–ca. 733) referred to the Annunciation "as the 'springtime feast of feasts.'"[112]

The feast of the Annunciation is believed to have been introduced in Constantinople in 550, and from there it spread.[113] It was instituted in Rome around 660 and contained the themes of salvation through the incarnation ("the entire mystery of Christ") as well as Mary's virginity and her role in bearing Christ.[114] Much like the feast of the Presentation, the title has varied according to the theological focus; before Vatican II, the feast of the Annunciation was called the "Annunciation of the Angel to the Blessed Virgin Mary," while after the liturgical reforms of Vatican II, the christological focus was emphasized with the title the "Annunciation of the Lord."[115]

---

110. On the correlation of the nine-month space between the Annunciation and Christmas, see Thomas J. Talley, *The Origins of the Liturgical Year* (Collegeville, MN: Liturgical Press, 1991), 91–99. Bradshaw and Johnson add a disclaimer: "Although 25 March is important in the computation hypothesis for determining the 25 December date of Christmas, there is no evidence for this date being a commemoration specifically of the annunciation until the middle of the sixth century in the Christian East and only later in the West." See Bradshaw and Johnson, *The Origins of Feasts, Fasts and Seasons in Early Christianity*, 210.

111. Calabuig, "The Liturgical Cult of Mary in the East and West," 256.

112. Rubin, *Mother of God*, 72.

113. Calabuig, "The Liturgical Cult of Mary in the East and West," 256.

114. Ibid., 263.

115. O'Donnell, *At Worship with Mary*, 56.

The Feast of the Assumption (August 15),[116] which is "the oldest Marian feast," has its roots in Jerusalem, where it was celebrated as a feast of Mary *Theotokos*.[117] It is sometimes identified as the "oldest" Marian feast because the first indication of it comes from the fifth-century *Armenian Lectionary*, which describes the liturgies that took place "in late-fourth century Jerusalem."[118] This feast was first celebrated at the Kathisma, which is believed to be the place where Mary rested on her way to Bethlehem.[119] At the end of the fifth century the feast moved to the basilica in Gethsemane "where people venerated the tomb of the Virgin."[120] The feast then became known as the "Dormition of the Theotokos," and Emperor Maurice (582–602) "decreed that it be celebrated throughout the Empire."[121]

Reaching Rome around 650, the feast celebrated the "end of the earthly life of the Virgin"; although she died, "she could not be vanquished by death."[122] At the time when the feast came to Rome, the Western Church was still uncertain about the "bodily nature of the assumption of the Virgin."[123] Calabuig notes that "at Rome the doctrine of the bodily assumption of Mary made slow progress," and this is seen in the theology of the prayers of the Gregorian formulary that speaks only of the "glorification" of Mary's body as well as her "role as intercessor in heavenly glory."[124]

Indeed, this is certainly the case, as belief in Mary's assumption was based on apocryphal literature; Rubin notes that there are some

116. The reason for the August 15 date is still uncertain. Johnson says it may have been "the date of the Kathisma's dedication" among other possibilities. He also puts forth the work of Walter Ray in the pre-Christian, Essene *Book of Jubilees*, centering on the date of the festival of Pentecost as well as the birth of Isaac (May 15) and his conception by Sarah nine months earlier (August 15). The *Armenian Lectionary* had a feast of "Holy Innocents" on May 18, so it is possible that May 15 commemorated Christ's nativity and August 15 commemorated his conception. See Johnson, "*Sub Tuum Praesidium*," 264–66.

117. Johnson, "*Sub Tuum Praesidium*," 263.

118. Ibid.

119. Jounel, "The Veneration of Mary," 131.

120. Ibid.

121. O'Donnell, *At Worship with Mary*, 129.

122. Calabuig, "The Liturgical Cult of Mary in the East and West," 262.

123. Ibid.

124. Ibid., 262–63.

sixty accounts of Mary's *transitus*, all written before 1000.[125] She also describes two goals of these accounts of Mary's end: "praise of Mary and her miraculous end—a Dormition followed by an Assumption to heaven—and the disparagement of the Jews as Mary's enemies."[126] There is only one account of her end that does not include the polemical story of Jews trying to disrupt her funeral procession.[127] As was the case regarding the miracle story of the Jewish boy, Mary "continued to demarcate the difference between Christians and Jews."[128]

Another similarity to the miracle story of the Jewish boy is the significance of the power of Mary's intercession; the feast of the Assumption was instrumental in assuring the faithful of Mary's intercession, as her ability to intercede was heightened by the fact that she was "seated alongside her son in heaven."[129] Because Mary had been assumed into heaven, the faithful were unable to venerate her body, and so her "veneration was mediated by objects that had been close to her body."[130] These relics included Mary's milk, her girdle, "which she dropped to earth as she was assumed into heaven," and her robe.[131]

Although there has been a strong belief in Mary's bodily assumption throughout the ages, it was not declared to be the official dogma of the Catholic Church until 1950. Christopher O'Donnell notes that today this is the "only marian feast to have a vigil";[132] this is as a sign of how important this feast continues to be in the Catholic Church.

125. Rubin, *Mother of God*, 55.

126. Ibid.

127. Similar to the account of the unbelieving Salome in the *Protoevangelium of James*, in addition to Jewish people being blinded, one had his hand cut off by an angel and it stuck to Mary's funeral bier. They then asked for Mary's help, and "many converted." See Rubin, *Mother of God*, 56–57.

128. Ibid., 43.

129. Ibid., 139.

130. Ibid., 60.

131. Ibid. The story of how Mary's robe was acquired is what Rubin describes as "a classic narrative of Christian triumph over Judaism, dramatized as a move from the Holy Land to Constantinople." Two brothers tricked a Jewish woman and they took Mary's robe from her and brought it to Constantinople where it was housed in Blachernae. The relic would be "credited with saving the city from destruction by the Avars, the Muslims and the Russians." Here again Mary is used as a weapon and protectress against heretics. See ibid., 60–61.

132. O'Donnell, *At Worship with Mary*, 130.

It makes sense that the feast would be so popular, as other saints have their liturgical feasts "on the day of their entry into glory," and so the Assumption marks this day for Mary.[133]

In fact, there are hymns that continue to be written about the assumption, including "Sing, sing, ye angel bands." This hymn was written before the dogma was declared in 1950 (in the mid-nineteenth century), and, as many hymns, while not referencing the assumption explicitly, speaks of Mary both as she "ascends" and as she is enthroned in heaven looking down on us and caring for us:

1. Sing, sing, ye angel bands,
   All beautiful and bright;
   For higher still, and higher,
   Through fields of starry light,
   Your Virgin Queen ascends,
   Like the sweet moon at night.

2. O happy angels! look,
   How beautiful she is!
   See! Jesus bears her up!
   Her hands are locked in his.
   Oh! who can tell the height
   Of that fair Mother's bliss?

3. On through the countless stars
   Proceeds the bright array;
   And Love Divine comes forth
   To light her on the way,
   Through gloom of earthly night,
   Into celestial day.

4. Swifter and swifter grows
   That wondrous flight of love,
   As though her heart were drawn
   More veh'mently above;
   While joyful angels part
   A pathway for the Dove.

133. McDonnell, "The Marian Liturgical Tradition," 390.

5. Hark! hark! through highest heaven
　　What sounds of mystic mirth!
Mary, by God proclaimed
　　The Queen of spotless birth.
And diademed with stars
　　The lowliest of the earth.

6. And shall I lose thee then—
　　Lose my sweet right to thee?
Oh! no; the Angels' Queen,
　　Man's Mother still will be;
And thou upon thy throne
　　Wilt keep thy love for me. Amen.[134]

The final of these four Marian feasts, the Nativity of Mary (September 8), also has its origins in Jerusalem. O'Donnell cites the Constantinople new year of September 1 as influencing the date of the feast, which would later lead to the December 8 date for Mary's conception nine months earlier.[135] Paul Bradshaw and Maxwell Johnson posit that September 8 may have been the anniversary date for the dedication of a church to Mary in Jerusalem "next to the pool of Bethesda and near to the house of Anne, in which Mary was presumably born."[136] Calabuig also mentions this church dedicated to Mary was located near a healing pool, which he says may have been the pool Anna went to in order to be healed of her infertility.[137]

---

134. Frederick W. Faber, "Sing, sing, ye angel bands," Hymnary.org, http://www.hymnary.org/text/sing_sing_ye_angel_bands, accessed February 2014. Taken from Alfred Young, ed., *The Catholic Hymnal: Containing Hymns for Congregational and Home Use, and the Vesper Psalms, the Office of Compline, the Litanies, Hymns at Benediction, Etc.* (New York: Catholic Publication Society, 1885), 136.

135. O'Donnell, *At Worship with Mary*, 159.

136. Bradshaw and Johnson, *The Origins of Feasts, Fasts and Seasons in Early Christianity*, 211–12. While they offer this as a probable explanation, they also say that "the mere fact that the church was built on this site may suggest, alternatively, that there was already a commemoration of Mary's birth on 8 September in Jerusalem at this site that gave rise both to the feast and to the dedication of the church on this date, rather than the other way around."

137. Calabuig, "The Liturgical Cult of Mary in the East and West," 254. This corresponds to the healing ritual described in the *Protoevangelium of James* in chaps. 1–4.

The emperor Justinian (d. 565) brought the feast from Jerusalem to Constantinople.[138] The feast then made its way to Rome between 680 and 695, and the texts of the feast show Mary's birth as pointing toward the "mystery of the birth of Christ, in who is the mystery of our salvation."[139] Pierre Jounel describes how the Nativity of Mary, like the Nativity of John the Baptist, is a feast that is celebrated with joy because "salvation was about to dawn."[140] These four Marian feasts stood alone until the fourteenth century, when they were joined by the feasts of the Visitation and the Conception of Mary, as well as the Presentation of Mary in the Temple, Our Lady of the Snow, and the Sorrows of Mary.[141]

Early Marian Hymnody

The Akathist[142]

The *Akathist* is a Greek alphabetic acrostic of twenty-four stanzas (one for each letter of the alphabet) that comes from sometime between the mid-fifth or early sixth century. *Akathist* means not sitting, so this prayer is to be recited while standing.[143] The rich imagery found in this text made its way to the West when the text was translated into Latin in the ninth century.[144] The *Akathist* features

---

138. Ibid.

139. Ibid., 264.

140. Jounel, "The Veneration of Mary," 136.

141. Ibid., 138–41. Our Lady of the Snow commemorates the legend that the ground plan of St. Mary Major in Rome was "outlined by a snowfall in the middle of the Roman Summer."

142. For the full text of the *Akathist*, see: Luigi Gambero, *Mary and the Fathers of the Church: The Blessed Virgin Mary in Patristic Thought* (San Francisco, CA: Ignatius Press, 1999), 342–51.

143. Graef, *The Devotion to Our Lady*, 31. Daw makes the interesting point that "a standing position, especially in Orthodox practice, is associated with the affirmation of the Resurrection (in Greek, *anastasis*, [literally 'to stand again']). That is why the Council of Nicea made failure to stand in church during Easter Season an excommunica[ble] offense." Carl P. Daw, Jr., e-mail message to author, February 4, 2012.

144. Ibid., 31–32.

antithesis and hyperbole, two devices that were particularly popular with the Greek and Syriac writers.[145]

The twenty-four stanzas are divided into two parts, with the first part devoted to the story of Christ's birth and the second to praising Mary, or as Calabuig describes it, "a short *summa* on Mariology: the virginal life of Mary, the virginal conception, the divine motherhood, the virgin birth, Mary as the defender and model of virgins, Mary as source of the sacred mysteries of baptism, Mary as the protector of the Christian empire."[146] The *Akathist* also describes Mary as the "inviolate spouse of God,"[147] an image that will become popular after the first millennium, when many looked to interpret the Song of Songs through a Marian lens. Graef also notes that this text reinforces Mary's power as intercessor because she is "the heavenly ladder by which God descended as well as the bridge that leads from earth to heaven."[148]

Venantius Fortunatus

Moving from Marian hymns in the East to the West, we find Venantius Fortunatus (ca. 530–ca. 600), who is described as an "intelligent and subtle poet who took his inspiration from classical forms but whose content was deeply Christian."[149] Known for such classic hymns as *Vexilla Regis produent* and *Pange, lingua, gloriosi*, Fortunatus also allegedly wrote such well-known Marian texts as "The God whom earth and sea and sky/The Lord whom earth and stars" and "*O gloriosa Virginum*/O glorious Maid." "The God whom earth and sea and sky" is often referred to by its Latin text, *Quem terra, pontus, aethera*, which Calabuig aptly describes as an "awestruck meditation on the motherhood of Mary of Nazareth, in whose womb there is

145. Rubin, *Mother of God*, 25, 72. Rubin writes of their propensity for "praise in contradiction," particularly around the paradox of the incarnation, where you have "a god made flesh, a virgin giving birth, the creator being created." One example is Andrew of Crete (ca. 660–ca. 740), who called Mary the "container of the uncontainable" (ibid., 72).

146. Calabuig, "The Liturgical Cult of Mary in the East and West," 257.

147. Gambero, *Mary and the Fathers of the Church*, 338.

148. Graef, *The Devotion to Our Lady*, 31–32.

149. Calabuig, "The Liturgical Cult of Mary in the East and West," 250.

the universe and to whom heaven, earth, and sea render praise."[150]
Here is the English translation of the text by John Mason Neale
(1818–1866):

1. The God whom earth and sea and sky
   Adore and laud and magnify,
   Whose might they own, whose praise they swell,
   In Mary's womb vouchsafed to dwell.

2. The Lord whom sun and moon obey,
   Whom all things serve from day to day,
   Was by the Holy Ghost conceived,
   Of her who, through His grace, believed.

3. How blest that Mother, in whose shrine
   The world's Creator, Lord divine,
   Whose hand contains the earth and sky,
   Once deigned, as in His ark, to lie!

4. Blest in the message Gabriel brought,
   Blest by the work the Spirit wrought,
   From whom the great Desire of earth
   Took human flesh and human birth.

5. O Lord, the Virgin-born, to Thee
   Eternal praise and glory be!
   Whom, with the Father, we adore,
   And Holy Ghost for evermore.[151]

Fortunatus also composed *In laudem sanctae Mariae*.[152] In this
text, comprising 360 verses, Gambero points out that there is a passage where Fortunatus attributes "something to the Virgin Mother
that, properly speaking, ought to be attributed to her son" when

---

150. Ibid., 251.

151. Venantius Honorius Clementianus Fortunatus, "The God whom earth
and sea and sky," Hymnary.org, http://www.hymnary.org/text/the_god_whom
_earth_and_sea_and_sky, accessed February 2014. Taken from Philip Schaff, ed.,
Christ in Song (New York: Anson D. F. Randolph, 1871), 99–100.

152. Calabuig, "The Liturgical Cult of Mary in the East and West," 250.

he writes, "Destroying hell, you bring back captives to their na-
tive land; / And restore their freedom, after breaking their yokes"
(329–330).[153] Gambero writes that speaking of Mary in this manner
"is fairly widespread" and that "it presupposes the implicit view
that certain expressions have to be understood as referring only to
Christ the Redeemer, in a strict sense, even if they may be applied
to Mary indirectly."[154]

It will be important to keep this notion in mind when examining
Marian congregational songs that verge on being heretical because
they too contain expressions applied to Mary that are generally reserved for Christ. The distinction was made by John Damascene (ca.
650–ca. 750) between *latria*, adoration "owed to God alone," and
the "honor or veneration that ought to be given to the holy Virgin,"
later known as *dulia*.[155] This is where the term "Mario-latry" would
come from during the Reformation, when Protestants would ac-
cuse Catholics of giving too much *latria* to Mary. Thomas Aquinas
(1225–1274), however, felt that Mary was owed more than *dulia* or
"reverence," and so her adoration was given the term *hyperdulia*.[156]

The Ave maris stella

One of the most enduring Marian hymns from before the first
millennium is the *Ave maris stella* ("Hail, Star of the Sea"), a text first
seen in manuscripts from the ninth century, but most likely from
the eighth century.[157] Graef describes this hymn as "an epitome of
medieval man's devotion to the Mother of God, expressing both his
insecurity in a troubled world and his limitless confidence in the
protection of her who is the 'star of the sea' that guides the traveler
safely into the port of heaven."[158] Pelikan tells how the title *maris stella*
came about: apparently Jerome described the etymology of Mary as

153. Gambero, *Mary and the Fathers of the Church*, 362.
154. Ibid.
155. Ibid., 406.
156. Pelikan, *Mary through the Centuries*, 102.
157. Hilda Graef, *Mary: A History of Doctrine and Devotion; With a New Chapter Covering Vatican II and Beyond by Thomas A. Thompson* (Notre Dame, IN: Ave Maria Press, 2009), 136.
158. Graef, *The Devotion to Our Lady*, 40–41.

"a drop of water from the sea [*stilla maris*]," and *stilla* (drop) became *stella* (star) when the notion was taken up by Isidore of Seville (ca. 560–636).[159]

This hymn contains many of the doctrines associated with Mary by this point in time: her divine motherhood, her perpetual virginity, the Mary/Eve parallel, her mercy, and her intercession.[160] Just as Mary's mantle was seen "as a sign and pledge of protection" that "symbolizes the ideal of a mother's love and concern for her children"[161] in the story of the Jewish boy, again one can see the notion of "Mary's motherly protection" coming up throughout this text.[162] Graef summarizes all that Mary is to do: "she is to show herself a true mother who presents our prayers to her Son."[163] This notion that Mary should "show herself a true mother," found in stanza 4 of this hymn, is one that is found in Bernard of Clairvaux (1090–1153) and also quite often in Marian congregational songs before Vatican II.

Another notion that was popular in the Middle Ages and continued to be so for centuries is the nautical imagery of "Mary as the star guiding the ship of faith," the "lodestar of voyagers through life."[164] Bernard of Clairvaux, who had a great devotion to Mary, "called on his hearers to look to the star that was Mary."[165] In addition to being described as the "gate of heaven" in stanza 1, in stanza 6 she is described as someone who will help us navigate a safe way to Jesus. Here is the Gregorian chant tune that most commonly goes with the text, along with the Latin text and Edward Caswall's (1814–1878) English translation, "Hail! bright star of ocean":

159. Pelikan, *Mary through the Centuries*, 94.

160. Calabuig, "The Liturgical Cult of Mary in the East and West," 273.

161. Gambero, *Mary and the Fathers of the Church*, 356–57.

162. Graef, *The Devotion to Our Lady*, 40.

163. Ibid., 41.

164. Pelikan, *Mary through the Centuries*, 93–94.

165. Graef, *The Devotion to Our Lady*, 41.

1. A - ve ma - ris Stel - la, De - i
Ma - ter al - ma, At - que sem - per
Vir - go, Fe - lix cæ - li por - ta.

Figure 1. *Ave maris Stella*. Text: Anonymous, ninth century. Tune: Plainchant, Mode 1. (From Socias and Stepansky, eds., *Cantate et Iubilate Deo*, 23.)

1. Ave maris stella,
    Dei Mater alma,
    Atque semper Virgo,
    Felix cæli Porta.
	1. Hail! bright Star of Ocean,
	    God's own Mother blest,
	    Ever-sinless Virgin,
	    Gate of heavenly rest.

2. Sumens illud Ave
    Gabriélis ore,
    Funda nos in pace,
    Mutans Hevæ nomen.
	2. Taking that sweet Ave
	    Which from Gabriel came,
	    Peace confirm within us,
	    Changing Eva's name.

3. Solve vincla reis,
    Profer lumen cæcis,
    Mala nostra pelle,
    Bona cuncta posce.
	3. Break the captive's fetters;
	    Light on blindness pour;
	    All our ills expelling,
	    Every bliss implore.

4. Monstra te esse matrem:
    Sumat per te preces,
    Qui pro nobis natus
    Tulit esse tuus.
	4. Show thyself a mother;
	    May the Word divine,
	    Born for us thine Infant,
	    Hear our prayers through thine.

5. Virgo singuláris,
    Inter omnes mitis,
    Nos, culpis solútos,
    Mites fac et castos.
	5. Virgin all excelling,
	    Mildest of the mild,
	    Freed from guilt, preserve us
	    Meek and undefiled.

6. Vitam præsta puram,
    Iter para tutum:
    Ut vidéntes Iesum,
    Semper collætémur.
	6. Keep our life all spotless,
	    Make our way secure,
	    Till we find in Jesus
	    Joy for evermore.

7. Sit laus Deo Patri,	7. Through the highest heaven,
Summo Christo decus,	To the Almighty Three,
Spirítui Sancto,	Father, Son, and Spirit,
Tribus honor unus. Amen.[166]	One same glory be. Amen.[167]

This hymn's popularity and the idea of Mary as "Star of the Sea" carried throughout the ages (at least up until Vatican II). "Hail, Queen of Heaven, the Ocean Star" contains some of the themes more commonly found in Marian congregational songs that date before Vatican II, in addition to the older *Ave maris stella*. This text by John Lingard (1771–1851)—described by J. Vincent Higginson as "one of the oldest English vernacular hymns commonly found in Catholic hymnals"—although inspired by the *Ave maris stella* it is not a translation of the Latin text.[168]

1. Hail, Queen of Heaven, the Ocean Star,
   Guide of the wand'rer here below!
Thrown on life's surge, we claim thy care,
   Save us from peril and from woe.
      Mother of Christ, Star of the Sea,
      Pray for the wand'rer, pray for me.

2. O gentle, chaste, and spotless Maid!
      We sinners make our prayers to thee;
   Remind thy Son that He has paid
      The price of our iniquity.

166. Socias and Stepansky, eds., *Cantate et Iubilate Deo*, 22–23.

167. Edward Caswall, "Hail, bright star of ocean, God's own mother," Hymnary.org, http://www.hymnary.org/text/hail_bright_star_of_ocean_gods_own _mothe, accessed February 2014. Taken from Roman Catholic Church, *Hymns and Songs for Catholic Children* (New York: Catholic Publication Society, 1870),126–27. This text is also known as "Gentle star of ocean" or "Hail, thou star of ocean," and Caswall revised it to "Hail, bright star of ocean" in his 1873 collection *Hymns and Poems*. J. Vincent Higginson, *Handbook for American Catholic Hymnals* (New York: The Hymn Society of America, 1976), 76. The earlier version appeared in his 1849 collection, *Lyra Catholica*. Emma Hornby, "Ave maris stella," *The Canterbury Dictionary of Hymnology*, http://www.hymnology.co.uk/a /ave-maris-stella, accessed March 2014.

168. Higginson, *Handbook for American Catholic Hymnals*, 79. Lingard's text is usually paired with STELLA (ca. 1850), a tune that Henri F. Hemy (1818–88) arranged from a folksong.

Virgin most pure, Star of the Sea,
Pray for the sinner, pray for me.

3. Sojourners in this vale of tears,
    To thee, blest Advocate, we cry;
   Pity our sorrows, calm our fears,
     And soothe with hope our misery.
    Refuge in grief, Star of the Sea,
    Pray for the mourner, pray for me.

4. And while to Him who reigns above,
    In Godhead One, in Persons Three,
   The Source of life, of grace, of love,
     Homage we pay on bended knee;
    Do thou, bright Queen, Star of the Sea,
    Pray for thy children, pray for me.[169]

Many of the pre–Vatican II texts speak of Mary as "Star of the Sea," a beacon[170] or guiding star, who will help to navigate our way[171] and be a "Guide of the wand'rer here below."[172] It is often mentioned how life is like a "tempestuous sea,"[173] but, when we are "Thrown on life's surge"[174] Mary will calm the seas of life for us[175] and be a port

---

169. John Lingard, "Hail, queen of heaven, the ocean star," Hymnary.org, http://www.hymnary.org/text/hail_queen_of_heaven_the_ocean_star, accessed March 2014. Taken from Roman Catholic Church, *Hymns and Songs for Catholic Children* (New York: Catholic Publication Society, 1870), 138–39.

170. See stanza 3 of #105, "Mother of Christ," in *The Standard Catholic Hymnal: Complete Edition*, ed. James A. Reilly (Boston, MA: McLaughlin & Reilly Co., 1921), 117–18.

171. See stanza 3 of "Ah, her smile, makes Heaven rejoice" in *Sunday School Hymn Book*, ed. Sisters of Notre Dame (Philadelphia, PA: Oliver Ditson Company; Theodore Presser Co., Distributors, 1915), 112.

172. See stanza 1 of "Hail Queen of Heaven, the ocean star," as quoted above.

173. See stanza 1 of "Mother dear, oh pray for me," as quoted below.

174. See stanza 1 of #102, "Hail Queen of Heaven, the ocean star," in *St. Basil's Hymnal: An Extensive Collection of English and Latin Hymns for Church, School and Home*, ed. the Basilian Fathers (Chicago: John P. Daleiden Co., 1918), 119.

175. See stanza 2 of #136, "Daily, daily sing to Mary," in *The Catholic Hymnal: Containing Hymns for Congregational and Home Use, and the Vesper Psalms, the Office of Compline, the Litanies, Hymns at Benediction, Etc. The Tunes by Rev. Alfred Young,*

of rest.[176] Richard Mouw offers a helpful study on "Nautical Rescue Themes in Evangelical Hymnody" which can, despite some differences, be applied to Marian congregational song.[177] While the Evangelical hymnody he explores tends to be more mission oriented, some of the nautical Marian congregational songs share similar themes. For instance, both cases address the theme of "life as a stormy sea,"[178] as noted above in "Mother dear, oh pray for me." "The plea for a reliable pilot/navigator,"[179] is also found in this case except here, the navigator is Mary, Star of the Sea, instead of God or Jesus. Mary is the "guiding star of the sea, / And trusting ever we look on thee."[180] The "quest for safety" is also a shared theme, as seen above when Mary calms the waters and brings us safely home.[181]

Mouw points to John Paul II's reference to Paul VI in *Redemptor Hominis* "as the 'helmsman of the Church, the bark of Peter'" referring to the Church as a ship, or the boat (bark) of Peter.[182] He also looks to the work of Gertrude Grace Sill who describes the "central portion of a church building as the 'nave'" which comes "from the ancient practice of depicting the church as a sailing vessel, that, as

---

Priest of the Congregation of St. Paul the Apostle. The Words Original and Selected, ed. Alfred Young (New York: Catholic Publication Society Co., 1884), 130.

176. See the chorus of #99, "Ave Maria, Guardian dear," in *St. Basil's Hymnal: Containing Music for Vespers of All the Sundays and Festivals of the Year. Three Masses and over Two Hundred Hymns, Together with Litanies, Daily Prayers, Prayers at Mass, Preparation and Prayers for Confession and Communion, and the Office and Rules for Sodalities of the Blessed Virgin Mary*, ed. the Basilian Fathers, 10th ed. (Toronto and Medina, NY: St. Basil's Novitiate and James Brennan, 1906), 186–87.

177. Richard J. Mouw, "'Some Poor Sailor, Tempest Tossed': Nautical Rescue Themes in Evangelical Hymnody," in *Wonderful Words of Life: Hymns in American Protestant History and Theology*, ed. Richard J. Mouw and Mark A. Noll (Grand Rapids, MI: William B. Eerdmans Publishing Company, 2004), 234–50.

178. Ibid., 235.

179. Mouw, "'Some Poor Sailor, Tempest Tossed,'" 235.

180. From the first stanza of #109, "Bright Queen of Heaven, Virgin all fair," in *Psallite: Catholic English Hymns. With an Appendix of Prayers and Devotions*, ed. Alexander Roesler, 8th ed. (St. Louis, MO: B. Herder Book Company, 1918), 123.

181. See stanza 2 of #136, "Daily, daily sing to Mary," 130; and the refrain of # 99, "Ave Maria, Guardian dear," 186–87.

182. John Paul II, as quoted in Mouw, "'Some Poor Sailor, Tempest Tossed,'" 237.

St. Hippolytus put it, 'is beaten by the waves, but not submerged.'"[183]
The corporate notion of the Church as a ship was transferred to an individual sailing on life's sea in a ship, both in Evangelical hymns and
in Marian congregational song.[184] This motif is found, for instance,
in the first stanza of "Mother dear, oh pray for me":

> Mother dear, oh pray for me,
> Whilst, far from Heav'n and thee,
> I wander in a fragile bark
> O'er life's tempestuous sea.
> O Virgin Mother, from thy throne,
> So bright in bliss above,
> Protect thy child and cheer my path
> With thy sweet smile of love.[185]

While these nautical images were popular before Vatican II when
travel by sea was more common (and dangerous), they seem to have
fallen out of favor as fewer people travel by sea and more travel by
plane. Mouw argues that these images can still be meaningful today,
even though we do not live in an age where we might be as "conscious of the dangers of the sea, so that images of angry waters and
vulnerable barks and the real threat of shipwreck are appropriate
vehicles for some deep spiritual impulses"[186] as they were to those
who sang to Mary, Star of the Sea in the past. The impending end
of the first millennium would raise new fears and create dramatic
shifts in devotions to Jesus, and therefore also to Mary.

---

183. Gertrude Grace Sill, *A Handbook of Symbols in Christian Art* (New York: Macmillan, 1975), 134, as quoted in Mouw, "'Some Poor Sailor, Tempest Tossed,'" 237.

184. In her work on Marian poetry, de Flon points to Margaret Johnson's de-
scription of how the Tractarians used "the ship 'as an image of spiritual journey-
ing.'" Margaret Johnson, *Gerard Manley Hopkins and Tractarian Poetry* (Aldershot:
Ashgate, 1997), 209, as quoted in Nancy de Flon, "Mary in Nineteenth-Century
English and American Poetry," in *Mary: The Complete Resource*, ed. Sarah Jane
Boss (Oxford: Oxford University Press, 2007), 507n8.

185. "Mother dear, O pray for me," Hymnary.org, http://www.hymnary.org
/text/mother_dear_o_pray_for_me, accessed March 2014. Taken from #86 in *The
De La Salle Hymnal: For Catholic Schools and Choirs*, ed. Christian Brothers (New
York: La Salle Bureau, 1913), 86–87.

186. Mouw, "'Some Poor Sailor, Tempest Tossed,'" 249.

Chapter Two

The Face That Most Resembles Christ[1]

Ecclesia, flush with rapture! Sing
for Mary's sake, sing
for the maiden, sing
for God's mother. Sing![2]
    —Hildegard of Bingen, "Ave generosa"

Introduction

The cult of Mary blossomed during the Middle Ages, a period in which Dante Alighieri (1265–1321), in his work *The Divine Comedy*, would refer to Mary as "the face that most resembles Christ." This flourishing was largely a result of the increased emphasis on the humanity of Jesus and Mary, as well as a new attitude toward Christ's

---

1. Dante, *Paradiso* 32:85–86, as quoted in Vincent A. Lenti, "The Face That Most Resembles Christ," *The Hymn* 45, no. 2 (April 1994): 19.

2. Hildegard of Bingen, "Ave generosa," stanza 7, as translated in Hildegard of Bingen, *Symphonia: A Critical Edition of the* Symphonia armonie celestium revelationum [*Symphony of the Harmony of Celestial Revelations*], introduction, translations, and commentary by Barbara Newman, 2nd ed. (Ithaca and London: Cornell University Press, 1998), 123.

passion and death, and Mary's role at the foot of the cross. Around the eleventh and twelfth centuries, the focus of devotion shifted from the resurrection to the passion.[3] These changes were reflected in the tone of the funeral liturgy at that time, as it moved from one of joyful hope and expectation to one of fear of judgment and desire for absolution.[4] As Rachel Fulton argues, this shift was not only reflected in the people's sense of unworthiness and fear of impending judgment heightened by the passing of the "millennial anniversaries of Christ's birth and death"; it also created a context where Mary "provided the model for compassionate response to Christ's pain."[5]

This focus on Mary's grief at the foot of the cross was expressed in the artwork, music, and liturgy of the time, including the *Pietà*, *Stabat Mater*, and the Stations of the Cross. These changes, in addition to the shift in mediation from Christ to that of Mary and the saints, led the faithful to look to Mary for help, guidance, protection, and her intercession to Christ, bridging the gap between heaven and earth, divinity and humanity. All of this helped to create the medieval cult of the Blessed Virgin.

Medieval Marian Devotions, Music, and Liturgy from the Millennium up to Trent

Shifts in Devotion to Christ and Mary

From the Beato Passio to the Bitter Passion

A few hundred years after the institution of the four Marian feasts, a change in Christian prayer led to an even greater proliferation of Marian devotion. There was a great outpouring of devotion to Mary in the form of prayers, music, and artwork, fueled by the prayers and sermons of many great figures of the time, including Anselm of Canterbury (1033–1109), Bernard of Clairvaux, and

---

3. Joseph A. Jungmann, *Christian Prayer through the Centuries* (New York: Paulist Press, 1978), 96–98.

4. Richard Rutherford, *The Death of a Christian: The Order of Christian Funerals* (Collegeville, MN: Liturgical Press, 1990), 61–65.

5. Rachel Fulton, *From Judgment to Passion: Devotion to Christ and the Virgin Mary, 800–1200* (New York: Columbia University Press, 2002), 78, 199.

Bonaventure (1221–1274).[6] The roots of this change go back to the Arian controversies in Spain in the fifth and sixth centuries.

As a reaction to the Arian controversy, the Church was forced "to stress in every possible way the equality in essence of the Son with the Father" since the Arians believed that Jesus was subordinate to God.[7] This new emphasis created a gap for the faithful in that they were distanced from God and could not look to Christ as their Mediator; they could no longer pray to God through Christ, as that could be seen by the Arians as the "subordination of the Son to the Father."[8] Joseph Jungmann cites this distancing from Christ as the origin of kneeling in church (first mandated at the Synod of Tours in 813), created by a sense of "misery and sinfulness."[9] The Christian faithful had no choice but to look for another mediator, leading them to look to "Mary, the angels, the saints and relics" as their new source of help.[10]

Another dramatic shift occurred in the eleventh and twelfth centuries. Instead of an emphasis on the victory over the cross, the focus was now on Jesus' life: "interest is focused on the person of him who achieved the redemption, on the external facts of his appearance in this world and his career as reported in the gospels."[11] The high points of interest were Christmas and Easter, or more specifically, Jesus' birth by Mary and the suffering of both Mary and Jesus during the passion. Jungmann describes this as a shift from the *beato passio* (the blessed passion) to the bitter passion, with the focus moving from Easter to Christmas and Good Friday.[12] It is not a coincidence that it is also around the tenth century that crosses are first made bearing a *corpus*.[13]

---

6. Jungmann, *Christian Prayer through the Centuries*, 109–15. Jungmann credits St. Bernard with giving Mary the title *Domina nostra* (Our Lady).

7. Ibid., 69.

8. Ibid., 69–70.

9. Ibid., 70.

10. Ibid., 71.

11. Ibid., 96.

12. Ibid., 96–97.

13. Elizabeth C. Parker, "Architecture as Liturgical Setting," in *The Liturgy of the Medieval Church*, ed. Thomas J. Heffernan and E. Ann Matter (Kalamazoo, MI: Medieval Institute Publications, 2001), 296. One of the earliest of these crucifixes with a *corpus* that remains today is the Gero crucifix (ca. 975–99) in Cologne Cathedral. See Fulton, *From Judgment to Passion*, 62.

This emphasis on "Christ's human nature" and "the earthly life which he had assumed" was one of two effects of what Jungmann refers to as the "second phase" of piety in the Middle Ages; the other effect was the search for "secondary mediators."[14] The "first phase" was the result of Arianism as noted above; here the emphasis is on the "oneness in essence of the three Divine Persons."[15] The "second phase" is a result of the same issue—the controversy of Christ's divinity brought on by Arianism—but this time "the glorified God-man is obscured and dimmed to a greater and greater degree."[16] As a result in this shift, the faithful turned to Mary both as a mediator and as someone who shared in the human nature of Christ, especially in his birth and death.

But why did this shift occur in what Jungmann labels the "second phase" of piety in the Middle Ages? Rachel Fulton does well in attempting to answer this question, one that is very significant in understanding Marian devotion because it sets up the framework for devotion to Mary for centuries to come. As Fulton describes it, her research "sets out to explain the origins and initial development of a devotion at the heart of medieval European Christianity: the imitative devotion to Christ in his suffering, historical humanity and to his mother, Mary, in her compassionate grief."[17] Prior to this shift, as seen in the work of Hrabanus Maurus (780–856), there was not a feeling of compassion toward Christ, but rather a feeling of "gratitude and awe—awe at his strength in overcoming the powers of darkness, gratitude for his humbling himself so as to overcome the forces of death."[18]

Fulton says that the catalyst for this eleventh-century shift from gratitude and awe to a desire to share in Christ's pain and imitate him was the calendar with the years 1000 and 1033, the millennial anniversaries of Christ's birth and death.[19] These anniversaries brought increasing fear that Christ would return in judgment, leading people to believe they needed to placate and repay "the all-powerful,

---

14. Jungmann, *Christian Prayer through the Centuries*, 98.
15. Ibid.
16. Ibid.
17. Fulton, *From Judgment to Passion*, 1.
18. Ibid., 55.
19. Ibid., 64.

all-seeing crucified Judge."[20] Following the passing of these anniversaries, the "nonevent of the Apocalypse" brought nostalgia for the past and a sense of uncertainty and loss in addition to threatening the efficacy of images and the liturgy.[21]

This uncertainty began to focus on the image of the crucifix: as crucifixes begin to portray the image of a dead Christ hanging on them, people such as Peter Damian (ca. 1007–1072) begin to advocate for a severe form of imitating Christ in self-flagellation. Because the cross reminds the viewer of "the debt incurred by Christ's Passion" they should imitate "Christ as Judge"; through the act of self-flagellation the sinner was able both to "discharge the balance of his debts" as well as "act as judge against himself prior to the judgment, thus removing the need for Christ to judge him at all."[22] This desire for imitation was also seen in the priesthood, as it is during this time that there was a move for priests to remain celibate in an effort to have them imitate Christ's purity.[23] Fulton also argues that the anxiety and instability of "Tradition" brought about by the "failure of the Apocalypse" led to the debates over the presence of Christ in the Eucharist.[24]

The effects of this way of thinking impacted Marian devotion as well, especially in the work of Anselm of Canterbury. As Fulton describes, unlike Peter Damian, Anselm had a different response to the fear of Christ's judgment, for he "had convinced himself that there was, in fact, no debt to be repaid because there was nothing, not even fear, with which he could pay. There were, rather, only love and mindfulness and a diet of tears."[25] This is extremely important because it sets the stage for the devotion to Mary at the foot of the cross. It is the example of Mary's grief at the foot of the cross that will be the ultimate example for sinners as they seek to respond to Christ's sacrifice with "love and mindfulness and a diet of tears."

The prayers of Anselm draw from "earlier Carolingian and Anglo-Saxon collections of private prayers."[26] Fulton points out that while

20. Ibid.
21. Ibid., 78, 80.
22. Ibid., 87, 91, 103.
23. Ibid., 107–8.
24. Ibid., 119, 140.
25. Ibid., 146.
26. Ibid., 150.

prayers addressed to Christ were "liturgically rare"—most likely as a reaction to the Arian controversy—they were "relatively common as private devotions" in the eleventh century and under the Carolingians.[27] These prayers, focused on Christ on the cross or Mary at the foot of the cross, have the sinner asking for Christ's compassion, since he is the Judge.[28] A similar notion can be observed in Marian congregational songs from the mid-nineteenth to mid-twentieth century in which the sinner admits unworthiness and asks for Mary's help in attaining Christ's forgiveness.

Another concept is the "great distance between Christ and the sinner."[29] Fulton gives examples of where the sinner is actually shouting to be heard because the distance between Christ's suffering and ours is so great.[30] As was seen previously in regard to Mary's assumption, her place in heaven next to Christ helped to bridge that gap, in terms of both the distance between heaven and earth and the distance between divinity and humanity. Fulton describes how Mary is now at the Judge's throne and that it is her "prerogative now, to pray for those whom she has left behind on earth, and so her Son encourages her, 'Open to me.'"[31]

The structure of Anselm's prayers, which were meant to lead the sinner to devotion and love (as Fulton argues), is similar to the structure of many Marian congregational songs, particularly those written before Vatican II which focus on Mary's suffering at the foot of the cross and her role as intercessor in heaven. Fulton draws from the work of René Roques in outlining the structure of Anselm's prayers

27. Ibid.

28. Ibid.

29. Ibid., 153.

30. Ibid., 153–54.

31. Ibid., 275, 278. The image of Mary interceding to Christ on behalf of sinners continued "in fourteenth-century iconography," where "Mary's breasts are revealed in order to turn Christ away from a judgement of death upon a sinful humanity. A variant of the same theme is found in the widespread representation of Mary interceding for a petitioner by showing one of her breasts to Christ, who in turn shows the wound in his side to God the Father. The breast and the wound are emblems of Christ's humanity and reassurances of his mercy." See Sarah Jane Boss, *Empress and Handmaid: On Nature and Gender in the Cult of the Virgin Mary* (London and New York: Cassell, 2000), 38.

as containing praises of the intercessor, self-loathing of the sinner, the hope that the "loving relationship" between the sinner and the intercessor and/or God will keep the sinner from being forgotten, and praise to God and the saints, "confident in the compassion of a merciful Judge."[32] This structure also reflects Anselm's notion that we can never repay the debt owed to God; therefore, the "only appropriate response" was "love and praise."[33]

In conjunction with Anselm's shift from fear of judgment to meditation on Christ's passion, there is also a shift in the understanding of Mary's response at the foot of the cross. Before Anselm's time, Mary was depicted as being stoic at the scene of Christ's passion.[34] Anselm, however, describes Mary not only as grieving but also as weeping, and this weeping "becomes the model for the contemplative's own experience of grief."[35] The intense suffering that Mary experienced during the passion led to new devotions such as the Sorrowful Mysteries of the rosary, the *Stabat Mater*, and the *Planctus Mariae*.

This suffering was often depicted in artwork in which Mary's heart was pierced with a sword as foretold by Simeon in Luke 2:35, which was known as Our Lady of Sorrows. Fulton notes that while Christ experienced spiritual and physical pain, Mary suffered the "pain of remembrance" as all Christians did.[36] Since no Christian could suffer as Christ did for our sins, Mary's pain "provided the model for compassionate response to Christ's pain, her pain that taught Christians what it was like to have seen Christ die on the cross."[37] Fulton aptly summarizes how this new devotion to Mary's suffering goes hand in hand with the new devotion to Christ's human suffering:

> In other words, devotion to Christ in his suffering humanity depended not only on devotion to the Mother from whom he became incarnate; it also depended upon empathy with that Mother in both her sorrow

32. Fulton, *From Judgment to Passion*, 173–74.

33. Ibid., 176. This is Anselm's satisfaction theory of atonement.

34. Ibid., 206. Ambrose of Milan said that Mary stood at the foot of the cross, but she didn't weep.

35. Ibid., 191–92.

36. Ibid., 199. Fulton also describes this as "interpreted through the wound of love suffered by the beloved in the Song of Songs (2:5 LXX)."

37. Ibid.

and her joy. The translation of the crucified Judge into the suffering man went hand in hand with the translation of the queenly Intercessor into the grieving Mother—and this mutual translation was and is nowhere more urgent or visible than in Anselm's prayers.[38]

Not only were these prayers new in their focus on Mary's suffering but they also display a greater sense of urgency. As Fulton points out, "begging for Mary's intercession with her Son the Lord God had long been a standard motive in Marian prayer"; in the eleventh century, however, a greater urgency in the need for Mary's intercession arose since people feared Christ's imminent return in judgment.[39] For some, such as Eadmer of Canterbury (ca. 1064–ca. 1124), a disciple of Anselm, this sense of urgency was met by the idea that, in his words, "salvation is quicker if we remember Mary's name than if we invoke the name of the Lord Jesus."[40]

The notion that one should go to Mary first, or go to Mary in order to reach Jesus, is one that was expanded on by Bernard of Clairvaux and one that is extremely prominent in Marian congregational songs before Vatican II. Graef describes how Bernard's works focus on "Mary's mediation between her Son and his faithful," and his thoughts caught on not because they were groundbreaking but as a result of the "force and beauty with which he, the 'Mellifluous Doctor,' expressed his love of Mary."[41] Bernard's prayer to Mary to "show yourself to be a mother" is one repeated quite often in Marian congregational songs in the mid-nineteenth and mid-twentieth centuries.[42]

38. Ibid., 205.

39. Ibid., 205, 218. Fulton cites as an example the prayers of Fulbert of Chartres written for the feast of Mary's Nativity. She also notes that in these prayers of Fulbert is the new idea of associating Christ's pain on the cross with Mary's intercession. See Fulton, 221.

40. Eadmer, *Liber de excellentia virginis Mariae*, chap. 6, as quoted in Fulton, *From Judgment to Passion*, 246.

41. Hilda Graef, *Mary: A History of Doctrine and Devotion; With a New Chapter Covering Vatican II and Beyond by Thomas A. Thompson* (Notre Dame, IN: Ave Maria Press, 2009), 185.

42. Rubin describes how Bernard prayed this prayer "in front of a statue of Mary and child," and it was during this experience that "Mary offered the milk of her breast to his prayerful lips" in what is known as the lactation of St.

In his *Sermon on the Aqueduct,* written for the feast of Mary's Nativity, Bernard likens Mary's mediation between Christ and his followers on earth to an "aqueduct which leads the divine waters to earth," allowing "floods of grace" to reach the earth through Mary.[43] Bernard was also fond of the image of Mary as Star of the Sea, as is found in one of his homilies on the Annunciation. Graef quotes the following passage to show the "universal efficacy" of Mary's intercession. It is quoted at length here because there are many similarities between Bernard's language and that of Marian congregational songs before Vatican II. There are countless hymns that not only refer to Mary as Star of the Sea (e.g., *Ave maris stella*) but also use the imagery of one's life being tossed on the tempest-filled waters of life:

> If you will not be submerged by tempests, do not turn away your eyes from the splendor of this star! If the storms of temptations arise, if you crash against the rocks of tribulation, look to the star, call upon Mary. If you are tossed about on the waves of pride, of ambition, of slander, of hostility, look to the star, call upon Mary. If wrath or avarice or the enticements of flesh upset the boat of your mind, look to Mary. If you are disturbed by the immensity of your crimes . . . if you begin to be swallowed up by the abyss of depression and despair, think of Mary! In dangers, in anxiety, in doubt, think of Mary, call upon Mary. Let her name not leave your lips nor your heart, and that you may receive the help of her prayer, do not cease to follow the example of her conduct. . . . If she holds you, you will not fall, if she protects you, you need not fear.[44]

Graef goes on to note that Bernard's works, as exemplified in this quote, were just as influential, if not more so, as the continued use

---

Bernard, which has been depicted in artwork. See Miri Rubin, *Mother of God: A History of the Virgin Mary* (New Haven, CT, and London: Yale University Press, 2009), 150, 350.

43. Graef, *Mary,* 186. Expanding on the notion of "floods of grace" flowing between Mary and her children on earth, Graef tells us that by the time of Thomas Aquinas, Mary's "direct mediation of grace by her activity in heaven had become almost a commonplace of Marian teaching and preaching." See Hilda Graef, *The Devotion to Our Lady* (New York: Hawthorn Books, 1963), 52.

44. Bernard, *Homiliae Super Missus Est,* as quoted in Graef, *Mary,* 185–86.

of the miracle story of Theophilus in building up people's faith in Mary's "all-powerful intercession."[45]

Bernard's works continued to influence popes throughout the ages, as his notion that God "willed us to have everything through Mary" is one that is seen in the nineteenth and twentieth centuries in the writings of Popes Pius IX, Leo XIII, and Pius XII.[46] The reason that one can go "through Mary" is because she is "the most efficacious advocate"; while Christ is our advocate, he is also our Judge, and so Bernard felt that it was easier for those who are "timid" and scared of the Judge to go through Mary.[47] Being a compassionate mother, Mary is able to take our gifts and make them "more acceptable to him [God] than if they had been offered directly."[48] In addition, Mary is human and "only sweet and gentle; she judges no one and therefore no one need be afraid of her."[49] Here in the writings of Bernard is another popular idea that emerged during the Middle Ages: that Christ was solely seen as the Judge, while Mary was the dispenser of mercy. This notion is closely tied to changing ideas about death.

Shifts in Beliefs Surrounding Death

Graef describes how the "idea that Mary appeases the wrath of God, the Judge," which she claims to be "one of the most popular themes of medieval Marian devotion," can be traced to Germanus of Constantinople (631/649–ca. 733).[50] This idea is seen in the West in the work of Ambrose of Autpert (ca. 730–84), who writes in a prayer to Mary, "we find no one more powerful in merit to placate the wrath of the Judge than you, who have merited to be the mother of the Redeemer and Judge."[51] In her discussion of the Franciscans, Graef finds this understanding also in a homily attributed to Bonaventure;

---

45. Ibid., 186. In her other book, Graef refers to this faith as "childlike trust in the all-powerful help of the Mother of God" (*The Devotion to Our Lady*, 44).

46. Graef, *Mary*, 187. Pius IX, for example, uses this saying in *Ubi Primum* (1849).

47. Graef, *Mary*, 187; and Graef, *The Devotion to Our Lady*, 44–45.

48. Graef, *The Devotion to Our Lady*, 44.

49. Ibid., 44–45.

50. Ibid., 39.

51. Ibid., 39.

he wrote that "Christ reserved to himself the realm of justice while giving to his mother the kingdom of mercy."[52] The result of this belief is that people feared Christ and sought Mary's protection, since she could "stay the revenge of her Son."[53]

This fear of Christ and reliance on Mary's help was seen very strongly in beliefs and practices surrounding death in the Middle Ages. Karen Westerfield Tucker notes a shift in the twelfth and thirteenth centuries in the West as death was approached not with "confidence, but rather with fear."[54] Evidence is found in such factors as the use of the sequence *Dies irae, dies illa* ("Day of wrath, O dreadful day") in the *Requiem* Mass for the dead that developed in the thirteenth century, the "need for absolution and intercession at the point of death and *post mortem*," the increasing belief in purgatory, and the development of the *ars moriendi* in the late Middle Ages, "a means by which persons could prepare for the inevitable judgment at death by learning and practicing the 'art' of dying (and living) well."[55] Richard Rutherford observes how this "new medieval spirituality viewed Christ's coming in judgment as a cause for fear, whereas formerly it was a source of consolation," and that this was reflected in medieval art and music.[56]

Where does Mary play a role in this new understanding of death? Rubin writes that Mary is "associated with the preparation for death" by the fifteenth century.[57] Christians believed that Mary could help smooth the transition from life to death and make it "less frightening" and so they looked to Mary's death as a model for their own.[58] Mary also began to play a role in the time of judgment. In Philippe Ariès's work on death, he describes a shift during the twelfth and

52. Ibid., 53.

53. Ibid.

54. Karen B. Westerfield Tucker, "Christian Rituals Surrounding Death," in *Life Cycles in Jewish and Christian Worship*, ed. Paul F. Bradshaw and Lawrence A. Hoffman (Notre Dame, IN: University of Notre Dame Press, 1996), 199.

55. Westerfield Tucker, "Christian Rituals Surrounding Death," 199. Mary's ability to intercede for those in purgatory was seen not only in the legend of Theophilus but also in Dante's *Inferno*. See Graef, *The Devotion to Our Lady*, 61–62.

56. Rutherford, *The Death of a Christian*, 64.

57. Rubin, *Mother of God*, 322.

58. Ibid.

thirteenth centuries similar to that described by Westerfield Tucker; the increasing fear of death that Westerfield Tucker describes is most likely associated with the shift that Ariès describes in that the Second Coming of Christ is now linked to the Last Judgment, and the focus becomes "the weighing of souls and the judgment."[59]

Mary had the ability to play a very important role as an intercessor in this process of judgment, as Ariès describes:

> However, the judgment does not always follow the decision of the scales. Intercessors step forward and play a role not anticipated by the passage from Saint Matthew, the double role of the advocate (*patronus*) and suppliant (*advocare Deum*) who appeal to the pity, that is, the mercy, of the sovereign judge. The judge is the one who pardons the guilty person as well as the one who condemns him, and it is the function of certain of his familiars to sway him to pardon. Here this role belongs to his mother and to the disciple who was also present with him at the foot of the cross, Saint John the Evangelist.[60]

The image of Mary in the weighing of souls was depicted in iconography, often "painted on the walls of sickrooms to console the dying."[61] The image included Michael the Archangel weighing the souls, the dead in one side, "straining devils in the other"; behind Michael was "a gentle (and often diminutive) Virgin" who "decides the struggle by laying her rosary on the sinner's side."[62] This shows the belief held by many, and voiced by Conrad of Saxony (d. 1279) that Mary was the only person who could placate her Son: "she 'prevents her Son from striking sinners; for before Mary there was no one who dared thus hold back the Lord.'"[63]

Drawing on the idea that Mary could plead for her children at the time of judgment comes the notion that because of Mary's

---

59. Philippe Ariès, *The Hour of Our Death: The Classic History of Western Attitudes toward Death over the Last One Thousand Years*, trans. Helen Weaver (New York: Vintage Books, 1981), 101.

60. Ibid.

61. Eamon Duffy, *The Stripping of the Altars: Traditional Religion in England 1400–1580* (New Haven, CT: Yale University Press, 2005), 319.

62. Ibid.

63. Graef, *The Devotion to Our Lady*, 53.

"unique relationship with Christ . . . the son could refuse his mother nothing."[64] Even though the sinner could use this belief to feel confident that Christ would listen to anything that Mary asked for, there is still often in prayers "a sense of shame and unworthiness when facing Mary" in what Rubin describes as "a tone of self-abjection in the unburdening of sin."[65] In Marian congregational songs before Vatican II it is very common to come across both the idea that no son could refuse his mother as well as the need to speak in a self-deprecating manner when approaching Mary.

In addition to functioning as an intercessor to Christ, the Judge, Mary was also present at the time of death, acting as an integral part of the *ars moriendi*, which focused on the specific "hour of death" in the *Ave Maria*.[66] In fact, it was around this time that the phrase "now and at the hour of our death" was added to the prayer. Eamon Duffy shows how important Mary was at this moment of transition, referring to her as the "saint of the deathbed."[67] Many of the Marian congregational songs, especially those before Vatican II, draw on Mary's role as intercessor and protectress as people ask for her presence at the time of death and to help those who have already died (especially those in purgatory). Medieval prayers articulate these shifts, among them the *Ave Maria*, which Buono describes as a prayer asking Mary's help both now and at death, hoping for "passage to our heavenly home" and "the grace of a happy death."[68]

Medieval Devotion, Hymns, and Prayers to Mary

The Ave Maria

The *Ave Maria* (in English the "Hail Mary"), the "child's first prayer, the dying person's last," is almost certainly the most popular prayer to Mary in the history of Christianity.[69] Jungmann points to

64. Rubin, *Mother of God*, 132.

65. Ibid.

66. Ariès, *The Hour of Our Death*, 301, 607.

67. Duffy, *The Stripping of the Altars*, 318.

68. Anthony M. Buono, *The Greatest Marian Prayers: Their History, Meaning, and Usage* (New York: Alba House, 1999), 7–8.

69. Rubin, *Mother of God*, 319.

Peter Damian as being "first to testify that the Ave Maria (the angelical salutation to Mary, combined with that of her cousin Elizabeth; Luke 1:28, 42) had become a favorite prayer with the people."[70] In 1210 the *Statuta Synodalia* of Paris pronounced "episcopal ordinances" that "express the wish that the faithful, in addition to reciting of the Our Father and the Creed, should also learn the Ave Maria."[71] Following this decree can be seen the growth of the "Marian Psalter," consisting of one hundred and fifty *Ave Marias*.[72] The prayer, as we know it today, consists of two parts: "(1) the Evangelical Salutation (see Luke 1:28 and 42) and (2) the Supplication of the Church."[73] This second part, "Holy Mary, Mother of God, pray for us sinners, now and at the hour of our death" was not added until the fifteenth century—which corresponds to the development of the *ars moriendi* and the association of Mary with the time of death—and was finalized in the form known today in the Breviary of Pius V in 1568.[74]

The Hail Mary is also associated with the practice of the *Angelus*. The *Angelus* consists of sets of versicles and responses relating to the annunciation—interspersed with Hail Marys—and closes with a prayer.[75] The *Angelus* was recited at the ringing of the *Angelus* bell morning, noon, and night, and was used throughout the Middle Ages to pray for peace and the success of the Crusades.[76] Here is yet another example of the use of Mary in the fight against "heretics" or "infidels." To this day, the Hail Mary continues to be one of the most well-known prayers, and this is reflected in the numerous musical settings of the texts, from Franz Schubert's setting for solo voice and piano to multiple hymn settings to the famous Gregorian chant setting here:

---

70. Jungmann, *Christian Prayer through the Centuries*, 102.

71. Ibid.

72. Ibid., 106–8.

73. Buono, *The Greatest Marian Prayers*, 1.

74. Jungmann, *Christian Prayer through the Centuries*, 102. Jungmann identifies the Carthusians as adding this second part around 1530, while Buono places its addition earlier in the fifteenth century.

75. See Buono, *The Greatest Marian Prayers*, 57–62.

76. Ibid., 58–60. The midday *Angelus* became popular in "the fifteenth century, when the danger of the Turkish invasion led the people to ever more pressing recourse to Mary." See Graef, *The Devotion to Our Lady*, 58.

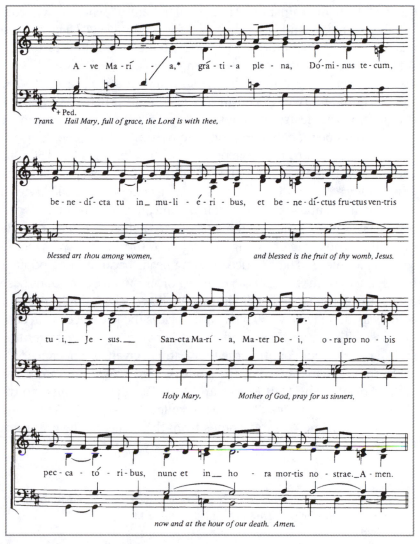

Figure 2. *Ave Maria.* Text: St. Luke's gospel and tradition. Tune: *Ave Maria,* Plainchant, Mode 1. Accompaniment by Theodore Marier. (From Marier, ed., *Hymns, Psalms, and Spiritual Canticles,* 199. Courtesy of Boston Boy Choir, Inc.).

The Rosary

The rosary—which prominently features the Hail Mary—has a complicated history, stemming from two traditions. The first comes from St. Dominic, who is said to have been given the rosary by Mary during "the fight against the Albingensian heresy" when he was told to take the rosary and "preach it as a form of prayer."[77] The second tradition, which is "more widely acceptable" according to Joseph Agbasiere, sees the devotion stemming from the "tender devotion to Jesus and Mary,"[78] prompted by the shift in Christian prayer around the eleventh and twelfth century. According to Michael O'Carroll, this led to "the desire to give the laity a form of common prayer which would be modeled on monastic prayer."[79]

This desire led to the development of the "psalters" of 150 Our Fathers or Hail Marys in an imitation of the 150 psalms recited in the Divine Office.[80] Sarah Boss discusses the use of beads to facilitate in counting these prayers; in early Christianity, prayers may have been counted by "moving pebbles from one pile to another, and subsequently by pulling beads or knots along a string or by turning a prayer wheel a spoke at a time."[81] The practice of using beads became more popular in helping to count the 150 *Pater Nosters* or *Ave Marias*, and soon these beads were strung together "in lines as well as circles, and the number could vary quite widely."[82] Hilda Graef places the use of beads in conjunction with the rosary around the early twelfth century, stemming from a practice "for counting the Our Fathers given as a penance."[83]

In the same manner that the psalms were broken up into three groups of fifty, the Hail Marys and Our Fathers were also so divided, and these groups of fifty were called "chaplets."[84] According to Graef, the name "rosary" comes from the name for the groups of fifty *Aves* that were called "*rosarium* after Mary's title of *rosa mystica*."[85]

---

77. Joseph Therese Agbasiere, "The Rosary: Its History and Relevance," *African Ecclesial Review (AFER)* 30 (August 1988): 243.

78. Ibid.

79. Michael O'Carroll, *Theotokos: A Theological Encyclopedia of the Blessed Virgin Mary* (Wilmington, DE: Michael Glazier, 1986), 313.

80. Agbasiere, "The Rosary," 243.

81. Sarah Jane Boss, "Telling the Beads: The Practice and Symbolism of the Rosary," in *Popular Devotions*, ed. Lawrence S. Cunningham (London: The Way Publications, 2001), 67.

82. Ibid., 67–68.

83. Graef, *The Devotion to Our Lady*, 57.

84. Agbasiere, "The Rosary," 243.

85. Graef, *The Devotion to Our Lady*, 57.

Furthermore, the 150 *Aves* were meant to imitate the 150 psalms in the Psalter; originally the antiphons were Marian, the psalms were "replaced by the Hail Mary" and then "the antiphons were left out, the *Gloria Patri* was interspersed and the one hundred and fifty Hail Mary's were divided into groups of fifty."[86] Agbasiere credits H. Kalper, a Carthusian monk, with breaking the prayers into groups of ten, or "decades," with the addition of an Our Father after each decade.[87] It was the Carthusians and Dominicans who helped to spread the popularity of the rosary in the fifteenth century, especially with the founding of rosary confraternities.[88] After Mary's apparition at Fátima (1917) the following prayer, to be said after each decade, was also added: "O my Jesus, forgive us our sins, save us from the fires of hell, lead all souls to heaven, especially those in greatest need."

The mysteries of the rosary developed over time, and in the words of Jungmann, gave the Marian Psalter a christological character.[89] The mysteries began as the addition of "a phrase based on the psalms, referring to Jesus or Mary" that was added to each decade of the rosary.[90] These then turned into phrases about the mysteries of Jesus' and Mary's life, from the annunciation to "the glorification of both of them in heaven."[91] O'Carroll says in the early stages of the mysteries the "joys" were at the fore, including the annunciation, which soon came to be associated with the first chaplet.[92] In the fourteenth century, the Sorrows were contemplated during the second chaplet, "and heavenly joy during a third."[93] It is not a coincidence that the Sorrowful Mysteries came into being during the fourteenth century when the devotion to the passion and Mary as *Mater Dolorosa* was at its height.

The sixteenth century saw the finalization of the fifteen mysteries familiar today, as "officially approved" by Pius V in 1569, who also approved "the addition of the second half of the Hail Mary and the

86. Ibid.
87. Agbasiere, "The Rosary," 244.
88. Rubin, *Mother of God*, 333.
89. Jungmann, *Christian Prayer through the Centuries*, 108.
90. Agbasiere, "The Rosary," 244.
91. Ibid.
92. O'Carroll, *Theotokos*, 313.
93. Ibid.

Glory to the Father."[94] The rosary was also given the honor of a feast day (October 7) in 1573 to give thanks for the victory at Lepanto on October 7, 1571.[95] It was said that the Christians defeated the Turks at Lepanto because the Roman confraternities had recited rosaries on that day, even prompting the title "Help of Christians" to be added to the Litany of Loreto.[96] The use of the rosary as a weapon "crusading against 'infidels' and 'heretics' alike"[97] is continued after Lepanto, as will be discussed later, and is seen particularly in "The clouds hang thick o'er Israel's camp," a Marian congregational song from the late nineteenth century. Stanzas 2 and 4 will be discussed in chapter 4, but stanzas 1 and 3, seen below, can be seen as particularly related to the victory at Lepanto.

Stanza 1 looks to St. Dominic, who, as discussed earlier, was said to have been given the rosary to fight heresy. Stanza 3 refers specifically to the victory over the Turks at Lepanto in 1571, and has a very strong anti-Muslim tone, referring to "The Moslem's dark array." It describes how invoking the names of Jesus and Mary led to victory at this particular battle, and will lead to victory in the future as well.

1. The clouds hang thick o'er Israel's camp
   As dawns the battle day,
   Arise! bright star of Dominic,
   And chase the gloom away:
   And where the foemen fiercest press
   Thy radiance let us see;
   Shine o'er the banners of thy sons,
   And lead to victory.

---

94. Ibid., 314. The Joyful Mysteries are: the Annunciation, the Visitation, the Nativity, the Presentation in the Temple, and the Finding of Jesus in the Temple. The Sorrowful Mysteries are: the Agony in the Garden, the Scourging at the Pillar, the Crowning with Thorns, the Carrying of the Cross, and the Crucifixion. The Glorious Mysteries are: the Resurrection, the Ascension, the Descent of the Holy Spirit, the Assumption of Mary, and the Coronation of Mary. Pope John Paul II's addition of the Luminous Mysteries are discussed in chap. 7.

95. Ibid.

96. Graef, *The Devotion to Our Lady*, 70.

97. Rubin, *Mother of God*, 401.

3. See o'er Lepanto's water spread
   The Moslem's dark array:
   A voice to Christendom went forth,
   And gave the word to pray:
   Jesus and Mary! names of strength
   Invoked, and not in vain;
   They conquered in the hour of need,
   And conquer shall again.[98]

In addition to being used as a weapon against heresy, the rosary has also been used by many as a source of protection and comfort, much like the *Ave Maria*, as they approach death. Pamphlets outlined the "merits of the rosary" and how to obtain "a good death."[99] The rosary was later associated with images of purgatory because praying it could lessen the time one would spend there.[100] It also developed close associations with death, as the hands of the deceased "were entwined in a rosary, a practice that has come down to our time."[101]

Notwithstanding its biblical references, the rosary is a devotion that seems to have fallen out of favor with many in the wake of Vatican II. After the council, many Marian devotions were disputed because they were based on apocryphal texts (such as the *Protoevangelium of James*), were not biblical, or were not christological. One twentieth-century hymn, however, has become quite popular despite the fact that it reflects on the mysteries of the rosary (although the stanza that speaks to them specifically is often omitted in hymnals). "Sing of Mary, pure/meek and lowly," written by Roland Palmer, SSJE

98. Augusta T. Drane, "The clouds hang thick o'er Isr'l's camp," Hymnary.org, http://www.hymnary.org/text/the_clouds_hang_thick_oer_isrls_camp, accessed March 2014. Taken from A. Edmonds Tozer, ed., *Catholic Church Hymnal with Music* (New York: J. Fischer & Bro., 1905), 163. This text by Augusta T. Drane (Mother Frances Raphael [1823–94]) is found in: Catholic Church, ed., *St. Dominic's Hymn-Book with the Office of Compline According to the Dominican Rite* (London: Burns and Oates, 1885). See J. Vincent Higginson, *Handbook for American Catholic Hymnals* (New York: The Hymn Society of America, 1976), 91.

99. Duffy, *The Stripping of the Altars*, 78.

100. Ariès, *The Hour of Our Death*, 305–6.

101. Ibid., 306.

(1891–1985), was originally written for the *Book of Common Praise*, the 1938 hymnal of the Church of England in Canada.[102]

Palmer entered the Society of St. John the Evangelist (SSJE), an Anglican monastic community, in 1919, and lived at their congregation in the Cowley Monastery in Cambridge, Massachusetts until 1927 when he left for Canada "to open a house there and become provincial superior and then superior of the Canadian congregation."[103] The beautiful worship space at the Cowley Monastery, designed by Ralph Adams Cram (1863–1942), includes stained glass windows depicting the mysteries of the rosary; perhaps it was these windows that inspired Palmer to write this text.[104] Palmer describes the genesis of this text:

> I was on the Committee for the production of that hymnal [*Book of Common Praise*] and was asked to find another good hymn for the festivals of the Blessed Virgin. I finally set to work and built "Sing of Mary" around the Joyful, Sorrowful, and Glorious mysteries. I submitted it anonymously so that they could reject it without embarrassment. They accepted it. It appeared Anon. with some mistake as to the date. The date should be in the 1930's.[105]

While most hymnals tend to only print three stanzas, Palmer's original text contained five. Here are all five of Palmer's original

---

102. Raymond F. Glover, ed., *Hymns 1 to 384*, vol. 3A of *The Hymnal 1982 Companion* (New York: The Church Hymnal Corporation, 1994), 537.

103. Raymond F. Glover, ed., *Service Music and Biographies*, vol. 2 of *The Hymnal 1982 Companion* (New York: The Church Hymnal Corporation, 1994), 559.

104. The stained-glass window on the cover of this book is of the Annunciation to the Blessed Virgin Mary from the Cowley Monastery. Many thanks to Br. Curtis Almquist and all the brothers at SSJE for their generosity in sharing this image. Even though Cram building was not finished until 1936, it is still possible that Palmer returned to the Cowley Monastery after 1936. Thanks to Peter Scagnelli for pointing this out.

105. Palmer to Glover, June 15, 1984, Church Hymnal Corporation Papers as quoted in Glover, *Hymns 1 to 384*, 537. Some hymnals attribute this text to "Anon" because the text has its origins as an "anonymous poem in an Ilkeston, Derbyshire parish pamphlet, ca. 1914," and Palmer based his text on this poem and originally had his text published anonymously (ibid.).

stanzas (the hymnals that print three stanzas tend to print stanzas 1, 2, and 5, omitting 3 and 4):[106]

1. Sing of Mary, pure and lowly,
   Virgin-mother undefiled;
   Sing of God's own Son most holy,
   Who became her little child.
   Fairest child of fairest mother,
   God the Lord who came to earth,
   Word made flesh, our very brother,
   Takes our nature by his birth.

2. Sing of Jesus, son of Mary,
   In the home at Nazareth,
   Toil and labor cannot weary
   Love enduring unto death.
   Constant was the love he gave her,
   Though he went forth from her side,
   Forth to preach, and heal, and suffer,
   Till on Calvary he died.

3. Sing of Mary, sing of Jesus,
   Holy Mother's holier son.
   From his throne in heaven he sees us,
   Thither calls us every one,
   Where he welcomes home his Mother
   To a place at his right hand,
   There his faithful servants gather,
   There the crowned victors stand.

4. Joyful Mother, full of gladness,
   In thine arms thy Lord was borne.
   Mournful Mother, full of sadness,
   All thy heart with pain was torn.

106. Glover notes that in the *Hymnal 1940*, an alteration was made in line 6 stanza 2, where "it drove him from her side" was changed to "though he went forth from her side" (ibid.), and this alteration appears to have been made in Catholic hymnals as well. This text is usually set to the tune PLEADING SAVIOR, but in *The Hymnal 1982* it is set to the lovely tune RAQUEL.

Glorious Mother, now rewarded
　　With a crown at Jesus' hand,
Age to age thy name recorded
　　Shall be blest in very [*sic*] land.

5. Glory be to God the Father;
　　Glory be to God the Son;
Glory be to God the Spirit;
　　Glory to the Three in One.
From the heart of blessed Mary,
　　From all saints the song ascends,
And the Church the strain re-echoes
　　Unto earth's remotest ends.[107]

It is interesting to note that this particular Marian congregational song, although written in the 1930s, does not seem to find its way into Catholic hymnals until the 1960s.[108] Perhaps this is because by the 1960s the effects of the ecumenical movement are evident, as is the work of Omer Westendorf (1916–1997), the founder of the World Library of Sacred Music who published *The People's Hymnal* (where "Sing of Mary" is first found in US Catholic hymnals in 1961). Westendorf's experience in Europe during World War II gave him a broader, international perspective on sacred music, which led him to introduce congregational songs in his hymnals that were new to the standard Catholic repertoire in the United States.[109] It makes it all the more impressive, and speaks to the popularity of "Sing of Mary," that this text is written by a non-Catholic and does not seem to have entered the US Catholic repertoire until the 1960s, and yet it has gained widespread acceptance throughout a range of US Catholic hymnals.

---

107. "Sing of Mary," Stanzas 1, 2, and 5 are from #277 in *The Hymnal 1982: According to the Use of the Episcopal Church* (New York: Church Hymnal Corp., 1985); stanzas 3 and 4 are from Glover, *Hymns 1 to 384*, 538. The last line of stanza 4 contains an error; it should be "Shall be blest in every land."

108. The text seems to first appear at #R-10 in *The People's Hymnal: Voice Book*, ed. the People's Hymnal Committee, 2nd ed. (Cincinnati, OH: World Library of Sacred Music, 1961), 136–37. See Higginson, *Handbook for American Catholic Hymnals*, 90–91.

109. Donald Boccardi, *The History of American Catholic Hymnals Since Vatican II* (Chicago: GIA Publications, 2001), 4, 12.

The Memorare

One of the prayers that may be said at the end of the rosary is the *Memorare*. The prayer is often attributed to Bernard of Clairvaux, but now it is believed to have come from a longer Eastern prayer sometime between the eighth and tenth centuries.[110] Here is an anonymous translation of the entire text:

> Remember, O most gracious Virgin Mary,
> that never was it known,
> that anyone who fled to thy protection, implored thy help,
> sought thy intercession, was left unaided.
> Inspired with this confidence, I fly unto thee,
> O Virgin of virgins, my Mother,
> to thee I come, before thee I stand,
> sinful and sorrowful.
> O Mother of the Word incarnate, despise not my petitions,
> but in thy mercy, hear and answer me.[111]

The *Memorare* has been set to music, both in Latin and in English. Many of the texts contain the notion that anyone who seeks Mary's help will not be turned away (a notion that is quite common in Marian congregational songs from before Vatican II). "Remember, holy Mary," is by the Rev. Matthew Russell, SJ (1834–1912). His text includes the belief that Mary won't abandon anyone who asks for her help (stanza 1); the scene of Jesus and Mary at the foot of the cross (stanza 2); the popular image of Mary throwing her mantle over her children (stanza 3); and a tone of self-deprecation and unworthiness (stanzas 3 and 4).

> 1. Remember, holy Mary,
>   'Twas never heard or known
>   That any one who sought thee
>   And made to thee his moan,
>   That any one who hastened
>   For shelter to thy care

---

110. Buono, *The Greatest Marian Prayers*, 82.

111. "Memorare" in *The Pius X Hymnal: For Unison, Two Equal or Four Mixed Voices*, ed. Pius Tenth School of Liturgical Music (Boston, MA: McLaughlin & Reilly Co., 1953), 100.

Was ever yet abandoned
And left to his despair.

2. And so to thee, my Mother,
   With filial faith I call,
   For Jesus dying gave thee
   As Mother to us all
   To thee, O Queen of virgins,
   O Mother meek, to thee
   I run with trustful fondness,
   Like child to mother's knee.

3. See at thy feet a sinner,
   Groaning and weeping sore__
   Ah! throw thy mantle o'er me,
   And let me stray no more.
   Thy Son has died to save me,
   And from His throne on high
   His Heart this moment yearneth
   For even such as I.

4. All, all His love remember,
   And, oh! remember too
   How prompt I am to purpose,
   How slow and frail to do.
   Yet scorn not my petitions,
   But patiently give ear,
   And help me, O my Mother,
   Most loving and most dear.[112]

Russell's text points to the moment during the passion when Jesus gave Mary "As Mother to us all." The rosary helped strengthen the association between Mary and the passion with the contemplation of the mysteries of the rosary. As Rubin describes, "by the fifteenth century it had become all but impossible to tell the Passion

112. Matthew Russell, "Remember, holy Mary," Hymnary.org, http://www .hymnary.org/text/remember_holy_mary, accessed March 2014. Taken from *American Catholic Hymnal: An Extensive Collection of Hymns, Latin Chants, and Sacred Songs for Church, School, and Home, Including Gregorian Masses, Vesper Psalms, Litanies . . .*, ed. Marist Brothers (New York: P.J. Kenedy & Sons, 1913), 192.

fully and movingly without also addressing Mary's pain."[113] Christ's and Mary's suffering at the scene of the crucifixion became deeply intertwined, making the two almost "inseparable."[114]

The Stabat Mater dolorosa

The *Stabat Mater dolorosa* is one of the most enduring prayers that describe Mary's suffering at the foot of the cross. Over the course of twenty stanzas, the *Stabat Mater dolorosa* ("Sorrowfully His Mother Stood"), one of the most powerful Marian prayers of the Middle Ages, not only depicts the utter sorrow Mary experienced as she stood at the foot of the cross but also asks that we may share in Mary's suffering as we plead for her help through her crucified Son. Attributed to Pope Innocent II (1130–1143), Bonaventure, and Jacapone da Todi (1228–1306), the text was originally used as the sequence for the Mass of Our Lady of Sorrows, celebrated on September 15.[115] This text has been set to music throughout the centuries by such composers as Giovanni Battista Pergolesi (1710–1736) and Francis Poulenc (1899–1963).

The *Stabat Mater* is a result of the emphasis on the humanity of Jesus and Mary as well as the suffering they both experienced during the passion. Duffy describes how the *Stabat Mater* reflects this emphasis on contemplation: "Here the Virgin's grief is presented, not as an end in itself, but as a means of arousing and focusing sympathetic suffering in the heart of the onlooker."[116] The text also reflects the despair many people felt during that time as they lost loved ones to illness on a grand scale; as a result of the Black Death (1347–1350), one-third to one-half of the population in Europe died.[117] Indeed, in his discussion

---

113. Rubin, *Mother of God*, 338.

114. Ibid.

115. Buono, *The Greatest Marian Prayers*, 72, 75. Buono notes that there were well over 5,000 sequences in the Middle Ages until Pius V's *Roman Missal* eliminated all but four: *Victimae Paschali Laudes* (Easter), *Veni, Sancte Spiritus* (Pentecost), *Lauda Sion* (Corpus Christi), and *Dies Irae* (funerals). The *Stabat Mater* was officially added to the Missal in 1727. Paul VI's reforms after Vatican II eliminated the *Dies Irae* and made the *Stabat Mater* and *Lauda Sion* optional. See Buono, *The Greatest Marian Prayers*, 71–72.

116. Duffy, *The Stripping of the Altars*, 259.

117. Rubin, *Mother of God*, 249.

of the cult of the "Sorrows of the Virgin, or the Mater Dolorosa," Duffy says that one of the main functions of this devotion was "serving as an objective correlative for the discharge of grief and suffering in the face of successive waves of plague sweeping through Christendom."[118] It is around this time that the *Pestkreutz* (plague cross) begins to appear, particularly in the German Rhineland. Also known as a forked cross (because the cross is in a shape of a Y or a fork rather than a T or a bar), this is a "strongly expressive work" where "the wracked body of the crucified Christ" himself is "covered with plague boils and bursting ulcers."[119] By bearing the marks of the plague, Jesus partakes in the suffering of so many dying from the disease.

Throughout Edward Caswall's (1814–1878) translation of the *Stabat Mater*, we are asked to partake in Mary's suffering as she herself shared in Christ's anguish while standing at the foot of the cross. There is also reference to the "awful Judgment day" in stanza 18, and in stanza 19 Mary is asked to be an intercessor for the sinner in front of Christ, the Judge. The notion of participating in Mary's suffering and her acting as an intercessor to Christ, the Judge, both draw from the thinking of Anselm of Canterbury. Here is Caswall's translation of all twenty stanzas of the *Stabat Mater*:

1. At the Cross her station keeping,
   Stood the mournful Mother weeping,
   Close to Jesus to the last:

2. Through her heart, His sorrow sharing,
   All His bitter anguish bearing,
   Now at length the sword had passed.

3. Oh, how sad and sore distress'd
   Was that Mother highly blest
   Of the sole-begotten One!

4. Christ above in torment hangs;
   She beneath beholds the pangs
   Of her dying glorious Son.

118. Duffy, *The Stripping of the Altars*, 259.

119. Helmut Wessels, *Neuss and St. Quirin on Foot*, trans. John Sykes (Cologne: J.P. Bachem Verlag, 2005), 17. The church of St. Quirinius in Neuss, Germany, houses a plague cross from around 1360.

5. Is there one who would not weep,
   Whelmed in miseries so deep
   Christ's dear Mother to behold?

6. Can the human heart refrain
   From partaking in her pain,
   In that Mother's pain untold?

7. Bruised, derided, cursed, defiled,
   She beheld her tender Child
   All with bloody scourges rent;

8. For the sins of His own nation,
   Saw Him hang in desolation
   Till His Spirit forth He sent.

9. O thou Mother! fount of love!
   Touch my spirit from above,
   Make my heart with thine accord:

10. Make me feel as thou has felt;
    Make my soul to glow and melt
    With the love of Christ my Lord.

11. Holy Mother! pierce me through;
    In my heart each wound renew
    Of my Saviour crucified:

12. Let me share with thee His pain,
    Who for all my sins was slain,
    Who for me in torments died.

13. Let me mingle tears with thee,
    Mourning Him who mourned for me,
    All the days that I may live:

14. By the Cross with thee to stay;
    There with thee to weep and pray;
    Is all I ask of thee to give.

15. Virgin of all virgins blest!
    Listen to my fond request:
    Let me share thy grief divine;

16. Let me, to my latest breath,
     In my body bear the death
     Of that dying Son of thine.

17. Wounded with His ev'ry wound,
     Steep my soul till it hath swooned
     In His very Blood away.

18. Be to me, O Virgin, nigh,
     Lest in flames I burn and die,
     In that awful Judgment day.

19. Christ, when Thou shalt call me hence,
     Be Thy Mother my defence,
     Be Thy Cross my victory;

20. While my body here decays,
     May my soul Thy goodness praise,
     Safe in Paradise with Thee.[120]

In addition to a heightened focus on depicting Jesus' suffering, numerous images during this period depict Mary and John at the crucifixion. The writings of Anselm of Canterbury and Bernard of Clairvaux "reflect the heightened devotion to the suffering of the Virgin."[121] Indeed, it was during the fourteenth and fifteenth centuries that depictions of the *spasimo* or "Mary's swooning at the foot of the cross" are seen.[122] One of the most famous artistic renderings associated with Mary and the crucifixion is the *Pietà*.

The *Pietà and* Planctus Mariae

While Hilda Graef calls the *Stabat Mater* the "perfect transposition into poetry of the contemporary images of the *Pietà*, the sorrowing

---

120. "At the Cross her station keeping" in *The Pius X Hymnal*, 245.
121. Parker, "Architecture as Liturgical Setting," 322–23.
122. Rubin, *Mother of God*, 362. Rubin also notes this "new emphasis on Mary's distress directed attention to its cause—the Jews" and this was also seen in the inclusion of "Jews of ill intent" in artwork depicting the crucifixion. See Rubin, *Mother of God*, 252, 255, 314.

Virgin holding her dead Son in her arms,"[123] the *Pietà* "was the most cherished image of her" during the Middle Ages, when the faithful had a "tendency to dwell on the periphery and to indulge in excessive elaboration," and this "appears most of all in devotion to the Mother of God."[124] Although it was originally used by religious women for private contemplation, the *Pietà* was, and remains, an image that many can relate to, as Rubin calls it "the quintessential figure of bereavement and loss."[125] Michelangelo's (1475–1564) sculpture of the *Pietà* remains one of the most famous pieces of art in the world.

The *Planctus Mariae*, what can be described as "poetry of complaints of Mary" contains similar themes as the *Stabat Mater* and *Pietà*.[126] According to Elizabeth Parker, this devotion "expressed the idea central to the Marian devotion of the Late Medieval period: her compassion, her ability to share in the suffering of her son, gave her the role of co-redemptrix and intercessor on behalf of the believer."[127] While many of these devotions focused on the private contemplation of Mary, some, such as the Stations of the Cross, could be practiced corporately.

The Stations of the Cross

Drawing from the "Way of the Cross" that was practiced in Jerusalem since early Christianity, pilgrims had the desire to recreate this experience in their homeland as well.[128] This impetus grew during the Crusades, when devotions to sacred places and Christ's passion

123. Graef, *The Devotion to Our Lady*, 58.

124. Jungmann, *Christian Prayer through the Centuries*, 125.

125. Rubin, *Mother of God*, xxv, 313. Rubin also points out that this moment is not recorded in Scripture, yet it is a "condensation of Mary's pain and her son's sacrifice—his beginning in her lap, and his end there, with an invitation to the compassionate viewer to join." See Rubin, *Mother of God*, 313.

126. Jaroslav Pelikan, *Mary through the Centuries: Her Place in the History of Culture* (New Haven, CT: Yale University Press, 1996), 127.

127. Parker, "Architecture as Liturgical Setting," 323.

128. Christopher Walsh, "Stations of the Cross," in *The New Westminster Dictionary of Liturgy and Worship*, ed. Paul Bradshaw (Louisville and London: Westminster John Knox Press, 2002), 450. All the information and quotations in this section on the Stations of the Cross come from this source and are taken from page 450.

increased, leading people to make a "tableaux of the places they had visited in the Holy Land." In 1342 the Franciscans took custody of these "holy places," and they encouraged the faithful to make these tableaux, which at this point varied in subject as well as the number of stations, ranging from five to thirty.[129] This devotion was "regulated by Clement XII in 1731," when it stabilized at fourteen stations (nine from the gospel and "five from popular tradition"). By the nineteenth century it was common to find Catholic churches with "a set of fourteen [stations] ranged around the internal walls (or occasionally out of doors in church grounds)."

There are many ways in which this devotion can be practiced; it can be done privately and also publicly with clergy, often with people moving from station to station. It is the latter form that is particularly important in a study of Marian hymnody because the *Stabat Mater* is often sung as people move from station to station. During Lent, it is common for people to celebrate the Stations of the Cross publicly with clergy, singing the Latin *Stabat Mater* or an English translation or paraphrase of the Latin text as they move from station to station. During the nineteenth and twentieth centuries, in addition to singing the *Stabat Mater* in the vernacular, the meditations of Alphonsus Liguori were also very popular. The theology of Vatican II has had an effect on the Stations of the Cross, with the "recovered theology of the paschal mystery stressing the integral unity of Christ's death and resurrection," leading many to add a fifteenth station that represents the resurrection. The Vatican II focus on Scripture has also led to the use of more scriptural meditations than those that are nonscriptural. Walsh states that "this devotion has probably waned somewhat" as a result of the liturgical movement, but is "still practiced in Lent and as a supplementary service on Good Friday."

The Litany of Loreto

Similar to the Stations of the Cross, the Litany of Loreto is another devotion that seems to have fallen out of favor following Vatican II. The litany is a form of prayer found in Marian devotion that became

---

129. Walsh writes that the first time there are fourteen stations is in the sixteenth century in the Low Countries.

very popular in the Middle Ages. Jungmann credits the *Akathist* hymn as leading to the "development of the litanies to Mary"; he believes the *Ora pro nobis* in Marian litanies was a replacement of the *Chaire* used in the *Akathist* hymn to greet Mary.[130] In the twelfth century there are examples of litanies of *Kyrie eleison*, followed by "Mary's titles of honor."[131] From these developed the most famous Marian litany, the Litany of Loreto, also known as the Litany of the Blessed Virgin Mary.

Based on the Litany of the Saints (which originated in the seventh century), the Litany of Loreto, dating from the sixteenth century and originally sung at the Shrine of Our Lady of Loreto, praised Mary with seventy-three titles.[132] According to legend, it was at the house located at the shrine in Loreto that the annunciation occurred. In 1291, "Angels" moved the house from Nazareth to Dalmatia, and then finally to Loreto in 1294.[133] The litany, approved by Pope Sixtus V in 1587, has received the support of popes through the ages, even meriting their additions. This might well be a result of the strong biblical, patristic, and theological roots of the litany.[134] Some noteworthy additions to the litany include: "Queen conceived without original sin," by "universal spontaneous initiative" after the definition of the Immaculate Conception in 1854; "Queen of the Most Holy Rosary" and "Mother of Good Counsel" by Pope Leo XIII in 1883 and 1903; "Queen of Peace" by Benedict XV in 1916 during World War I; "Queen assumed into heaven" by Pope Pius XII in 1951 following his definition of Mary's Assumption in 1950; and "Mother of the Church" by Pope John Paul II in 1980.[135]

The Four Marian Antiphons

The "Four Marian Antiphons" are beautiful examples of Marian devotion that have found expression in Gregorian chant, polyphony,

---

130. Jungmann, *Christian Prayer through the Centuries*, 103–4.

131. Ibid.

132. Ibid., 104.

133. Buono, *The Greatest Marian Prayers*, 91. According to Buono, the word "Angels" is "now believed to refer to Crusaders" (ibid.).

134. Ibid., 91.

135. Ibid., 92–94.

and organ music, to name a few examples. These antiphons are used during the Liturgy of the Hours, sung during Compline throughout the liturgical year. They were first used together as "a series of four seasonal Marian antiphons" by the Franciscans in the thirteenth century, and soon spread throughout the Roman Use.[136]

The best known of these four, the *Salve Regina* ("Hail, O Holy Queen"), dates from the eleventh century and is attributed to a few authors, including Hermannus Contractus (1013–1054). The *Salve Regina* was added to the liturgy by Peter the Venerable around 1135 and was made popular with the Cistercians and Dominicans.[137] Since the thirteenth century, "it has been the last evening chant of many religious communities," a practice that continues to this day, as it is the Compline antiphon from Trinity Sunday up until Advent.[138]

According to Graef, "it is not surprising that the *Salve Regina* should have attained such popularity, for it expresses in touching and beautiful imagery men's earthly condition and their trust in Mary's motherly protection, so deeply felt in the Middle Ages."[139] Dante also attests to the popularity of this hymn in his *Divine Comedy* as he describes how "the suffering souls never cease to chant the *Salve Regina*" in purgatory.[140] The *Salve Regina* touches on common themes found in Marian hymnody including addressing Mary as "Advocate," a call for Mary to be compassionate to sinners and show them Jesus when life is over, and a description of our time here on earth as "exile" in a "vale of tears." Here is the text set to the simple Gregorian chant tone:

---

136. John Harper, *The Forms and Orders of Western Liturgy from the Tenth to the Eighteenth Century: A Historical Introduction and Guide for Students and Musicians* (Oxford: Clarendon Press, 2001), 131–32.

137. Graef, *The Devotion to Our Lady*, 56.

138. Buono, *The Greatest Marian Prayers*, 49–50.

139. Graef, *The Devotion to Our Lady*, 56.

140. Ibid., 62. This is yet another example of the belief that Mary had the ability to help souls in purgatory: "Mary, on her part, sends angels to guard them [the souls in purgatory] against the wiles of the devil who is trying still to corrupt the holy souls in the earthly paradise which lies between purgatory and heaven" (ibid.).

Figure 3. *Salve Regina/Hail, O Holy Queen!* (Compline Anthem During Ordinary Time). Text: Hermann Contractus + 1054. English adaptation by Theodore Marier © in "Pius X Hymnal," © 1953 by Summy-Birchard Music division of Birch Tree Music Group Ltd. Used with permission. Tune: Plainchant, Mode 5. Accompaniment by Theodore Marier. (From Marier, ed., *Hymns, Psalms, and Spiritual Canticles,* 260–61. Courtesy of Boston Boy Choir, Inc.).

℣. Pray for us, O holy Mother of God.
℟. That we may become worthy of the promises of Christ.

℣. *Ora pro nobis Sancta Dei Génitrix.*
℟. *Ut digni efficiámur promissiónibus Christi.*

Figure 3. *Salve Regina/Hail, O Holy Queen!* (continued).

"Hail, Holy Queen enthroned above/Salve Regina coelitum, O Maria!" is an English translation of a Latin paraphrase ("Salve Regina coelitum, O Maria!") of "Salve Regina, Mater misericordiae" (see pages 70–71). Since it is a paraphrase of the Latin chant, many of the themes contained in the chant are also here in the English text, which is an anonymous translation that comes from the *Roman Hymnal* (1884).[141] Most often paired with the German tune Salve Regina Coelitum, the text has an especially rousing chorus: "Triumph all ye Cherubim, / Sing with us, ye Seraphim, / Heav'n and earth resound the hymn: / *Salve, salve, salve Regina!*"[142] This continues to be one of the most popular and well-known Marian congregational songs today.

The first of the other three antiphons, *Alma Redemptoris Mater* ("Loving Mother of Our Savior," eleventh century; see pages 72–73), reflects on the annunciation and incarnation and is used in Compline from Advent to the Presentation (February 2). This antiphon, also attributed to Hermannus Contractus, echoes the *Ave maris stella* in that Mary is referred to as the "gate of heaven" and "star of the sea."[143] The text also mentions Mary's virginity before and after giving birth to Jesus ("*Virgo prius ac posterius*" or "Virgin before and after").

The *Ave Regina Caelorum* ("Hail Mary, Queen of Heaven," twelfth century; see page 74), is used at Compline from the Presentation through Holy Thursday, and references Mary as the "root" (Isa 11:1) and the "gate" (Ezek 44:2).[144]

The final antiphon, *Regina Coeli* ("Mary, Queen of Heaven," fourteenth century; see page 75), is used at Compline from Easter day through Pentecost, and reflects the Easter joy of Mary at the resurrection and during the entire paschal mystery.[145]

141. Higginson, *Handbook for American Catholic Hymnals*, 90.

142. The anonymous German tune comes from the *Choralemelodien zum heiligen Gesänge* (1808). See entry #702 in Marilyn Kay Stulken and Catherine Salika, *Hymnal Companion to Worship—Third Edition* (Chicago: GIA Publications, 1998), 415.

143. Graef, *The Devotion to Our Lady*, 55–56.

144. Buono, *The Greatest Marian Prayers*, 44.

145. Ibid., 63–64.

Figure 4. *Hail! Holy Queen, enthroned above*. Text: *Salve Regina* paraphrase; anonymous translation from *The Roman Hymnal*, 1884. Tune: Salve Regina Coelitum; *Choralmelodien zum Heiligen Gesänge*, 1808. (Reprinted from Montani, ed., *The St. Gregory Hymnal and Catholic Choir Book* [1920], 129–30). Image courtesy of Hymnary.org.

Figure 4. *Hail! Holy Queen, enthroned above* (continued).

Figure 5. *Alma Redemptoris Mater/Loving Mother of Our Savior* (Compline Anthem During Advent). Text: Ascribed to Hermann Contractus + 1054. English adaptation by Theodore Marier © in "Pius X Hymnal," © 1953 by Summy-Birchard Music division of Birch Tree Music Group Ltd. Used with permission. Tune: Plainchant, Mode 5. Accompaniment by Theodore Marier. (From Marier, ed., *Hymns, Psalms, and Spiritual Canticles*, 330–31. Courtesy of Boston Boy Choir, Inc.).

Vir - gin be - fore and vir - gin al - ways who re - ceived from Ga-briel's mouth
Vir - go pri - us ac po - sté - ri - us, Ga - bri - é - lis ab o - re

this mes - sage from heav - en, take pit - y on us poor sin - ners.
su - mens il - lud A - ve, pec - ca - tó - rum mi - se - ré - re.

℣. The angel of the Lord declared unto Mary.
℟. And she conceived of the Holy Ghost.

℣. *Angelus Dómini nuntiávit Maríae.*
℟. *Et concépit de Spíritu Sancto.*

Figure 5. *Alma Redemptoris Mater/Loving Mother of Our Savior* (continued)

Figure 6. *Ave Regina Caelorum/Hail Mary, Queen of Heav'n* (Compline Anthem During Lent). Text: twelfth century, anon. English adaptation by Theodore Marier © in "Pius X Hymnal," © 1953 by Summy-Birchard Music division of Birch Tree Music Group Ltd. Used with permission. Tune: Plainchant, Mode 6. Accompaniment by Theodore Marier. (From Marier, ed., *Hymns, Psalms, and Spiritual Canticles,* 262. Courtesy of Boston Boy Choir, Inc.).

Figure 7. *Regina Coeli/Mary, Queen of Heav'n* (Compline Anthem During Eastertide). Text: fourteenth century, anon. English adaptation by Theodore Marier © in "Pius X Hymnal," © 1953 by Summy-Birchard Music division of Birch Tree Music Group Ltd. Used with permission. Tune: Plainchant, Mode 6. Accompaniment by Theodore Marier. (From Marier, ed., *Hymns, Psalms, and Spiritual Canticles*, 332. Courtesy of Boston Boy Choir, Inc.).

Mary in Sacred and Secular Song

Marian hymnody from this period often utilizes nature imagery. Hildegard of Bingen, who is said to have "realized the idea of Mary as a song," is an important representative of this type.[146] Hildegard was very fond of the "Eva/Ave motif," so much so that Barbara Newman writes that "the notion that Mary's purity and obedience reversed the corruption and rebellion of Eve . . . occurs in at least half the Marian songs" of Hildegard.[147] This ties into the notion of Mary's *viriditas* or "greenness" which Hildegard often focused on in her hymns to Mary:

> By remaining inviolate yet divinely fruitful, Mary regains the lost heritage of Eve. Her body becomes the emblem of paradise regained as well as a path to it . . . For this reason Hildegard constantly associates Mary images of growth, greenness, flowering: she is the "shining lily" (no. 17), "the greenest branch" (no. 19), and so forth.[148]

Another place the association of Mary with nature is found is in thirteenth-century France, where Daniel O'Sullivan finds "signs of unprecedented growth" in Marian devotion.[149] He describes how it is nearly impossible to differentiate between devotional and secular song in this setting, because they both "share melodies as well as rhyme and metrical schemes."[150] The Latin text *Concordi laetitia* comes from the thirteenth century, and the accompanying chant tune is attributed to Pierre de Corbeil (d. 1222), archbishop of Sens. This hymn shows the joining of nature imagery, Mary, and Eastertide, particularly in the second stanza:

146. Rubin, *Mother of God*, 147. Heidi Epstein sounds a similar praise of Hildegard: "Hildegard emphasizes that it was only from the (musical) 'instrument' of a woman's body that God's incarnate song could resound." See Heidi Epstein, *Melting the Venusberg: A Feminist Theology of Music* (New York: Continuum, 2004), 125.

147. Hildegard of Bingen, *Symphonia*, 47.

148. Ibid.

149. Daniel O'Sullivan, *Marian Devotion in Thirteenth-Century French Lyric* (Toronto: University of Toronto Press, 2005), 3.

150. Ibid., 4. This observation could also be applied to some Marian congregational songs before Vatican II that focus on Mary and nature imagery.

2. Quæ felici gaudio,
   Resurgente Domino,
   Floruit ut lilium,
   Vivum cernens Filium:
   Virgo Maria![151]
	2. Who, with happy joy—
	   the Lord having risen—
	   flowered like a lily,
	   beholding her Son alive.
	   O Virgin Mary![152]

David Rothenberg, in his study of polyphonic songs that combined secular texts with sacred chant, describes how the lines between sacred and secular, the beloved and Mary (a notion from the bridal imagery in the Song of Songs), blurred during this time.[153] Both in secular music describing the beloved and in sacred music describing Mary, a red rose symbolized virginity and a white lily symbolized purity. The celebration of Easter during springtime "viewed the spring blossoms as an earthly sign of the salvation made possible by Christ's resurrection." When describing someone as a "sweet rose or a fair lily," they were also being compared to Mary, and by describing Mary in this way, it showed that she was human, like everyone else. By invoking spring, "the salvific potential of the Resurrection" was brought to bear on the person being described.

Further expanding on the connection between Mary and nature imagery, she was also referred to as a garden enclosed, in reference to her virginity.[154] There is also the influence of the nature imagery of the Song of Songs (a common text for exegesis during this time), one of the readings for the feast of the Assumption. The blessing of

151. From "Concordi lætitia," #257 in Richard Rice, ed., *The Parish Book of Chant: A Manual of Gregorian Chant and a Liturgical Resource for Scholas and Congregations; Including Order of Sung Mass for Both Ordinary and Extraordinary Forms of the Roman Rite with a Complete* Kyriale, *along with Chants and Hymns for Ocasional and Seasonal Use and Their Literal English Translations*, 2nd exp. ed. (The Church Music Association of America, 2012), 275. This hymnal is available online at http://media. musicasacra.com/book/pbc_2nd.pdf, accessed April 2014.

152. Ibid.

153. David J. Rothenberg, "The Marian Symbolism of Spring, ca. 1200–ca. 1500: Two Case Studies," *Journal of the American Musicological Society* 59, no. 2 (Summer 2006): 319–20. All quotations and information from this paragraph are taken from this source.

154. Thanks to Dr. Francine Cardman for making this connection.

flowers, grasses, and herbs often occurred in conjunction with this Marian feast.[155]

Mary in Medieval Liturgy

Little Office of the Virgin

As was discussed earlier, during the Middle Ages, Mary became the focus of attention as people were becoming more reliant on her for protection.[156] This led to the development of special liturgies devoted to her praise. In 1215 at the Fourth Lateran Council, it was decreed that there should be Masses for Mary not only on Saturday but also every day, as requested by Pope Urban II.[157] The desire to praise Mary on a daily basis also spread to the Divine Office, and so between the twelfth and sixteenth centuries it was common to find the daily recitation of the Little Office of the Virgin.[158] The Little Office contained seasonal and principal texts (including the Hail Mary), and could be recited or sung.[159] Rubin outlines the Hours and their Marian associations: "Matins and Annunciation, Lauds and Visitation, Prime and Nativity, Terce and Annunciation to the Shepherds, Sext and the Adoration of the Magi, None and the Presentation in the Temple, Vespers and the Flight into Egypt, and Compline with the Coronation of the Virgin."[160] In some foundations, there was a special chapel set aside, a Lady chapel, where groups of singers had the sole responsibility of reciting the Little Office.[161]

---

155. Fulton, *From Judgment to Passion*, 267. See also the following website which describes the history of this practice: http://communio.stblogs .org/2009/08/herb-blessing-on-the-solemnity.html. Thanks to Peter Scagnelli for pointing out this source.

156. Graef, *The Devotion to Our Lady*, 54.

157. Parker, "Architecture as Liturgical Setting," 323.

158. Harper, *The Forms and Orders of Western Liturgy from the Tenth to the Eighteenth Century*, 133. Jungmann notes the Little Office was fixed in the Roman Breviary in 1568 (*Christian Prayer through the Centuries*, 149).

159. Harper, *The Forms and Orders of Western Liturgy from the Tenth to the Eighteenth Century*, 133–34; and Graef, *The Devotion to Our Lady*, 54.

160. Rubin, *The Mother of God*, 221.

161. Harper, *The Forms and Orders of Western Liturgy from the Tenth to the Eighteenth Century*, 134.

Graef describes that there began to be stories that "reported favours attached to the recitation of the Little Office or punishments attending on negligence in this. The main object of most of these legends was to inculcate trust in the Mother of Mercy who was always willing and able to help those who called on her."[162] In addition to obtaining Mary's favor, the Little Office was used "in order to obtain Mary's help" during the First Crusade.[163]

Commemorative Office and Mass of the Virgin

It is important to note the difference between the Little Office and the Commemorative Office and Mass of the Virgin: "The Little Office was said in addition to the main Office of the day: the Commemorative Office displaced the Office of the day once a week, most often on Saturday."[164] The Commemorative Office contained seasonal antiphons that were divided liturgically, much like the Four Marian Antiphons, and the texts "corresponded with those of the Feasts of the Virgin," as was the case with many of the Marian feasts.[165] Holding a Mass in honor of Mary on Saturday emphasized the medieval perspective that while Sunday was the Lord's Day, Saturday was Mary's day.[166]

It seems that this practice came about when Alcuin received the Gregorian Sacramentary from Pope Adrian sometime between 784 and 791.[167] During Ordinary Time, there were only Masses for Sunday, so in order to avoid repeating them during the week, Alcuin "compiled a double series of Masses for the seven days of the week." Each day had two different intentions except for Saturday, when both of the intentions were for Mary. The themes for the first formulary

---

162. Graef, *The Devotion to Our Lady*, 60.

163. Graef, *Mary*, 181.

164. Harper, *The Forms and Orders of Western Liturgy from the Tenth to the Eighteenth Century*, 134.

165. Ibid., 135.

166. Ibid., 134.

167. Ignazio M. Calabuig, "The Liturgical Cult of Mary in the East and West," in *Liturgical Time and Space*, vol. 5 of *Handbook for Liturgical Studies*, ed. Anscar J. Chupungco (Collegeville, MN: Liturgical Press, 2000), 277–79. All quotations and information in this paragraph are taken from this source.

sound very familiar to the themes found in Marian congregational songs before Vatican II: "Thematically, the formulary contrasts the dangers of the present life and its essential sadness with the assurance of receiving, by means of the intercession of the Virgin, the security, ease, and peace of the life to come."

Feasts of the Visitation and Presentation of Mary

From the seventh to the fourteenth century, "the Roman Church felt no need of increasing the number of its Marian feasts and kept to the traditional four."[168] Later in the Middle Ages two more feasts were added: the feast of the Visitation and the feast of the Presentation of Mary.[169] The visitation story of Mary's journey to Elizabeth (Luke 1:39-56) has its origins in the Roman liturgy of the sixth century, when "the episode was celebrated on Friday of the *tempora* of Advent."[170] Because the feast had its roots in the East, it was only gradually accepted by the West beginning in the thirteenth century.[171] During the Crusades, the Latins became familiar with the feast, but "profoundly changed the object of the feast" and focused on the gospel reading of the visitation.[172] Pope Urban VI fixed the feast in 1389 on July 2; he did so hoping that Mary's intercession would bring peace and an end to the Great Schism with the antipope Clement VII.[173] With the liturgical changes of Vatican II, the feast was moved to May 31 which had previously been celebrated as the Queenship of Mary (which was moved to August 22). One of the more famous

---

168. Pierre Jounel, "The Veneration of Mary," in *Liturgy and Time*, vol. 4 of *The Church at Prayer: An Introduction to the Liturgy*, ed. Aimé Georges Martimort (Collegeville, MN: Liturgical Press, 1986), 138.

169. For a more in-depth look at the development of these feasts, see R.W. Pfaff, *New Liturgical Feasts in Later Medieval England* (Oxford: Clarendon Press, 1970), 40–61, 103–15.

170. Calabuig, "The Liturgical Cult of Mary in the East and West," 292.

171. The Eastern celebration on July 2 did not focus on the visitation, but rather on "the memorial of the deposition of the burial urn in which the mortal remains of the Mother of Christ rested in the church called Blacherne." Another tradition says it was a feast for the "deposition of Mary's clothing" (ibid., 292).

172. Calabuig, "The Liturgical Cult of Mary in the East and West," 292.

173. Ibid., 293.

hymns written specifically for this feast is the Latin hymn *Quo sanctus ador te rapit* by Jean-Baptiste de Santeuil (1630–1697) which was translated into English by Edward Caswall as "Whither thus, in holy rapture":

1. Whither thus, in holy rapture,
     Princely Maiden, art Thou bent?
   Why so fleetly art Thou speeding
     Up the mountain's rough ascent?

2. Fill'd with the eternal Godhead!
     Glowing with the Spirit's flame!
   Love it is that bears Thee onward,
     And supports thy tender frame.

3. Lo! thine aged cousin claims Thee,
     Claims thy sympathy and care;
   God her shame from her hath taken;
     He hath heard her fervent prayer.

4. Blessed Mothers! joyful meeting!
     Thou in her, the hand of God,
   She in Thee, with lips inspired,
     Owns the Mother of her Lord.

5. As the sun his face concealing,
     In a cloud withdraws from sight,
   So in Mary then lay hidden
     He who is the world's true light.

6. Honor, glory, virtue, merit,
     Be to Thee, O Virgin's Son!
   With the Father and the Spirit,
     While eternal ages run.[174]

---

174. Jean-Baptiste de Santuel, "Whither thus, in holy rapture," Hymnary. org, http://www.hymnary.org/text/whither_thus_in_holy_rapture, accessed March 2014. Taken from Roman Catholic Church, *Lyra Catholica: Containing All the Hymns of the Roman Breviary and Missal, with Others from Various Sources* (New York: E. Dunigan & Bro., 1851), 314–15.

The feast of the Presentation of Mary (November 21), based on the story from the *Protoevangelium of James*, has its roots in Jerusalem in the sixth century with the dedication of the Nea Church, built on Temple ruins by Emperor Justinian I in Mary's honor.[175] It slowly spread to the West, by way of the Italian monasteries in the ninth century and to England in the twelfth century. Philip de Mézières was the great proponent for bringing the feast more fully into the West, and he worked with Gregory XI in 1372 to create liturgical texts for the Mass.[176] "The idea behind the formulary was the preparation of the Virgin for her role as Mother of God. Mary is in the Temple, Israel's holiest place, because, having conceived the Son of God within her womb, she is herself the holy temple of the Most High."[177] Just as the feast of the Visitation had hopes for peace associated with it, Mézières, a French knight who had lived in the East, in a spirit of ecumenism, hoped to spread the feast to the West.[178]

In addition to these two feasts, there are also a few other Marian feasts, as well as feasts associated with Mary, that came into being during this time. The Conception of Mary, which had been celebrated in the East since the eighth century, made its way to England in the eleventh century and France in the twelfth century.[179] The debate over Mary's immaculate conception would go on for centuries. In 1854, Pope Pius IX defined it as dogma. The feast of the Sorrows of Mary, now celebrated on September 15, developed in the twelfth century "under the influence of St. Anselm and St. Bernard."[180] This feast, later known as the Seven Sorrows of the Blessed Virgin, is a product of the Marian devotion of Anselm and Bernard, as acknowledged ear-

---

175. Calabuig, "The Liturgical Cult of Mary in the East and West," 254. It was called the "new" church "in order to distinguish it from the earlier church, also dedicated to Mary, that had been built near the Sheep Pool opposite the Temple." See Calabuig, "The Liturgical Cult of Mary," 255. Unless otherwise noted, the following information is taken from ibid., 295–96.

176. For more information on de Mézières, see William E. Coleman, ed., *Philippe de Mézières' Campaign for the Feast of Mary's Presentation* (Toronto: Centre for Medieval Studies by the Pontifical Institute of Medieval Studies, 1981).

177. Calabuig, "The Liturgical Cult of Mary in the East and West," 296.

178. Jounel, "The Veneration of Mary," 140.

179. Ibid., 139.

180. Ibid., 141.

lier, and the *Stabat Mater* is the sequence for this day.[181] This period also saw a greater popularity in the cults of Mary's husband, Joseph, and her mother, Anne. Anne's feast began to be celebrated in the twelfth and thirteen centuries on July 25, while Joseph's March 19 feast spread in the fifteenth century.[182]

This increase in Marian feasts coincides with the increase in Marian visions, pilgrimages, and shrines; during the thirteenth and fourteenth centuries, Mary's cult was at its height in terms of the number of Marian visions experienced and Marian pilgrimages made.[183] Many of these pilgrimage sites (or the relics housed there), were said to have miraculous powers. These sites and all of Marian devotion were about to become a line in the sand between Protestants and Catholics as a result of the Reformation.

181. For the later development of the Seven Sorrows of the Blessed Virgin, see Jounel, "The Veneration of Mary," 146.

182. Ibid., 143–44. The Feast of St. Anne is celebrated on July 26 in the West, and July 25 in the East.

183. Graef, *The Devotion to Our Lady*, 61. This surge in visions and pilgrimages would be seen again in the nineteenth and twentieth centuries with visions and pilgrimages associated with such places as Lourdes, Fátima, and Medjugorje.

Chapter Three

Through Mary to Jesus

Daily, daily sing to Mary;
   Sing, my soul, her praises due;
All her feasts, her actions worship
   With the heart's devotion true.
Lost in wond'ring contemplation,
   Be her majesty confessed;
Call her Mother, call her Virgin—
   Happy Mother, Virgin blest![1]

      —Tr. Henry Bittleston, "Daily, daily sing to Mary"

Introduction

Despite the fact that Marian devotion was challenged by many of the Reformers, it continued to flourish after the Council of Trent (1545–1563) as it was strengthened by the continuing popularity of

---

1. Stanza 1 of Henry Bittleston, "Daily, daily sing to Mary," Hymnary.org, http://www.hymnary.org/text/daily_daily_sing_to_mary, accessed March 2014. Taken from Roman Catholic Church, *Hymns and Songs for Catholic Children* (New York: Catholic Publication Society, 1870), 136. This is Bittleston's translation of *Omni die dic Marie.* The text comes from the sixteenth-century *Mariale,* while some attribute it to either St. Anselm (d. 1109) or St. Bernard of Cluny (twelfth century). See Higginson, *Handbook for American Catholic Hymnals,* 77.

the rosary and novenas, the addition of new Marian feasts, and by supporters of devotion to Mary, including Louis-Marie Grignion de Montfort (1673–1716) and Alphonsus Liguori (1696–1787). This fervent devotion to the Blessed Mother was carried by Catholics to the United States, and at the First National Synod in Baltimore in 1791, Mary was named "principal patroness of the diocese" and the feast of her Assumption was declared the "principal feast of the diocese."[2] Here is the solid foundation for Marian devotion in the US Catholic Church that would flourish in the nineteenth century and the first half of the twentieth century.

The Reformation, the Council of Trent, and Beyond

Mary, the Reformers, and the Council of Trent (1545–1563)

The Reformers

The Reformers felt that in "taking from Mary the false honors with which she had been burdened in the Middle Ages" they were actually doing her a service by liberating her and allowing her to become "a supreme model of faith in the word of God."[3] Martin Luther (1483–1546) and the other first generation Reformers did not completely abandon Mary—at first. Luther's views on Mary changed throughout his life, moving away from the veneration of Mary and from nonbiblical devotions to a focus on her "Christological dimensions" (*sola Scriptura* and *solus Christus*) as he transformed her from a "queenly advocate" to a "woman full of faith and scriptural certitude" and a "model of faith" (*sola fide*).[4] In 1523 he allowed the feasts of

---

2. Peter Guilday, *A History of the Councils of Baltimore, 1791–1884* (New York: MacMillan Co., 1932), 67–69.

3. Jaroslav Pelikan, *Mary through the Centuries: Her Place in the History of Culture* (New Haven, CT: Yale University Press, 1996), 153.

4. Miri Rubin, *Mother of God: A History of the Virgin Mary* (New Haven, CT: Yale University Press, 2009), 355; James F. White, *Protestant Worship: Traditions in Transition* (Louisville, KY: Westminster John Knox Press, 1989), 44; and Pelikan, *Mary through the Centuries*, 155, 159. For a fuller understanding of Luther's biblical grounding of Mary as a woman of faith and humility, see Jaroslav Pelikan, ed., *Luther's Works*, vol. 21: *The Sermon on the Mount (Sermons) and The Magnificat* (Saint Louis: Concordia Publishing House, 1955), 297–355.

the Purification (which showed Mary's modesty) and Annunciation (which showed her humility), because they were feasts of Christ, and also permitted the observance of the Assumption and Mary's Nativity; these last two feasts he kept at first because he knew that it would have been too difficult to strip them from people's devotions right away.[5]

Although Luther was clearly against the veneration of Mary and the saints as is seen in the Confessions of Augsburg (1530), he knew just how strong devotion to Mary was.[6] This strong devotion was also found in the hymnody of the time, seen in a telling quote from a Protestant music-master of Joachimsthal in Bohemia:

> I will speak only of the songs, from which the state of religion may be readily understood. These were for the most part intended for the invocation of the highly-praised Virgin Mary and the dead saints. No one knew how to sing or speak about the Lord Jesus Christ. He was regarded and set forth only as a strict judge, from whom no grace could be expected, but only wrath and punishment.[7]

This account attests to Mary's popularity in the hymnody of the time as well as the belief earlier noted that Christ, the Judge, is inapproachable, such that people must go to Mary instead.

If Luther tried to give Mary a less elevated status, then John Calvin (1509–1564) gave her "an even lower place."[8] Because Calvin believed that grace was predestined and everything depended on God's will, he completely rejected the veneration of Mary and the notion that she could "obtain grace for us."[9] Ulrich Zwingli (1484–1531) continued the trend of reducing Mary's role as he believed Christ is the sole Mediator, so there was no need for other mediators like

---

5. Hilda Graef, *Mary: A History of Doctrine and Devotion; With a New Chapter Covering Vatican II and Beyond by Thomas A. Thompson* (Notre Dame, IN: Ave Maria Press, 2009); and Rubin, *Mother of God*, 369.

6. Graef, *Mary*, 287.

7. Christopher Boyd Brown, *Singing the Gospel: Lutheran Hymns and the Success of the Reformation* (Cambridge, MA: Harvard University Press, 2005), 157, as quoted in Rubin, *Mother of God*, 368.

8. Graef, *Mary*, 286.

9. Ibid.

Mary.[10] Similar to Luther, Zwingli focused on Mary's lowliness, and it is also interesting to note that he kept the *Ave Maria* in his Sunday service until 1563.[11] The Church of England also took strong action against Marian devotion, condemning the recitation of the rosary (Injunctions in 1538 and 1547) and forbidding the invocation of the saints (Article 22 of the *Thirty-Nine Articles*, 1563).[12] These strong positions against Mary were somewhat modified by Queen Elizabeth I (1533–1603), who helped restore the cult of Mary (and the saints) as she herself was compared to Mary and was called the "Virgin Queen," similar to the "Virgin Queen of Walsingham."[13]

The Documents of Trent

According to Graef, the Catholic Church "had too much on its hands to deal explicitly with questions of Mariology" during the Council of Trent.[14] In his foreword to the English translation of the documents of Trent, H. J. Schroeder describes the council's twofold purpose: "to define the doctrines of the Church in reply to the heresies of the Protestants, and to bring about a thorough reform of the inner life of Christians."[15] As seen above, two criticisms the Reformers brought against the Catholic Church addressed the veneration of Mary and the saints, and brief references to these points are found in the documents of Trent.

Graef points out that the Council of Trent defended the veneration of the saints in Session XXII in December 1563, saying "it was good and useful to invoke them in order to obtain benefits from God through his Son Jesus Christ, without mentioning, but neces-

---

10. Pelikan, *Mary through the Centuries*, 154.

11. Graef, *Mary*, 287; and White, *Protestant Worship*, 61. Graef also notes that "he objects to a false trust in the recitation of *Hail Marys* without a corresponding Christian life" (*Mary*, 287).

12. Eamon Duffy, *The Stripping of the Altars: Traditional Religion in England 1400–1580* (New Haven, CT: Yale University Press, 2005), 450, 462; and Graef, *Mary*, 289.

13. Pelikan, *Mary through the Centuries*, 161.

14. Graef, *Mary*, 289.

15. Catholic Church, *The Canons and Decrees of the Council of Trent*, trans. H. J. Schroeder (Rockford, IL: Tan Books and Publishers, 1978), iii.

sarily including, her [Mary] in this general defence of prayer to the saints."[16] The two places where Mary is specifically mentioned have to do with her conception and whether or not she was born without sin, a topic that had been argued over for hundreds of years and had been brought into question by the Reformers. In Session V in June 1546, the council declared, that "blessed and immaculate Virgin Mary" was not included in the discussion of original sin.[17] Mary was also considered in the discussion of justification and sin in Session VI held in January 1547, where it describes in Canon 23 how she was given "a special privilege from God," so she was the one person who was able to refrain from sin throughout her entire life.[18]

The Aftermath of Trent

As Nathan Mitchell points out in his foreword to James White's study of Catholic worship, there were actually no liturgical reforms at Trent: "Instead, in a momentous decision, they turned the reform of 'the missal and breviary' over to the pope. The so-called 'Tridentine liturgy' is thus a collection of rites reformed *after* Trent under papal auspices."[19] Mitchell goes on to note that it was not the pope who put together the Breviary in 1568 and the Missal in 1570; rather, it was a "panel of scholarly experts" who worked under the five principles of the papal bull *Quo primum*:

> (1) That a *single rite* for Mass and Office should be used throughout the Latin Church; (2) that *qualified scholars* should determine the antiquity and probity of the new books' contents; (3) that the rites should be restored according to the "pristine norm of the Fathers" (*ad pristinam Patrum normam*); (4) that from now on, this "norm" will be *regulated strictly by the pope* through *editions typicae* that he

---

16. Graef, *Mary*, 289–90.
17. Catholic Church, *The Canons and Decrees of the Council of Trent*, 23.
18. Ibid., 45.
19. James F. White, *Roman Catholic Worship: Trent to Today*, foreword by Nathan Mitchell, 2nd ed. (Collegeville, MN: Liturgical Press, 2003), ix.

promulgates; and (5) that *nothing can be added or subtracted from the text without the pope's approval.*[20]

So what effect did the soon-to-be-called *Missal of Pius V* have on Marian devotions? What did it mean that all churches, which in the past had used different liturgies, were now all required to pray from the same rite and could not change anything without the pope's approval?

Joseph Jungmann gives a very descriptive and powerful account of what he believes happened as a result of the new rite, so I quote him at length:

> After fifteen hundred years of unbroken development in the rite of the Roman Mass, after the rushing and the streaming from every height and out of every valley, the Missal of Pius V was indeed a powerful dam holding back the waters or permitting them to flow through only in firm, well-built canals. At one blow all arbitrary meandering to one side or another was cut off, all floods prevented, and the safe, regular and useful flow assured. But the price paid was this, that the beautiful river valley now lay barren and the forces of further evolution were often channeled into the narrow bed of a very inadequate devotional life instead of gathering strength for new forms of liturgical expression.[21]

Jungmann clearly believes that by forcing everyone to use the same rite, all creative energies could now only be expressed through devotions, rather than liturgical innovations in the Mass.

Edmund Bishop gives a similar interpretation as to why devotions became so popular in the wake of the Council of Trent. In his work "The Genius of the Roman Rite," Bishop describes how the attempt at unification by the *Missal of Pius V* left less freedom in the

20. Ibid., Mitchell's emphasis. Daw makes the interesting point that principle number five "gives these liturgical texts the same status as the Law delivered through Moses; cf. Deuteronomy 4:2, 12:32 as well as that of God's own handiwork: Ecclesiastes 3:14b." Carl P. Daw, Jr., e-mail message to author, February 4, 2012.

21. Joseph A. Jungmann, *The Mass of the Roman Rite: Its Origins and Development (Missarum Sollemnia)*, 2 vols., trans. Francis A. Brunner (Westminster, MD: Christian Classics, 1986), 1:140–41.

liturgy, in addition to the fact that the people's ability to participate in the liturgy was greatly reduced, perhaps leading them to look for devotions that would allow their participation.[22] He explains how before the reforms of the Missal in 1570 there was

> variety and diversity of the rituals, missals, and breviaries of later mediaeval times; and it explains also how the books of devotion of those days, contrary to what is common now, were drawn up on the lines of the official service books themselves; or as some people have put it, "there were no popular devotions in those days." But this was only because the popular devotional spirit expressed itself with freedom and liberty in the strictly liturgical services of the various local churches.

This all changed, however, with Pius V's reforms and the establishment of the Congregation of Rites, which were "designed to keep observances on the lines laid down in those books, such manipulation of the public service books of the Church as was common in the middle ages in every country in Europe was destined to be finally put an end to." Bishop concludes by arguing that the "spirit" once found in the liturgy was still active, but it had to find a new outlet, and that outlet was devotions; for in words similar to Jungmann's, "unable to act inside and on the liturgy itself, it acts with yet greater freedom without. One path shut up, it seeks its ends by another."

The assessments of "popular devotions" by Jungmann and Bishop are helpful in understanding the trends of Marian devotion following the Council of Trent. Much of what may have been able to be expressed in a local liturgy was now not allowed, and this "devotional spirit" had to seek another outlet. This surge in devotions created a trend of distancing people from the liturgy; they were already distanced by their lack of ability to participate as the Mass was in Latin (and parts of it were spoken silently), so when they found a devotion that met their personal needs and allowed them to participate actively, they latched on to it.

22. The following information is taken from Edmund Bishop, "The Genius of the Roman Rite," in *Liturgica Historica: Papers on the Liturgy and Religious Life on the Western Church* (Oxford: Clarendon Press, 1962), 1–19. All quotations in this and the following paragraph are taken from page 18.

Marian Devotions and Feasts

Baroque and Enlightenment Characteristics

The effects of the Council of Trent continued to be felt in the Baroque and Enlightenment periods. A "chief feature of the baroque era was the standardization of the rites" following the establishment of the Congregation of Rites in 1588 to police liturgical activity and to implement the new Breviary, Missal, and *Roman Ritual* (1614).[23] The standardization of the rites led to what Jungmann describes as a contrast between the "Baroque spirit and that of the traditional liturgy," leading to a dualism between the liturgy and popular piety.[24] Mark Francis blames this dualism on clericalism and individualism; the increased clericalism along with a liturgy that was inaccessible and incomprehensible to the people forced the faithful to turn to devotions which allowed them to cultivate "an affective relationship with God, the Blessed Virgin, and the saints."[25]

The Baroque period of the seventeenth century was one of "artistic brilliance," and this played out in the liturgy, particularly in the visual aspects of "procession, benediction, and exposition."[26] Popular cults arose from this focus on visual images, including the Sacred Heart of Mary and the Sacred Heart of Jesus.[27] Relics and the cult of the saints were taken over by devotions to Mary and by visually oriented eucharistic devotions such as Benediction and exposition, where the "Blessed Sacrament and the monstrance" were the focus.[28] The Host could be regarded as the "relic par excellence" because the Mass was now extremely visually oriented: people did not receive communion by receiving wafers in their mouths, rather, they received by looking at the raised Host at the moment of elevation.[29]

---

23. White, *Protestant Worship*, 30.
24. Ibid.; and Mark R. Francis, "Liturgy and Popular Piety in a Historical Perspective," in *Directory on Popular Piety and the Liturgy: Principles and Guidelines. A Commentary*, ed. Peter C. Phan (Collegeville, MN: Liturgical Press, 2002), 19–43.
25. Francis, "Liturgy and Popular Piety in a Historical Perspective," 25–26.
26. White, *Protestant Worship*, 31.
27. Ibid.
28. Ibid.
29. White, *Roman Catholic Worship*, 34.

In the Enlightenment period Rome became even "more defensive" in light of rationalism as well as from the push by some for such changes as vernacular liturgy (including Archbishop John Carroll in the United States), reception of communion for all, and "restraints" on popular devotions, including those to Mary.[30] In addition to the continued dualism between liturgy and popular piety, there appears to have been a widening gap "between the religious practices of the learned and those of the 'simple people,'" which became especially prominent.[31] While the upper class disdained popular religion, the rest of the faithful appreciated having devotions outside of the liturgy that they could understand (in the vernacular) and that were meaningful to their spirituality.[32] This is important for Marian congregational song, especially before Vatican II, because many of these songs were in the vernacular and were sung at services held outside of regular Sunday Mass, such as Benediction and exposition of the Blessed Sacrament.

New Marian Devotions

In addition to confraternities founded under Mary, the Jesuits also organized "Marian Congregations," groups living under the motto *"Per Mariam ad Iesum* (through Mary to Jesus)."[33] The phrase "through Mary to Jesus" caught on quickly, and writers such as Alphonsus Liguori and Louis-Marie Grignion de Montfort (1673–1716) were very popular in this period. Montfort's *Treatise on True Devotion to the Blessed Virgin* was rediscovered in 1842, and it may have had an influence on Marian congregation songs of the mid- to late nineteenth century. Many of the themes he writes about, such as being afraid of Christ and the need to approach God through a mediator (Mary), are very common in the songs of this time.[34] Liguori's works, such as *The*

---

30. White, *Protestant Worship*, 31–32. It is interesting to note that many of these changes sought are those that would be brought up again during the liturgical movement in the twentieth century.

31. Francis, "Liturgy and Popular Piety in a Historical Perspective," 22.

32. Ibid., 21, 26.

33. Hilda Graef, *The Devotion to Our Lady* (New York: Hawthorn Books, 1963), 69.

34. Ibid., 72–73.

Glories of Mary, remained popular through the nineteenth century and also contained themes common to Marian congregational song during that era, including Mary's ability to placate God's wrath as she saves the sinner from her Son's "avenging arm" and the notion that Mary was omnipotent because she obtains all she asks for from her Son.[35]

In addition to his devotional writings, Liguori also helped to foster devotion to Mary through the praying of different novenas, or prayers repeated for nine days.[36] This would often take the form of the recitation of the rosary, and in addition to asking for "particular favors" or receiving indulgences, they were often prayed to the rising devotions to the Sacred Heart of Jesus and the Immaculate Heart of Mary.[37]

New Marian Feasts

By the end of the seventeenth century, Marian feasts began to be added to the calendar quite regularly, marking a "new phase in the liturgical cult of Mary" as some feasts were actually based on historical events while others were the result of religious orders looking to have their particular devotion to Mary approved in the liturgy.[38] One such feast from the Carmelites is Our Lady of Mount Carmel, celebrated on July 16 and added to the Roman Calendar in 1726 by Pope Benedict XIII.[39] The hymn *Salve, Mater misericordiae* comes from the Carmelite tradition, addressing Mary as "Mother of Mercy" and as one who pardons and is full of grace. This anonymous text, written in the thirteenth or fourteenth century, comes from the *Iubilus aureus B.M.V.*, a song from the Middle Ages composed of one hundred stanzas; here there are four stanzas and the refrain:[40]

---

35. Ibid., 76.

36. White, *Roman Catholic Worship*, 60.

37. Ibid., 61, 96. During this period it was common for devotions to Jesus to be paralleled with devotions to Mary (*Roman Catholic Worship*, 34).

38. Pierre Jounel, "The Veneration of Mary," in *Liturgy and Time*, vol. 4 of *The Church at Prayer: An Introduction to the Liturgy*, ed. Aimé Georges Martimort (Collegeville, MN: Liturgical Press, 1986), 144–46.

39. Ibid., 146.

40. Anselmo Lentini, *Te decet hymnus: l'innario della "Liturgia horarum"* (Città del Vaticano: Typis Polyglottis Vaticanis, 1984), 236. This hymn appears with

R. Salve, Mater misericordiæ, Mater Dei, et Mater veniæ, Mater spei, et Mater gratiæ, Mater plena sanctæ lætitiæ, O Maria!	**R.** Hail, Mother of mercy, Mother of God, and Mother of pardon, Mother of hope, and Mother of grace, Mother full of holy happiness, O Mary!
1. Salve, decus humani generis, Salve, Virgo dignior ceteris, Quæ virgines omnes transgrederis, Et altius sedes in superis, O Maria! **R.**	1. Hail, O honor of the human race, Hail, Virgin more worthy than the others, You who excel all other virgins, And sit higher in the heavens, O Mary! **R.**
2. Salve, felix Virgo puerpera: Nam qui sedet in Patris dextera, Cælum regens, terram et æthera, Intra tua se clausit viscera, O Maria! **R.**	2. Hail, blessed Virgin mother: For he sits at the Father's right hand, King of heaven, earth and skies, Shut himself within your womb, O Mary! **R.**
3. Te creavit Pater ingenitus, Obumbravit te Unigenitus, Fecundavit te Sanctus Spiritus, Tue es facta tota divinitus, O Maria! **R.**	3. The unbegotten Father created you, The Only-begotten overshadowed you, The Holy Spirit made you fruitful, You became completely full of divinity, O Mary! **R.**

varying numbers of verses. The four verses here are the same printed (albeit in a different order) as those found in the post–Vatican II Carmelite Proper Offices printed jointly by the Carmelites (O. Carm.) and Discalced Carmelites (O.C.D.). See Catholic Church, *Proper of the Liturgy of the Hours of the Order of the Brothers of the Blessed Virgin Mary of Mount Carmel and of the Order of Discalced Carmelites* (Rome: Institutum Carmelitanum, 1993), 473–74. Many thanks to Peter Scagnelli for his help in obtaining this information.

4. Esto, Mater, nostrum solatium; Nostrum esto, tu Virgo, gaudium; Et nos tandem post hoc exsilium, Lætos iunge choris cæletium, O Maria! **R.**[41]	4. Mother, be our solace; O Virgin be our joy; and at length, After this exile, join us joyful With the choirs of heavenly hosts, O Mary! **R.**[42]

The seventeenth century saw the addition of the feasts of the Holy Name of Mary (held the Sunday after Mary's Nativity on September 8) and Our Lady of Mercy (September 24), while the feast of the Rosary of the Virgin Mary emerged in the eighteenth century. Although the victory at Lepanto had been attributed to the recitation of the rosary in 1571 and the accompanying feast was made obligatory in Rome in 1573, the feast spread to the entire Roman Rite in 1716 when Pope Clement XI made the declaration in thanksgiving for another victory over the Turks, this time at Peterwardein.[43] Here is yet another instance where Mary is associated with defeating the "infidels."

The Feast of the Seven Sorrows of the Blessed Virgin (originally celebrated on the third Sunday of September but moved to September 15 by Pius X in 1913) was expanded to the entire Roman Rite in 1814 after Pope Pius VII returned to Rome following his time as a prisoner at Fontainebleau when France took over the Papal States. The reason for this feast was "as an act of thanksgiving to the Virgin Mary for having safeguarded the Church through the trials of the preceding twenty years."[44] Similar offerings of thanks to Mary will follow the "captivity" of the papacy in Rome later in the nineteenth century with Pius IX, among others.

O quot undis is a hymn associated with the Feast of the Seven Sorrows of Mary, a feast that focuses on the "compassionate sorrow that pierces [Mary's] heart."[45] This hymn reflects on the sixth sorrow

---

41. James Socias and Christian F. Stepansky, eds., *Cantate et Iubilate Deo: A Devotional and Liturgical Hymnal* (Princeton, NJ: Scepter Publishers, 1999), 112.
42. Ibid.
43. Jounel, "The Veneration of Mary," 145.
44. Ibid., 146.
45. Graef, *Mary*, 241.

(Jesus is taken down from the cross),[46] describing the great tears and sorrows that Mary experienced while holding her crucified son, an image familiar to us from the *Stabat Mater* and *Pietà*.

1. What a sea of tears and sorrows
    Did the soul of Mary toss
  To and fro upon its billows,
    While she wept her bitter loss;
  In her arms her Jesus holding,
    Torn but newly from the Cross.

2. Oh, that mournful Virgin Mother!
    See her tears how fast they flow
  Down upon His mangled body,
    Wounded side and thorny brow;
  While His hands and feet she kisses,
    Picture of immortal woe!

3. Oft and oft His arms and bosom
    Fondly straining to her own;
  Oft her pallid lips imprinting
    On each wound of her dear Son,
  Till at last, in swoons of anguish,
    Sense and consciousness are gone.

4. Gentle Mother, we beseech thee,
    By thy tears and troubles sore;
  By the death of thy dear Offspring;
    By the bloody wounds He bore;
  Touch our hearts with that true sorrow
    Which afflicted thee of yore.

5. To the Father everlasting,
    And the Son, who reigns on high,

---

46. The Seven Sorrows of Mary are: "at the prophecy of Simeon; at the flight into Egypt; having lost the Holy Child at Jerusalem; meeting Jesus on his way to Calvary; standing at the foot of the Cross; Jesus being taken from the Cross; and at the burial of Christ." See Frederick Holweck, "Feasts of the Seven Sorrows of the Blessed Virgin Mary," vol. 14 of *The Catholic Encyclopedia* (New York: Robert Appleton Company, 1912), available from http://www.newadvent.org/cathen/14151b.htm, accessed April 2014.

With the coeternal Spirit,
     Trinity in Unity,
  Be salvation, honor, blessing,
     Now and through eternity.[47]

Early Marian Devotion in the United States

Mary in Early US Catholic Homilies

It is fitting that the first Catholic Mass held in the thirteen colonies was in Maryland on the feast of the Annunciation, March 25, 1634.[48] Mary would hold an important place in the devotion of Catholics in their new home, as John Carroll, who was the first bishop/archbishop of Baltimore (and the United States) from 1789 to 1815, placed his diocese under Mary's protection and dedicated the first cathedral in the United States to her, the Cathedral of the Assumption.[49] The dedication of the cathedral to Mary was not "an anomalistic event in the age of the Enlightenment," but was rather a reflection of the devotion to Mary that already existed.[50]

In a survey of homilies from 1750 to 1787, Michael Sean Winters paints a picture of an already strong devotion to Mary in the colonies and fledging United States. In fact, he is able to say Mary's "prominent role" in the US Catholic Church "was not a nineteenth century import" brought over by the immigrants, but one that is found back to the time of Archbishop Carroll (1789–1815) and even earlier.[51] These homilies also show that many of the Marian themes and devotions from earlier centuries were carried to the colonies:

---

47. F. Campbell, "What a sea of tears and sorrows," Hymnary.org, http://www
.hymnary.org/text/what_a_sea_of_tears_and_sorrows, accessed February 2014.
Taken from #228 in *American Catholic Hymnal: An Extensive Collection of Hymns, Latin Chants and Sacred Songs for Church, School, and Home, Including Gregorian Masses, Vesper Psalms, Litanies . . .*, ed. Marist Brothers (New York: P. J. Kenedy & Sons, 1913), 256.

48. James J. Hennesey, *American Catholics: A History of the Roman Catholic Community in the United States* (New York: Oxford University Press, 1981), 39.

49. Michael Sean Winters, "Marian Spirituality in Early America," in *American Catholic Preaching and Piety in the Time of John Carroll*, ed. Raymond J. Kupke (Lanham, MD: University Press of America, 1991), 87.

50. Ibid., 102–3.

51. Ibid., 102.

for example, the notion that Mary reversed what Eve did; that Mary acts as a mediatrix and our advocate to God because of "her proximity to the Lord in heaven"; that God cannot refuse his Son, and the Son cannot refuse his Mother; the advantages of praying the rosary; and the use of the Hail Mary at the beginning and end of sermons.[52]

The Patroness of a New Diocese

At the First National Synod in Baltimore in 1791, Archbishop Carroll gave a very strong reasoning as to why he was naming Mary as the patroness of the diocese:

> At the beginning of our episcopate, we have been impelled by an ardent desire to make the Blessed Virgin Mary the principal patroness of our diocese, so that by Her intercession, faith and love of God and sanctity of life in the people committed to our care may flourish and increase more and more. We were consecrated first Bishop of Baltimore on the feast of the Assumption and we are led to honour Her as our patron and we exhort our venerable colleagues to venerate Her with a great devotion and often and zealously commend this devotion to their flock, so that in Her powerful patronage they may rely on Her protection from all harm.[53]

In addition to placing his flock under Mary's protection, Archbishop Carroll and the members of the Synod prescribed that the "Litany of the Blessed Virgin was to be recited before Mass, since the Mother of God was the principal patroness of the diocese."[54] Also, if multiple priests were available, they were to hold Benediction after Mass (with hymns in English), and if only one priest was available, they were to "recite with him the *Pater Noster, Ave Maria, Apostles' Creed,* and the *Acts of Faith, Hope* and *Charity.*"[55] Marian devotion found its way into the Sunday Mass, albeit before and after the actual Mass.

---

52. Ibid., 90, 93–96, 101.

53. Ibid., 101–2. The decree goes on to mention that the Assumption is the "principal feast of the diocese" and that on the Sunday within the octave of the Assumption (or if the feast falls on a Sunday) "the people should be excited to receive piously and religiously the Sacraments of Penance and Holy Eucharist." See Guilday, *A History of the Council of Baltimore 1791–1884,* 68–69.

54. Guilday, *A History of the Council of Baltimore 1791–1884,* 67–68.

55. Ibid., 68.

At the Sixth Provincial Council held in 1846, the "Blessed Virgin Mary Immaculate" was decreed as "Patroness of the Church in the United States."[56] The council also asked the Holy See to add the word "Immaculate" to the Office and Mass on December 8, as well as permission to insert in the "Litany the invocation: *Queen, conceived without original sin, pray for us.*"[57] In September 1846 the Catholic Church in the United States received word from Pope Pius IX that they were given permission to declare "the *Blessed Virgin, conceived without sin,* as the patroness of the Church in the United States of America."[58] Finally, in the Seventh Provincial Council in 1849, they voted to "petition the pope to make a doctrinal declaration on the Immaculate Conception of the Blessed Virgin Mary."[59] Regarding devotion to the immaculate conception of Mary, they wrote in a report sent to the Holy See that this devotion "was practiced with great fervor" in the United States.[60] From these council documents, there is the sense that the devotion to Mary's immaculate conception was quite strong, even before the pronouncement of the dogma in 1854.

A text from the early nineteenth century that hints at the growing focus on Mary's immaculate conception is *O sanctissima.*[61] In addition to praising Mary as holy, sweet, and beloved while asking for her help, there is also the focus on traits associated with the immaculate conception: in stanzas 1 and 3, Mary is described as "undefiled," and in stanza 3 it is stated that "no stain of sin is in thee." This Latin phrase, "macula non est in te," will serve as a refrain "Daughter of a mighty Father," which will be looked at in the next chapter. Following the declaration of the Immaculate Conception in 1854, more Marian congregational songs would come to focus on her freedom from sin while describing her as spotless, sinless, and pure.

---

56. Ibid., 148.

57. Ibid., 149. It is impressive that the council requested this action eight years before Pius IX defined Mary's Immaculate Conception as dogma in 1854 (see p. 150).

58. Ibid., 151 (emphasis in the original).

59. Ibid., 157.

60. Ibid., 159.

61. This hymn originally appeared in J.G. Herder's *Stimmen der Völker in Liedern* from 1807. It can subsequently be found in multiple versions with different combinations of the Latin stanzas. This text is often set to the tune Sicilian Mariners. Higginson, *Handbook for American Catholic Hymnals*, 88.

1. O sanctissima, O piissima, Dulcis Virgo Maria! Mater amata, intemerata, Ora, ora pro nobis!	1. O most holy, O most loving, O sweet Virgin Mary! Mother best beloved, undefiled: Pray, O pray for us!
2. Tu, solatium et refugium, Virgo Mater Maria! Quiquid optamus, per te speramus; Ora, ora pro nobis!	2. Thou art our comfort, and our refuge, Virgin Mother Mary! All that we long for, through thee we hope for: Pray, O pray for us!
3. Tota pulchra es, O Maria, et Macula non est in te; Mater amata, intemerata, Ora, ora pro nobis.	3. Thou art all fair, O Mary, and no stain of sin is in thee; Mother best beloved, undefiled: Pray, O pray for us.
4. In miseria, in angustia, Ora, Virgo, pro nobis; Pro nobis ora in mortis hora, Ora, ora pro nobis.	4. In misery, in anguish, pray, for us, O Virgin; pray for us in the hour of death: Pray, O Pray for us.
5. Ecce debiles, perquam flebiles, Salva nos, O Maria! Tolle languores, sana dolores, Ora, ora pro nobis!	5. See how weak we are, lost in tears; save us, O Mary! Lighten our anguish, soothe our sorrows: Pray, O pray for us!
6. Virgo, respice, Mater, aspice, Audi nos, O Maria! Tu, medicinam, portas divinam, Ora, ora pro nobis![62]	6. Virgin, turn and look; Mother behold us; hear us, O Mary! Thou art the bearer of health divine: Pray, O pray for us![63]

62. "O Sanctissima," #222 in Richard Rice, ed., *The Parish Book of Chant: A Manual of Gregorian Chant and a Liturgical Resource for Scholas and Congregations; Including Order of Sung Mass for Both Ordinary and Extraordinary Forms of the Roman Rite with a Complete* Kyriale, *along with Chants and Hymns for Ocasional and Seasonal Use and Their Literal English Translations*, 2nd exp. ed. (The Church Music Association of America, 2012), 224.

63. Ibid.

The Catholic Church in the United States was clearly bound up in its devotion to Mary: the first Mass in the colonies was held on the feast of the Annunciation, the first bishop was consecrated on the feast of the Assumption, the first cathedral was dedicated to her, and the Catholic Church in the United States was placed under her protection, first as the Blessed Virgin Mary and later as the Immaculate Conception. In the next chapter the declaration of Mary as the Immaculate Conception by Pope Pius IX will be looked at, a devotion that already had great support in the United States.

Chapter Four

No Grace Comes to Us except through Mary[1]

Immaculate, Mary!
Our hearts are on fire;
That title so wondrous
Fills all our desire!
Ave, Ave, Ave, Maria!
Ave, Ave, Maria![2]

—Anonymous, "Immaculate Mary, our hearts"

Introduction

So begins one of the most popular Marian congregational songs, drawing its inspiration from a processional hymn sung by pilgrims

---

1. Hilda Graef, *Mary: A History of Doctrine and Devotion; With a New Chapter Covering Vatican II and Beyond by Thomas A. Thompson* (Notre Dame, IN: Ave Maria Press, 2009), 379. Graef says this in reference to Leo XIII's encyclical on the rosary *Octobri Mense* given September 22, 1891.

2. Stanza 1 of "Immaculate Mary, our hearts," Hymnary.org, http://www .hymnary.org/text/immaculate_mary_our_hearts_are_on_fire, accessed February 2014. Taken from #95 in *Catholic Church Hymnal with Music*, ed. A. Edmonds Tozer (New York: J. Fischer & Bro., 1905), 128.

at Lourdes. The apparition of Mary at Lourdes in 1858, along with the declaration of her Immaculate Conception in 1854, begin what Barbara Pope has described as "a popular and official resurgence in the veneration of Mary throughout the Catholic world" leading many to "call the years between 1850 and 1950 the Marian Age."[3] This "Marian Age" is filled with multiple Marian apparitions and punctuated by the definition of two new Marian dogmas: Mary's Immaculate Conception in 1854 and Mary's Assumption in 1950. The result of these declarations and apparitions is what Hilda Graef describes as "one tremendous wave of enthusiasm that did not spend itself for over a century."[4] This "tremendous wave of enthusiasm" will also be seen in the great outpouring of new Marian congregational songs.

In order to understand better Marian theology and devotion through the lens of hymnody during this time, many of the contextual factors that had an effect on Marian theology and devotion will be considered. First, the declaration of the Immaculate Conception in 1854 will be looked at, including the history of the theology of the Immaculate Conception and the circumstances surrounding the declaration. Then, a few of the most popular Marian apparitions during this period will be investigated. Finally, developments in the world of Catholicism during the "Marian Age" are surveyed, including the popes and their many encyclicals, new Marian feasts, and new popular devotions to Mary.

Mary's Immaculate Conception

A Brief History of the Doctrine of the Immaculate Conception

As the history of the doctrine of the immaculate conception is traced, the history of the corresponding feast must also be followed, for in the case of Mary's immaculate conception, the celebration of the feast was intimately bound up with the arguments over the the-

---

3. Barbara Corrado Pope, "Immaculate and Powerful: The Marian Revival in the Nineteenth Century," in *Immaculate & Powerful: The Female in Sacred Image and Social Reality*, ed. Clarissa W. Atkinson, Constance H. Buchanan and Margaret R. Miles (Boston, MA: Beacon Press, 1985), 173.

4. Graef, *Mary*, 340.

ology of the doctrine: "discussion over Mary's freedom from original sin was initiated by liturgical practice, rather than by problems of theory."[5] Since the time of early Christianity, the belief was that Mary had remained sinless, never sinning during her life.[6] In addition to this belief, "the doctrine of the immaculate conception states that even at the first moment of her existence, Mary was free of the condition of original sin which is the inheritance of humanity in general."[7]

This debate over Mary was mostly found in the West, where Augustine was expounding on original sin.[8] Augustine's mentor, Ambrose of Milan, was the person "probably responsible for the definitive establishment of a firm 'causal connection between the virginal conception and the sinlessness of Christ . . . the combination of the ideas of the propagation of original sin through sexual union and of the sinlessness of Christ as a consequence of his virginal conception.'"[9] In Augustine's discussion of original sin, *On Nature and Grace*, he briefly mentions how Mary is an exception:

> We must make an exception of the holy Virgin Mary, concerning whom I wish to raise no question when it touches the subject of sins, out of honor to the Lord. For from him we know what abundance of grace for overcoming sin in every particular [*ad vicendum omni ex parte peccatum*] was conferred upon her who had the merit to conceive and bear him who undoubtedly had no sin.[10]

Pelikan points out that "Augustine did not describe this great exception"; Augustine only hints at Mary's "great exception" rather than explaining in detail how it actually happened, and as a result, the debate over Mary's conception would continue for centuries.[11]

5. See Sarah Jane Boss, *Empress and Handmaid: On Nature and Gender in the Cult of the Virgin Mary* (London: Cassell, 2000), 126.

6. Ibid., 124.

7. Ibid.

8. Jaroslav Pelikan, *Mary through the Centuries: Her Place in the History of Culture* (New Haven, CT: Yale University Press, 1996), 189–90.

9. Joseph Huhn, *Das Geheimnis der Jungfrau-Mutter Maria nach dem Kirchenvater Ambrosius*, 79–80, as quoted in Pelikan, *Mary through the Centuries*, 190.

10. Augustine, *On Nature and Grace*, xxxvi.42, as quoted in Pelikan, *Mary through the Centuries*, 191.

11. Pelikan, *Mary through the Centuries*, 191.

While the West debated the theology of Mary's conception, the East had been celebrating a feast on December 9 in honor of Mary's conception since the eighth century, known as the "Conception of St. Anna, mother of the *Theotokos*."[12] It is also important to note here the theological differences between the East and West; while the East never dealt with the Pelagian controversy as Augustine did in the West, the East also had a different understanding of original sin, "connecting it far more with mortality and general human weakness than with a mortal stain."[13] The feast of Mary's conception gradually spread to the West, however, and by the eleventh century it was celebrated in England on December 8, where the focus of the feast was shifting from Anna, "the one who conceived," to Mary, "the one who was being conceived."[14] After the Norman occupation the feast was suppressed, but it was restored in the twelfth century by Anselm the Younger (d. 1148), and once again the focus of the feast shifted, this time from Mary's body to her soul.[15]

At this point in time the feast spread from England to France. Bernard of Clairvaux spoke out against the feast, arguing that this was "a rite of which the Church knows nothing, of which reason cannot approve and for which there is no authority in tradition."[16] The debates continued, with Thomas Aquinas and Bonaventure siding with Bernard ("Christ alone did not need to be redeemed"), while Eadmer and John Duns Scotus (ca. 1265–1308) took the opposite stance (the

---

12. Ignazio M. Calabuig, "The Liturgical Cult of Mary in the East and West," in *Liturgical Time and Space*, vol. 5 of *Handbook for Liturgical Studies*, ed. Anscar J. Chupungco (Collegeville, MN: Liturgical Press, 2000), 284.

13. Hilda Graef, *The Devotion to Our Lady* (New York: Hawthorn Books, 1963), 35.

14. Calabuig, "The Liturgical Cult of Mary in the East and West," 285–86.

15. Ibid., 286–87.

16. Bernard of Clairvaux, *Epistola* 174, 1, as quoted in Calabuig, "The Liturgical Cult of Mary in the East and West," 287. While most saints were celebrated on the day of their death (their entry into eternal life), Mary and John the Baptist were exceptions because they were sanctified before birth; the celebration of their births was acceptable because they were not "born in a state of sin." See Boss, *Empress and Handmaid*, 126.

immaculate conception was possible and God wanted it).[17] It is not surprising that Aquinas and his fellow Dominicans—known for their intellectual prowess—would be against the doctrine, since it "was frequently proposed as an outcome of devotion rather than of theological considerations,"[18] while Scotus was a Franciscan, and his defense of the doctrine drew from his Franciscan tradition that respected all of God's creation, focusing on "an optimistic understanding of humanity's, and the physical world's, capacity for goodness and redemption."[19]

Scotus's defense of Mary's immaculate conception drew from the theology of Anselm of Canterbury, which stated that "original sin was the absence of the original justice with which the world was created," and this "propensity towards evil . . . does not take effect until a child has reached the age at which it should have the possibility of exercising free will."[20] Drawing from Anselm's argument that "the seed which generates new human life is intrinsically neither sinful nor meritorious," and thus it is the will and not the seed that is sinful, Scotus argued that while baptism washes away original sin, the flesh is still contaminated but the soul is not; therefore the "sanctification of the soul" does not depend on the "purification of the flesh," so "God could have sanctified Mary's soul at the first moment of her conception notwithstanding the fact that she had been engendered by her parents in the natural way."[21]

---

17. Calabuig, "The Liturgical Cult of Mary in the East and West," 288; and Boss, *Empress and Handmaid*, 127–29.

18. Graef, *Mary*, 244–45.

19. Boss, *Empress and Handmaid*, 132.

20. Ibid., 126.

21. Ibid., 130–31. Scotus also drew from his teacher, William of Ware (d. *c.* 1305), who discussed "two kinds of debt: that which is contracted and must be paid, and that which is not contracted when it could have been." Mary, who never sinned, belongs in the second category, and so Scotus argued that "preservation from sin is better than deliverance. Consequently, to claim that Mary was preserved from contracting original sin is to say not that she did not need to be redeemed, but on the contrary, that she was the object of Christ's most perfectly redemptive action. Thus, the doctrine of the Immaculate Conception teaches that Christ's salvific power reaches to the fullest possible extent." See Boss, *Empress and Handmaid*, 129.

Following Scotus's arguments for Mary's immaculate conception, the feast continued to spread, and the doctrine received attention from both councils and popes. The Council of Basel (1431–1437) supported the doctrine, but at the point when it was discussed in 1438, the council was in schism, so its declaration "had no canonical standing."[22] Pope Sixtus IV (1471–1484), a Franciscan, followed the Council of Basel with his support of the feast, approving the Mass and Office for the feast that was written by Leonardo Nogarolo.[23]

The doctrine was also developing through art: "as it has done with the doctrine of Mary throughout history, Christian art often anticipated the development of dogma, which eventually caught up with the iconography."[24] At first Mary's conception was depicted as the meeting of Anne and Joachim at the Golden Gate, or Mary was shown in Anne's womb.[25] In the seventeenth century, the artwork moved from a focus on the physical aspects of Mary's conception to the spiritual, such as Diego Velázquez's (1599–1660) *The Immaculate Conception*. Boss describes this depiction as typified by portraying Mary

> as a young girl standing alone, sometimes at prayer, sometimes treading on a serpent, sometimes standing on the moon, sometimes crowned with the stars—but not in physical contact with another human being, although having some limited association with those aspects of the physical creation which appear alongside her.[26]

Velázquez's image also calls to mind Genesis 3:15 as Mary is often depicted crushing the serpent, and "in both art and theology, the motif of the woman trampling the serpent underfoot was applied to

22. Calabuig, "The Liturgical Cult of Mary in the East and West," 289–90.

23. Ibid., 290. While Sixtus IV's 1477 bull *Cum praecelsa* "did not make the feast of December 8 obligatory and universal," it did help to spread the feast and it was "the first time that a pope had officially intervened" in the matter of the feast of the Immaculate Conception. Nogarolo's Mass expressed the belief in Mary's immaculate conception so well "that it inspired the Bull *Ineffabilis Deus* of Pius IX." See Pierre Jounel, "The Veneration of Mary," in *Liturgy and Time*, vol. 4 of *The Church at Prayer: An Introduction to the Liturgy*, ed. Aimé Georges Martimort (Collegeville, MN: Liturgical Press, 1986), 140.

24. Pelikan, *Mary through the Centuries*, 194.

25. Boss, *Empress and Handmaid*, 141.

26. Ibid.

Mary's immaculate conception, since her freedom from sin was a sign of the devil's total defeat."[27] Boss also notes that these images often draw from Revelation 12:1 as Mary is seen standing on the moon with a crown of twelve stars. It interesting that as the artwork begins to depict Mary alone, there are a great deal of Marian congregational songs from the late nineteenth and early twentieth centuries that focus on Mary alone, often without referencing Jesus at all. Mary's triumph over the devil in Genesis 3:15 will play an important part in Pope Pius IX's definition of the Immaculate Conception in 1854.

Ubi Primum *and* Ineffabilis Deus

The Context of Ineffabilis Deus

In 1830, Catherine Labouré (1806–1876), a Daughter of Charity of St. Vincent de Paul in Paris, France, had a vision of Mary similar to the artwork described above. She saw Mary "standing on a globe, her hands giving out rays of light, spread out towards earth," and around Mary was an oval frame which said "O Mary, conceived without sin, pray for us who have recourse to thee."[28] Labouré says a voice told her to strike a medal of this vision and "promised that its wearers would receive many graces."[29] The medal, soon to be known as the Miraculous Medal, was struck in 1832. Many miracles were attributed to it, and it "greatly stimulated interest in the Immaculate Conception, and demands for the definition of the doctrine multiplied."[30]

In addition to Labouré's vision and the popularity of the Miraculous Medal, several political issues swirled around the Catholic Church leading up to the declaration of Mary's Immaculate Conception in 1854. Sarah Butler points out that unlike other papal pronouncements that were usually given to combat heresy, the declaration of Mary's Immaculate Conception was not a reaction to heresy; instead, she believes Pope Pius IX (1846–1878) responded to three factors:

---

27. Boss, *Empress and Handmaid*, 141–42.
28. Graef, *The Devotion to Our Lady*, 77–78.
29. Ibid., 78.
30. Ibid.

he acted first of all to respond to the insistent petitions of the Catholic people and to express his and their filial devotion to the Blessed Virgin; second, to announce revealed truth in the face of "modern errors" that denied the supernatural and the very concept of revelation; and third, to exercise the papal office decisively in the face of external threats to the spiritual as well as the temporal authority of the Church.[31]

By 1847, all of the religious orders, including the Dominicans—holdouts because of their loyalty to Thomas Aquinas—had accepted the celebration of Mary's immaculate conception.[32] In 1849, Pius IX asked bishops in his encyclical *Ubi Primum* (On the Immaculate Conception) to report on "the sentiments in their dioceses" regarding Mary's immaculate conception.[33] The pope received a mostly favorable response to *Ubi Primum,* in addition to many petitions from the faithful. Butler describes the *sensus fidelium* (sense of the faithful) in this response to the pope as not only a "powerful motive" behind Pius IX's definition but also "the ultimate warrant for the definition."[34]

Butler suggests that Pius IX had a "desire to confront certain errors of the day."[35] In fact, the original approach was to argue for Mary's immaculate conception and write a "syllabus of modern errors" all in the same document.[36] While this dual approach was dropped in 1853, in his address to the cardinals the day after he declared Mary's

---

31. Sara Butler, "The Immaculate Conception: Why Was It Defined as a Dogma? And What Was Defined?" in *Studying Mary: The Virgin Mary in Anglican and Roman Catholic Theology & Devotion: The ARCIC Working Papers,* ed. Adelbert Denaux and Nicholas Sagovsky (New York and London: T & T Clark, 2007), 147. While some claim that Pius IX used the declaration of Mary's Immaculate Conception in 1854 to set up his declaration of papal infallibility in 1870, Butler does not agree with this argument.

32. Graef, *Mary,* 340.

33. Ibid. In addition to the support of a theological consulta and pontifical commission Pius IX put together in 1848 (the consulta voted 17 for and 3 against), 603 bishops were for the declaration and 56 were against.

34. Butler, "The Immaculate Conception," 148.

35. Ibid.

36. Ibid., 149. While Pius IX did abandon this approach in 1853, he went on to give his *Syllabus of Errors* in 1864, condemning what he saw as errors in the "modern" world, which led people to call him "Pio No No," a play on his name in Italian, "Pio Nono."

Immaculate Conception, Pius IX scolded "those who take 'reason' for 'an infallible mistress.'"[37] He also declared his wish that "the 'greatness of [Mary's] privilege will be a powerful means of confuting those who deny that human nature was corrupted by the first sin and who exaggerate the forces of reason in order to deny or lessen the benefit of Revelation.'"[38] Calling upon Mary as the "conqueror of heresies," Pius IX hoped Mary would "'uproot and destroy this dangerous error of Rationalism' which afflicts not only civil society but also the Church."[39] In Pius IX's mind, the best way to combat the errors of rationalism and those who upheld reason was to declare a dogma that could not be proven by reason, but only by divine revelation. Here again, Mary, the "conqueror of heresies," was being used as a weapon to combat those seen to be in error by the Catholic Church. This reinforces Barbara Pope's point that "defensive antimodernism may be the most distinct legacy of the church-defined Marian cult of the nineteenth century."[40]

In addition to invoking Mary as a weapon against the "evils" of his time, Pius IX was also using Mary to fight back against the effects of the French Revolution and the "Roman Question" in an attempt to show the might of a religious institution that was rapidly losing its power in the secular world. The trauma of the French Revolution shook the "old marriage of throne and altar," powered by the Enlightenment which John O'Malley describes as "rabidly anticlerical, anti-Christian, and especially anti-Catholic."[41] The "Roman Question" refers to the dispute between the Italian Government and the Catholic Church over the ownership of the Papal States. This is an issue that would plague the papacy beginning in 1861 until the matter was resolved with Benito Mussolini (1883–1945) in 1929. Mary was often called on by the popes to protect them during this tumultuous time.[42] Because these issues threatened

37. Ibid.

38. Ibid.

39. Ibid. Butler also quotes George Tavard who refers to the definition as "a piece in the papal arsenal against modernity" (ibid., 162n11).

40. Pope, "Immaculate and Powerful," 195.

41. John O'Malley, *What Happened at Vatican II* (Cambridge, MA: The Belknap Press of Harvard University Press, 2008), 54.

42. For more information, see David I. Kertzer, *Prisoner of the Vatican: The Popes' Secret Plot to Capture Rome from the New Italian State* (Boston, MA: Houghton Mifflin Company, 2004).

the pope's spiritual and temporal authority, Butler argues that these "external challenges" only gave Pius IX "added incentive to exercise his spiritual authority as head of the universal Church [by declaring Mary's Immaculate Conception], and by this means to strengthen and encourage the bishops and the faithful."[43]

The Content of Ineffabilis Deus

Mary's Immaculate Conception was declared on December 8, 1854. For many outside the Catholic Church, there was issue with not only what the declaration said but also how it was declared. While *Ineffabilis Deus*, the apostolic constitution that defined the Immaculate Conception, drew from Scripture, tradition, and liturgical practices to defend the declaration,[44] some people were more concerned with the "procedural and juridical question of the authority of the pope on his own to define a dogma for the entire church."[45] Non-Catholics "reacted violently" to the declaration, with Protestants believing that Mary "shares the law of sin with all mankind," and the Orthodox—not influenced by Augustine like the Latin West—held a different understanding of original sin altogether.[46]

At the core of *Ineffabilis Deus* is the actual definition of Mary's Immaculate Conception:

> We declare, pronounce, and define that the doctrine which holds that the most Blessed Virgin Mary, in the first instance of her conception, by a singular grace and privilege granted by Almighty God, in view of the merits of Jesus Christ, the Savior of the human race, was pre-

---

43. Butler, "The Immaculate Conception," 149.

44. See sections in the document such as "Interpreters of Sacred Scripture," "Testimonies of Tradition," and "Liturgical Argument." It is also important to note that under "Veneration of the Immaculate," the document refers to the principle of *lex orandi, lex credendi* when it points to the use of the title "Immaculate Conception" in the Litany of Loreto, the preface of the Mass for the Immaculate Conception, and the Office for the Immaculate Conception to show "that the rule of prayer might thus serve to illustrate the rule of belief."

45. Pelikan, *Mary through the Centuries*, 200. This issue would come up again at the First Vatican Council in 1869–70 with the declaration of the pope as infallible.

46. Graef, *The Devotion to Our Lady*, 79.

served free from all stain of original sin, is a doctrine revealed by God and therefore to be believed firmly and constantly by all the faithful.[47]

Butler points out that this definition is a "negative formulation," in that the focus is on Mary's preservation from original sin instead of her "fullness of grace."[48] Elizabeth Johnson chooses to take a more positive stance, thinking of the doctrine not "in the language of the absence of sin," but rather "in essence it is all about the presence of grace."[49] However, in many of the Marian congregational songs written in the wake of the 1854 declaration, there is much more of a focus on the absence of the stain of sin, and Mary is often described as spotless, sinless, and pure.

Ineffabilis Deus *Reflected in Marian Congregational Song*
"O Heart of Mary, Pure and Fair, There Is No Stain in Thee"[50]

There are quite a few references to Mary's purity and freedom from the stain of sin in *Ineffabilis Deus*. In the very first paragraph, Mary is described as "ever absolutely free of all stain of sin, all fair

---

47. Pius IX, *Ineffabilis Deus*, http://www.papalencyclicals.net/Pius09/p9ineff.htm, accessed June 2014. Because the paragraphs in this encyclical are not numbered, references will be made using the titles of the headings under which the quoted passage appears. In this case, the definition is in the first paragraph under the heading "The Definition." See Graef, *Mary*, 341. It is interesting to note, as Graef does, that the definition does not comment on whether "the act by which Mary was conceived was without sin nor that she had no need of a redeemer." See Graef, *Mary*, 343. The document relies on the theological work of John Duns Scotus. See Graef, *The Devotion to Our Lady*, 79.

48. Butler, "The Immaculate Conception," 158.

49. Elizabeth Johnson, *Truly Our Sister: A Theology of Mary in the Communion of the Saints* (New York: Continuum, 2003), 108.

50. Sisters of Notre Dame, "O heart of Mary, pure and fair," Hymnary.org, http://www.hymnary.org/text/o_heart_of_mary_pure_and_fair, accessed 2014. Taken from #80 in Christian Brothers, ed., *The De La Salle Hymnal: For Catholic Schools and Choirs* (New York: La Salle Bureau, 1913), 80. This Marian congregational song is found in Sisters of Notre Dame, Cincinnati, ed., *May Chimes: A Collection of Hymns to the Blessed Virgin* (Boston, MA: Oliver Ditson Co., 1871). The text and tune are attributed to a Sister of Notre Dame. See J. Vincent Higginson, *Handbook for American Catholic Hymnals* (New York: The Hymn Society of America, 1976), 86.

and perfect."[51] In the paragraphs under "Interpreters of the Sacred Scripture," the focus is again on Mary's purity, as she is described as possessing "most excellent innocence, purity, holiness, and freedom from every stain of sin" as well as being a "spotless dove" that is "entirely perfect, beautiful, most dear to God and never stained with the least blemish."[52] In discussing the "truly marvelous style of speech" used by people throughout the ages to describe Mary, the section on "Of a Super Eminent Sanctity" tells how

> they have frequently addressed the Mother of God as immaculate, as immaculate in every respect; innocent, and verily most innocent; spotless, and entirely spotless; holy and removed from every stain of sin; all pure, all stainless, the very model of purity and innocence; more beautiful than beauty, more lovely than loveliness; more holy than holiness, singularly holy and most pure in soul and body; the one who surpassed all integrity and virginity; the only one who has become the dwelling place of all the graces of the most Holy Spirit. God alone excepted, Mary is more excellent than all, and by nature fair and beautiful, and more holy than the Cherubim and Seraphim. To praise her all the tongues of heaven and earth do not suffice.[53]

It is clear that there is a strong focus on the notion of Mary's purity and freedom from the stain of sin. This emphasis is also seen in many Marian congregational songs from the late nineteenth and early twentieth centuries, revealing the impact of *Ineffabilis Deus*. In the Sisters of Notre Dame's text "O Heart of Mary, pure and fair, There is no stain in thee," Mary's purity is emphasized throughout, as she is described as "some fair lily 'midst the thorns" who possesses a "chaste and holy heart" (stanza 2). In the refrain, the singer asks Mary to help them to be "pure in heart," just as she is.

1. O Heart of Mary pure and fair,
     There is no stain in thee;
   In Adam's fall thou hast no share,
     From sin's taint thou art free.

---

51. Pius IX, *Ineffabilis Deus*.
52. Ibid.
53. Ibid.

Refrain: O Heart of Mary, pure and fair,
          No beauty can with thine compare!
     From ev'ry stain of sin thou'rt free;
          Oh make us pure in heart like thee.

  2. As some fair lily 'midst the thorns,
          Thou 'mongst Eve's daughters art;
     Celestial purity adorns
          Thy chaste and holy heart. **R.**

  3. Dear heart, within thy depths so pure,
          We'll dwell and ne'er depart,
     Till thou our souls hast linked secure
          To Jesus' Sacred Heart. **R.**

  4. And when from thy loved heart we'll go
          To that of thy dear Son,
     Oh shall we leave thee then?
          Ah, no; His Heart and thine are one. **R.**[54]

It does not seem to be a coincidence that Frederick William Faber (1814–1863) wrote two texts which focus on Mary's purity in 1854, the year of the declaration of the Immaculate Conception, "O purest of creatures" and "O Mother! I could weep for mirth."[55] In addition to having the recurring phrase "sweet Star of the Sea" at the end of each stanza, "O purest of creatures" describes the "one spotless womb wherein Jesus was laid" (stanza 1), as well as describing Mary as the "One spot where His [God] Spirit untroubled could be" (stanza 2). Faber also heralds Mary's newly promulgated title in stanza 3, writing " 'Conceived without sin' thy new title shall be."

  1. O purest of creatures, sweet Mother, sweet Maid!
     The one spotless Womb wherein Jesus was laid!
     Dark night hath come down on us, Mother and we
     Look out for thy shining, sweet Star of the Sea!

54. Sisters of Notre Dame, "O heart of Mary, pure and fair," Hymnary.org, http://www.hymnary.org/text/o_heart_of_mary_pure_and_fair, accessed 2014.

55. Both of these texts come from Frederick W. Faber, *Oratory Hymns and Oratory Hymn Tunes* (London: Burns and Lambert, 1854). See Higginson, *Handbook for American Catholic Hymnals*, 87.

2. To sinners what comfort, to angels what mirth;
   That God found one creature unfallen on earth;
   One spot where His Spirit untroubled could be,
   The depths of thy shining, sweet Star of the Sea!

3. Oh, shine on us brighter than ever, then, shine;
   For the greatest of honors, dear Mother, is thine;
   "Conceived without sin," thy new title shall be,
   Clear light from thy birthspring, sweet Star of the Sea!

4. So worship we God in these rude latter days;
   So worship we Jesus our Love, when we praise
   His wonderful grace in the gift He gave thee,
   The gift of clear shining, sweet Star of the Sea!

5. Deep night hath come down on us, Mother, deep night,
   And we need more than ever the guide of thy light;
   For the darker the night is, the brighter should be
   Thy beautiful shining, sweet Star of the Sea![56]

Faber's other text, "O Mother! I could weep for mirth" is a song of praise to Mary, focusing on the joy at her immaculate conception. The refrain lifts up Mary's majesty and state, lauding her as "Immaculate! Immaculate! Immaculate!" The fourth stanza comments on how the immaculate conception is not only a joy for Mary but also a "great joy for me!"

1. O Mother! I could weep for mirth;
     Joy fills my heart so fast.
   My soul today is heav'n on earth,
     Oh! could the transport last!

56. Frederick W. Faber, "O purest of creatures, sweet mother, sweet maid," Hymnary.org, http://www.hymnary.org/text/o_purest_of_creatures_sweet _mother_sweet, accessed April 2014. Taken from #279 in *American Catholic Hymnal: An Extensive Collection of Hymns, Latin Chants, and Sacred Songs for Church, School, and Home, Including Gregorian Masses, Vesper Psalms, Litanies . . .*, ed. Marist Brothers (New York: P. J. Kenedy & Sons, 1913), 319. This hymn is comprised of many stanzas, and different hymnals include different groupings of stanzas. The last line of each stanzas is also repeated in this particular hymnal to match it to the tune. The most common tune this text is set to is PADERBORN.

Refrain: I think of thee, and what thou art,
      Thy majesty, thy state;
    And I keep singing in my heart,
      Immaculate! Immaculate! Immaculate!

2. When Jesus looks upon thy face,
      His Heart with rapture glows,
   And in the Church, by His sweet grace,
      Thy blessed worship grows. **R.**

3. The angels answer with their songs,
      Bright choirs in gleaming rows;
   And saints flock round thy feet in throngs,
      And heaven with bliss o'erflows. **R.**

4. Conceived, conceived, immaculate!
      Oh, what a joy for thee!
   Conceived, conceived immaculate!
      Oh, greater joy for me! **R.**

5. It is this thought to-day that lifts
      My happy heart to heaven,
   That for our sakes thy choicest gifts
      To thee, dear Queen, were given. **R.**[57]

Another text drawing from the language of spotlessness is "Daughter of a mighty Father." At the end of each stanza is the Latin phrase "Macula non est in te," meaning "There is no stain in thee."[58] This phrase—seen previously in *O sanctissima*—constitutes the entire text of the chorus, where it is repeated four times. Here is the first of six stanzas, followed by the refrain:

1. Daughter of a mighty Father,
      Maiden patron of the May,
   Angel forms around thee gather:
      Macula non est in te.

---

57. Frederick W. Faber, "O mother, I could weep for mirth," Hymnary.org, http://www.hymnary.org/text/o_mother_i_could_weep_for_mirth, accessed April 2014. Taken from #148 in *American Catholic Hymnal*, 183.

58. The Latin word "macula" can mean stain, blemish, spot, or blot. See Leo F. Stelten, *Dictionary of Ecclesiastical Latin: With an Appendix of Latin Expressions Defined and Clarified* (Peabody, MA: Hendrickson Publishers, 2006), 155.

Refrain: Macula non est in te,
Macula non est in te,
Macula non est in te,
Macula non est in te.[59]

"Thy Heel Hath Crush'd the Serpent's Head"[60]

The reference to Genesis 3:15 (the punishment in the Garden of Eden) and the comparison of Mary with Eve are themes found in *Ineffabilis Deus* that are also popular in Marian congregational song in the late nineteenth and early twentieth centuries. Under the section "Interpreters of the Sacred Scripture," following the reference to Genesis 3:15 ("I will put enmities between you and the woman, between your seed and her seed"), it is stated that "the most holy Virgin, united with him [Christ] by a most intimate and indissoluble bond, was, with him and through him, eternally at enmity with the evil serpent, and most completely triumphed over him, and thus crushed his head with her immaculate foot."[61] There is also a section titled "Mary Compared with Eve," which tells how Mary is exalted above Eve because while both are virgins, Eve "listened to the serpent with lamentable consequences," while Mary, "on the contrary, ever increased her original gift, and not only never lent an ear to the serpent, but by divinely given power she utterly destroyed the force and dominion of the evil one."[62]

In the song that provides the title of this section, "Most noble Queen of Victory," Mary's power over evil is praised when she is

---

59. "Daughter of a mighty Father," Hymnary.org, http://www.hymnary.org/text/daughter_of_a_mighty_father, accessed April 2014. Taken from #58 in *The Catholic Youth's Hymn Book: Containing the Hymns of the Seasons and Festivals of the Year, and an Extensive Collection of Sacred Melodies; to which are Added an Easy Mass, Vespers, and Motets . . .*, ed. Christian Brothers (New York: P. O'Shea, 1871), 61. This text is anonymous and comes from the hymnal *Sacred Wreath* (1863). See Higginson, *Handbook for American Catholic Hymnals*, 77.

60. From the second stanza of #127, "Most noble Queen of Victory," in Ludwig Bonvin, ed., *"Hosanna" Catholic Hymn Book: With an Appendix of Prayers and Devotions*, 4th ed. (St. Louis, MO: B. Herder, 1914), 155. The author of the text is anonymous. See Higginson, *Handbook for American Catholic Hymnals*, 84.

61. Pius IX, *Ineffabilis Deus*. The crushing of the serpent's head is in reference to Genesis 3:15: "he will crush your head, and you will strike his" (NIV).

62. Ibid.

described as someone who will "be our sword and shield" in battle in the first stanza. In the second stanza, there is reference to the serpent from Genesis when it is told that Mary's heel has "crush'd the serpent's head."

> 1. Most noble Queen of Victory, Maria!
>   Enthron'd in peerless majesty, Maria!
>   When we arm to take the field,
>   Thou shalt be our sword and shield.

> **Refrain:** Oh, be thou near to us
>   To aid and cheer us
>   By word and deed,
>   In ev'ry need,
>   Maria.

> 2. Thy heel hath crush'd the serpent's head, Maria!
>   Thy hand hath laid the foe-man dead, Maria!
>   Oft thy modest look has cowed
>   Lustful souls and demons proud. **R.**

> 3. The God of battle honored thee, Maria!
>   And made thee Queen of Victory, Maria!
>   At thy pray'r the foes of God
>   Prostrate fell beneath His Rod. **R.**[63]

There are also references to Mary and the serpent in such texts as "Mary Immaculate, Star of the Morning," which describes in stanza 1 how Mary will bring "Woe to the serpent and rescue to man." In stanza 5 the "wiles of the serpent" are attacking the faithful, but Mary's "immaculate merit" will be there to protect them, for their weakness only gives Mary a chance to prove her might.

> 1. Mary Immaculate, Star of the Morning,
>   Chosen before the creation began,
>   Chosen to bring, in the light of thy dawning,
>   Woe to the serpent and rescue to man:

---

63. #127, "Most noble Queen of Victory," in Bonvin, ed., *"Hosanna" Catholic Hymn Book,* 155.

5. See how the wiles of the serpent assail us,
   See how we waver and flinch in the fight:
   Let thine immaculate merit avail us,
   Make of our weakness a proof of thy might.[64]

"O Maiden! Mother mild!," a text by Isaac Williams (1802–1865), also refers to the serpent. In stanza 2 the destructive work of the serpent is described, but then there is Mary, who came in and crushed the serpent's head with her heel, bringing about "redemption to man."

Refrain: O Maiden, Mother mild!
Behold thy trusting child,
Before thee kneels in supplication;
Direct me lest I stray,
In devious paths away,
Thou art my help, my salvation.

1. The angels arose in their pride,
   Refusing their God obey;
   They seek now o'er earth far and wide,
   To draw souls beneath Satan's sway. **R.**

2. The serpent in Eden's fair vale,
   His work of destruction began;
   His head thou didst crush 'neath thy heel,
   And so brought redemption to man. **R.**

3. In all times and ages thou'lt be,
   Of Christians the help and the guide;
   Keep me close to Jesus and thee,
   In safety and peace to abide. **R.**[65]

64. F.W. Weatherell, "Mary immaculate, star of the morning," Hymnary .org, http://www.hymnary.org/text/mary_immaculate_star_of_the_morning, accessed April 2014. Taken from #154 in *A Treasury of Catholic Song: Comprising Some Two Hundred Hymns from Catholic Sources Old and New*, ed. Sidney S. Hurlbut (New York: J. Fischer & Bro., 1915). In this hymnal, there are six stanzas for this hymn. This text is by F. W. Weatherell. See Higginson, *Handbook for American Catholic Hymnals*, 84.

65. Isaac Williams, "O Maiden! Mother Mild!," Hymnary.org, http://www .hymnary.org/text/the_angels_arose_in_their_pride, accessed April 2014. Taken from #139 in *American Catholic Hymnal*, 174.

The play on Mary and Eve's name, "Eva/Ave" commented on earlier in chapter 1, is also found in many texts. These tend to be English translations of the *Ave maris stella* which speak of Mary reversing the wrongs of Eve, such as Edward Caswall's "Hail! bright star of ocean" which speaks of "Taking that sweet Ave / Which from Gabriel came, / Peace confirm within us, / Changing Eva's name."[66]

"Chosen before the Creation Began"[67]

Mary's predestination is discussed in the very first paragraph of *Ineffabilis Deus*: "From the very beginning, and before time began, the eternal Father chose and prepared for his only-begotten Son a Mother in whom the Son of God would become incarnate and from whom, in the blessed fullness of time, he would be born into this world."[68] Under the section "Explicit Affirmation," it is also mentioned that Mary "was chosen before the ages, prepared for himself by the Most High, foretold by God when he said to the serpent, 'I will put enmities between you and the woman.'"[69] The topic of Mary's predestination is a common theme in Marian congregational songs written during the period from 1854 up until Vatican II.

The title of this section comes from a text looked at just above, "Mary Immaculate, Star of the Morning." In stanza 1 Mary is de-

---

66. From stanza 2 of Edward Caswall, "Hail, bright Star of ocean, God's own mother," Hymnary.org, http://www.hymnary.org/text/hail_bright_star_of_ocean_gods_own_mothe, accessed February 2014. Taken from Roman Catholic Church, *Hymns and Songs for Catholic Children* (New York: Catholic Publication Society, 1870), 126–27.

67. From stanza 1 of #154, "Mary Immaculate, Star of the Morning," in *A Treasury of Catholic Song*.

68. Pius IX, *Ineffabilis Deus*. Boss points out that the "understanding of Mary's predestination" in *Ineffabilis Deus* differs from that of Scotus: "Duns Scotus taught that before the sin of Adam was foreseen, God intended that the Word should become flesh in Christ in order that human nature should be glorified. Later Scotists argued that if God willed from eternity that the Word should take human flesh, then the woman from whom that flesh was to be taken must likewise have been predestined from eternity to be the Mother of God. Mary therefore shares in the predestination of Christ." See Boss, *Empress and Handmaid*, 154n55 and 138–39.

69. Ibid.

scribed as being "Chosen before the creation began." There are also reference to Mary's predestination in other texts. In "Sing, sing, ye angel bands," a text that was looked at earlier in conjunction with the discussion of the feast of the Assumption, one version speaks of Mary sitting "On her predestined throne."[70] In "Hail! Thou first begotten daughter," Mary's predestination is pointed to in the title. Mary is described in stanza 2 as someone who has been "Loved before the world was made!"

1. Hail! Thou first begotten daughter
   Of th'Almighty Father's love!
   Temple of eternal glory,
   Pure and spotless turtle dove!
   Mistress of the earth and skies,
   Hail! Thou Queen of Paradise!
   Salve, Regina!

2. Hail to Thee whose deep foundations
   On the holy hills are laid!
   Joy of endless generations,
   Loved before the world was made!
   Treasure in salvation's scheme,
   Clothed in dignity supreme!
   Salve, Regina!

3. Who can count the starry jewels
   Set about Thy crown of light?
   Who can estimate Thy greatness,
   Who can guess Thy glory's height?
   All that is of glory known
   Is for Thee and for Thy throne!
   Salve, Regina!

70. See stanza 6 of #66, "Sing, sing, ye angel bands," *St. Basil's Hymnal: An Extensive Collection of English and Latin Hymns for Church, School and Home. Arranged for Feasts and Seasons of the Ecclesiastical Year: Gregorian Masses, Vespers, Motets for Benediction, Litanies, Etc.*, ed. The Basilian Fathers (Chicago: John P. Daleiden Co., 1918), 77. The text is by Frederick Faber. See Higginson, *Handbook for American Catholic Hymnals*, 91. This stanza does not appear in the version that is discussed in chap. 1.

4. Thou hast power for us sinners
Grace and pardon to implore
Of Thy Son Whose love hath crowned Thee,
"Help of Christians" evermore!
Thro' Thee God's most loving plan
Gave a Saviour unto man!
Salve, Regina![71]

"When Wicked Men Blaspheme Thee, I'll Love and Bless Thy Name"[72]

Another theme in *Ineffabilis Deus*: the evils and heresies of the world and Mary as the one to protect individuals and the Catholic Church. Under the section "Hoped-For Results," Mary is described as one who has

> destroyed all heresies and snatched the faithful people and nations from all kinds of direst calamities; in her do we hope who has delivered us from so many threatening dangers. We have, therefore, a very certain hope and complete confidence that the most Blessed Virgin will ensure by her most powerful patronage that all difficulties be removed and all errors dissipated, so that our Holy Mother the Catholic Church may flourish daily more and more throughout all the nations and countries, and may reign "from sea to sea and from the river to the ends of the earth," and may enjoy genuine peace, tranquility and liberty. We are firm in our confidence that she will obtain pardon for the sinner, health for the sick, strength of heart for the weak, consolation for the afflicted, help for those in danger; that she will remove spiritual blindness from all who are in error, so that they may return to the path of truth and justice, and that here may be one flock and one shepherd.[73]

71. "Hail! Thou First Begotten Daughter," #114 in *Psallite: Catholic English Hymns. With an Appendix of Prayers and Devotions*, ed. Alexander Roesler, 8th ed. (St. Louis, MO: B. Herder Book Company, 1918), 129.

72. From stanza 1 of #64, "I'll sing a hymn to Mary," in *St. Basil's Hymnal*, 74. The text was written by Fr. John Wyse (1825–98). See Higginson, *Handbook for American Catholic Hymnals*, 81.

73. Pius IX, *Ineffabilis Deus*.

Mary is clearly seen as the one who is to be called on to fight heresy and "spiritual blindness" while saving faithful Catholics from the "direst calamities."

The song that provides the title of this section, "I'll sing a hymn to Mary" by John Wyse (1825–1898), is interesting because many of the stanzas end with the line "When wicked men blaspheme thee, / I'll love and bless thy name." It is almost like a spiritual fight song for Mary, assuring that no matter what heresy or "spiritual blindness" one might be confronted with, one will always defend Mary. This theme is carried throughout the hymn; for example in stanza 5 it describes how Mary is brighter than all the saints, seemingly referencing her immaculate conception and those who do not believe in it when it says "Oh! that which God did give thee / Let mortals ne'er disclaim." This "wondrous gem" that lies in Mary's crown is more fully described in stanza 6 as a direct statement of faith: "No sin hath e'er defiled thee." Finally, in stanza 7, it goes so far as to say that if "others jeer and mock" Mary, her followers will be willing to lay down their lives to defend her.

1. I'll sing a hymn to Mary,
     The Mother of my God,
   The Virgin of all virgins,
     Of David's royal blood.
   Oh, teach me, holy Mary,
     A loving song to frame;
   When wicked men blaspheme thee,
     To love and bless thy name.

5. The Saints are high in glory,
     With golden crowns so bright;
   But brighter far is Mary
     Upon her throne of light.
   Oh! that which God did give thee
     Let mortals ne'er disclaim;
   When wicked men blaspheme thee
     I'll love and bless thy name.

6. But in the crown of Mary
     There lies a wondrous gem,

As Queen of all the angels,
  Which Mary shares with them.
"No sin hath e'er defiled thee,"
  So doth our faith proclaim;
When wicked men blaspheme thee
  I'll love and bless thy name.

7. And now, O Virgin Mary,
    My Mother and my Queen,
  I've sung thy praise, so bless me
    And keep my heart from sin.
  When others jeer and mock thee,
    I'll often think how I,
  To shield my Mother, Mary,
    Would lay me down and die.[74]

It seems that those who are in "spiritual blindness" and speak ill of Mary (perhaps non-Catholics who were against the high place that Mary held in the Catholic Church?) are to be countered with love for Mary. Frederick Faber, in his text "Mother Mary, at thine altar," speaks of Mary as someone who will "guide us, / With a mother's fondest care" and "whate'er in life betide us, / We will seek a refuge there."[75] Mary is the Mother who will help us during our time on this "earth so waste and wide."[76] While Marian congregational songs were one means of reiterating the doctrine of Mary's Immaculate Conception, another facet of Marian devotion would soon burst onto the scene to further support Pius IX's declaration: the apparition of Mary as the Immaculate Conception at Lourdes.

74. John Wyse, "I'll sing a hymn to Mary," Hymnary.org, http://www.hymnary
.org/text/ill_sing_a_hymn_to_mary, accessed April 2014. Taken from #105 in
Catholic Church Hymnal with Music, ed. A. Edmonds Tozer (New York: J. Fischer
& Bro., 1905), 144. This hymnal notes that stanzas 2, 3, and 4 may be omitted.

75. Stanza 2 of Frederick W. Faber, "Mother Mary, at thine altar We thy
loving children kneel," Hymnary.org, http://www.hymnary.org/text/mother
_mary_at_thine_altar_we_thy_loving, accessed April 2014. Taken from #278 in
American Catholic Hymnal, 318.

76. Ibid. This text is taken from the chorus.

Marian Apparitions

The Proliferation of Marian Apparitions during the Marian Age

George Tavard describes "two additional characteristics" associated with Marian devotion in the Marian Age. Along with the declaration of Marian doctrines, including Mary's Immaculate Conception and her Assumption, this is a "period of visions and apparitions."[77] The proliferation of Marian apparitions that led to the building of new shrines and countless pilgrimages compelled faithful Catholics to embrace a popular devotion that "assumes that the mother of Christ not only listens and responds to prayers addressed to her, but also intervenes directly in this world through recurring apparitions."[78]

These apparitions, many of which occurred in France, came on the heels of the French Revolution and rationalism. Throughout history, it is often found that "when one development has reached its saturation point its antithesis begins to appear or to reappear."[79] In this case, the antithesis to the rationalism of the Enlightenment and the French Revolution was romanticism, which Graef describes as "an attitude of mind that was favourable once more to irrational and suprarational influences, to emotional as well as mystical experiences."[80] In addition to a mindset that made people more open to apparitions, the timing is also important; many of the apparitions occurred during chaotic periods in history, lending "political significance" to many of the visions.[81] David Blackbourn points out that the messages contained in the apparitions, such as at Knock in 1879, were often apocalyptic, yet they offered "emotional consolation" by helping to assure people that even though times were tough, Mary

---

77. George Tavard, *The Thousand Faces of the Virgin Mary* (Collegeville, MN: Liturgical Press, 1996), 171.

78. Ibid.

79. Graef, *Mary*, 339.

80. Ibid.

81. Tavard, *The Thousand Faces of the Virgin Mary*, 178. Michael Carroll does an excellent job of describing not only the social and political context of many of these apparitions, but also the personal contexts of the seers in Part II "Marian Apparitions." See Michael P. Carroll, *The Cult of the Virgin Mary: Psychological Origins* (Princeton, NJ: Princeton University Press, 1986).

was there to console as well as give comfort and hope, because repentance would lead to restoration.[82]

Barbara Pope lists some of the most famous apparitions in France as Catherine Labouré's vision of Mary in Paris (1830), along with those at "La Salette (1846), Lourdes (1858), and Pontmain (1871)."[83] Outside of France, she points to the apparitions in "Fátima, Portugal (1917); and Beauraing (1932) and Banneaux (1933) in Belgium."[84] In addition to arousing "great hopes and fears," these apparitions also helped to birth what Pope describes as "the onset of the modern French pilgrimage movement in 1873"[85] as people took advantage of their increased mobility brought on by technological advances in transportation that allowed them easier access to pilgrimage sites. The Augustinian Fathers of the Assumption in France helped spur this pilgrimage movement with their periodical *Le Pèlerin*, which reported on people's pilgrimages, as well as their organization of mass pilgrimages to Lourdes, beginning in 1873.[86]

During this "great century of Marian apparitions" from the 1830s through the 1930s, Mary seemed to mostly appear to "laypeople and peasants." Some might see this as Mary "fulfilling her proclamation and prophecy in the Magnificat"[87] by looking "with favor on the lowliness of his servant" and "lifting up the lowly" (Luke 1:48, 52)—in this case women and children. One of the first women to receive an apparition during this time is Catherine Labouré, who received the

---

82. David Blackbourn, "Apparitions of the Virgin Mary in Nineteenth-Century Europe," in *Marpingen: Apparitions of the Virgin Mary in a Nineteenth-Century German Village* (New York: Vintage Books, 1993), 19.

83. Pope, "Immaculate and Powerful," 173.

84. Ibid. To this list could be added the apparition at Knock, Ireland in 1879, among others. While not all apparitions are "ecclesiastically acknowledged," Pelikan writes that in 1962 there were ten that had received official recognition: Guadalupe, Mexico (1531); Catherine Labouré's vision in Paris (1830); La Salette, France (1846); Lourdes, France (1858); Filippsdorf, in what is now the Czech Republic (1866); Pontmain, France (1871); Pompeii, Italy (1876); Fátima, Portugal (1917); Beauraing, Belgium (1932–33); and Banneux, Belgium (1933). See Pelikan, *Mary through the Centuries*, 178–79.

85. Pope, "Immaculate and Powerful," 174.

86. Ibid., 185, 187.

87. Pelikan, *Mary through the Centuries*, 179.

vision of the Miraculous Medal in 1830. The medal became almost like a talisman, in that those who wore it received Mary's protection from harm. It was so popular that by 1842, only ten years after it was first struck, one hundred million medals had been made.[88]

The image of Mary on the Miraculous Medal—standing on a globe, trampling a snake, with her arms extended—helped to promote "a uniform, even universal notion of what she [Mary] looked like."[89] It was so well known that Bernadette, the seer at Lourdes, and the children at Pontmain said that their visions of Mary looked "like the Miraculous Medal, but without the rays."[90] One of the most famous Marian apparitions that followed Catherine Labouré was at Lourdes in 1858.

"Rome Is the Head of the Church but Lourdes Is Its Heart"[91]

Lourdes, which has been described as the "most popular of all Christian shrines and the most important site of miraculous healing in the world," is where in 1858 Bernadette Soubirous (1844–1879), a poor, young girl, received multiple visions of Mary, who at one point identified herself as the Immaculate Conception.[92] At the grotto where Bernadette received her apparitions, a fountain began to flow and miracles began to occur. Mary asked to have a chapel built on the site, and as the church was built and a train station constructed at Lourdes, pilgrims began to flock to Lourdes, seeking miraculous

---

88. Blackbourn, "Apparitions of the Virgin Mary in Nineteenth-Century Europe," 23.

89. Pope, "Immaculate and Powerful," 176. Note the connection between the image of Mary trampling the snake on the Miraculous Medal and the connection with the reference to Mary crushing the serpent in relation to Genesis 3:15 as described in *Ineffabilis Deus*.

90. Ibid.

91. Andrea Dahlberg, "The Body as a Principle of Holism, Three Pilgrimages to Lourdes," in *Contesting the Sacred: The Anthropology of Christian Pilgrimage*, ed. John Eade and Michael J. Sallnow (New York: Routledge, 1991), 35, as quoted in Pelikan, *Mary through the Centuries*, 184.

92. Pope, "Immaculate and Powerful," 173 and Graef, *Mary*, 355.

cures in the waters of the grotto.[93] " 'All the elements of the classic modern apparition' had 'fused' at Lourdes: 'The simplicity of the humble visionary, the delivery of a message, the initial skepticism of the parish priest, the hostile reaction of the civil authorities, claims of miraculous cures, and finally the purposive creation of an official cult by the church.' "[94] As well as serving as a model for future Marian apparitions, Lourdes also helped to spread devotion to Mary's immaculate conception; in fact, Pius IX saw Lourdes as affirming his declaration of the dogma four years earlier.[95]

The Effect of Marian Apparitions on Devotions

Following the Enlightenment, nationalism and the secularization of the state had "challenged Catholic beliefs in tradition, revelation, and miracles."[96] Pius IX was forced to flee Rome in 1848 as a result of the revolution in Italy, and although he would return to Rome, this experience "hardened Pius's resolve to combat what he saw as the sins and heresies of the modern world."[97] This steadfastness can be seen in many of Pius IX's actions: in his declaration of Mary's Immaculate Conception in 1854, described by Pope as a "gauntlet flung at the proud pretensions of his enemies"; in his 1864 *Syllabus of Errors* against "the sins and heresies of the modern world"; and finally, in 1870, in the "culmination of his strategic efforts within the hierarchy . . . the declaration of papal infallibility" at Vatican I (1869–1870).[98]

---

93. By 1862 the bishop of Tarbes had investigated the apparitions and authorized the cult of Our Lady of Lourdes for the diocese (Graef, *Mary*, 355). By 1866 a train station had been built in Lourdes (Pope, "Immaculate and Powerful," 187).

94. Blackbourn, "Apparitions of the Virgin Mary in Nineteenth-Century Europe," 5, as quoted in Pelikan, *Mary through the Centuries*, 179.

95. Blackbourn, "Apparitions of the Virgin Mary in Nineteenth-Century Europe," 36.

96. Pope, "Immaculate and Powerful," 181.

97. Ibid.

98. Ibid., 181–82. The unstable political situation in Italy caused Vatican I to end abruptly.

This led to the notion of ultramontanism, or "the belief that one should look to Rome for leadership in all spiritual matters."[99] In a world that was increasingly hostile to the Catholic hierarchy, those in positions of power in the Catholic Church sought to regulate the one realm over which they felt they had authority, and that was the laity. The method of their control was

> the successful promotion of a certain kind of piety. Pius and his immediate successors advocated new or renewed devotions that emphasized the affective rather than the rational or ethical aspects of faith. That is, they chose to direct rather than to condemn or ignore emotional and potentially subversive religious impulses in order to maintain and increase Catholic influence.[100]

This is important because many of the criticisms of Marian congregational songs before Vatican II are that they are too sentimental or focused on feelings; yet it was precisely the goal of the Catholic hierarchy to support emotional and affective devotions, and so it was only natural that this would spill over into Marian congregational songs which were often sung in conjunction with these devotions supported by the hierarchy.

Pius IX and Leo XIII—who both had a particularly strong devotion to Mary—supported emotional cults, such as those of Mary, and did so by confirming apparitions and offering indulgences for those who made pilgrimages to the sites of these miracles.[101] For Pius IX, Lourdes was "heaven-sent verification" of his declaration of the Immaculate Conception, in his mind proving him right, and that Catholicism was "the one true faith."[102] As a result, it only made sense that he would support devotions to an apparition that showed the world that Catholicism was correct in declaring Mary's Immaculate Conception.

---

99. Ibid., 182.

100. Ibid., 182–83.

101. Ibid. Blackbourn points to the visions of Labouré and Lourdes as an instance where "changing doctrine and popular piety reinforced each other." See Blackbourn, "Apparitions of the Virgin Mary in Nineteenth-Century Europe," 30.

102. Ibid.

Marian Apparitions Reflected in Marian Congregational Song
"Hail, Sweet Notre Dame de Lourdes"[103]

In 1894, Émile Zola wrote *Lourdes*, a critique of what he saw as the hierarchy's manipulation of "the invincible ignorance of the unenlightened masses."[104] Over one hundred years later, Mark Francis describes how, at least in Europe and America in the nineteenth century, popular piety was used "as an instrument of 'Romanization.'"[105] By offering indulgences for properly performed devotions, the Roman hierarchy was able to standardize the devotions by requiring them to be performed in a certain manner, and the attachment of indulgences to these devotions was a way to link them to the pope's authority.[106] This can be seen as the co-opting of popular piety by the papacy in an effort to "bolster an ultramontane Catholicism that sought to equate the universality of the church with a standard discipline that came from Rome."[107] It is true that many went on pilgrimage to seek cures or miracles. But by also offering indulgences—often promising a certain number of days to be released from purgatory—the hierarchy was able to give the laity even more incentive to practice devotions and participate in pilgrimages.

These indulgences were often linked to pilgrimages to Marian shrines. It was common for groups to go on pilgrimage together where they would develop a sense of *communitas* or "unmediated communion" as described by Edith and Victor Turner.[108] The singing of hymns was one form of community building that would take place during these pilgrimages, and at Lourdes the most famous of

---

103. From the refrain of #118, "Hail! all hail! sweet Notre Dame de Lourdes," in *St. Basil's Hymnal*, 138. This anonymous text comes from the Sisters of Notre Dame (Philadelphia), *Sunday School Hymn Book* (Boston, MA: O. Ditson, 1887). See Higginson, *Handbook for American Catholic Hymnals*, 78.

104. Pelikan, *Mary through the Centuries*, 180.

105. Mark R. Francis, "Liturgy and Popular Piety in a Historical Perspective," in *Directory on Popular Piety and the Liturgy: Principles and Guidelines. A Commentary*, ed. Peter C. Phan (Collegeville, MN: Liturgical Press, 2002), 39.

106. Ibid., 40.

107. Ibid., 41.

108. Pope, "Immaculate and Powerful," 187–88.

these became known as the "Lourdes Processional."[109] In the United States, a text came into popularity that was paired with the tune Lourdes Hymn, "Immaculate Mary, our hearts."

Two different versions of the tune resulted when in Edmonds Tozer's *Catholic Hymns* (1898) Tozer altered the refrain "to give the proper accent to '*Ave, Ave.*'"[110] One can see below in Figure 8, which shows this hymn in the 1905 version of Tozer's *Catholic Hymns*, that there is a note at the bottom saying that "In the chorus to this hymn, as arranged above, the Latin words receive their proper accent, or quantity. The 'popular' rendering of the melody, as sung in other countries, makes this impossible."

In addition to "Immaculate Mary, our hearts," there was another text set to the Lourdes tune, "Immaculate Mary, thy praises we sing." This 1952 text was a "considerably revised version" of Jeremiah Cumming's (1814–1866) "Hail, Virgin of Virgins, thy praises we sing" written for his *Songs for Catholic Schools* (1860).[111] The most common form of this text and tune in a twentieth- or twenty-first-century hymnal would be "Immaculate Mary, your praises we sing," as found in *Worship IV* (2011) which retains an altered version of Cummings's text in the first stanza, with stanzas 2 through 7 written by Brian Foley (1919–2000) in 1970.[112] It remains one of the most popular Marian congregational songs to this day.

109. This tune comes from a "traditional French cantique to which the refrain *Ave Maria* had been added, evidently for the Lourdes Processional." See Higginson, *Handbook for American Catholic Hymnals*, 241. The original text sung at Lourdes, by Abbe Gaignet, was originally eight stanzas, but in order to accommodate the lengthy processions at Lourdes, it was extended to sixty stanzas. The text told the "Lourdes story." See Higginson, *Handbook for American Catholic Hymnals*, 81.

110. Higginson, *Handbook for American Catholic Hymnals*, 241. To this day, there are still some Catholic parishes in the United States that sing Tozer's altered version, while others retain the "French" version.

111. Ibid., 80, 82.

112. #893 in *Worship*, ed., Kelly Dobbs-Mickus, 4th ed. (Chicago: GIA Publications, 2011). For information on the Cummings/Foley text, see Marilyn Kay Stulken and Catherine Salika, *Hymnal Companion to Worship*, 3rd ed. (Chicago: GIA Publications, 1998), 417–18.

Figure 8. *Immaculate Mary! Our hearts are on fire.* Text: Anonymous. Tune: Lourdes Hymn. (From Tozer, ed., *Catholic Church Hymnal with Music,* 128). Image courtesy of Hymnary.org.

"Thy Feeble Child Implores Thee"[113]

The emphasis of dependence on both Mary and Rome led the laity to follow both in a childlike manner. In addition to depending on Rome to dispense rewards for saying devotions properly, Boss describes how Mary, seen as Mother, was often "associated with that sense of continuing comfort and nourishment which recalls the devotees' infant desires."[114] In his work on Victorian hymnody, Ian Bradley describes how some hymns became "over-sentimental," not only to create an "emotional effect" but also to allow those who sang them a chance to forget their problems.[115] This "over-sentimental approach" led both children and adults to feelings of dependence and infantilism through the singing of hymns.[116]

It is no wonder then, with the combination of dependence on Mary and the Catholic Church—coupled with the infantilism often found in Victorian hymnody—that these themes would appear in Marian congregational song of the late nineteenth and early twentieth centuries. One example of this is the common use of the word "lisping" to describe one's prayers. In the second stanza of "On this day, O beautiful Mother," Mary is asked to hear "Lisping children's humble pray'r." There is also throughout this text a great sense of dependence on Mary, as we stay close to Mary, hovering near her in the refrain. Also, in stanza 1, Mary's care is asked for to help keep us from straying from her "guiding way."

Refrain: On this day, O beautiful Mother,
On this day we give thee our love.
Near thee, Madonna, fondly we hover,
Trusting thy gentle care to prove.

113. From the refrain of "My mother dear, my queen divine," Hymnary.org, http://www.hymnary.org/text/my_mother_dear_my_queen_divine, accessed April 2014. Taken from #2 in *May Blossoms, A Collection of Hymns to the Blessed Virgin*, ed. Sisters of Notre Dame (Cincinnati: Oliver Ditson & Co., 1872), 5.

114. Boss, *Empress and Handmaid*, 22.

115. Ian Bradley, *Abide with Me: The World of Victorian Hymns* (Chicago: GIA Publications, 1997), 132.

116. Ibid.

1. On this day we ask to share,
   Dearest Mother, thy sweet care;
   Aid us ere our feet astray,
   Wander from thy guiding way. **R.**

2. Queen of angels, deign to hear,
   Lisping children's humble pray'r;
   Young hearts gain, O Virgin pure,
   Sweetly to thyself allure. **R.**[117]

It is also common in these texts that the narrator often describes herself or himself as weak. This emphasis on weakness occurs twice in "O Mary, my mother most tender." In the first stanza, Mary is asked to "Look graciously down on thy weak, lowly child," who is calling out to her "From this land of exile." In the third stanza, the difficulties in life in the "land of exile" are described, but the text ends by stating there is no need to fear, for "I know I am weak, but my Mother is near."

1. O Mary, my Mother, most tender, most mild,
   Look graciously down on thy weak, lowly child.
   From this land of exile I call upon thee;
   Then Mary, my Mother, look kindly on me.

2. If thou dost forsake me, where-to shall I go?
   My comfort and hope in this valley of woe.
   The world and its dangers with terror I see,
   But sweet hope will cheer me in thinking of thee.

---

117. "On this day we ask to share," Hymnary.org, http://www.hymnary.org /text/on_this_day_we_ask_to_share-2, accessed April 2014. Taken from #51 in *The Catholic Youth's Hymn Book*, 54. There are multiple version of this text in various hymnals containing differing numbers of stanzas. In this hymnal there are five stanzas. This anonymous text is found in: Philip Rohr's *Favorite Catholic Melodies* (1857). The author was unable to find more bibliographic information for this hymnal, but Higginson does list the 1851 edition of Rohr's *Favorite Catholic Melodies* as being published in Boston, MA by Patrick Donahue. See Higginson, *Handbook for American Catholic Hymnals*, 89, 303.

3. In sorrow, in darkness, be still at my side,
   My light and my refuge, my helper and guide.
   Though snares surround me, yet, why should I fear?
   I know I am weak, but my Mother is near.[118]

Finally, many of these texts exhibit a strong dependence on Mary for protection. While "Look down, O Mother Mary" (*Dal tuo celeste trono, Maria*) was written by Alphonsus Liguori (1696–1787), it was translated into English by Edmund Vaughan (1827–1908) and made popular in an 1863 collection of Liguori's works.[119] The first stanza asks for "One only glance of love" from Mary, and goes on to rather harshly say that if Mary does not pity her children, then she should "turn away" and "look on us no more." Stanza 4 begins with the familiar image of being asked to be enfolded in Mary's mantle because we can stay there "without fear." This is followed by the often used phrase, "What evil can befall us, / If, Mother, thou art near?," displaying the notion that Mary has the ability to protect one from any and all harm. Finally, Mary is asked to "Look down on us with pity. / Who thy protection crave."

1. Look down, O Mother Mary,
      From thy bright throne above;
   Cast down upon thy children
      One only glance of love.
   And if a heart so tender
      With pity flows not o'er,
   Then turn away, O Mother,
      And look on us no more.

4. Unfold to us thy mantle,
      There stay we without fear:

---

118. #123, "O Mary, my Mother most tender," in *Psallite*, 139. This text is a paraphrase of the *Memorare*. For more information on this text, see the entry "O Mary, my Mother, so tender, so true" in Higginson *Handbook for American Catholic Hymnals*, 87.

119. Alphonso Liguori and Robert A. Coffin, *Hymns and Verses on Spiritual Subjects: Being the Sacred Poetry of St. Alphonso Maria Liguori* (London: Burns and Lambert, 1863). See Higginson, *Handbook for American Catholic Hymnals*, 83.

> What evil can befall us,
>   If, Mother, thou art near?
> O kindest, dearest Mother,
>   Thy sinful children save;
> Look down on us with pity,
>   Who thy protection crave.[120]

The dependence on Mary for protection is a theme that will continue to be at the forefront of Catholic thought—from the pope all the way down to the laity—during the pontificates of Leo XIII through Pius XII.

Worldwide Catholic Developments

As mentioned earlier in this chapter, ultramontanism played a large role in the realm of devotions during this period. It was also greatly influencing the theology of the time:

> Within Ultramontane Catholicism, however, the notion of tradition had been in danger of narrowing to mean little more than the current Roman theology. Pio Nono's notorious 1870 aphorism *"I am the tradition,"* was a telling reflection of the day-to-day reality of an increasingly powerful central authority, which strangled Catholic theology (and episcopal teaching) for a century.[121]

The notion that the Catholic Church possessed the truth in its (unchanging) tradition went hand in hand with the antimodernism that dominated the reign of Pope Pius IX.

Philip Gleason points out in his work on the "Mythic Middle Ages" that the search for truth and a notion of immutability continued during the reign of Pope Leo XIII, especially in his support of

---

120. Alfonso M. de Liguori, "Look down O mother Mary," Hymnary.org, http://www.hymnary.org/text/look_down_o_mother_mary, accessed April 2014. Taken from #126 in *American Catholic Hymnal*, 160. Here are stanzas 1 and 4. The hymnal itself has a total of four stanzas printed.

121. Eamon Duffy, *Faith of Our Fathers: Reflections on Catholic Tradition* (London & New York: Continuum, 2004), ix.

neoscholasticism and Neo-Thomism in his 1879 encyclical *Aeterni Patris* (On the Restoration of Christian Philosophy).[122] The romantic holding up of the Middle Ages can be seen in the work of Dom Prosper Guéranger (1805–1875), one of the forerunners of the twentieth-century liturgical movement, and someone who could be described as a "romantic medievalist who made Solesmes Abbey into a miniature Middle Ages."[123] The Middle Ages were also upheld in the face of social critique, citing it as an "alternative social model against which the effects of the modern world would be contrasted."[124] In fact, Virgil Michel (1890–1938), one of the key figures in the liturgical movement in the United States, relied heavily on Aquinas in his work on social justice.[125] Gleason attempts to address the question of why medievalism was so attractive: "the obvious answer perhaps—is that Catholic medievalism is the obverse of Catholic antimodernism and its intensity reflects the degree of uneasiness felt by Catholics about the dominant tendencies of the modern world."[126] Antimodernism dominated the papacy of Pius IX, and this trend continued into the late nineteenth and early twentieth centuries.

122. Philip Gleason, *Keeping the Faith: American Catholicism Past and Present* (Notre Dame, IN: University of Notre Dame Press, 1987). See also Leo XIII, On the Restoration of Christian Philosophy (*Aeterni Patris*), August 4, 1879, Papal Encyclicals Online, http://www.papalencyclicals.net/Leo13/l13cph.htm, accessed June 2014. O'Malley describes the encyclical in this manner: "The encyclical rode the tide of nineteenth-century Romantic enthusiasm for the Middle Ages that was by no means confined to Catholics, and it provided a stimulus for Catholics to claim the Middle Ages, now the 'Ages of Faith,' as peculiarly their own. Thus began the powerful Neo-Thomist movement in Catholicism." See O'Malley, *What Happened at Vatican II*, 62. Leo XIII is also widely known for his encyclical defending worker's rights, *Rerum Novarum* (On Capital and Labor), May 15, 1891, Papal Encyclicals Online, http://www.papalencyclicals.net/Leo13/l13rerum.htm, accessed June 2014.

123. Gleason, *Keeping the Faith*, 24. Louis Bouyer (1913–2004), one of the important figures in the twentieth-century liturgical movement, pointed to the work of Guéranger as an example of what liturgical renewal *shouldn't* be, "warning specifically against the temptation to romanticize the medieval Church."

124. Ibid., 20.

125. See Virgil Michel, "Defining Social Justice," *The Commonweal* 23 (1936): 425–26.

126. Gleason, *Keeping the Faith*, 26.

In addition to combating modernism, the turn back to the Middle Ages also helped to emphasize the notion that the Catholic Church was immutable, possessing *"perennially* valid principles" as well as "embod[ying] *timeless* truths."[127] This view can be described as antihistoricist "in that it ruled out altogether the possibility that the passage of time and changing circumstances might require any *essential* modification of St. Thomas's synthesis of natural knowledge and supernatural revelation. Truth was truth and remained the same, despite changing outward circumstances."[128] In a time when the Catholic Church felt under attack—the papacy was "beleaguered and on the defensive"[129]—the holding up of the "Mythic Middle Ages" was seen as an antidote to all the ills that the Catholic Church was struggling with at this time.

Papal Encyclicals, Pronouncements, and Marian Devotion

Leo XIII (1878–1903)

Pope Leo XIII continued to fight against the errors of the modern world as did his predecessor. Both Pius IX and Leo XIII were fond of writing encyclicals; Pius IX wrote thirty-eight and Leo XIII produced seventy-five.[130] This trend of increasingly writing encyclicals as "a response to the enemy" of Liberalism showed that "the popes became teachers" through their encyclicals.[131] In reflecting on these encyclicals, René Laurentin writes that they were not so much focused on doctrine as on fostering devotion, and their style was not

---

127. Ibid. (emphasis Gleason).

128. Ibid., 27 (emphasis Gleason). This notion of immutability is one that will resurface in chapter 7 in the debate over changes in liturgy and social teachings at Vatican II. There will also be a return to the focus on "Truth" in the papacy of Benedict XVI. His search for "Truth" resonates with the neoscholastic desire to show who was right and wrong and *"redeem the modern world by converting it from error to truth."* Gleason, *Keeping the Faith*, 27 (emphasis Gleason).

129. O'Malley, *What Happened at Vatican II*, 53–54.

130. Ibid., 56.

131. Ibid., 55. O'Malley points out that at the end of Pius IX's *Syllabus of Errors*, one of the errors listed is "That the Roman Pontiff can and should reconcile himself and make peace with progress, with Liberalism, and with modern culture" (ibid. 60).

so much "homiletical" as "oratorical, full of images, and sometimes more generous than rigorous. . . . It would be a bad mistake if one were to take pastoral utterances of this kind and turn them into dogmatic theses."[132]

It is precisely for this devotional purpose that Leo XIII—who possessed a very strong devotion to Mary and was referred to as the "pope of the rosary,"—wrote eleven of his encyclicals on the topic of the rosary.[133] The rosary was "a devotion which he recommended very strongly in those bad times when the Church and especially the pope were so violently attacked."[134] For ten years in a row, Leo XIII wrote an encyclical during the month of October, and he encouraged the praying of the rosary (even during Mass), especially during the month of October, in what came to be known as October devotions.[135]

Through these encyclicals, Leo XIII encouraged some long-held notions associated with Mary. In his 1891 encyclical *Octobri Mense* (On the Rosary), he upholds the medieval notion that "as we have no access to the Father save through the Son, so also the Son can best be reached through the Mother, who judges no one and was given to us under the Cross."[136] In his 1883 encyclical *Supremi Apostolatus Officio* (On Devotion of the Rosary), Leo XIII reminded people that just as the rosary had "saved the church from heresy and from the Turks" in the sixteenth century, "he hoped that contemporary devotion to Mary would similarly help Catholics to defeat secularism and materialism."[137] Here again is the notion that Mary, who can "destroy all heresies," may be used as a weapon—a theme that will continue into the twentieth century.[138] Leo's devotion to the rosary, for ex-

132. René Laurentin, *Mary's Place in the Church*, as quoted in Graef, *Mary*, 397.

133. J. N. D. Kelly, *The Oxford Dictionary of Popes* (Oxford: Oxford University Press, 2006), 312.

134. Graef, *Mary*, 379.

135. Pope, "Immaculate and Powerful," 183; and Graef, *The Devotion to Our Lady*, 88–89.

136. Ibid., 88. This is similar to the medieval notion explored in chap. 2 where Christ is the Judge and Mary is the sympathetic Mother who intercedes for humankind through her Son.

137. Pope, "Immaculate and Powerful," 183.

138. Leo XIII, *Supremi Apostolatus Officio* (On Devotion of the Rosary) in Catholic Church, *1878–1903*, vol. 2 of *The Papal Encyclicals*, ed. Claudia Carlen

ample, has been described as a "warfare of prayer" and the rosary as "an effective weapon in defending the faith against the aggressions of heresy."[139] In his 1895 encyclical *Adiutricem* (On the Rosary), Leo XIII called for Mary's intercession to help with Christian unity, especially with those in Eastern Christianity who also held Mary in high esteem.[140] The hope that Mary can be an agent in promoting Christian unity will resurface again during Vatican II.

As can be seen in his writings, Leo XIII believed the rosary was the devotion that "pleases her [Mary] best and most effectively insures her intercession with God"; in fact, in his introduction to Leo XIII's writings on the rosary, William Lawler writes that "the surest way to the merciful heart of God is through the Mother of His only-begotten Son; and the surest way to the heart of his Mother most merciful is through her Rosary."[141] In addition to promoting the recitation of the rosary and offering indulgences for such devotions, Leo XIII also consecrated the month of October to the "Holy Queen of the Rosary," and added "Queen of the Most Holy Rosary" to the Litany of Loreto.[142]

In addition to his encyclicals on the rosary, Leo XIII also fostered Marian devotion through what are known as the "Leonine Prayers." This collection of prayers, originally introduced by Pius IX in the Papal States during difficult political times, were expanded by Leo XIII in 1884 when he asked that they be said at the end of Low Mass all over the world to ask for "divine assistance" during trying times.[143] Jungmann describes them as "intercessory prayers in time of stress, pleas for the great needs of the Church, appeals in which

---

(Ann Arbor, MI: The Pierian Press, 1990), 83. All of Leo XIII's encyclicals mentioned may be found in this source.

139. Leo XIII, *The Rosary of Mary: Translations of the Encyclical and Apostolic Letters of Pope Leo XIII*, ed. William Raymond Lawler (Paterson, NJ: St. Anthony Guild Press, 1944), x–xi.

140. Michael O'Carroll, "Leo XIII," in *Theotokos: A Theological Encyclopedia of the Blessed Virgin Mary* (Wilmington, DE: Michael Glazier, 1986), 219.

141. Leo XIII, *The Rosary of Mary*, v, vii.

142. Leo XIII, *Supremi Apostolatus Officio*, 83 and Leo XIII, *The Rosary of Mary*, vii.

143. R. E. Brennan, "The Leonine Prayers," *American Ecclesiastical Review* 125 (1951): 85.

the people should share and which therefore are recited with the faithful in their own language."[144]

The Leonine Prayers included saying (in Latin or the vernacular) the *Ave Maria* three times, the *Salve Regina*—added to "further enforce the tone of supplication"—followed by a versicle and response, and a collect.[145] After 1886, the collect was changed and a prayer to St. Michael was added.[146] In 1904, Pius X allowed the addition of saying "Most Sacred Heart of Jesus, have mercy on us" three times, and in 1930 Pius XI "ordered that the Leonine Prayers be said *for Russia*, charging the bishops and other clergy carefully to inform the people of this and frequently to recall it to their minds."[147] This is particularly important as it shows a growing trend of associating Mary and prayers to her, including the rosary, with political controversies involving Russia and Communism.

Pius X (1903–1914)

Pope Pius X did not write as many encyclicals on Mary as Leo XIII did; instead, much of his papacy was focused on reform—particularly of the liturgy and music—as he sought to fulfill his papal motto, "to

144. Jungmann, *The Mass of the Roman Rite*, 2:455.

145. Ibid., 2:457 and Brennan, "The Leonine Prayers," 85–86. A 300 days indulgence was attached to these prayers. Pius X increased this to "7 years and 7 quarantines" and Pius XI increased it to ten years "to encourage the faithful to forego the premature exit which seems to be so appealing and to remain to join in the recitation of the prayers after Mass." See Brennan, "The Leonine Prayers," 87. These prayers, along with the final gospel, were suppressed by the directive *Inter Oecumenici* (1964). See Annibale Bugnini, *The Reform of the Liturgy 1948–1975*, trans. Matthew J. O'Connell (Collegeville, MN: Liturgical Press, 1990), 831–34. The author grew up in a Catholic Church where it was the practice to say a Hail Mary at the end of Mass, and the story goes that a former pastor instituted this practice in order to keep people from leaving Mass early, as Pius XI mentioned.

146. Brennan, "The Leonine Prayers," 86. Jungmann writes that there is a legend that "this prayer was introduced by Leo XIII after a dream or vision (!) of the powers of hell." See Jungmann, *The Mass of the Roman Rite*, 2:458n15 (emphasis Jungmann).

147. Brennan, "The Leonine Prayers," 88–89.

restore all things in Christ."[148] He did, however, write an encyclical on the Immaculate Conception in 1904, *Ad Diem Illum Laetissimum*. The encyclical was written for the fiftieth anniversary of Pius IX's declaration of the Immaculate Conception. Pius X articulated a "very definite teaching on the right devotion to the Mother of God,"[149] which is not surprising given his interest in liturgical reform. He writes that "for to be right and good, worship of the Mother of God ought to spring from the heart; acts of the body have here neither utility nor value if the acts of the soul have no part in them."[150] Here he seems to attack those who practice devotions to Mary that may be done mechanically and/or without feeling, a critique that will be heard again from those involved in the liturgical movement.

Benedict XV (1914–1922) and Fátima

Benedict XV spent much of his pontificate dealing with World War I (1914–1918) and its aftermath.[151] He also oversaw the completion of the revision of canon law in 1917, a project begun by Pius X, and one that O'Malley sees as not only "augment[ing] papal authority" but also shoring up the centralization of the hierarchy.[152] While he did not have any significant teachings on Mary, one of the most popular Marian apparitions of the twentieth century occurred during his pontificate.

In 1917 in Fátima, Portugal, the Virgin Mary appeared to three children, Lucia, Francisco, and Jacinta, on the thirteenth day of the month for six months. Describing herself as "the Lady of the Rosary," Mary asked the children to "say the Rosary every day in honour of our Lady of the Rosary to obtain peace."[153] In addition to showing the children visions of hell and telling them "secrets," Mary also gave the children a prayer to be said at the end of each decade of

---

148. Kelly, *The Oxford Dictionary of Popes*, 313. His motto was based on Eph 1:10.

149. Graef, *Mary*, 380.

150. Pius X, *Ad Diem Illum Laetissimum*, February 2, 1904, 17, Papal Encyclicals Online, http://www.papalencyclicals.net/Pius10/p10imcon.htm, accessed June 2014.

151. Kelly, *The Oxford Dictionary of Popes*, 315.

152. Ibid., 315–16 and O'Malley, *What Happened at Vatican II*, 65.

153. Graef, *Mary*, 387–88.

the rosary, promised a miracle, and many that came to be with the children at the time of the apparitions saw different phenomena associated with the sun.[154] Pilgrims began to flock to the shrine built at Fátima, and in 1931 the shrine and the "cult of our Lady of the Rosary of Fátima" were given official recognition.[155] The apparitions at Fátima helped encourage devotion to the rosary and would go on to create an association between the praying of the rosary, fighting Communism, and the conversion of Russia as a result of the claim of one of the seers, Lucia dos Santos, that if Russia and the entire world was consecrated to the Immaculate Heart of Mary, then "the conversion of Russia was promised *unconditionally.*"[156]

Pius XI (1922–1939)

In his 1931 encyclical *Lux Veritatis*, Pius XI celebrated "Mary's twofold motherhood of Christ and of Christians" as he also had the entire Church celebrate a Mass and Office in honor of her divine Motherhood.[157] Pius XI also wrote on Mary in his 1937 encyclical, *Ingravescentibus Malis*, where he "urged the recitation of the Rosary as a remedy for the evils of the time: for it was the age of National Socialism, well-established communism, and the immanence of another world war."[158] While Pius XI mentions some common themes about Mary that have appeared before, for example that she "destroys all heresies in the world" and as St. Bernard said "we should have all things through Mary," he now focused the praying of the rosary against the "error" of Communism: "The Holy Virgin who once victoriously drove the terrible sect of the Albigenses from Christian countries, now suppliantly invoked by us, will turn aside the new errors, especially those of Communism, which remind us in many ways, in its motives and misdeeds, of the ancient ones."[159]

154. Ibid., 388.
155. Graef, *The Devotion to Our Lady*, 82.
156. Graef, *Mary*, 389 (emphasis Graef).
157. Graef, *The Devotion to Our Lady*, 89.
158. Graef, *Mary*, 394.
159. Pius XI, *Ingravescentibus Mali*, September 29, 1937, 2, 8, 19, Papal Encyclicals Online, http://www.papalencyclicals.net/Pius11/P11GRAVE.HTM, accessed June 2014.

Pius XII (1939–1958)

Graef describes Pius XII as the pope "who has done more for the spread of Marian devotion than any pope before him except perhaps Pius IX."[160] J. N. D. Kelly also writes that Pius XII was "the first to appreciate the Marian importance of Fátima."[161] It was in 1942, on the twenty-fifth anniversary of the Marian apparitions at Fátima, that Pius XII consecrated the world to the Immaculate Heart of Mary.[162] In 1952 he further fulfilled the wish of Lucia, one of the visionaries at Fátima, who had reported that Mary told her that if Russia was consecrated to the Immaculate Heart of Mary, then Russia would be converted.[163]

Fátima was increasingly associated with Russian Communism during the reign of Pius XII because of the belief that Russia could be converted through the praying of the rosary.[164] As a result, groups such as the Blue Army were formed in 1947 to encourage the praying of the rosary in an effort to "vanquish the 'red army of atheists.'"[165] As Barbara Pope describes the situation at the time, "the Rosary said against the Turks in the sixteenth century and against impiety in the nineteenth, was being recited in the 1950s over the radio for the conversion of Russia."[166] In addition to promoting Fátima and its message of the conversion of Russia through Marian devotion, Pius XII also fostered devotion to Mary by affirming her bodily assumption into heaven—a belief held for many centuries, but never clearly defined—and overseeing the celebration of the one hundredth anniversary of Pius IX's declaration of Mary's Immaculate Conception.

Pius XII defined the dogma of Mary's bodily Assumption into heaven with the 1950 apostolic constitution *Munificentissimus Deus*. In the document, he expresses hope for "a still greater increase in Marian devotion" in response to defining her Assumption and for a

---

160. Graef, *Mary*, 394.
161. Kelly, *The Oxford Dictionary of Popes*, 319.
162. Graef, *Mary*, 389.
163. Ibid.
164. Ibid., 405.
165. Pope, "Immaculate and Powerful," 195.
166. Ibid.

strengthening in the "belief in our own resurrection."[167] The actual definition says: "we pronounce, declare, and define it to be a divinely revealed dogma: that the Immaculate Mother of God, the ever Virgin Mary, having completed the course of her earthly life, was assumed body and soul into heavenly glory."[168] Graef declares this definition "studiously vague" because it does not clarify if Mary died before she was taken to heaven.[169] She also raises the question why Pius XII would choose 1950 as the year to define Mary's Assumption, when it was certain to become an ecumenical issue, although more so with the Protestants than with the Orthodox, who have long celebrated Mary's dormition.[170] To this question she responds:

> Two world wars and the horrors of the concentration camps of the twentieth century, as well as the accompanying immorality, had made men callous and outraged the respect due not only to the soul but also to the body of one's neighbour. By solemnly defining the glory of the body of a purely human being Pius XII wished to "make our faith in our own resurrection both stronger and more active," so that men should be more careful in preserving the integrity of their own as well as other neighbour's bodies.[171]

Pius XII anticipated the one hundredth anniversary of the definition of Mary's Immaculate Conception in his 1953 encyclical *Fulgens Corona* by announcing the Marian Year from December 8, 1953, to December 8, 1954, thereby connecting the 1854 dogma with the dogma he defined in 1950.[172] Graef describes the purpose of the Marian Year as "a way to increase the faith of the people and to deepen their devotion to the Virgin Mother" through sermons by bishops, prayers for peace, and visits to shrines, especially at Lourdes.[173] "The

---

167. Pius XII, *Munificentissimus Deus*, 7, 42.

168. Ibid., 44.

169. Graef, *Mary*, 395.

170. Graef, *The Devotion to Our Lady*, 91; and Graef, *Mary*, 395.

171. Graef, *The Devotion to Our Lady*, 91–92.

172. Ibid., 92.

173. Ibid., 93.

response to the pope's call was tremendous" and popular devotion to Mary "reached a new height."[174]

The Marian Year concluded with Pius XII's 1954 encyclical *Ad Caeli Reginam* in which he declared the title of Mary's Queenship and established a feast to celebrate this aspect of Marian devotion.[175] Graef's interpretation of the purpose of this encyclical harkens back to earlier notions of Mary: "The Pope's intention was to renew the ancient devotion to Mary as Queen, whose royal dignity rests on her divine motherhood and who 'plays a unique part in the work of our eternal salvation.'"[176] In the midst of all that he did to foster Marian devotion, including the encouragement in *Ad Caeli Reginam* to crown images of Mary, Pius XII still warns against "unfounded opinions and exaggerated expressions which go beyond the truth" as well as "excessive narrowness of mind" concerning Mary.[177]

Liturgical and Devotional Developments

New Feasts

There are four feasts that were instituted or allowed to be celebrated throughout the Catholic Church during the late nineteenth and early twentieth centuries: The Apparition of the Immaculate Virgin Mary at Lourdes (February 11); The Motherhood of Mary (October 11); the Immaculate Heart of Mary (August 22); and the Queenship of Mary (May 31).[178] Pius X added the celebration of the apparitions at Lourdes to the Roman Calendar in 1907, one year before the fiftieth anniversary of Bernadette's apparitions.[179] As observed earlier in this chapter, Pius XI instituted the feast of Mary's motherhood in *Lux veritatis* (1931) "as a memorial of the fifteen-hundredth anniversary of

174. Ibid.

175. Ibid.

176. Graef, *Mary*, 396.

177. Pius XII, *Ad Caeli Reginam*, October 11, 1954, 33, 34, Papal Encyclicals Online, http://www.papalencyclicals.net/Pius12/P12CAELI.HTM, accessed June 2014.

178. Jounel, "The Veneration of Mary," 146–47.

179. Ibid., 146.

the Council of Ephesus."[180] The diocese of Rome had celebrated the feast of Mary's Immaculate Heart since 1880 during the reign of Leo XIII, and in 1944 Pius XII, in honor of his dedication of the world to Mary's Immaculate Heart in 1942, mandated the feast to the entire Roman Rite.[181] Pius XII instituted the feast of Mary's Queenship in 1954 in *Ad Caeli Reginam*.[182]

May Devotions

One particular devotion supported by popes of this period was the crowning of statues of Mary. Leo XIII crowned a statue of Mary at La Salette, and Pius XII crowned a statue of Mary at Fátima.[183] During the late nineteenth and early twentieth centuries, the crowning of statues of Mary, along with other devotions, became part of what are known as May devotions.

> Each May throughout the United States, as the national sodality magazine observed, millions of Catholic schoolchildren, seminarians, college students, and parishioners walked in processions and ceremonies for the Virgin Mary to honor her during her sacred month. They decorated Maypoles, marched together and assembled at a statute of Mary which they crowned with flowers. Together they recited prayers, sang hymns, and delivered petitions for their special intentions.[184]

180. Ibid. October 11 "was mistakenly thought to have been the date when the Council of Ephesus ended," and it was also the date John XXIII chose for the opening of Vatican II in 1962.

181. Ibid., 147.

182. Ibid. While the feast was originally celebrated on May 31, following the liturgical changes of Vatican II it was moved to August 22 and the Feast of the Visitation was moved from July 2 to May 31. The Feast of the Immaculate Heart of Mary was moved from August 22 to the "Saturday following the Second Sunday after Pentecost." See "Feasts and Prayers of The Blessed Virgin Mary," Women for Faith & Family, http://www.wf-f.org/MarianFeast.html, accessed June 2014.

183. Graef, *Mary*, 394.

184. Paula M. Kane, "Marian Devotion Since 1940: Continuity or Casualty?," in *Habits of Devotion: Catholic Religious Practice in Twentieth-Century America*, ed.

While the May devotions to Mary date back to the sixteenth century, it is clear they have many pagan influences.[185] While the name May "is a form of 'Mary,' the name comes from the Latin for the 'month of Maia,' the Roman goddess of grain." In ancient Rome, May 1 was celebrated in honor of Flora, "the goddess of flowers, who was represented by a small statue wreathed in garlands. A procession of singers and dancers carried the statue past a sacred tree decorated with blossoms." This sounds surprisingly similar to the May processions that were very popular, especially in the first half of the twentieth century, when statues of Mary were crowned with flowers and paraded through the streets. In fact, Caryl Rivers's memory of participating in such a May procession even mentions how it must have seemed to others to be a scene from ancient Rome:

> To someone looking in from outside, I can well imagine that the spectacle of the May procession, with all the children dressed in white marching through the streets of Silver Spring with the Virgin carried aloft, must have smacked a bit of the spring festival to Aphrodite in suburban Rome around 202 B.C. . . . The smell of incense floated on the air, and as we walked with our rosaries in our hands we chanted the "Hail Mary" in cadence or we sang: "Bring Flowers of the Fairest."[186]

The festivals celebrated in ancient Rome later spread to Europe, and in the Middle Ages they were particularly popular in England.[187] The festivities included "dances around a May pole" (similar to the description above) and also the choosing of a May queen. Philip Neri (1515–1595) seems to be the first to have transformed these pagan celebrations into Christian celebrations, making Mary the new May

---

James M. O'Toole (Ithaca, NY: Cornell University Press, 2004), 89. Sodalities were groups of laity formed around certain devotions, often focused on Mary.

185. Monica and Bill Dodds, "May," in *Encyclopedia of Mary* (Huntington, IN: Our Sunday Visitor Publishing Division, 2007), 183. All quotations and information in this paragraph come from this source.

186. Caryl Rivers, *Aphrodite at Mid-Century: Growing Up Catholic and Female in Post-War America* (Garden City, NY: Doubleday, 1973), 157–58.

187. Dodds and Dodds, "May," 183–84. All quotations and information in this paragraph are taken from this source.

queen as statues of her were decorated with flowers. In the eighteenth century, the Jesuit priest Annibale Dionisi was credited with encouraging devotions to Mary throughout the month as the pagan May festivities were transformed into Christian practices. These Christian May devotions included "floral tributes, processions, and the crowning of a statue."

The crowning of a statue of Mary became one of the central practices associated with the May devotions. The Dodds note that the fifth Glorious Mystery of the rosary is the crowning of Mary as "Queen of Heaven and Earth."[188] As seen earlier, Pius XII supported the act of crowning statues of Mary in *Ad Caeli Reginam*.[189] The crowning of statues of Mary dates back to the late sixteenth century, and this devotion had the support of subsequent popes.[190] In the seventeenth century a rite was composed for the "coronation of religious images of Jesus, Mary, and the saints," and in the nineteenth century a rite was prepared solely for "crowning images of Mary."[191] In 1981 the Congregation for the Sacraments and Divine Worship approved a new rite, which was translated into English and published by the United States Conference of Catholic Bishops in 1986.[192] This rite suggests the following Marian congregational songs—all of which were discussed earlier—to be sung (either in Latin or English) during the rite: the *Salve Regina*; *Sub tuum praesidium*; *Ave, Regina caelorum*; *Alma Redemptoris Mater*; and *Regina coeli*.[193]

It is important to note the difference between this official rite and the popular "May crowning":

> A similar custom—although not an official liturgical act—is a coronation popularly known as a "May crowning" because often it takes place during that month. In parishes and schools, and at Marian

188. Monica and Bill Dodds, "Coronation of the Blessed Virgin Mary," in *Encyclopedia of Mary* (Huntington, IN: Our Sunday Visitor Publishing Division, 2007), 73.

189. Pius XII, *Ad Caeli Reginam*, 33.

190. Dodds and Dodds, "Coronation of the Blessed Virgin Mary," 73.

191. Ibid.

192. National Conference of Catholic Bishops, *Order of Crowning an Image of the Blessed Virgin Mary* (New Jersey: Catholic Book Publishing Corp., 2005).

193. Ibid., 18–20.

shrines and grottos, an individual is chosen to place a wreath of flowers on Mary's image. It often takes place during Benediction, the recitation of the Rosary, or at the end of Mass.[194]

This "May crowning" seems to be more popular than the official rite, and it is this devotion, along with the month of May in general, for which many Marian congregational songs were written.

Papal Piety and Devotional Developments Reflected in Marian Congregational Song

"To the Fairest of Queens, Be the Fairest of Seasons, Sweet May"[195]

The popularity of May devotions is reflected in the great number of Marian congregational songs that are devoted to Mary and the month of May. Although the Marian rituals these songs were associated with may not have required a priest or held the "sacramental power" associated with other rituals such as the Eucharist, these practices were extremely popular.[196] As discussed earlier, people's devotional needs were often met outside of the Mass before Vatican II, and it was mostly outside the context of the Mass that Marian congregational songs were sung; those associated with the month of May and May crownings (at least before Vatican II) fall into this category.

In her work "Mary in Nineteenth-Century English and American Poetry," Nancy de Flon makes a few observations regarding nineteenth-century English poetry devoted to Mary: (1) the poems can be polemical (in reaction to people being hostile to Catholicism); (2) the dogma of the Immaculate Conception is frequently mentioned; (3) there was often an attempt to defend against claims of "Mariolatry" by emphasizing Mary's role in the incarnation; (4) nature symbolism is regularly used, particularly when discussing Mary's month of May;

194. Dodds and Dodds, "Coronation of the Blessed Virgin Mary," 74.

195. From the refrain of "'Tis the month of our Mother, the sweet month of May," Hymnary.org, http://www.hymnary.org/text/tis_the_month_of_our_mother_the_sweet_mo, accessed April 2014. Taken from Sisters of Notre Dame, ed., *Sunday School Hymn Book* (Boston: Oliver Ditson Co., 1907), 152. This anonymous text is found in: Sourin and Barbelin, ed., *Sacred Wreath* (1863). See Higginson, *Handbook for American Catholic Hymnals*, 92.

196. Kane, "Marian Devotion since 1940," 89.

(5) the ballad and other medieval forms of poetry were commonly used; (6) the "Victorian ideal of womanhood" can be detected; and (7) these different features often appear together, not separately, in one poem.[197] Many of these features have been seen thus far in looking at Marian congregational song in this chapter, often intertwined as de Flon mentions. As noted in the section on Mary's immaculate conception, many of the Marian congregational songs were polemical, pointed frequently to the immaculate conception, and rallied against critics of Marian devotion, saying "When wicked men blaspheme thee, I'll love and bless thy name."[198]

In writing about the month of May in northern Europe (and one can argue in most of the United States as well),[199] de Flon describes it as a time where there is an

> awareness of nature, due to the signs of its return to life after winter's dormancy being most obvious at this time. . . . Given the ancient popular significance of May in its connection with nature, along with the importance of Mary in Catholic devotion, it was inevitable that these things should be conflated in the Catholic poetic mind.[200]

Nature imagery was also common in Marian congregational songs that did not specifically refer to the month of May; there are references to Mary as the Mystical Rose, which de Flon describes as the "rose without thorns that symbolizes the innocent human condition before the fall," and to Mary as the "garden in which the flower grows."[201]

197. Nancy de Flon, "Mary in Nineteenth-Century English and American Poetry," in *Mary: The Complete Resource*, ed. Sarah Jane Boss (Oxford: Oxford University Press, 2007), 504–5.

198. From stanza 1 of "I'll sing a hymn to Mary."

199. It is important to note that these notions of spring only hold true in the northern hemisphere; during this time of year it is autumn in the southern hemisphere.

200. de Flon, "Mary in Nineteenth-Century English and American Poetry," 510.

201. Ibid., 514. The issue of flower imagery as being erotic and symbolizing women's bodies and genitals is a topic brought up by June Hadden Hobbs, but one which there was not space to explore in this study. See June Hadden Hobbs, *"I Sing for I Cannot Be Silent": The Feminization of American Hymnody, 1870–1920* (Pittsburgh, PA: University of Pittsburgh Press, 1997), 92.

John Henry Newman (1801–1890), a convert to Catholicism and hymn writer, further elaborates on why May is the month devoted to Mary. His first response is based on nature; as de Flon describes, "May is, quite simply, an extraordinarily beautiful month."[202] Newman also sees May as "quasi liturgical" in that, in the words of de Flon, "it is a joyous time of year": following the penitential seasons of Advent and Lent, the liturgical year moves to the celebratory feasts of the Easter season (including Ascension and Pentecost) which are celebrated in May (except when Easter falls late; then they are celebrated in June).[203]

"Green are the leaves," a hymn text by Newman, is full of nature imagery, describing the blue sky, the green grass, and the flowers that smile. While all these things will fade because they have "an end," Mary "dost not fade" because she is forever "throned," possibly a reference in stanza 2 to Mary's assumption and the belief that her body never decayed because it was assumed into heaven. The flowers placed on Mary, however, will not waste away, as is described in stanza 3.

1. Green are the leaves, and sweet the flowers,
    And rich the hues of May;
We see them in the gardens round
    And market-panniers gay;
And e'en among our streets and lanes
    And byways we descry,
By fitful gleams, the sunshine fair,
    The blue transparent sky.
        O Mother-Maid, be thou our aid,
          Now in the opening year,
       Lest sights of earth to sin give birth,
        And bring the tempter near.

2. Green is the grass; yet wait awhile—
    'Twill grow, and then will fade;
The flowrets, brightly as they smile,
    Will droop, and then decay.

202. John Henry Newman, "Meditations on the Litany of Loreto for the Month of May," as quoted in de Flon, "Mary in Nineteenth-Century English and American Poetry," 511.
    203. Ibid.

The merry sun, you sure would say,
    Could never set in gloom;
But earth's best joys have all an end,
    And sin a heavy doom.
        But Mother-Maid, thou dost not fade;
            With stars above thy brow,
        The moon beneath thy queenly feet,
            For ever throned art thou.

3. Green leaves, sweet flowers, and glittering grove,
        And heaven's majestic dome,
    All image forth a brighter bower,
        A more refulgent home;
    They tell us of that Paradise
        Of everlasting rest,
    And that high Tree, all flowers and fruit,
        The sweetest, yet the best.
            O Mary pure and beautiful!
                Thou art our Queen of May!
            Our garlands wear about thy hair,
                And they will ne'er decay.[204]

There are many texts that specifically make references to Mary and the month of May. The chorus of "Hail Virgin, dearest Mary," praises Mary as "Our lovely Queen of May." The verses join together the themes of May and nature imagery as they describe children praying at Marian shrines, the earth in full blossom, and the crowning of Mary with a wreath of flowers.

204. "Green are the leaves, and sweet the flowers," Hymnary.org, http://www.hymnary.org/hymn/SH1887/248, accessed April 2014. Taken from E. F. MacGonigle, ed., *The Sodalist's Hymnal: Containing a Collection of Catholic Hymns Set to Original and Selected Harmonized Melodies, also The Little Office of the Immaculate Conception, The Vesper Compline Office . . .* (Philadelphia, 1887), 248–49. Higginson writes that this text dates from 1850 and was included in: John Henry Newman, *Verses on Religious Subjects* (Dublin: J. Duffy, 1853). See Higginson, *Handbook for American Catholic Hymnals*, 78.

Refrain: Hail, Virgin dearest Mary!
Our lovely Queen of May.
O spotless, blessed Lady,
Our lovely Queen of May.

1. Thy children, humbly bending,
Surround thy shrine so dear;
With heart and voice ascending,
Sweet Mary, hear our prayer. **R.**

2. Behold earth's blossoms springing
In beauteous form and hue;
All nature gladly bringing
Her sweetest charms to you. **R.**

3. We'll gather fresh, bright flowers,
To bind our fair Queen's brow;
From gay and verdant bowers,
We haste to crown thee now. **R.**

4. And now, our blessed Mother,
Smile on our festal day,
Accept our wreath of flowers,
And be our Queen of May. **R.**[205]

The title of this section comes from "'Tis the month of our mother," which in stanza 1 enthusiastically describes May as the month of "The blessed and beautiful days, / When our lips and our spirits / Are glowing with love and with praise." The refrain ends with a joining together of the praise of Mary and the month of May: "To the fairest of Queens, / Be the fairest of seasons sweet May." Stanza 4 is also interesting in that it almost borders on the heretical, indicating that Mary is divine and has been clothed with human nature.

---

205. "Hail, virgin, dearest Mary," Hymnary.org, http://www.hymnary.org/text /hail_virgin_dearest_mary, accessed April 2014. Taken from #143 in Marist Brothers, ed., *American Catholic Hymnal* (1913), 178. This anonymous text is found in: A Catholic Priest, ed., *The Sacred Wreath: Or a Collection of Hymns and Prayers for the Use of the Members of the Sodality of the Blessed Virgin Mary* (Philadelphia, PA: Eugene Cummiskey, 1844). See Higginson, *Handbook for American Catholic Hymnals*, 80.

Figure 9. *'Tis the Month of Our Mother.* Text: Anonymous. Tune: Louis Lambillotte, SJ (1796–1855). (From Sisters of Notre Dame, ed., *Sunday School Hymn Book* [1907], 152). Image courtesy of Hymnary.org.

In Caryl Rivers's quote previously cited, she recounts singing "Bring flowers of the fairest/rarest."[206] This Marian congregational song is probably the one that is most closely associated with the May processions and crownings, particularly because of its refrain: "O Mary! we crown thee with blossoms today, / Queen of the Angels, Queen of the May, / O Mary we crown thee with blossoms today, / Queen of the Angels, Queen of the May." Throughout the text there is the joining of nature imagery with Mary and the month of May, as well as praise of Mary, including the final line of stanza 4 which states "How dark without Mary, life's journey would be." Not much is known about Mary E. Walsh, who wrote the text and tune, except that she is also famous for writing the very popular "Black Hawk Waltz," which might explain much of the chromaticism in the piece, which was quite common for the Victorian period. While many of these Marian congregational songs have fallen out of favor, some continue to be sung by younger generations, such as "Bring flowers of the fairest/rarest," which is often sung at churches that still hold May crowning services.[207]

206. Mary E. Walsh, "Bring flowers of the rarest," Hymnary.org, http://www.hymnary.org/text/bring_flowers_of_the_rarest, accessed April 2014. Taken from Sisters of Notre Dame, ed., *Sunday School Hymn Book* (1907), 156–57. The text and tune is by Mary E. Walsh and is found in: Sisters of Notre Dame, ed., *Wreath of Mary: Companion to the May Chimes; A Collection of Hymns to the Blessed Virgin* (Boston, MA: Oliver Ditson & Co., 1883). Higginson writes that this Marian congregational song is often known as the "Crowning Hymn" and "is used for the May Processions" for which its refrain is "particularly appropriate." See Higginson, *Handbook for American Catholic Hymnals*, 76.

207. There were attempts at replacing these Marian congregational songs with newer, more "theological" texts such as "In this your month, creation's Queen" in *The New St. Basil Hymnal* (1958) and Melvin Farrell's "Holy Mary, now we crown you," first seen in the *People's Hymnal* (1955) and subsequent World Library Publications (World Library of Sacred Music) hymnals. These texts, however, did not seem to catch on and never became as popular as "Bring flowers of the fairest/rarest."

Figure 10. *Bring flow'rs of the rarest.* Text: Mary E. Walsh. Tune: Mary E. Walsh. (From Sisters of Notre Dame, ed., *Sunday School Hymn Book* [1907], 156–57). Image courtesy of Hymnary.org.

Their Lady they name thee, their mistress proclaim thee,
Oh grant that thy children on earth be as true;
As long as the bowers are radiant with flowers,
As long as the azure shall keep its bright hue.

4

Our voices ascending, in harmony blending,
Oh thus may our hearts turn, dear Mother, to thee.
Oh! thus shall we prove thee, how truly we love thee;
How dark without Mary, life's journey would be.

Figure 10. *Bring flow'rs of the rarest* (continued).

"The Rosary Our Weapon Still, to Wield in Holy War"[208]

It wasn't just Marian congregational songs devoted to the month of May that explored nature imagery; "O Queen of the Holy Rosary" by Emily M. C. Shapcote (1828–1909) is replete with nature imagery, describing how Mary is offered garlands of roses, "Buds white and red and gold."[209] As stated earlier in this chapter, Pope Leo XIII dedicated the month of October to Mary, "Holy Queen of the Rosary," in *Supremi Apostolatus Officio* (1883); it seems that this title caught on quickly as only two years later Shapcote's text was composed incorporating the title. Shapcote's text also touches on the mysteries of the rosary in stanza 2, as she describes how Jesus' life was intertwined with Mary's and Mary was also a mirror, reflecting Jesus.

1. O Queen of the Holy Rosary!
       Oh bless us as we pray,
   And offer thee our roses,
       In garlands day by day.
   While from our Father's garden,
       With loving hearts and bold,
   We gather to thine honor,
       Buds, white, and red, and gold.

2. O Queen of the Holy Rosary!
       Each mystery blends with thine,
   The sacred life of Jesus,
       In ev'ry step divine.
   Thy soul was His fair garden,
       Thy virgin breast His throne,
   Thy thoughts His faithful mirror,
       Reflecting Him alone.

208. From the fourth stanza of "The clouds hang thick o'er Israel's camp," Augusta T. Drane, "The clouds hang thick o'er Isr'l's camp," Hymnary.org, http://www.hymnary.org/text/the_clouds_hang_thick_oer_isrls_camp, accessed March 2014.

209. As seen in the discussion of Rothenberg's work in chap. 2, red and white roses and lilies symbolize Mary's virginity and purity.

3. Sweet Lady of the Rosary!
     White roses let us bring,
   And lay them round thy footstool
     Before our Infant King.
   For nestling in thy bosom
     God's Son was fain to be,
   The Child of thy Obedience
     And spotless purity.

4. O Queen of the Holy Rosary!
     What radiancy of love,
   What splendour and what glory
     Surround thy court above!
   Oh, in thy tender pity,
     Dear source of love untold,
   Refuse not this our offering,
     Our flowers white, red, and gold.[210]

"Hail, full of grace and purity" is a text that reflects more specifically on the Joyful Mysteries of the rosary.[211] In each of the first five stanzas, one of the mysteries of the rosary is reflected on, as well as a characteristic the mystery represents: stanza 1 is the annunciation (humility); stanza 2 is the visitation (charity to our neighbor); stanza 3 is the birth of our Lord (poverty); stanza 4 is the presentation in the temple (obedience); stanza 5 is the finding of our Lord (love of Him and His service); and stanza 6, the concluding stanza, asks Mary to look down "With tender love" and to "bless the hearts that offer thee / This chaplet for thy crown." In this particular hymnal,

210. Emily M. C. Shapcote, "O queen of the holy rosary! O bless us as we pray," Hymnary.org, http://www.hymnary.org/text/o_queen_of_the_holy _rosary_o_bless_us_as, accessed April 2014. Taken from *Sunday School Hymn Book*, 92–93. This text is often set to the tune ELLACOMBE. The text is found in: *St. Dominic's Hymn-Book with the Office of Compline According to the Dominican Rite* (1885). See Higginson, *Handbook for American Catholic Hymnals*, 88.

211. John Placid Conway, "Hail, full of grace and purity," Hymnary.org, http://www.hymnary.org/text/hail_full_of_grace_and_purity, accessed April 2014. Taken from #197 in Marist Brothers, ed., *American Catholic Hymnal* (1913), 230. The text is found in: *The Dominican Hymn Book: With Vespers and Compline* (London: Burns and Oates, 1881). See Higginson, *Handbook for American Catholic Hymnals*, 78.

it suggested that children might learn the rosary better if they sing the indicated verse that corresponds to each mystery of the rosary (see Figure 11 below). The author of this text, John Placid Conway (1855–1913), also wrote texts that associate moral characteristics with the Sorrowful ("Lord, by Thy prayer in agony") and Glorious Mysteries ("All hail, great Conqueror, to Thee").[212]

The juxtaposition of the mysteries of the rosary with moral qualities is interesting because Leo XIII often referred to how praying the rosary could lead to living well. For example, in his 1894 encyclical *Iucunda semper Expectatione*, Pope Leo writes that the mysteries and prayers of the rosary are "thus a kind of prayer that requires not only some raising of the soul to God, but also a particular and explicit attention, so that by reflection upon the things to be contemplated, impulses and resolution may follow for the reformation and sanctification of life."[213]

212. These may be found in the *American Catholic Hymnal* (1913) at #198 and #199, respectively.

213. Leo XIII, *Iucunda semper Expectatione* in Catholic Church, *1878–1903*, 357, 7.

Figure 11. *Hail, full of grace and purity.* Text: Fr. John Placid Conway, OP (1855–1913). Tune: German Melody. (From Marist Brothers, ed., *American Catholic Hymnal* [1913], 230). Image courtesy of Hymnary.org.

The rosary has often been used as a weapon against evil, heresy, and—in association with the apparitions at Fátima—Communism.

These first two "enemies" are reflected in "The clouds hang thick o'er Israel's camp," a text mentioned earlier in relation to the battle of Lepanto in 1571 and which also provides the title for this section.[214] Stanza 2 reflects on the rosary's use as a weapon against "error and sin." Stanza 4 appears to connect Pius V's teachings about the rosary in regards to the victory at Lepanto in 1571 with Leo XIII's teachings on the rosary through his many encyclicals, as well as his call for the rosary to fight the heresies of the day.

> 2. The weapon which our Father gave
>   Each hand shall fearless wield:
> Who bear our Lady's Rosary
>   Need neither sword nor shield:
> With dauntless faith the ranks they face
>   Of error and of sin,
> And, armed with those blest beads alone,
>   The victory they win.

> 4. As Pius then to Europe spake,
>   So Leo speaks once more;*
> The Rosary our weapon still
>   To wield in holy war:
> Ave Maria! from each tongue
>   Shall rise the pleading word;
> Oh! doubt not that the prayer of faith
>   Will now, as then, be heard.[215]

214. This text was written in 1885, well before the apparitions at Fátima.

215. Augusta T. Drane, "The clouds hang thick o'er Isr'l's camp," Hymnary.org, http://www.hymnary.org/text/the_clouds_hang_thick_oer_isrls_camp, accessed March 2014. Taken from #115 in *Catholic Church Hymnal with Music*, 163. Line 2 of stanza 4 seems to be altered in this version by Tozer. In Tozer's 1905 *Catholic Church Hymnal with Music*, stanza 4 begins "As Pius then to Europe spake, / So Pius spake once more." When this hymn appears in various editions of the *St. Basil's Hymnal*, it appears as printed here, "As Pius then to Europe spake / So Leo speaks once more." This version of the text also appears in an earlier edition of Tozer's hymnal *Catholic Hymns* (1898), so it seems that this is an alteration that Tozer made himself by the time of the 1905 *Catholic Church Hymnal with Music*, perhaps in reference to the then-current Pope Pius X, whose papacy began in 1903.

The rosary will continue to be wielded as a weapon against the "enemies" of Catholicism, particularly Communism as the Church takes part in the Cold War in the 1950s. There are other factors, however, that will also play an important role in Marian theology and devotion including cultural and religious ideals about gender roles and death, as well as a movement focused on the liturgy that would help lead the Church into the Second Vatican Council.

Chapter Five

So We Take Thee for Our Mother[1]

Mother Mary at thine altar
  We thy loving children kneel;
With a faith that cannot falter,
  To thy goodness we appeal.
We are seeking for a mother,
  O'er the earth so waste and wide,
And from off the Cross our Brother
  Points to Mary by His side.[2]
—Frederick W. Faber, "Mother Mary at thine altar"

Introduction

Following a look at developments in the Catholic Church at a more international level, this chapter focuses on exploring Marian devotion and theology more specifically in the United States,

---

1. From stanza 3 of Frederick W. Faber, "Mother Mary, at thine altar We thy loving children kneel," Hymnary.org, http://www.hymnary.org/text/mother _mary_at_thine_altar_we_thy_loving, accessed March 2014. Taken from #278 in *American Catholic Hymnal: An Extensive Collection of Hymns, Latin Chants, and Sacred Songs for Church, School, and Home, Including Gregorian Masses, Vesper Psalms, Litanies . . .*, ed. Marist Brothers (New York: P.J. Kenedy & Sons, 1913), 318.

2. Ibid., stanza 1.

including the rise of missions and devotional books, the Victorian notion of True Womanhood, changing attitudes toward death, and the liturgical movement. Marian congregational songs from this era—such as the above text from Faber—will be looked at in order to understand the effect of these developments on Marian piety. Also, musical movements and documents from this period up until the eve of Vatican II in 1962 will be looked into in order to understand their impact as well.

Catholic Developments in the United States

Spirituality in the United States

The Household of Faith and Treasury of Merit

Ann Taves's study of nineteenth-century Catholic devotions centers on her notion of "the household of faith" which she describes as "the network of affective, familial relationships between believers and supernatural 'relatives,' such as Jesus and Mary, presupposed by devotions."[3] These relationships were built up by devotions, and one way to promote these devotions was through devotional guides. These guides—printed in great numbers during the 1850s—were often distributed at parish missions, which also became popular in the 1850s.[4] The goal of these missions was "to revitalize the faith of the laity by inducing in them a desire for confession and communion, and an eagerness to persevere in the faith."[5] Parish missions were not only opportunities to increase the faith but also occasions for mission preachers to introduce new devotions to parishes—often times devotions that included Mary, such as the rosary and scapulars.[6]

3. See Ann Taves, *The Household of Faith: Roman Catholic Devotions in Mid-Nineteenth Century America* (Notre Dame, IN: University of Notre Dame Press, 1986), viii.

4. Ibid., 5, 12.

5. Ibid., 11.

6. Ibid. Taves goes on to describe how "parish-based confraternities and sodalities, intended to foster the devotional life of the ordinary Catholic, were often established in conjunction with parish missions" (p. 14).

Many Marian devotions appeared in the devotional guides, particularly after 1840, and while the rosary was "in all the most popular American prayer books," other Marian devotions included were "the seven dolors, the Immaculate Conception, the Sacred Heart of Mary, and one or more scapulars."[7] Marian devotions often had indulgences attached to them, and these indulgenced devotions had an important effect on the creation of the "household of faith." By encouraging indulgenced devotions, the hierarchy was able to better control the laity through (1) a process of centralization and standardization of practices and (2) "by creating symbolic associations and patronage relationship between supernatural beings, the pope, and the institutional church."[8]

What exactly did the laity gain from these indulgences? Taves describes the "mutual interchange and sharing" that took place within the "household of faith."[9] A "treasury of sacred goods" was exchanged, and this

> treasury was filled with vaguely defined benefits or power derived in some way from the superabundant holiness of Jesus, the saints, and Mary. These benefits could be dispensed by God in the form of graces and favors, or by the hierarchy in the form of indulgences. Devotions played an integral part in the acquisition of benefits.[10]

While prayers were thought to be especially effective in the presence of the consecrated Host, devotions to Mary—such as the rosary—"were also touted as especially efficacious means of acquiring graces and favors."[11] In looking at the "favors obtained" sections in devotional magazines such as the *Ave Maria* and *The Messenger of the Sacred Heart*, Taves discerned that the most common results asked for were "conversions; cures; resolution of family difficulties; moral reform, particularly of the intemperate; and happy deaths."[12] Clearly devotions helped facilitate communication between those

7. Ibid., 36, 24.
8. Ibid., 89.
9. Ibid., 50.
10. Ibid., 50–51.
11. Ibid., 52.
12. Ibid., 55–56.

on earth and heaven in the "household of faith," and any "favors obtained" became "tangible proof of the reality of the relationships that devotional acts and objects presupposed," as well as proof of the intercessory power of those called upon.[13]

These devotions emphasized an "affective spirituality" as represented in the writings of Alphonsus Liguori and Frederick William Faber. Both were influenced by the writings of Francis de Sales (1567–1622), but while de Sales wrote in a restrained manner with the goal of "direct[ing] emotions generated by meditation into ethical action," Liguori and Faber wrote in a more emotional, affective manner, and "used meditations to form affective bonds between human and supernatural beings."[14] This is reflected in their Marian congregational songs, as well as many of the Marian congregational songs of the pre–Vatican II era. Instead of focusing on how prayer can lead to action, to help those in need, and to live out the Christian faith, these texts are centered on individual needs, emotions, and relationships with members of the "household of faith." The desire to foster these relationships was emphasized by the notion of the "treasury of merit" and the belief that Mary (and Christ and the saints) could dispense graces and favors.[15] This dependence on Mary and others in the "household of faith" for graces helped to encourage "feelings of dependence" often associated with parental figures, leading to infantilism.[16]

Mary and Death

The "treasury of merit" was also strongly tied to death. Mary has often been associated with practices surrounding death, with the scapular being one devotion particularly tied to Mary's intercession at the time of death.[17] Liguori had a strong devotion to Mary, his patron, as he depended on her "for a 'good' death."[18] This can

---

13. Ibid., 69.

14. Ibid., 71–74.

15. Ibid., 76, 91.

16. Ibid., 86.

17. Ibid., 39. String scapulars came in different colors for different devotions; for example one of the more famous is the brown scapular associated with Our Lady of Mount Carmel.

18. Ibid., 76.

be seen in the third stanza of Liguori's hymn "Mother Mary, Queen most sweet" where he describes how he will call out Mary's name on his deathbed just before he dies:

> 3. When the demon hosts invade,
>   When temptation rages high,
>   Crying "Mary, Mother, aid;"
>   I will make the tempter fly.
>   This shall be my comfort sweet,
>   When the hand of death is nigh,
>   "Mary! Mary!" to repeat
>   Once again, and then, to die.[19]

Mary was also associated with the souls in purgatory because there was a belief that by making an offering to her, "she may distribute them in behalf of those souls whom it is her good pleasure to deliver from the pains of purgatory."[20] The connection between those on earth and those in purgatory led to the popularity of devotions specifically for those in purgatory, including the use of scapulars, the rosary, and the singing of Marian congregational songs specifically written for souls in purgatory. Another reason for the increase in prayers for others is a shift to what Philippe Ariès calls the "death of the other," in which survivors were more upset over "physical separation from the deceased" as opposed to "the fact of dying," leading them to want to maintain connections with the deceased.[21]

True Womanhood

In addition to fostering emotions and affective bonds, Marian devotions and congregational songs from the Victorian period also

19. Alfonso M. de Liguori, "Our Lady's dear name," Hymnary.org, http://www.hymnary.org/text/mother_mary_queen_most_sweet, accessed March 2014. Taken from #131 in *American Catholic Hymnal*, 166. Here is printed stanza 3; in this hymnal there are three stanzas total.

20. *The Raccolta*, 368–69, as quoted in Taves, *The Household of Faith*, 40.

21. Philippe Ariès, *The Hour of Our Death: The Classic History of Western Attitudes toward Death over the Last One Thousand Years*, trans. Helen Weaver (New York: Vintage Books, 1981), 610.

helped to enforce the "four cardinal virtues" of True Womanhood: "piety, purity, submissiveness, and domesticity."[22] If a woman possessed these virtues, "she was promised happiness and power," yet "without them, no matter whether there was fame, achievement, or wealth, all was ashes."[23] While all of these virtues seem problematic and oppressive to women by way of our twenty-first-century mindset, some were particularly difficult to grasp—even for those living in the nineteenth century—when many of these virtues were the norm and what was expected of women.

In discussing the dilemma over the virtue of purity, Barbara Welter writes that a "woman must preserve her virtue until marriage and marriage was necessary for her happiness. Yet marriage was, literally, an end to innocence. She was told not to question this dilemma, but simply to accept it."[24] This paradox is similar to the inability for any woman besides Mary to be both a virgin and a mother. Welter describes another highly problematic virtue, submission, as "perhaps the most feminine virtue expected of women" and one that was decreed by God; this hierarchy of gender (i.e., the subordination of women to men) was not to be "tampered with" because if women did so, "they tampered with the order of the Universe."[25]

While Welter is describing a secular phenomenon, the notion of True Womanhood clearly spilled over into the religious realm, particularly in its association with Mary. Darris Saylors explores this association, describing how the four cardinal virtues outlined by Welter correspond to those seen in Mary. Saylors concludes that while Mary may have been associated with True Womanhood, this is a "problematic correlation" because Mary "over-fulfills the requirements of True Womanhood in ways that other women could never achieve, even if they are expected to do so."[26]

---

22. Barbara Welter, "The Cult of True Womanhood: 1820–1860," *American Quarterly* 18, no. 2 (Summer, 1966): 152.

23. Ibid.

24. Ibid., 158.

25. Ibid., 159. Welter describes how although women "were separate, they were equal."

26. Darris Catherine Saylors, "The Virgin Mary: A Paradoxical Model for Roman Catholic Immigrant Women of the Nineteenth Century," *Journal of the National Collegiate Honors Council* (Spring/Summer, 2007): 109.

While the holding up of these virtues associated with Mary could be oppressive, they could also be consoling because, on the one hand, Mary understood all that motherhood entailed. Yet on the other hand, she was also a figure that was used to reinforce oppressive cultural structures, leading Mary to be for women both "the source of their comfort" as well as "the source of their entrapment."[27] Robert Orsi aptly summarizes this paradox: "Women found the Madonna's azure cloak, so ceremoniously draped over their shoulders, a heavy one indeed."[28] In the end, the oppressive models for women, embodied as True Womanhood or the Virgin Mary, mutually enforced each other, with virginity and purity upheld as ideals and Mary as the exemplary.[29]

Factors in the United States Reflected in Marian Congregational Song

"None Have Ever, Ever Found Thee Wanting, Who Have Called upon Thy Aid"[30]

Mary was an integral member of the "household of faith," granting graces and favors from the "treasury of merit." Many claimed that Mary's ability to dispense from the "treasury of merit" was particularly strong, perhaps drawing on "Catholics' certainty that their requests to a loving mother could not be refused. As one popular devotional prayer phrased it, 'never was it known that any one who sought her intercession was left unaided.'"[31] The notion that prayers to Mary cannot be refused—one acknowledged earlier in this study—is reflected in the hymn that provides the title for this section, "Wilt thou look upon me, Mother." In fact, the refrain specifically mentions the fact that this idea is traced back to St. Bernard of Clairvaux,

27. Varacalli and Primeggia, *The Saints in the Lives of Italian-Americans: An Interdisciplinary Investigation*, 82; and Robert Orsi, *The Madonna of 115th Street*, 180, as quoted in Saylors, "The Virgin Mary," 125.

28. Robert Orsi, *The Madonna of 115th Street: Faith and Community in Italian Harlem, 1880–1950* (New Haven, CT: Yale University Press, 1985), 204–5.

29. Saylors, "The Virgin Mary," 136.

30. From the refrain of "Wilt thou look upon me, Mother."

31. Paula M. Kane, "Marian Devotion Since 1940: Continuity or Casualty?," in *Habits of Devotion: Catholic Religious Practice in Twentieth-Century America*, ed. James M. O'Toole (Ithaca, NY: Cornell University Press, 2004), 93.

reminding Mary that no one who calls on her is turned away, as the "sainted Bernard said."

1. Wilt thou look upon me, Mother,
   Thou who reignest in the skies,
   Wilt thou deign to cast upon me,
   One sweet glance, from those mild eyes.

Refrain: O, my Mother Mary, still remember,
What the sainted Bernard said,
None have ever, ever found thee wanting,
Who have called upon thy aid,
Who have called upon thy aid.[32]

The idea that prayers to Mary cannot be refused is often found in settings of the *Memorare*. One example is "O Mother blest, whom God bestows," a text by Alphonsus Liguori that was translated by Edmund Vaughan. In the refrain there is the call to Mary to "remember me." This is echoed in the second stanza, when Mary is asked to remember that no one who has asked for her care has ever left "unconsoled."

1. O Mother blest! whom God bestows
   On sinners and on just,
   What joy, what hope thou givest those,
   Who in thy mercy trust.

Refrain: Most holy Mary! at thy feet
Thy children bend a suppliant knee;
Dear Mother of my God,
Do thou remember me.

---

32. "Petitions to Mary," Hymnary.org, http://www.hymnary.org/text/wilt _thou_look_upon_me_mother, accessed accessed April 2014. Taken from #23 in *May Blossoms, A Collection of Hymns to the Blessed Virgin*, ed. Sisters of Notre Dame (Cincinnati, OH: Oliver Ditson & Co., 1872), 38. Here is only printed the first stanza and refrain; in the hymnal there are four stanzas with the refrain. The author of this text is anonymous. See J. Vincent Higginson, *Handbook for American Catholic Hymnals* (New York: The Hymn Society of America, 1976), 93.

2. Remember, Mary, Virgin fair,
      It never yet was told
That he who humbly sought thy care,
      Departed unconsoled. **R.**

3. O Mother blest! for me obtain,
      Ungrateful though I be,
To love that God, Who first could deign
      To show such love to me. **R.**[33]

The themes from the *Memorare* are often coupled with the idea discussed in chapter 2, that one must go through Mary to reach Christ because Mary is seen as the kind mediatrix while Christ is the stern Judge. This sentiment is found in "Queen and Mother! many hearts" where Mary is repeatedly referred to as the "Gate of Heav'n." Stanza 5 specifically describes how it is only possible to reach Christ by going through Mary, while stanza 6 seems to refer to Mary's role at the time of death.

1. Queen and Mother! many hearts
      Cast themselves before thy throne,
But we call ourselves by right
      Very specially thine own.
Oh, then be to each one here
The *"Gate of Heav'n,"* O Mother dear,
Oh, then be to each one here
The *"Gate of Heav'n,"* O Mother dear.

2. We have pledged ourselves to fight
      In the battles of thy Son,
We would pass by thee to Him
      When the dusty fight is won.

---

33. Alfonso M. de Liguori, "Memorare," Hymnary.org, http://www.hymnary .org/text/o_mother_blest_whom_god_bestows, accessed April 2014. Taken from #66 in *English and Latin Hymns, or Harmonies to Part I of the Roman Hymnal: for the Use of Congregations, Schools, Colleges, and Choirs*, ed. J. B. Young (New York: Fr. Pustet and Co., 1884), 95. For more information, see Higginson, *Handbook for American Catholic Hymnals*, 87.

Be to all enlisted here
The *"Gate of Heav'n,"* O Mother dear,
Be to all enlisted here
The *"Gate of Heav'n,"* O Mother dear.

5. Thou unto the King of Kings
    Wert a Gate to earth and us.
We must go to Christ thro' thee,
    We can reach Him only thus.
Oh, be thou to each one here
The *"Gate of Heaven,"* O Mother dear.
Oh, be thou to each one here
The *"Gate of Heaven,"* O Mother dear.

6. When the midnight cry is heard,
    Do not let us be too late,
Do not let thy children call,
    "Open, open, Lord, Thy Gate,"
But, because we loved thee here
Let us in, O Mother dear.
But, because we loved thee here
Let us in, O Mother dear.[34]

"And My Dying Words Shall Be 'Virgin Mother, Pray for Me!'"[35]

Marian congregational song also articulates the theme of Mary's companionship and prayers at the deathbed. Bradley reinforces the fact that "death was a much more common experience for Victorian children than it is for young people today," so much so that in the nineteenth century, of every one hundred babies born, fifteen would die within their first year.[36] In Caswall's "Hail, Queen of the Heavens,"

34. "Queen and mother many hearts," Hymnary.org, http://www.hymnary.org/text/queen_and_mother_many_hearts, accessed April 2014. Taken from #128 in *American Catholic Hymnal*, 162. Here are printed stanzas 1, 2, 5, and 6; in the hymnal there are six stanzas total. The text is attributed to "S.N.D." (Sister of Notre Dame). See Higginson, *Handbook for American Catholic Hymnals*, 89.

35. From stanza 3 of "O Maiden Mother, tender and mild."

36. Ian Bradley, *Abide with Me: The World of Victorian Hymns* (Chicago: GIA Publications, 1997), 113.

a translation of the Latin hymn *Salve mundi Domina* for the feast of the Immaculate Conception, the last two stanzas in particular refer to Mary and her role at death. In stanza 3, Mary is referred to as "Light of the grave" and one that we must go through in order to reach the "haven of rest." In stanza 4, Mary is asked not only to guide us through the pilgrimage on earth but also to be with us at the time of death.

1. Hail Queen of the Heavens: hail Mistress of earth:
   Hail Virgin most pure of immaculate birth.
   Clear Star of the Morning, in beauty enshrined,
   O, Lady, make speed to the help of mankind.

3. O Mother of mercy, O Star of the wave,
   O Hope of the guilty, O Light of the grave:
   Through thee may we come to the haven of rest,
   And see Heaven's King in the courts of the blest.

4. These prayers and these praises I lay at thy feet,
   O Virgin of virgins, O Mary most sweet.
   Be thou my true Guide through this pilgrimage here,
   And stand by my side when my death shall draw near.[37]

"This is the image of our Queen," another text by Caswall, also solicits Mary's help at the end of life. In stanza 3, Mary is asked to remember the narrator when he or she is lying on death's bed. Then in stanza 4 is the familiar notion of asking Mary to intercede for someone while they are at the Judgment-seat standing in front of Christ.

3. Full sweet the flowrets we have culled
   This image to adorn,
   But sweeter far is Mary's self,
   That rose without a thorn.

37. Edward Caswall, "Hail, queen of the heavens," Hymnary.org, http://www.hymnary.org/text/hail_queen_of_the_heavens, accessed April 2014. Taken from #171 in *A Treasury of Catholic Song: Comprising Some Two Hundred Hymns from Catholic Sources Old and New*, ed. Sidney S. Hurlbut (New York: J. Fischer & Bro., 1915). Here are printed stanzas 1, 3, and 4; in the hymnal there are four stanzas total. This text appeared in: Edward Caswall, *Lyra Catholica* (London, 1849). See Higginson, *Handbook for American Catholic Hymnals*, 79–80.

Most holy Mary, at thy feet I bend a suppliant knee:
When I on bed of death shall lie,
By Him Who did for sinners die,
Do thou remember me.

4. O Lady, by the stars that make
A glory round thy head,
And by thy pure uplifted hands
That for thy children plead,
When at the Judgment-seat I stand
And my Redeemer see,
When waves of night around me roll
And hell is raging for my soul,
O then remember me.[38]

In addition to Mary's prayers at the time of death, Mary is also implored to intercede for the souls in purgatory, as seen in Frederick Faber's text "O turn to Jesus, Mother, turn." In the first stanza, Mary is asked to call out to Jesus as she prays for the souls in purgatory. In stanza 4, she is reminded that they are her children who are suffering, so she must go and help them. The sixth and final stanza tells Mary that her prayers will be heard by God, for they are "His law of charity."

1. Oh! turn to Jesus, Mother, turn,
   And call Him by His tend'rest names;
Pray for the holy souls that burn
   This hour amid the cleansing flames.

4. They are the children of thy tears;
   Then hasten, Mother, to their aid.
In pity think each hour appears
   An age while glory is delayed.

---

38. Edward Caswall, "This is the image of the Queen," Hymnary.org, http://www.hymnary.org/text/this_is_the_image_of_the_queen, accessed April 2014. Taken from #166 in *A Treasury of Catholic Song*. Here are printed stanzas 3 and 4; in this hymnal there are four stanzas total. This text is found in: Edward Caswall, *Masque of Mary and other Poems* (London: Burns and Lambert, 1858). See Higginson, *Handbook for American Catholic Hymnals*, 92.

5. O Mary! let thy Son no more
   His lingering spouses thus expect;
   God's children to their God restore,
   And to the Spirit His elect.

6. Pray, then, as Thou hast ever prayed;
   Angels and souls all look to thee;
   God waits thy prayers, for He hath made
   Those prayers His law of charity.[39]

A few Marian congregational songs also seek Mary's protection during the evening hours, a time of darkness and danger. The notion that evil would come during the night dates back to early Christianity. The texts that ask for Mary's protection at nighttime include "As the dewy shades of even," "Fading, still fading, the last beam is shining," and "When evening shades are falling."

"Ave Maria! Thou Virgin and Mother"[40]

Many of the Marian congregational songs from this period reflect the virtues of True Womanhood as described by Welter. "Ave Maria! thou Virgin and Mother" not only repeats the impossibility of any woman being both virgin and mother but also ends each stanza by referring to Mary as "Sinless and beautiful Star of the Sea." This is an example of yet another unattainable quality, as all humans (outside of Jesus and Mary) are sinful. Stanza 4 also includes the familiar image of fleeing to Mary for shelter and protection.

---

39. Frederick W. Faber, "O turn to Jesus, mother, turn," Hymnary.org, http://www.hymnary.org/text/o_turn_to_jesus_mother_turn, accessed April 2014. Taken from Roman Catholic Church, *Hymns and Songs for Catholic Children* (New York: Catholic Publication Society, 1870), 107–8. Here are printed stanzas 1, 4, 5, and 6; in this hymnal there are six stanzas total. While some hymnals print more, others print less. This text is found in: Frederick W. Faber, *Jesus and Mary* (London: J. Burns, 1849). See Higginson, *Handbook for American Catholic Hymnals*, 107.

40. "Ave Maria! thou Virgin and Mother," #93 in *The Standard Catholic Hymnal: Complete Edition*, ed. James A. Reilly (Boston, MA: McLaughlin & Reilly Co., 1921), 104.

1. Ave Maria! thou Virgin and Mother,
    Fondly thy children are calling to thee;
  Thine are the graces, unclaimed by another,
    Sinless and beautiful Star of the Sea.

4. Ave Maria! thy arms are extending,
    Gladly within them for shelter we flee;
  Are thy sweet eyes on thy lonely ones bending?
    Sinless and beautiful Star of the Sea.[41]

"How pure and frail and white," written by Adelaide Anne Procter (1825–1864), juxtaposes the image of the snowdrop flower with the description of Mary's annunciation. The snowdrop is a flower that normally blooms in the winter, so it would be in bloom by the time of March 25, the date of the feast of the Annunciation. It is often common that the flowers given to Mary have a meaning. In addition to being a symbol of hope—since this is a flower that blooms in the winter and is therefore an early sign of spring—there is also a legend linking this particular flower to Eve in the Garden of Eden, invoking the Mary/Eve parallel.[42] The flowers, which are described as "pure, frail, and white" might also be seen as referencing Mary's purity.

1. How pure, how frail, and white
    The snowdrops shine,
  Gather a garland bright
    For Mary's shrine.

41. "Ave Maria, thou virgin and mother," Hymnary.org, http://www.hymnary.org/text/ave_maria_thou_virgin_and_mother, accessed April 2014. Taken from #93 in *Catholic Church Hymnal with Music*, ed. A. Edmonds Tozer (New York: J. Fischer & Bro., 1905), 126. Here are printed stanzas 1 and 4; in this hymnal there are four stanzas total. This text by "Sr. M." is found in: Marist Brothers of St. Mungo's School, Glasgow, ed., *St. Patrick's Catholic Hymn Book* (London: Burns and Lambert and Oates, 1862). See Higginson, *Handbook for American Catholic Hymnals*, 75.

42. Apparently an angel turned snowflakes into snowdrop flowers to show Eve that the winter would soon end. See Martha the Floral Therapist, "Snowdrop Flower is the Symbol of Hope," The Floral Therapist http://thefloraltherapist.com/snowdrop-flower-is-the-symbol-of-hope/, accessed April 2014.

Refrain: Hail Mary, Hail Mary,
       Queen of Heav'n,
         Let us repeat,
       And place our snowdrop wreath,
         Here at her feet.

2. For on this blessed day
    She knelt at pray'r
When lo! before her shone
    An Angel fair. **R.**

3. Hail Mary! infant lips
    Lisp it today,
Hail Mary! with faint smile,
    The dying say. **R.**

4. Hail Mary! many a heart
    Broken with grief,
In that angelic prayer
    Has found relief. **R.**[43]

In "Maiden Mother, meek and mild"—ironically another text also written by a woman—there is a focus on Mary's submissiveness, one of the four cardinal virtues of True Womanhood. James White points out that in the nineteenth century, there was an emphasis on "Mary's submissiveness to the will of God" as well as her "subservience,"[44] and this is found throughout Cecilia M. Caddell's (1814–1877) text, as Mary is repeatedly referred to as "meek and mild."

1. Maiden Mother, meek and mild,
Take, oh, take me for thy child,
All my life, oh, let it be
My best joy to think of thee,
Virgo Maria!

43. Adelaide A. Procter, "How pure, how [and] frail, and white," Hymnary .org, http://www.hymnary.org/text/how_pure_how_and_frail_and_white, accessed April 2014. Taken from #14 in *May Blossoms*, 25.

44. James F. White, *Roman Catholic Worship: Trent to Today*, 2nd ed. (Collegeville, MN: Liturgical Press, 2003), 86.

3. Teach me also through the day
   Oft to raise my heart and say:
   "Maiden Mother, meek and mild,
   Guard, oh, guard thy faithful child!
   Virgo Maria!"[45]

Mary's lowliness is highlighted in Caswall's "What mortal tongue can sing your praise," a translation of the Latin text *Quis te canat mortalium* for the feast of the Annunciation. Beginning in the second stanza, the question is posed, "what sweet force" was it that led God to choose Mary as the dwelling place for God's Son? Stanza 3 replies that is was not simply Mary's "guileless faith," or her "pure, seraphic love," or her "peerless chastity." The full answer is given in stanza 4: it was Mary's *lowliness* that was "Well pleasing to the Lord" and made her "worthy to become / The Mother of the Word."

1. What mortal tongue can sing thy praise,
   Dear Mother of the Lord?
   To angels only it belongs
   Thy glory to record.

2. O Virgin, what sweet force was that,
   Which from the Father's breast
   Drew forth his co-eternal Son
   To be thy bosom's guest?

3. 'Twas not thy guileless faith alone,
   That lifted thee so high;
   'Twas not thy pure, seraphic love,
   Or peerless chastity;

4. But oh! it was thy lowliness,
   Well pleasing to the Lord,

45. Cecilia M. Caddell, "Maiden Mother, meek and mild," Hymnary.org, http://www.hymnary.org/text/maiden_mother_meek_and_mild, accessed April 2014. Taken from #150 in *American Catholic Hymnal*, 185. This text is found in: Henry Formby and John Lambert, eds., *Collection of Catholic Hymns: For the Use of Choirs and Congregations (Catholic Sacred Songs)* (London: Burns and Lambert, 1853). See Higginson, *Handbook for American Catholic Hymnals*, 83.

That made thee worthy to become
The Mother of the Word.[46]

The Liturgical Movement and Its Effect

Virgil Michel and the Liturgical Movement in the United States

Virgil Michel (1890–1938), the driving force behind the liturgical movement in the United States, wrote that "Pius X tells us that the liturgy is the indispensable source of the true Christian spirit; Pius XI says that the true Christian spirit is indispensable for social regeneration. Hence the conclusion: The liturgy is the indispensable basis of Christian social regeneration."[47] Drawing on the work of such Europeans as Prosper Guéranger and Lambert Beauduin, Michel sought to reform the liturgy to encourage active participation by the faithful. This reform meant favoring the corporate act of participating in the Mass over individual, private devotions, including "praying the rosary while the priest prayed the Mass."[48] Private, popular devotions—such as the Marian devotions in the months of May and October—had a tendency to overshadow corporate worship focused around the liturgical year. Mary's month of May, for example, would overshadow the Easter season happening at the same time, perhaps because it was during the popular devotions such as the rosary that the faithful had "the only possibility for some form of corporate prayer outside the context of the Mass."[49]

---

46. Jean-Baptiste de Santuel, "What mortal tongue can sing thy praise," Hymnary.org, http://www.hymnary.org/text/what_mortal_tongue_can_sing_thy _praise, accessed April 2014. Taken from #129 in *The Catholic Hymnal: Containing Hymns for Congregational and Home Use, and the Vesper Psalms, the Office of Compline, the Litanies, Hymns at Benediction, Etc.*, ed. Alfred Young (New York: Catholic Publication Society, 1885), 123. Here are printed stanzas 1 through 4; in the hymnal there are five stanzas total. Caswall's text is found in his 1849 *Lyra Catholica*. See Higginson, *Handbook for American Catholic Hymnals*, 93.

47. Virgil Michel, "Liturgy as the Basis of Social Regeneration," *Orate Fratres* 9 (1935): 545.

48. Keith Pecklers, *The Unread Vision: The Liturgical Movement in the United States of America: 1926–1955* (Collegeville, MN: Liturgical Press, 1998), 43.

49. Ibid., 42.

Michel focused on corporate worship and making the connection between liturgy and social justice: "Quite simply, liturgy demanded justice. In fact, liturgy was justice in action because it embodied that ideal and just society: the reign of God."[50] Drawing on the imagery of the Mystical Body of Christ, Michel believed that

> the renewal of the social order would come when the Church lived as the Mystical Body of Christ with full and active liturgical participation. The Christian, then, was called to live the life of Christ daily as an unceasing act of worship. . . . For the Christian, every action was already a social action, because the believer shared membership in the body of Christ.[51]

Michel felt that if one prayed individually, one would live an individualistic life, while if one prayed communally, one could "become sincerely social in prayer."[52] This communal focus meant the lifting up of the Eucharist while pushing individualistic devotions, such as the rosary, to the side. This had an effect not only on the decline in Marian devotion but also on Marian congregational song.

Marian Decline in the 1950s?

In their study of St. Philomena parish in Pittsburgh, Pennsylvania, Timothy Kelly and Joseph Kelly examine attendance at the novena to Our Lady of Perpetual Help. Their study finds that by the 1950s "the crowds began to thin," so much so that by the end of the decade "only 40 percent of the 1950 attendance" still went to the novena.[53] Because of their findings, Kelly and Kelly are able to conclude that the 1950s may not have been as conservative as history would have us believe, but rather, changes were happening at many levels be-

---

50. Ibid., 132.
51. Ibid., 133.
52. Ibid., 133n141.
53. Timothy Kelly and Joseph Kelly, "Our Lady of Perpetual Help, Gender Roles, and the Decline of Devotional Catholicism," *Journal of Social History* 32, no. 1 (Fall 1998): 5. They continue to explain that "the trend continued unmistakably and dramatically, so that over the next two decades attendance dwindled to only 10 percent of the 1950 average."

fore Vatican II.[54] For example, in the years leading up to the feminist movement, "Catholic women who once embraced a ritual that affirmed their roles as passive nurturers increasingly rejected that feminine ideal."[55] What exactly led to the decline in the novena to Our Lady of Perpetual Help?

As discussed earlier, many people in the late nineteenth and early twentieth centuries prayed novenas and participated in devotions to obtain favors or graces from the treasury of merit. The Redemptorists, a religious congregation founded by St. Alphonsus Liguori, published *Our Lady of Perpetual Help* magazine. It highlighted favors answered by Mary, allowing them to show "the value of 'faith' over 'reason.'"[56] The novena also focused on the idea of "real power as largely immaterial and as deriving from passivity."[57] This notion led to more of an emphasis on Mary's "willingness to help Catholics endure their distress" rather than to "remove suffering" or grant "material solutions to their worldly afflictions."[58]

One might characterize the Redemptorist worldview as one of submissiveness (one of the four cardinal virtues of True Womanhood). The Redemptorists taught that people should pray for the ability to "endure suffering with grace," as it was not their place to try to change their situation, but rather to ask "for the perseverance to tolerate it."[59] This sounds very similar to the idea described by Welter that women should accept their place in the hierarchy of the cosmos (i.e., a place of subordination) and not attempt to disrupt it. But what would happen if women disrupted this way of being and "replace[d] the discourse of faith with reason[?]"[60]

As women began to work and earn their own money, they also took control over their own families, leading them to realize they were in control of their own destinies and therefore did not need to

54. Ibid.

55. Ibid., 5–6.

56. Ibid., 12.

57. Ibid., 13.

58. Ibid., 14.

59. Ibid., 15. Kelly and Kelly describe this as an "ideology of passive endurance" (ibid., 16).

60. Ibid., 16.

seek Mary's help through the corresponding devotions.[61] Drawing on the work of William Chafe, Kelly and Kelly explain how at first, women going to work during and after World War II was a behavioral change; but with the feminist movement in the 1960s, work led to ideological changes as well.[62] With the rejection of traditional women's roles observed by Kelly and Kelly in their study, they are able to see the ideological seeds of the feminist movement that would blossom in the 1960s and 1970s.[63] They also see the decline in Marian devotion as a symptom of women's "rejection of the belief that power derives from passivity"; instead of asking Mary to help them passively endure the "temporal world," women realized that they had the ability to go out and make changes themselves as they ignored society's preconceived notions about gender roles.[64]

Perhaps the decline expressed by Kelly and Kelly might also be seen as a backlash to what Paula Kane describes as a war that had been waged against women after World War II in an attempt to force them back into domesticity and their "proper" gender roles.[65] In addition to being used as a weapon against Communism, Mary was also used as a weapon to enforce notions of purity like "motherhood, homemaking, and modesty" as people began to make a connection between the "rising sexual immorality" and "the decline in Marian devotion."[66] Some complained that "women were abandoning their God-given sexual roles, thereby emasculating husbands and sons and leaving families without their natural leaders."[67] Although the cardinal virtues upheld by the notion of True Womanhood were over one hundred years old, they still seemed to have a stranglehold on women, because of the fear of women not conforming to "their God-given sexual roles."

Kane notes that the concepts of Fátima and the Cold War also became intertwined with "the modesty crusade" as Mary was seen as someone who could help fight Communism because of the as-

---

61. Ibid.
62. Ibid., 18.
63. Ibid.
64. Ibid., 20–21.
65. Kane, "Marian Devotion since 1940," 104.
66. Ibid.
67. Ibid., 105.

sociation of the apparitions at Fátima with the conversion of Russia.[68] Even the way women dressed was somehow associated with Communism: "Seductive feminine fashion was not just a domestic menace, moreover; women were assured that cosmic issues were at stake and that their style of dress was a beacon of civilization against the immorality promoted by the 'Red Dragon of Russia.'"[69] These ideals associated with Mary in the 1950s made it difficult for Marian devotion (and congregational song) to survive the tumultuous and liberating times of the 1960s and 1970s.

Musical Developments

Musical Movements and Documents

The Formation of Societies

Prosper Guéranger began his reform of liturgical practices and Gregorian chant by looking to models of the past, particularly the "Mythic Middle Ages." In addition to Guéranger, there were others who also made an effort to move from the "'theatrical' music of the baroque and Romantic eras" to Gregorian chant in the Church's liturgy.[70] This work would be taken up by musical societies, such as the American Cecilian Society, founded in the United States in 1873. The goal of the Cecilian society was to move from "decadent church music" to "that of a liturgical character, revive classical polyphony, and encourage the use of the official Ratisbon chant."[71]

Anthony Ruff comments that "Cecilianism is important for its contribution to historical consciousness through its idealization of music of the past, especially Gregorian chant and Palestrina-style polyphony."[72] This "idealization of music from the past" can be seen as a symptom of Romanticism that was very popular in the nine-

68. Ibid.

69. Ibid., 106.

70. John O'Malley, *What Happened at Vatican II* (Cambridge, MA: The Belknap Press of Harvard University Press, 2008), 72.

71. Anthony Ruff, *Sacred Music and Liturgical Reform: Treasures and Transformations* (Chicago: Hillenbrand Books, 2007), 111.

72. Ibid., 76.

teenth century.[73] Musical societies were not the only ones interested in renewing the Catholic Church's music; several papal musical documents of the first half of the twentieth century supported the same type of music as the Cecilian movement: Gregorian chant and polyphony (in the style of Palestrina).

Tra le Sollecitudini *(1903)*

O'Malley describes how Pius X's instruction on sacred music, *Tra le Sollecitudini,* was representative of his larger goals to "rally the faithful against the spirit of the age by fostering modes of worship that purportedly prevailed in the Middle Ages or patristic era and that would effect the spiritual regeneration of society. Implicit in the decrees, therefore, was the principle that changes could legitimately be made to make the present conform to a normative past."[74] In *Tra le Sollecitudini,* one seems to see the "Mythic Middle Ages" creeping in. *Tra le Sollecitudini* called for "sacred music" over "profane" or "secular music," particularly the music of Gregorian chant and polyphony.[75] Although the congregational singing of Gregorian chant may not have caught on everywhere, O'Malley admits that Pius X did succeed "in promoting frequent, even daily" Eucharist, and his notions of liturgical and musical reform (including the more active participation of the laity) would be "take[n] to its logical conclusion" at Vatican II.[76]

Mediator Dei *(1947)*

Ruff describes Pius XII's encyclical on the Sacred Liturgy, *Mediator Dei,* as "a position of cautious affirmation" of the liturgical movement.[77] While affirming the liturgical movement's use of the image of the Mystical Body of Christ and describing the Latin language as a "sign of unity," *Mediator Dei* also said the vernacular "can often be of great pastoral use (MD 60)."[78] *Mediator Dei* continued the call of

---

73. Ibid., 78.
74. O'Malley, *What Happened at Vatican II*, 72.
75. Ibid., 72–73.
76. Ibid., 73.
77. Ruff, *Sacred Music and Liturgical Reform*, 293.
78. Ibid., 294.

Pius X and the liturgical movement for the laity's participation in the liturgy (MD 80).[79] In regard to music, *Mediator Dei* offered a "more favorable and tolerant attitude toward modern music" (MD 193) and uplifted congregational singing (MD 194).[80] This favorable attitude toward modern music, the vernacular, and the liturgical movement, while all important, would also contribute to the decline of Marian congregational songs in the years leading up to Vatican II.

Musicae Sacrae Disciplina *(1955) and* Instructio de Musica Sacra et Sacra Liturgia *(1958)*

Pius XII's encyclical on sacred music, *Musicae Sacrae Disciplina*, moved beyond *Tra le Sollecitudini* in allowing music that had previously been deemed "profane" as well as allowing for a greater use of vernacular music.[81] Pius XII's instruction on sacred music and Sacred Liturgy, *Instructio de Musica Sacra et Sacra Liturgia*, written weeks before his death, is described by Ruff as a "summary and codification of preceding directives presented in great detail" and therefore does not say much that is new.[82] Ruff does point out, however, that this document contains more of a "legalistic spirit" as well as "a desire to limit the influence of the Liturgical Movement."[83]

The Effect of Musical Movements and Documents in the United States

The Effect of the Liturgical Movement

In the United States, the leaders of the liturgical movement worked to implement Pius X's call for more active participation, and this included the realm of music and singing in the liturgy. Like Pius X, the liturgical movement used chant (from Solesmes, not Ratisbon) as the model to help in the "call for the restoration of congregational

---

79. Ibid.
80. Ibid., 295.
81. Ibid., 296.
82. Ibid., 305.
83. Ibid.

singing."[84] Introducing congregational song into the liturgy was not easy; in fact, some felt it was "superfluous to the liturgy itself" and even "interfered with their private devotions" that were said during Mass.[85] Keith Pecklers also describes how "American Catholics continued to resist chant as cold and uninteresting, compared with the more emotionally-charged operatic music in vogue during those years."[86]

With regard to Marian congregational song, while the liturgical movement welcomed Marian chants, other forms of Marian congregational songs were not as welcomed; in general, the leaders of the movement favored Gregorian chant over hymnody. When some would argue that they were "singing liturgically" through the corporate singing of "Bring flowers of the fairest/rarest," the response of those in the liturgical movement was that "all congregational singing was not necessarily liturgical."[87] The point of singing during corporate worship was to contribute "to the upbuilding of the Mystical Body of Christ" and to shift the focus from the individual to the community, which constituted the body of Christ.[88]

The Effect of Musical Documents on Hymnals

Many of the hymnals of this period were influenced by one or more of the papal encyclicals written on music. Some hymnals named Pius X in their title, such as the Marist Brothers' *American Catholic Hymnal* (1921), which in its complete title mentions that it is written "According to the Motu Proprio of his Holiness Pope Pius X."[89]

---

84. Pecklers, *The Unread Vision*, 256.

85. Ibid., 257.

86. Ibid.

87. Ibid., 258. It seems the liturgical movement was looking for "Catholic hymns that have been traditionally approved, or that ring with a true Catholic tone and spirit," particularly "parts of the Mass in Latin and in Gregorian melody."

88. Ibid. The liturgical movement also asserted that liturgical music should be "connected to the liturgical act of the assembly" as opposed to "music that was strictly performance." See Pecklers, *The Unread Vision*, 279.

89. Marist Brothers, ed., *American Catholic Hymnal: An Extensive Collection of Hymns, Latin Chants and Sacred Songs for Church, School and Home, Including Gregorian*

There is also the *Pius X Hymnal* (1956) that was compiled by the Pius Tenth School of Liturgical Music. Other hymnals, such as the *De La Salle Hymnal* (1913) and the *Treasury of Catholic Song* (1915) contain mention of *Tra le Sollecitudini* in the preface. In 1955 the *Mediator Dei Hymnal* was published, named for Pius XII's document.[90] *Our Parish Prays and Sings* (1959), as Boccardi points out, is based on *Musicae Sacrae Disciplina*, which had only come out four years before.[91]

Marian Congregational Song as Influenced by Musical Movements and Documents

When Were Marian Congregational Songs Sung?

When exactly were Marian congregational songs sung before Vatican II? Boccardi claims that "most devout Catholics knew singing and vernacular hymns . . . through attendance at novena services, Benediction, parish missions, Stations of the Cross, and May crownings."[92] Many of the Marian congregational songs already commented on were associated with these devotions, particularly novenas, Stations of the Cross, the May crownings, and other devotions related to the month of May. While the laity was able to participate through singing at these services, they were to be silent during the Mass, since the music (if there was any) was usually sung by the choir.[93] It was really not until Pius XII's 1955 encyclical on sacred music, *Musicae Sacrae Disciplina*, that vernacular music was given an "official" place in the Mass.[94]

Masses, Vesper Psalms, Litanies, Motets for Benediction of the Blessed Sacrament, Etc., According to the Motu Proprio of His Holiness Pope Pius X (New York: P. J. Kenedy and Sons, 1921).

90. Cyr de Brant, ed., *Mediator Dei Hymnal: For Unison Choirs and Congregations* (Toledo, OH: Gregorian Institute of America, 1955).

91. Donald Boccardi, *The History of American Catholic Hymnals Since Vatican II* (Chicago: GIA Publications, 2001), 16.

92. Ibid., 7.

93. Ibid., 7–8.

94. Thomas A. Thompson, "The Popular Marian Hymn in Devotion and Liturgy," *Marian Studies* XLV (1994): 124.

Metrical hymnody—outside of the Liturgy of the Hours—was never "a regular element in the Western Roman Catholic Eucharist."[95] Metrical hymnody was used, however, outside of the "official liturgy," thus creating a "dichotomy between official liturgy and popular religious music," a dichotomy that "remained in force until the twentieth century, and to some extent the distinction still holds."[96] Many Marian congregational songs from before Vatican II—like other hymns sung before Vatican II—were sung outside of the liturgy, were directed at peoples' emotions, were not in fact intended to be liturgical, were not very theological, and were in the vernacular.[97] Because many of the pre–Vatican II Marian congregational songs were tied to devotional practices outside the liturgy, they did not fit into a post–Vatican II theological and liturgical framework, and with the liturgical reforms brought on by Vatican II, there was no longer any place for them.

Some churches had a long tradition of using the vernacular during the Mass, such as in Germany, but in most countries, there was either the "sung/solemn/high Mass" (the *missa cantata*) where the choir sang all the music in Latin, or "read Mass" (the *missa lecta*).[98] It was during the *missa lecta* that there were increasing allowances for the use of vernacular, as well as congregational participation in spoken responses, leading to the "dialogue Mass."[99] The "dialogue Mass" or "low Mass"—approved by *Mediator Dei*—not only provided the people the opportunity to participate by reciting responses but also functioned as the vehicle through which "popular songs" and

95. Frank C. Quinn, "Liturgical Music as Corporate Song 2: Problems of Hymnody in Catholic Worship," in *Liturgy and Music: Lifetime Learning*, ed. Robin A. Leaver and Joyce Ann Zimmerman (Collegeville, MN: Liturgical Press, 1998), 310–11.

96. Ibid., 311. Carl Daw points out that the dichotomy Quinn refers to "parallels a comparable split in Protestant congregational song between less formal materials (associated with gospel songs and Sunday School songs) and more formal ones (strophic hymns used in Sunday worship)." Carl P. Daw, Jr., e-mail message to author, February 22, 2012.

97. Ibid., 311–12.

98. Ibid., 313.

99. Ibid.

metrical hymns came to be sung during the Mass.[100] These songs were often sung during the "procession moments of the Mass,"[101] or what Robert Taft refers to as the "soft points" of the Mass.[102]

Marian Congregational Songs on the "Black List"

Michael Malloy describes many of the congregational songs associated with "extra-liturgical activities" as being "largely of a sentimental, pietistic nature."[103] This type of music (as well as "overly theatrical music"), was challenged by Pius X in *Tra le Sollecitudini*.[104] As a result, dioceses attempted to regulate what music was being sung in churches. They created two lists of music: that which was approved (the "white" list), and that which was not approved (the "black" list).[105] In 1922, the Society of St. Gregory of America—founded by Nicola A. Montani among others—created such a "Black List" of music that was "not in accordance" with *Tra le Sollecitudini*.[106]

The list of banned music and hymnbooks included several which contained many popular Marian congregational songs, such as *May Chimes*, the *Wreath of Mary*,[107] and "all editions to date" of the *St. Basil's Hymnal*. *The New St. Basil Hymnal* (1958) sought to rectify this condemnation by changing the contents of the hymnal, even noting

100. Ibid.; and Higginson, *History of American Catholic Hymnals*, 207.

101. Quinn, "Liturgical Music as Corporate Song 2," 313–14.

102. Robert Taft, "How Liturgies Grow: The Evolution of the Byzantine 'Divine Liturgy,'" *Orientalia Christiana Periodica* 43 (1977): 8–30; available from http://jbburnett.com/resources/taft,%20evolution%20of %20ltg.pdf, accessed August 2014.

103. Michael James Molloy, "Liturgical Music as Corporate Song 3: Opportunities for Hymnody in Catholic Worship," in *Liturgy and Music: Lifetime Learning*, ed. Robin A. Leaver and Joyce Ann Zimmerman (Collegeville, MN: Liturgical Press, 1998), 328.

104. Pecklers, *The Unread Vision*, 256–57.

105. Ibid., 257.

106. Society of St. Gregory of America, "The Black List Disapproved Music," Musica Sacra Church Music Association of America, http://www.musicasacra .com/pdf/blacklist.pdf, accessed June 2014, 86.

107. The copy of the *Wreath of Mary* used for this study (from the Burns Library at Boston College) had a handwritten note on the inside cover page saying "Disapproved on 'White List.'"

that this new edition was "approved by The White List Committee of the Society of Saint Gregory of America."[108] On the list of "Miscellaneous Disapproved Music" are two Marian congregational songs that were very popular in the late nineteenth and early twentieth centuries: "Mother dearest, Mother fairest" and "Mother dear, O pray for me."[109]

There was a great deal of tension surrounding music and the liturgy in the years leading up to Vatican II, and Marian congregational song and devotion were right in the center of the debates. In fact, O'Malley describes the 1950s as a time when "behind the placid façade that Catholicism present[ed] to the world, a clash of epic proportions was waiting to happen."[110]

---

108. Boccardi, *The History of American Catholic Hymnals since Vatican II*, 15.
109. Society of St. Gregory of America, "The Black List Disapproved Music," 87.
110. O'Malley, *What Happened at Vatican II*, 89.

Chapter Six

The Madonna Is Not Pleased
When She Is Put above Her Son[1]

Mary the Dawn, Christ the Perfect Day;
Mary the Gate, Christ the Heav'nly Way!
. . . .
Mary the Mother, Christ the Mother's Son;
Both ever blest while endless ages run.[2]

—Justin Mulcahy, CP, "Mary the Dawn"

Introduction

This text, although written by Fr. Justin Mulcahy almost ten years before the beginning of Vatican II in 1962, points to what was to come: a more balanced Mariology in which Mary is discussed in rela-

---

1. John XXIII, as quoted in Hilda Graef, *Mary: A History of Doctrine and Devotion; With a New Chapter Covering Vatican II and Beyond by Thomas A. Thompson* (Notre Dame, IN: Ave Maria Press, 2009), v.

2. Stanzas 1 and 7 of #221,"Mary the Dawn," in *Hymns, Psalms and Spiritual Canticles: A Parish Music Manual* ed. Theodore Marier (Belmont, MA: BACS Publishing Co., 1983), 195. This text and tune by Justin Mulcahy (1894–1981) first appear in: Pius X School of Liturgical Music, *The Pius X Hymnal: For Unison, Two Equal or Four Mixed Voices* (Boston, MA: McLaughlin & Reilly, 1953). See J. Vincent Higginson, *Handbook for American Catholic Hymnals* (New York: The Hymn Society of America, 1976), 84. The authorship of "Mary the Dawn" often appears under the pseudonym "Paul Cross."

tion to Christ, rather than by herself, as well as the use of biblically based imagery to describe Mary. This move to a more minimalist approach to Mary did not come without a battle at Vatican II.

Following the "long nineteenth century,"[3] with its great devotion to Mary through the apparitions at Lourdes and Fátima, the promulgation of the Immaculate Conception in 1854, and twentieth-century developments—including the promulgation of the Assumption in 1950—there was much discussion during Vatican II about whether or not a new Marian doctrine would be defined.[4] According to John O'Malley, devotion to Mary "was in fact one of the most striking and distinguishing characteristics of Catholic piety that had never been stronger than on the eve of Vatican II."[5]

This chapter begins by examining the proceedings at Vatican II and the debates between the minimalists (progressives) and maximalists (conservatives) regarding the declaration of a new Marian doctrine, and whether a statement on Mary should be included in *Lumen Gentium* or developed in a separate document. Much attention was also given to the ecumenical consequences of any further declarations on Mary, as she was being hailed as the "Promoter of Christian union."[6] Finally, this chapter will conclude by studying what was said about Mary in the eighth chapter of *Lumen Gentium* (the Dogmatic Constitution on the Church).

Vatican II and Mary

The Context of Vatican II

John XXIII's announcement in early 1959 of his intention to hold a council came as quite a surprise to everyone.[7] At Vatican I, the pope

---

3. O'Malley defines "the long nineteenth century," as "the period stretching, for the Catholic Church, from the French Revolution until the end of the pontificate of Pius XII in 1958." See John W. O'Malley, "Introduction," in *Vatican II: Did Anything Happen?*, ed. David G. Shultenover (New York: Continuum, 2007), 11.

4. John O'Malley, *What Happened at Vatican II* (Cambridge, MA: The Belknap Press of Harvard University Press, 2008), 20.

5. Ibid., 188.

6. Giuseppe Alberigo, ed., *History of Vatican II*, English version ed. Joseph A. Komonchak, 4 vols. (Maryknoll, NY: Orbis; Leuven: Peeters, 1995–2003), 1:260.

7. O'Malley, *What Happened at Vatican II*, 15.

was declared infallible, so "some theologians predicted that there would never be another council because it seemed to them that now the pope could solve all problems."[8] Pius XI and Pius XII had thought about reopening Vatican I to complete it, but John XXIII—who may or may not have known of Pius XI and Pius XII's previous intentions—decided to call this council Vatican II, which he hoped would be a "new Pentecost."[9]

What exactly did John XXIII envision for this council? One word often associated with Vatican II is *aggiornamento*, a word that John XXIII used in reference to the council, which in Italian means "bringing up to date."[10] On January 25, 1959, John XXIII made the announcement that he would be calling a council, in which he outlined some of his goals: "the need to reaffirm doctrine and discipline"; "the enlightenment, edification, and joy of the entire Christian people"; and "to extend 'a renewed cordial invitation to the faithful of the separated communities to participate with us in this quest for unity and grace, for which so many souls long in all parts of the world.'"[11]

O'Malley describes John XXIII's announcement as "remarkable for two reasons."[12] The first is that John XXIII spoke "in altogether positive terms."[13] As O'Malley points out, the previous popes often spoke in a negative tone, condemning "the evils of the times."[14] John XXIII, however, was speaking in positive tones, particularly in the area of ecumenism, the second "remarkable" trait mentioned by O'Malley. "John's stated aims quite directly extended a hand in friendship to the other Christian churches, and they did so, it seemed, without

8. Ibid., 15–17.

9. Ibid., 17, and See J. N. D. Kelly, *The Oxford Dictionary of Popes* (Oxford: Oxford University Press, 2006), 321. Vatican I was never completed because of "the seizure of Rome by Italian troops in 1870." It was a "sudden inspiration from the Holy Spirit" that led to John XXIII's calling of the council (Kelly, 321).

10. O'Malley, *What Happened at Vatican II*, 9.

11. *Acta et Documenta Concilio Oecumenico Vaticano II Apparando, Series prima (Antepraeparatoria)* (Vatican City: Typis Polyglottis Vaticanis, 1960–1961), I:3–6, as quoted in O'Malley, *What Happened at Vatican II*, 17.

12. Ibid.

13. Ibid.

14. Ibid., 17–18.

strings attached."[15] In fact, John XXIII wrote in his diary that he chose the date of January 25 to announce the opening of the council because it fell at the end of the week of prayer for Christian unity. This was a "significant departure" from previous popes, such as Pius XI and Pius XII, who partook in the "papal policy of eschewing ecumenical encounters."[16] The concern for ecumenism would be very important in the discussion surrounding Mary at Vatican II.

On the Eve of "Development"

In looking at what happened at Vatican II, O'Malley makes the distinction between *ressourcement* and *ad fontes* in his discussion of the debate over continuity and discontinuity in Vatican II with regards to past councils.[17] He interprets *ressourcement* as a "return to the sources with a view to making changes that retrieve a more normative past," such as the changes made during the Gregorian Reform of the eleventh century.[18] *Ad fontes*, "the motto of the great humanist movement of the Renaissance," is, historically speaking, "a call to return to the good literature of antiquity to displace the Latin jargon or doggerel, as the humanists saw it, of 'the schools,' that is, the universities. It was a call to recover a more literary style of discourse."[19]

In the years immediately preceding Vatican II, there was a *ressourcement* seen in the theological movement in France known as *la nouvelle théologie* by those in Rome who opposed its teachings.[20] Many of these theologians were silenced by Pius XII and condemned in his 1950 encyclical *Humani Generis*.[21] What was at stake here was the issue of "development": could the teachings of the Church change over time? While many looked to John Henry Newman's *An Essay on the Development of Christian Doctrine*, there was also the understanding

---

15. Ibid., 18.

16. Ibid.

17. John W. O'Malley, "Vatican II: Did Anything Happen?," in *Vatican II: Did Anything Happen?*, ed. David G. Schultenover (New York: Continuum, 2007), 64–67.

18. Ibid., 64.

19. Ibid., 64–65.

20. Ibid., 65.

21. Ibid.

of "development" as "moving further along a given path."[22] In the case of Marian doctrine, there were the examples of the definition of the Immaculate Conception, the Assumption, and the hope for further declarations during the council.[23] It was precisely this hope for "development" that was sensed among the bishops in the antepreparatory documents of Vatican II.[24]

The Battle over Mary
De Beata Virgine Maria

From the time that Pope John XXIII announced the convening of Vatican II in 1959 to his opening address on October 11, 1962, much work was done preparing the documents and ideas to be discussed. Giuseppe Alberigo notes that the antepreparatory commission for Vatican II had over 600 *vota*[25] asking for "a document that would clarify the standing and role of the Virgin Mary."[26] Although the official *Quaestiones* did not include Mary among the topics of the Theological Commission, there were 350 bishops who raised the topic of "the Virgin's privileges, especially her mediation," some even asking for further Marian definitions, while on the other side, there were sixty bishops who had voiced their opinion against any further Marian definition, feeling that they were unnecessary and would keep those who had left the Catholic Church from returning.[27] Already a

22. Ibid., 65–66.

23. Ibid. In differentiating *ressourcement* from development, O'Malley writes that *ressourcement* "looks to the past for norms or practices or mind-sets that somehow are going to change or correct or at least qualify the direction of current developments" (ibid.).

24. Joseph Prior points out that "the planning of Vatican II involved two phases: antepreparatory and preparatory." See Joseph G. Prior, *The Historical Critical Method in Catholic Exegesis* (Rome: Pontifica Università Gregoriana, 1999), 135n12.

25. Prior describes the *vota* as "comments or opinions" that were collected during the antepreparatory work. These *vota* "would be solicited from the bishops of the world, from the Curia, and from the universities" and they "would contain items of issues which the contributor thought needed addressing by the council." See Prior, *The Historical Critical Method in Catholic Exegesis*, 135n12.

26. Alberigo, *History of Vatican II*, 2:480.

27. Ibid., 1:257n342.

division was evident among the bishops as to what to do regarding Mary: should there be a further definition of Mary or should they refrain from saying anything about her that would impede ecumenism?

Sebastian Tromp, the author of the original outline on Mary (*De deposito*), seemed to favor not having a separate schema for Mary: "the Blessed Virgin Mary belongs to the center and not to the periphery of the Church."[28] Luigi Ciappi, a member of the subcommission that was charged to "prepare the work of the TC [Theological Commission],"[29] elaborated the outline in *Schema compendiosum De deposito*: "The Blessed Virgin Mary. Not at the periphery but at the heart of Christianity: as the Mother of the Word Incarnate. Partner of Christ the Savior, Most holy Mother of all the members of Christ, Universal Mediatrix. Virgin before giving birth, while giving birth, after giving birth."[30] During the meeting on December 21, 1960, Tromp and the secretaries of the Theological Commission's subcommission put the schema for the Blessed Virgin Mary into the schema on the Church, *De Ecclesia*.[31]

Carl Balič, a mariologist who worked for the Holy Office, was given the task of preparing the text on Mary, and he presented his first draft in April 1961.[32] A few months later in July the second draft appeared "as the fifth chapter, 'De Maria Matre Iesu et Matre Ecclesiae' of the 'Capita varia' *De Ecclesia*."[33] Balič went about composing the three-page text with fourteen and a half pages of notes (mostly references to papal documents). Here was proposed a document that was not going to say anything new about Mary in an attempt to give Mary a role of unity, urging her to be prayed to as the "Promoter of Christian union"[34] in the ecumenical movement.

In the written comments from the September plenary session of that year, some wondered why this schema was in *De Ecclesia* and not

28. Ibid., 1:257n344.
29. Ibid., 1:227n246. The Theological Commission was asked by John XXIII to investigate "questions concerning Sacred Scripture, Sacred Tradition, faith and morals" (ibid.). Tromp served as the secretary of the Theological Commission.
30. Ibid., 1:258.
31. Ibid.
32. Ibid.
33. Ibid.
34. Ibid.

in a separate document.[35] Some felt the document was "excessive," while others felt it was not strong enough. It is also important to note that the title was changed from "Mater Ecclesiae" to "De Maria, Matre Corporis Christi Mystici"; this is another instance of the opposition created by the minimalists against saying something new about Mary, such as declaring her "Mother of the Church" (*Mater Ecclesiae*).

The text was revised again in March 1962, and Balič pointed out that it might be better to have a separate text so the schema could be "expanded."[36] The subcommission of *De Ecclesia* accepted the text and approved it. Tromp, however, objected to the "statements about the mediation of Mary," and the subcommission adjusted the statement, taking this into consideration. The Central Preparatory Commission (CPC) approved the text in April, but not without the intervention of Pope John XXIII.[37]

While some members of the CPC worried about the "assertion of the mediation of Mary," others, such as Cardinal Augustin Bea, did not: "We should not be afraid of offending the Protestants; today many of them sincerely venerate the Blessed Virgin."[38] The Theological Commission held firm on the issue of mediation, feeling that by not addressing it, they would be seen as bowing to the Protestants and also admitting that they had made an error in referring to Mary as mediator in the past.[39] Here is evidence of the growing conservative (maximalist) view of Mary. It seems, however, that this issue was not one of concern about devotion to Mary, but rather of refusing to compromise Catholic beliefs in order to make the Protestants comfortable, as well as avoiding admission of having proclaimed incorrect teachings for centuries. While most of the bishops seemed to be happy with *De Beata Maria Virgine*, there was still a "substantial minority," including the theologian Yves Congar, who asked the council to "not promulgate any new Marian doctrines, particularly because of the ecumenical implications."[40]

35. Ibid. All information in this paragraph comes from Alberigo, *History of Vatican II*, 1:258 and 1:258n349.

36. Ibid., 1:259. All information in this paragraph comes from this source.

37. It seems that someone did not want the text to be printed, possibly Tromp.

38. Alberigo, *History of Vatican II*, 1:259 and 1:259n354.

39. Ibid., 1:259.

40. Ibid., 1:260.

Genesis of the Document within the Council

"No part of the constitution on the Church gave rise to as many commentaries or elicited such a flood of publications as what the Council said about the Virgin Mary."[41] The document on Mary would lead to one of the closest votes in the entire council. The document's story within the council begins as it was sent to the CPC in June 1962. Vatican II opened in October 1962, and on November 10, 1962 the document on Mary was distributed to the members of the council, but was "not discussed during the first period of the Council." At the end of January 1963, the Conciliar Commission decided that the document would be separated from the schema on the Church and sent separately. It was distributed to the council fathers on April 22, 1963, and "was unchanged except in title, which had become 'The Virgin Mary, Mother of the Church.'" Many hoped for a further definition of Mary as coredeemer or "Mother of the Church."[42] This title had become a major "point of contention" at the council because, according to the Doctrinal Commission, although "it lacked any theological basis, it was nonetheless proclaimed, at the end of 1964, by a formal act of Pope Paul VI."[43]

The authors of the schema made it clear that they had worked objectively, seeking to avoid errors on both the maximalist and minimalist side.[44] They also wanted to show that they were working toward "ecumenical openness" by avoiding the use of terms that might be valid, yet "difficult for the separated brethren to understand."[45] Again the council attempted to put ecumenism first. This is a common theme in Vatican II; an open, friendly dialogue that would pervade the documents of the council.[46] This spirit of dialogue and engagement with the modern world started with the man who convened

---

41. This quote and the following material are taken from Alberigo, *History of Vatican II*, 2:480–81.

42. O'Malley, *What Happened at Vatican II*, 188.

43. Alberigo, *History of Vatican II*, 2:480–81n313.

44. Ibid., 2:481.

45. Ibid.

46. John O'Malley, *Four Cultures of the West* (Cambridge, MA: The Belknap Press of Harvard University Press, 2004). See especially chap. 3, "Poetry, Rhetoric, and the Common Good."

the council, Pope John XXIII. He set the tone for the council in 1959 not only by what he said but also by the style in which he said it. Vatican II was "Pope John XXIII's call to 'open a window and let in a little fresh air' to the Catholic Church."[47]

In his discussion of the "four phenomena in the history of the West" which he calls the "four cultures of the West,"[48] John O'Malley describes Vatican II as fitting into "Culture Three," which is more about open, friendly dialogue as opposed to "Culture Two." Culture Three, the "Humanistic Culture" is marked by dialogue and a penchant for the literary form, specifically the use of "a rhetorical, not a dialectical style," and its goal is "to change society for the better" by seeking "common ground" through compromise.[49] Culture Two, the "Academic/Professional Culture," on the other hand, is marked by a "style of discourse" that is "logical, rigorous, left-brain discourse that moves to resolution," and its goal is the "close examination of particulars that lead to precise distinctions formulated in sharply defined concepts."[50]

For O'Malley, *how* you say something is inseparable from *what* you say (the "spirit" and the "letter") because "the form conveys content."[51] The shift in style from what came before Vatican II, to the style that was used in the documents of Vatican II was quite marked—much like the difference that is being noted from Pope Francis as compared to Pope Benedict XVI—and as O'Malley writes, this change in style was deliberate:

> [a] style choice is an identity choice, a personality choice, a choice in this instance about the kind of institution the council wanted the church to be. The fathers chose to praise the positive aspects of

---

47. Colleen McDannell, *The Spirit of Vatican II: A History of Catholic Reform in America* (New York: Basic Books, A Member of the Perseus Books Group, 2011), x.

48. O'Malley, *Four Cultures of the West*, 1.

49. Ibid., 16, 175–76. The other two cultures are Culture One, "Prophetic Culture," and Culture Four, "Artistic Culture."

50. Ibid., 12. While Vatican II embodies Culture Three, the Council of Trent and its documents replete with "anathemas" would be an example of Culture Two. See O'Malley, *Four Cultures of the West*, 103–15.

51. O'Malley, "Introduction," 81, 83.

Catholicism and establish the church's identity on that basis rather than by making Catholicism look good by making others look bad. In this way and in others the style shift expressed and promoted a shift in values and priorities.[52]

Vatican II embodied Culture Three in its use of dialogue and desire for collegiality, particularly in the document *Gaudium et Spes* (the Pastoral Constitution on the Church in the Modern World).[53] Unlike previous Catholic documents, which had a mostly negative attitude toward the world (many of which were discussed in chapter 4), *Gaudium et Spes* also "raise[s] appreciation for the positive."[54] In addition to affirming "the dignity of the human person," *Gaudium et Spes* also speaks of "the need to work together for the common good—specifically to work together on issues such as poverty, war and peace, and the arms race."[55]

As the schema on the Church stood in March 1963, it represented the approach of the maximalists. Those who wanted the Marian schema in the Church schema represented the approach of the minimalists, who "located the Mother of God in the history of salvation."[56] Alberigo notes that "the final reintegration of the schema in *Lumen Gentium* would respond to the ecumenical concerns of Vatican II: veneration of the Blessed Virgin Mary would receive a christological foundation."[57] The minimalists desire to keep a hold on Marian devotion and doctrine, mostly in the name of ecumenism, would eventually win.

Debate during the Council and the Vote

The maximalists and minimalists continued to clash in the debate preceding the vote on the Marian document. Bishop García Martínez, titular bishop of Sululos, pointed out what the minimalists saw as the

---

52. O'Malley, *What Happened at Vatican II*, 305.
53. Unless otherwise indicated, all quotations in this book from the Vatican II documents come from Austin Flannery, ed., *Vatican Council II: The Conciliar and Postconciliar Documents* (Collegeville, MN: Liturgical Press, 2014).
54. O'Malley, *Four Cultures of the West*, 177.
55. Ibid.
56. Alberigo, *History of Vatican II*, 2:480–81.
57. Ibid., 2:481n316.

absurdity of some Marian devotion when he asked "how much longer the Church was to be embarrassed by such 'relics' as Our Blessed Lady's milk and veil, St. Joseph's sandals, and the like."[58] The theme of ecumenism, which preceded the debate on Mary, continued over into the Marian debate. Cardinal Alfredo Ottaviani,[59] who made a failed attempt to move the discussion on Mary before *De Ecclesia*, asserted, "As a matter of fact, we have many points in common with our separated brethren. We are united in our love for her. After discussing various points of difference, it is well for us to remember that she can serve to unite us."[60] Bishop Luigi Carli, the spokesman for Ottaviani, offered the stronger, more conservative, and uncompromising view in his complaints against the schemas for *De Ecclesia* and the document on revelation, saying that it did not matter if they "offend Protestants. Thus it seems as though we cannot speak of the Blessed Virgin Mary, nor may we talk of the Church Militant. We dare not mention communism. We can hardly mention ecumenism, and we will be outlawed if we bring up justice or chastity. Thus the council is slowly petering out before a series of taboos."[61]

Archbishop Ferrero di Cavallerleone, however, offered the minimalist view of attaching the schema on Mary to *De Ecclesia*, because he felt "it was not possible to speak of the Church without speaking of Mary."[62] The cardinal archbishop of Santiago de Chile spoke on behalf of the forty-four Latin American bishops, and he agreed with Archbishop Ferrero di Cavallerleone, saying it was common in Latin American countries for devotion to Mary to be "too far removed from

58. Xavier Rynne, *Vatican Council II* (Maryknoll, NY: Orbis Books, 1993), 58.

59. Ottaviani was "secretary (head) of the Holy Office from 1959" as well as a "member of the Central Preparatory Commission" and "president of the Preparatory Theological Commission and of the Doctrinal Commission." See O'Malley, *What Happened at Vatican II*, 325.

60. Rynne, *Vatican Council II*, 105. After extolling Lourdes, Fátima, "and other Marian apparitions with a view to winning acceptance for his proposal," Ottaviani said: "Those who explain my [Mary's] prerogatives, will have eternal life."

61. Ibid., 113.

62. Ibid., 159. Archbishop Ferrero di Cavallerleone was the Italian prelate of the Order of Malta.

the proper devotional life of the Church."[63] The theology of Mary
was to be placed within the "whole doctrine of Christian salvation,"
and therefore the schema should be a part of the schema on the
Church.[64] The bishop of Cuernavaca (Mexico) agreed, making an
interesting point about ecumenical dealings and misunderstandings
among Catholics and non-Catholics:

> It was desirable to demarcate the boundaries of Marian devotion to
> correct certain tendencies in popular devotion, and in order to ex-
> plain the matter better to non-Catholics who sometimes had wrong
> notions about the Church because of these excesses. "Devotion to
> Mary and the saints, especially in our countries, at times obscures
> devotion to Christ."[65]

It seems as though the great outpouring of devotion to Mary, following the "long nineteenth century" and the promulgation of the
two latest Marian dogmas had created too much emphasis on Mary
and not enough on Christ. This trend is certainly evident in regard
to the music devoted to Mary preceding Vatican II. There were those,
however, who wanted to maintain the maximalist perspective in Marian devotion. The cardinal archbishop of Tarragona argued against the
minimalist perspective as he spoke on behalf of the fifty-six Spanish
bishops. In his defense of Marian devotion, which was strong among
his flock of believers, he argued to keep Mary's document separate
from *De Ecclesia* because in his words, "the mystery of Mary is greater
than the mystery of the Church."[66]

During the council, Archbishop Pericle Felici[67] warned against
distributing pamphlets within the council hall. Fr. Balič, who wanted
a separate schema for Mary, continued to distribute his Marian pam-

63. Ibid., 160. This echoes a statement John XXIII made to the Roman clergy
in which he warned against the cultivation of "certain excessive devotional
practices, even with respect to devotion to the Madonna."

64. Ibid.

65. Ibid., 161.

66. Ibid.

67. Felici was an Italian canonist who served as "secretary of the Central
Preparatory Commission" and "secretary of the Council." See O'Malley, *What
Happened at Vatican II*, 323.

phlet within the council hall, abusing his powers by printing the pamphlet through the Vatican Press to make it look like an official schema.[68] Despite such underhanded tactics as those of Fr. Balič, the minimalists narrowly prevailed in what was taken by some as a vote "for" or "against" Mary when the vote was taken on October 29, 1963.[69] The final vote was 1,114 to include the Marian schema in *De Ecclesia* and 1,074 to keep the Marian schema separate, a margin of only forty votes. Following the announcement of the final results, "there was a profound silence."[70] This would be one of the closest votes during the entire council.[71]

Elizabeth Johnson describes this as marking a "seismic upheaval" in which the "theological earth shifted back to realignment with the pattern of the first millennium."[72] While Marian devotion in the first millennium may be described as objective, that is, focusing on Mary and the saints while belonging to "the spacious framework of biblical and creedal faith," Marian devotion in the second millennium is subjective—it is emotional, focusing solely on Mary and her "ability to obtain and dispense mercy."[73] The "clash of the titans" at Vatican II marked the battle between these two understandings of Mary, with the "curialist representatives of the 'Age of Mary'" supporting the second millennium approach, fighting against the "northern European alliance," who favored the first millennium approach, which included an open, rather than closed view to the modern world.[74] The question of Mary as a symbol of whether or not the Catholic Church is turning in on itself or allowing itself to "enter into history

---

68. Rynne, *Vatican Council II*, 175, 196, 212.

69. Ibid., 212.

70. Ibid., 214. Rynne notes that five votes were invalid because they forgot to use a "special magnetic pen" used to facilitate the counting of ballots by electronic computer. Thomas Thompson describes the silence after the vote as "a 'sepulchral silence.'" See Thomas A. Thompson, "Vatican II and Beyond," in *Mary: A History of Doctrine and Devotion. With a New Chapter Covering Vatican II and Beyond by Thomas A. Thompson* (Notre Dame, IN: Ave Maria Press, 2009), 412.

71. O'Malley, *What Happened at Vatican II*, 189.

72. Elizabeth Johnson, *Truly Our Sister: A Theology of Mary in the Communion of the Saints* (New York: Continuum, 2003), 128.

73. Ibid., 119.

74. Ibid., 128.

and engage the social and political implications of the gospel"[75] will be explored later.

Although Pope Paul VI—who was elected pope after John XIII's death in June 1963—did not interfere "on principle" with the proceedings dealing with Mary, he did later announce his favor for incorporating her into the schema on the Church, and later conferred the title "Mother of the Church" to Mary during his address to the council on November 21, 1964 at the closing of the third session.[76] Paul VI did not go as far as to please the maximalists by proclaiming a new Marian dogma, but he did spend much of his speech defending the new title he conferred, a title that was a point of contention from the earliest proceedings on Mary, even before the council opened in 1962.[77] Paul's speech was seen as "an indirect rebuke to the Theological Commission for having refused Mary the title which he now gave her."[78] O'Malley points out that the reasons why the title "Mother of the Church" had been left out of *Lumen Gentium* included that "the title was not traditional, it would displease Protestants, but, most fundamentally, it seemed to put Mary above the church rather than within it, where she was the preeminent model for Christians."[79] Despite the fear that this new title would create more clamor for another Marian dogma, the opposite seemed to happen, as the "moderate" position for ecumenism and restraint won out.[80] Paul VI would later speak further about Mary with his apostolic exhortation *Marialis Cultis* (For the Right Ordering and Development of Devotion to the Blessed Virgin Mary) in 1974.

75. Ibid.

76. Rynne, *Vatican Council II*, 265, 281–82, 425. See also O'Malley, *What Happened at Vatican II*, 246. O'Malley writes that Paul VI "said that now was the time to grant what so many of the faithful throughout the world desired, that during the council her maternal role in the lives of the Christian people be announced. Therefore, 'for the glory of the Blessed Virgin and for our consolation, we declare her Mother of the Church.' There was much applause from the crowd in the church. The pope had just officially conferred upon Mary a new title."

77. See Rynne, *Vatican Council II*, 425–26 for the Commission's comments on why the title was omitted from *Lumen Gentium*, including issues of ecumenism and the desire for a "persuasive, biblically-inspired" approach to Marian teachings.

78. Ibid., 425.

79. O'Malley, *What Happened at Vatican II*, 246.

80. Rynne, *Vatican Council II*, 444.

Chapter 8 of Lumen Gentium

After all the arguments about whether or not to say something new about Mary and give her a separate document or to include her in what became *Lumen Gentium,* what exactly was said about Mary at the council?[81] The chapter on Mary seems to have left the door open to further discussion:

> It does not, however, intend to give a complete doctrine on Mary, nor does it wish to decide those questions which the work of theologians has not yet fully clarified. Those opinions therefore may be lawfully retained which are propounded in Catholic schools concerning her, who occupies a place in the Church which is the highest after Christ and also closest to us. (LG 54)

The second section, "The Function of the Blessed Virgin in the Plan of Salvation," talks about Mary's place in the Hebrew Bible and New Testament, and Mary in her relationship to Christ from the incarnation as a "predestined mother" to her role at Pentecost (LG 55–59). Here again is mention of Mary's predestination, as well as the comparison between Mary and Eve, both themes that were prevalent in the declaration of the Immaculate Conception in 1854. The third section, "The Blessed Virgin and the Church," reiterates that there is only one Mediator, Christ, while still giving Mary the titles of "Advocate, Helper, Benefactress, and Mediatrix" (LG 60–62). After all the debate on the mediation of Mary and her overshadowing of Christ, the document tries to make it clear that Christ's place is first and foremost while Mary's role is only subordinate: "The Church does not hesitate to profess this subordinate role of Mary, which it constantly experiences and recommends to the heartfelt attention of the faithful, so that encouraged by this maternal help they may the more closely adhere to the Mediator and Redeemer" (LG 62). This section ends by discussing Mary as a model for the Church and describing her special relationship with the Church (LG

---

81. O'Malley points out that the inclusion of Mary within the document on the Church drew from Henri de Lubac's book *Splendour of the Church* (published in French in 1954) which had a final chapter on Mary, "The Church and Our Lady." See O'Malley, *What Happened at Vatican II,* 188.

63–65). Mary and the Church are compared as virgins both faithful to their spouses, themes that have been running through Christianity since the fourth century when Ambrose declared Mary "the type and image of the Church."[82]

The fourth section on "The Cult of the Blessed Virgin in the Church" notes that Mary is "above all angels and men" and "second only to her Son," which gives her the right to be honored by a "special cult in the Church" (LG 66). While Mary is accorded a special place, the document is quick to note that devotion to her should not be taken too far, warning of "false exaggeration"; here is the minimalist perspective, fearing a maximalist view that would hinder ecumenism: "Let them carefully refrain from whatever might by word or deed lead the separated brethren or any others whatsoever into error about the true doctrine of the Church" (LG 67). The chapter on Mary ends with the fifth and final section, "Mary, Sign of True Hope and Comfort for the Pilgrim People of God." Pope John Paul II would later pick up the idea of Mary as a "sign of certain hope and comfort to the Pilgrim People of God" in the second chapter of his encyclical *Redemptoris Mater*.[83] This section ends with a nod to the ecumenical impact of Mary by acknowledging the worship of Mary among "separated brethren . . . especially among the Easterns, who with devout mind and fervent impulse give honor to the Mother of God, ever virgin" (LG 69).

After such a contentious debate about Mary at Vatican II, what effect would this "seismic upheaval" have? What would it mean to have Marian theology and devotion shift back to a minimalist view after remaining in a maximalist view for so long? And what would all of this mean for Marian congregational song?

82. Luigi Gambero, *Mary and the Fathers of the Church: The Blessed Virgin Mary in Patristic Thought* (San Francisco, CA: Ignatius Press, 1999), 198. See the discussion of the Mary/Church parallel in chap. 1.

83. John Paul II, *Mary: God's Yes to Man—Pope John Paul II's Encyclical* Redemptoris Mater, introduction by Joseph Cardinal Ratzinger and commentary by Hans Urs von Balthasar (San Francisco: Ignatius Press, 1988), 95–122 (chap. 2, "The Mother of God at the Center of the Pilgrim Church").

Chapter Seven

Whatever Happened to Mary?[1]

Mary, Mary, quite contrary,
rebel, giving ear to God,
earth-soprano, singing freedom:
Zion's song in 'yes' and blood.[2]

—Fred Kaan, "Mary, Mary, quite contrary"

Introduction

Vatican II signaled the beginning of a new era in Marian devotion and theology as can be seen from Fred Kaan's above text. This chapter will look at what effects this had in Catholicism, both at an international level, and more locally, in the United States. First, there will

---

1. Taken from the Chumbawamba song, "Mary Mary" from the 1999 movie *Stigmata*. For complete lyrics see "Chumbawamba Mary Mary (stigmata mix) Lyrics," ST Lyrics, http://www.stlyrics.com/lyrics/stigmata/marymarystigmaticmix .htm, accessed June 2014.

2. Stanza 1 of Fred Kaan, "Mary, Mary, quite contrary," Hope Publishing Company, http://www.hopepublishing.com/html/main.isx?sitesec=40.2.1.0&h ymnID=3469, accessed April 2014. Reproduced by permission from Hope Publishing Company © 1999. This text is also known as "A tentative hymn to/about Mary with asterisks (stardust)." It is set to the tune STARDUST by Peter Churchill.

be an exploration of the Marian devotion and writings of the popes, beginning with John XXIII through Benedict XVI. Some of the Marian apparitions in the late twentieth century will be surveyed, along with developments in Marian feasts and liturgies. Post–Vatican II Catholic spirituality in the United States will be examined, particularly the perceived post–Vatican II "piety void" and the impact of the feminist movement on Marian devotion. Finally, the impact of some of the Catholic liturgical and musical documents published after Vatican II on US Catholic hymnals and Marian congregational song will be assessed. It should be noted that these final two chapters will offer a more critical view of Roman Catholic ecclesial documents and teachings as a more open and positive view of Marian theology and devotion is sought through the lens of hymnody.

Worldwide Catholic Developments

Papal Encyclicals, Pronouncements, and Marian Devotion
John XXIII (1958–1963)

John XXIII's Mariology, while not as strong as Pius XII's, still comes through in his *Journal of the Soul*, where his Marian devotion can be perceived as "sincere, authentic, and, in comparison with some tendencies of the time, restrained."[3] As is seen from the title of chapter 6, John XXIII was wary of Marian devotion that could be seen as "excessive" or "sentimental" and would lead to elevating Mary above Christ; instead he preferred "the simpler practices and doctrine of the early Church."[4]

Despite his restraint in Marian devotion as compared to Pius XII, John XXIII still valued Mary's intercession. In the week leading up to the opening of Vatican II (which was October 11, "the feast of the Divine Maternity of the Virgin Mary"), John XXIII visited the House of Loreto and spoke highly of Mary, calling her the "first

---

3. J. N. D. Kelly, *The Oxford Dictionary of Popes* (Oxford: Oxford University Press, 2006), 321; and Thomas A. Thompson, "Vatican II and Beyond," in Hilda Graef, *Mary: A History of Doctrine and Devotion; With a New Chapter Covering Vatican II and Beyond by Thomas A. Thompson* (Notre Dame, IN: Ave Maria Press, 2009), 407.

4. Thompson, "Vatican II and Beyond," 407.

star above the council."[5] He called on Mary's intercession, noting that "in future years, may it be said, that, through Mary's motherly intercession, the grace of God prepared, accompanied and crowned the twenty-first Ecumenical Council, imparting to all the children of the Holy Church new fervor, generosity, and firmness of intention."[6]

Paul VI (1963–1978) and Marialis Cultis (1974)

The kind-hearted man known as "Good Pope John"—now Saint John XXIII—was followed by Paul VI, a man who, as Cardinal Montini attending the first session of Vatican II, "spoke of Mary as 'Mother of the Holy Church'"[7] and later conferred that title on Mary in his new role as pope. Paul VI continued John XXIII's call for peace in the world, and in 1967 he visited Fátima "(at her [Mary's] personal bidding, he claimed), to pray for peace."[8] Paul VI also tried to quell the fear of some that Vatican II and its liturgical reforms were "not favorable to Marian devotion."[9] In *Signum Magnum* (1967), he wrote that "there need be no fear . . . that the reform of the liturgy . . . involves any diminution of the 'altogether singular' veneration of the Mother of God."[10]

After Vatican II, there was a perceived "piety void," particularly in the realm of Marian devotion. It was in response to this perceived decline, and the petitions of those like Fr. Patrick Peyton who asked "that the rosary be accepted as a liturgical prayer," that Paul VI wrote *Marialis Cultis* in 1974.[11] *Marialis Cultis* twice refers to the goal of "the right ordering and development of devotion to the Blessed Virgin Mary."[12] This seems to point to the emphasis throughout the document that any form of Marian devotion must be related to Christ

5. John XXIII, *Journal of a Soul*, 400, as quoted in Thompson, "Vatican II and Beyond," 408.

6. Ibid.

7. Thompson, "Vatican II and Beyond," 409.

8. Kelly, *Oxford Dictionary of Popes*, 323–24.

9. Thompson, "Vatican II and Beyond," 414.

10. Paul VI, *Signum Magnum*, as quoted in Thompson, "Vatican II and Beyond," 414.

11. Thompson, "Vatican II and Beyond," 417.

12. Ibid.

(a theme from Vatican II), because Marian devotion is Christian worship insofar as "it takes its origin and effectiveness from Christ, finds it complete expression in Christ, and leads through Christ in the Spirit to the Father" (MC introduction).[13] In the introduction to *Marialis Cultis*, Paul VI writes about the changes that devotions had undergone since Vatican II which necessitated the writing of this document: "Certain practices of piety that not long ago seemed suitable for expressing the religious sentiment of individuals and of Christian communities seem today inadequate or unsuitable because they are linked with social and cultural patterns of the past."

Marialis Cultis is divided into three sections which include reflections on (1) Mary in the liturgy, (2) "considerations and directives suitable for favoring the development of that devotion [to Mary]," and (3) the rosary (MC introduction). The section on liturgy explores Mary's place in the revised liturgical calendar and Lectionary. Here is expressed the need to balance the emphasis on Mary and Christ in worship in an effort to make sure that any devotion to Mary always points to Christ, because in the past "in certain forms of popular piety" Mary has been separated from Christ (MC 4). This is a tendency seen repeatedly in Marian congregational songs written before Vatican II, many of which do not mention Christ at all.

In the section on Marian devotion, Mary is offered as a model to the Church as she is described as the "attentive Virgin," the "Virgin in prayer," the "Virgin-Mother," the "Virgin presenting offerings," and as the "teacher of the spiritual life for individual Christians" (MC 16–21). Here again Mary is upheld as an unattainable model for women as no other woman can be both virgin and mother. In the section on Mary as the "Virgin in prayer," the *Magnificat* is described as "Mary's prayer par excellence" (MC 18), and the liberating qualities of the *Magnificat* will be further explored in the next chapter.

In addition to offering ways in which Mary is a model, the section on devotion also offers "principles" in an attempt to renew Marian devotion, which has been "subject to the ravages of time" (MC 24).

---

13. All references to *Marialis Cultis* come from: Paul VI, For the Right Ordering and Development of Devotion to the Blessed Virgin Mary (*Marialis Cultis*), 2 February 1974, Papal Encyclicals Online, http://www.papalencyclicals.net/Paul06/p6marial.htm, accessed June 2014.

As a result of this renewal, the elements that are "transient" should be replaced by an emphasis on "the elements that are ever new" as old Marian devotions are revised and new ones are created (MC 24).[14] Some of the principles listed include the need for Marian devotion to be trinitarian (including a christological and/or pneumatological orientation) and linked to the work of the Church, which reflects Mary's concerns (MC 25, 26, 28). The interests of the Church and Mary include those in "lowly circumstances," the "poor and weak," and a desire for "peace and social harmony" (MC 28).

Next is a discussion of "guidelines from Scripture, liturgy, ecumenism, and anthropology" which are to be used in revising any existing Marian devotions or the making of new devotions (MC 29).[15] This section includes a discussion of the proper relationship between Marian devotion and the eucharistic sacrifice as well as "modern anthropological studies" that can be applied to Marian devotion (MC 31, 34). The discussion of anthropology includes issues raised by the feminist movement as the document acknowledges that previous images of Mary presented in devotions "cannot easily be reconciled with today's life-style, especially the way women live today" (MC 34).

Marialis Cultis attempts to describe how Mary can be appreciated by "the modern woman" who is "anxious to participate with decision-making power in the affairs of the community" (MC 37). This statement comes across as somewhat condescending to women. *Marialis Cultis* also indicates how "the modern woman" can appreciate "Mary's choice of the state of virginity" as a "courageous choice which she made in order to consecrate herself totally to the love of God" (MC 37). Many women would find it difficult to find virginity as a "courageous choice," let alone the untold number of young girls who are forced to lose their virginity against their will at an all too young age. *Marialis Cultis* also describes how Mary can be appreciated by "the modern woman" because she is not "timidly submissive," but rather is "a woman of strength, who experienced poverty and

---

14. This sounds very similar to Vatican II's *Sacrosanctum Concilium*, which discusses the "changeable" and "unchangeable" (and "divinely instituted") elements of the liturgy. See SC 21.

15. Elizabeth Johnson explores the place of Mary in the communion of saints in *Truly Our Sister*.

suffering, flight and exile (cf. Mt. 2:13-23)" (MC 37). These themes of suffering, flight, and exile will be further reflected on in the next chapter, as they are experiences that, unfortunately, all too many women can relate to. In summary, *Marialis Cultis* feels that for all of these reasons, Mary is "the perfect model of the disciple of the Lord" (MC 37). This notion of Mary as the perfect disciple is one that would become prevalent in post–Vatican II Mariology.

After calling for the revisions of old Marian devotions and the creation of new ones (MC 40), *Marialis Cultis* discusses the *Angelus* and the rosary. First, *Marialis Cultis* uplifts the *Angelus* as a devotion that should be continued and one that does not need to be revised "because of its simple structure, its biblical character," and "its historical origin" (MC 41). It then commends "the renewal of the pious practice which has been called 'the compendium of the entire Gospel': the Rosary," a practice that is associated with prayers for peace (MC 42). Yet the recitation of the rosary during the Mass (a common practice before Vatican II) is called "a mistake"; *Marialis Cultis* instead advocates the praying of the rosary as a family (MC 48, 52). Many of the principles laid out in *Marialis Cultis* were important in directing post–Vatican II Mariology. However, as will be seen later in this chapter, there is uncertainty as to whether Paul VI's attempt to "revive" Marian devotion in the wake of Vatican II, in fact, succeeded.

John Paul I (1978)

While Paul VI "was always torn between his forward-looking vision and his suspicion of any innovation which might undermine the integrity and authority of the church's teaching,"[16] his successor, John Paul I, known as the "Smiling Pope," seemed poised to fulfill the desire of the cardinals who elected him. J. N. D. Kelly writes that "the majority of the cardinals wanted a completely new style of pope, without connections with the curial establishment," and so they chose Albino Luciani, whom they believed was "God's candidate."[17] Only three weeks after his election, John Paul I died, amid a shroud of mystery and claims that "he was poisoned because he planned

---

16. Kelly, *Oxford Dictionary of Popes*, 324.
17. Ibid., 325.

to clean up the Vatican Bank, demote important curial figures, and revise *Humanae Vitae.*"[18] It is impossible to know where John Paul I, the man who shocked the conservative-minded Vatican by referring to God as "our Mother,"[19] would have led the Catholic Church. From the little evidence he left behind, it seems it would have been in a progressive, forward-thinking path.

John Paul II (1978–2005)

While many have said that Pope John Paul II put an end to the "experimentation" that followed Vatican II, he held Mary in great esteem, somewhat in contrast to the developments surrounding Mary in Vatican II; some might even say he had a maximalist view of Mary. In fact, Mary was a part of his episcopal coat of arms; on it was "the letter *M* with the words, *Totus tuus,* an abbreviated version of the Marian consecration prayer of St. Louis Marie Grignion de Montfort: 'I am completely yours (*totus tuus ego sum*), and all that I possess is yours. I accept you in all that is mine. Give me your heart, O Mary.' "[20]

John Paul II declared a Marian Year from Pentecost 1987 to November 1, 1988, to prepare for the coming millennium, and his encyclical *Redemptoris Mater* (On the Blessed Virgin Mary in the Life of the Pilgrim Church)[21]—given on the feast of the Annunciation in 1987—set out a course for the Marian Year. Borrowing from the themes and images of Vatican II, the document declared that "the Church was to live consciously and intensely Mary's pilgrimage of

18. Ibid., 326. See the argument made by David Yallop that John Paul I was murdered: *In God's Name: An Investigation into the Murder of Pope John Paul I,* new ed. (New York: Basic Books, 2007). See also the History channel documentary on John Paul I and his death, where they recount the story that he visited Sister Lucia, one of the Fátima seers, who said something to John Paul I that appeared to shake him. The documentary writers wonder if Lucia told John Paul I the Third Secret of Fátima which, as we will see, depicts the death of a pope. Perhaps John Paul I feared that vision was a prediction of his own death. See Brad Meltzer's "Decoded," "Vatican Conspiracy–Pope John Paul I," YouTube, http://www.youtube.com/watch?v=HFewRC3oUX4, accessed June 2014.

19. Yallop, *In God's Name,* 147.

20. Thompson, "Vatican II and Beyond," 420.

21. John Paul II, *Mary: God's Yes to Man.*

faith."[22] The continued emphasis of Marian devotion in relation to Christ is visible in Joseph Cardinal Ratzinger's "Introduction" to the encyclical in which he describes the Marian Year as "center[ing] on the special presence of the Blessed Mother within the mystery of Christ and his Church" (RM 48).[23]

John Paul II—who grew up in communist Poland—also had a special devotion to Our Lady of Fátima, which corresponds to his fight to end Communism.[24] In 1981 John Paul II was shot in an assassination attempt. The date was May 13, "the anniversary of the first Fatima apparition," and John Paul II "credited his survival to Our Lady of Fatima: 'it was the mother's hand that guided the bullet's path and in his throes the Pope halted at the threshold of death.' "[25] He continued to generate interest in the apparitions at Fátima when he revealed the Third Secret of Fátima on June 26, 2000.[26] John Paul II interpreted the "bishop dressed in white" in the vision in the Third Secret as himself; he saw the Third Secret as foretelling the assassination attempt on his life in 1981, and he traveled to Fátima a year later in a pilgrimage of thanksgiving to Mary for saving his life.[27] Like Pius XII before him, John Paul II also "consecrated Russia to the Immaculate Heart of Mary" for the conversion of Russia, both in 1982 and 1984.[28]

In addition to his devotion to Our Lady of Fátima, John Paul II also had a strong dedication to praying the rosary, what he called his "favorite prayer."[29] He furthered devotion to the rosary by adding the

22. Thompson, "Vatican II and Beyond," 420.

23. Joseph Cardinal Ratzinger, "The Sign of the Woman: An Introduction to the Encyclical 'Redemptoris Mater,' " in John Paul II, *Mary: God's Yes to Man; Pope John Paul II's Encyclical* Redemptoris Mater, Introduction by Joseph Cardinal Ratzinger and Commentary by Hans Urs von Balthasar (San Francisco: Ignatius Press, 1988), 38.

24. Kelly, *The Oxford Dictionary of Popes*, 328.

25. Thompson, "Vatican II and Beyond," 422.

26. Congregation of the Doctrine of Faith, *The Message of Fatima* 26 June 2000, The Vatican, http://www.vatican.va/roman_curia/congregations/cfaith/documents/rc_con_cfaith_doc_20000626_message-fatima_en.html, accessed June 2014.

27. Thompson, "Vatican II and Beyond," 422–23.

28. Ann E. Matter, "Apparitions of the Virgin Mary in the Late Twentieth Century: Apocalyptic, Representation, Politics," *Religion* 31 (2001): 132.

29. Thompson, "Vatican II and Beyond," 422.

Luminous Mysteries in October 2002. The new "Mysteries of Light" include: "(1) his Baptism in the Jordan, (2) his self-manifestation at the wedding of Cana, (3) his proclamation of the Kingdom of God, with his call to conversion, (4) his Transfiguration, and finally (5) his institution of the Eucharist, as the sacramental expression of the Paschal Mystery."[30]

Finally, John Paul II came very close to promulgating the fifth Marian Dogma, that of Mary as "Co-Redemptrix, Mediatrix, and Advocate."[31] The movement of the *Vox Populi Mariae Mediatrici*, led by Dr. Mark Miravalle, is similar to the grassroots movements of the faithful that led to the definitions of the Immaculate Conception and Assumption of Mary. With the support of the faithful, bishops, cardinals, and even Mother Theresa, John Paul II used the term "Co-Redemptrix" in reference to the Blessed Virgin Mary multiple times during the course of his pontificate.[32]

Benedict XVI (2005–2013)

The Marian devotion of Benedict XVI is markedly different from that of the now canonized John Paul II.[33] While Benedict XVI has written on Mary (e.g., his introduction to *Redemptoris Mater* noted earlier in this chapter), he has much more of a minimalist view of Mary than did John Paul II, as well as a strong christocentric attitude which emphasizes Mary's place "at the center of the Church."[34]

---

30. John Paul II, *Rosarium Virginis Mariae*, October 16, 2002, 21, The Vatican, http://www.vatican.va/holy_father/john_paul_ii/apost_letters/documents/hf_jp-ii_apl_20021016_rosarium-virginis-mariae_en.html, accessed June 2014.

31. The other four Marian dogmas are: (1) Divine Motherhood; (2) Perpetual Virginity; (3) Immaculate Conception; and (4) Assumption. See Fr. Johann G. Roten, "The Marian Dogmas," The Marian Library/International Marian Research Institute, http://campus.udayton.edu/mary/mariandogmas .html, accessed June 2014.

32. "Letter from Mother Theresa," *Vox Populi Mariae Mediatrici*, http://www .fifthmariandogma.com/witnesses/saints-and-sensus-fidelium/letter-from -mother-teresa-2/, accessed June 2014; and Mark Miravalle, "Pope of Mary Co-Redemptrix," *Vox Populi Mariae Mediatrici*, http://www.fifthmariandogma.com /articles/881, accessed June 2014.

33. Thompson, "Vatican II and Beyond," 423.

34. Ibid.

While John Paul II incorporated Mary into his episcopal coat of arms and motto, Benedict XVI's choice of motto is also quite telling:

> He chose as his episcopal motto [in 1977]: "Cooperators of the truth." He himself explained why: "On the one hand I saw it as the relation between my previous task as professor and my new mission. In spite of different approaches, what was involved, and continued to be so, was following the truth and being at its service. On the other hand I chose that motto because in today's world the theme of truth is omitted almost entirely, as something too great for man, and yet everything collapses if truth is missing."[35]

This desire for the truth was seen throughout his conservative tenure as head of the Congregation for the Doctrine of the Faith and his pontificate, in which he upheld traditional positions.[36] In a move that surprised many, Benedict XVI, citing his advanced age, announced his retirement as pope in February 2013 amid questions of scandal in the Vatican. The last pope to retire willingly was Pope Celestine V in 1294. Pope Gregory XII had done so in 1415 to end a schism.

Francis (2013–)

Jorge Mario Bergoglio, previously the archbishop of Buenos Aires, was elected pope in March 2013. He has since taken the world by storm through his acts of humility and service. He is a pope of

---

35. "Biography of His Holiness, Pope Benedict XVI," The Vatican, http://www.vatican.va/holy_father/benedict_xvi/biography/documents/hf_ben-xvi_bio_20050419_short-biography_en.html, accessed June 2014. Kelly briefly describes Benedict XVI's "change of heart" from being liberal to conservative following the student riots in Tübingen in 1968. See Kelly, *The Oxford Dictionary of Popes*, 330.

36. This turn to conservatism can be related back to Philip Gleason's discussion of the "Mythic Middle Ages," seen in chap. 4, with the propensity to fight against modernism and the search for unchanging truths. As Prefect for the Congregation for the Doctrine of Faith under John Paul II "he was responsible for disciplining a number of important theologians, for issuing two documents heavily criticizing 'liberation theology,' and in 2000 for *Dominus Iesus*, which insisted on the superiority of Christianity, and specifically Roman Catholicism, over other world faiths." See Kelly, *Oxford Dictionary of Popes*, 329–30.

many firsts, being the first to take the name Francis, "the first non-European pope for a thousand years, the first pope from the Southern hemisphere, the first Jesuit pope, the first pope from the Americas where more than half of the planet's 1.2 billion Catholics live."[37] Francis has made it clear that one of the main themes of his pontificate is the care of the poor, as he said at his first press conference that he "would like a poor church for the poor."[38]

In addition to growing up in a family where devotion to the rosary and Mary was important,[39] Francis also has a particular devotion to Mary that he happened on while visiting Augsburg in 1986; it is to the painting *Mary Untier of Knots* by Johann George Schmidtner that hangs in St. Peter am Perlach in Augsburg, Germany. The story is that in 1610, Wolfgang Langenmantel went to see Jesuit Fr. Jakob Rem because he was having problems with his wife Sophia, and he brought the white ribbon with him from their wedding. Recalling Irenaeus, "who had written of how 'the knot of Eve's disobedience was loosed by the obedience of Mary,'" Rem took the wedding ribbon and asked Mary's protection over the couple, praying "I raise up the bond of marriage that all knots be loosed and resolved."[40] Afterward, the couple were happy and stayed together.

In 1700, their nephew commissioned the painting, which "shows Mary unravelling the entanglements in the ribbon, assisted by two angels and surrounded by cherubs, while her foot casually crushes the head of a serpent representing the Devil."[41] Francis was so taken with this painting that he brought a postcard of it with him back to Argentina where the devotion quickly caught on, so much so that a replica painting was made and now hangs in San José del Telar in Agronomeia.[42] As one priest describes it, "they all feel they are listened to and understood by the Virgin. As Mother she is very attentive to our problems. The knots are metaphors of the difficulties

37. Paul Vallely, *Pope Francis: Untying the Knots* (London: Bloomsbury, 2013), 163–64.

38. Ibid., 175.

39. Ibid., 25.

40. Ibid., x.

41. Ibid.

42. Ibid., xi–xii.

we have. She appeals to God to help us with them."[43] Having served the people in the slums of Argentina, Francis has shown an understanding of what popular piety—and particularly devotion to Mary—can mean to the faithful.[44]

Marian Apparitions

George Tavard writes that in the twentieth century there was a "tremendous inflation" in the number of Marian apparitions—despite guidelines given by the Congregation of the Doctrine of Faith in 1978 to help diocesan bishops regulate and determine their authenticity—and that the quality of the apparitions "had deteriorated fast," as a result of "the deterioration of the religious imagination."[45] Writing in 1996, Tavard posited that this phenomenon would be "diagnosed later as a sign of the great fear of the year 2000, the fear of the third millennium and of the mutation that will be required from the church if the faith is to survive under the conditions of the electronic age."[46] As seen in chapter 2, there was a great deal of fear that accompanied the arrival of a new millennium, the first millennium, and in chapter 4 it was pointed out that many of the Marian apparitions occurred during a time of social difficulty. Both of these factors seemed to be in play at the dawn of the third millennium.

Ann Matter examines the apocalyptic themes in late twentieth-century Marian apparitions. She writes that "between 1975 and 2000 there were, on every continent of the globe, an increasing number of reports of apparitions of the Virgin Mary."[47] Matter points out—as have many of the authors surveyed in chapter 4 who studied earlier apparitions—that Marian apparitions often occur during times of social anxiety, and many of the twentieth-century Marian apparitions are a direct response to these anxieties, particularly around the issues of Communism and the fear of nuclear war.[48] While earlier appari-

43. Ibid., xii.

44. Ibid., 135–37.

45. George Tavard, *The Thousand Faces of the Virgin Mary* (Collegeville, MN: Liturgical Press, 1996), 186; and Thompson, "Vatican II and Beyond," 432–33.

46. Tavard, *The Thousand Faces of the Virgin Mary*, 186.

47. Matter, "Apparitions of the Virgin Mary in the Late Twentieth Century," 125.

48. Ibid., 127.

tions such as at Lourdes focused on healing, and others, such as at La Salette, called for repentance, in the twentieth century, Fátima marked the beginning of apparitions accompanied by overtly political messages.[49] In fact, following Fátima, there would be a proliferation of apocalyptic, "less well-accepted manifestations."[50]

One such Marian apparition that "focus[ed] on the evils of Communism" was that of Mrs. Mary Ann Van Hoof, who received apparitions in Necedah, Wisconsin from 1950 to 1962 "which included warnings of Russian submarines in the St. Lawrence Seaway."[51] Another apparition that included the theme of "the godless State" began in 1981 at Medjugorje in Bosnia-Herzegovina, when Mary began appearing to six children with a message demanding "immediate conversion in order to avoid the punishment that God will otherwise send to the world."[52] These visions address the Communist context in which the children live and also include "secrets" given to the children, which are often given "apocalyptic interpretation."[53]

Matter points out that these secrets are similar to the Three Secrets of Fátima written down by Lucia in that they contain themes of anti-Communism and are apocalyptic.[54] The first two Secrets of Fátima have been revealed for many years, and these include "a vision of Hell," the foretelling of "the death of Francisco and Jacinta, the end of the First World War, and the spread of Communism."[55] Originally the Third Secret was to be revealed in 1960, but John XXIII chose

---

49. Ibid., 128.

50. Ibid.

51. Ibid., 129. Another anti-Communist Marian apparition is that of Veronica Lueken in Bayside, New York which occurred in the 1970s and 1980s. See Paula M. Kane, "Marian Devotion Since 1940: Continuity or Casualty?," in *Habits of Devotion: Catholic Religious Practice in Twentieth-Century America*, ed. James M. O'Toole (Ithaca, NY: Cornell University Press, 2004), 120.

52. Matter, "Apparitions of the Virgin Mary in the Late Twentieth Century," 129. The apparitions at Medjugorje continue to this day.

53. Ibid.

54. Ibid. Matter points out that it was after 1945 that Fátima began to be associated with "more militant, politicized, and even paranoid uses," such as the strong anti-Communism brought on by fears of the Cold War and atomic age. See Kane, "Marian Devotion since 1940," 119–20. This would make sense as McCarthyism was particularly strong in the 1950s.

55. Ibid., 129–30.

not to, and it was not revealed until 2000 when John Paul II visited Fátima for the beatification of Francisco and Jacinta Martos, two of the Fátima visionaries.[56] While many expected the Third Secret to be apocalyptic, the Vatican stressed that it was not, and as described earlier, it was interpreted to represent the "sufferings of the Popes, especially Pope John Paul II" and the 1981 assassination attempt on John Paul II's life.[57]

Some were disappointed by the revelation of the Third Secret and accused the Catholic Church of turning against the modern world—a theme repeated in this study—and this time the accusation was that the Catholic Church was "exalting the papacy against enemies real and imagined, such as the 'Pride 2000' celebration [Lesbian, Gay, Bisexual, and Transgender (LGBT) gay pride celebration] planned and carried out in Rome in July 2000, despite the Vatican outcry against the desecration of the Holy Year."[58] Here the "enemy" is the LGBT community as the Catholic Church continues its struggle with "deeper anxieties about the old and the new, traditionalism and modernity, in Christian culture."[59]

Matter makes the point that John Paul II not only allowed the space for Marian apparitions to flourish but also shared a conservative (and Marian maximalist) stance with many apparition followers, a position of "calling the Church back from the reformist path of the Second Vatican Council."[60] Just as pre–Vatican II apparitions, such as those at Lourdes, were used to uplift and verify conservative stances of the Catholic Church (e.g., antimodernism), so too were the Marian apparitions and their followers following Vatican II. Matter also points to those who blame a "lower profile of Thomistic theology" on Vatican II.[61] As noted in chapter 4, Philip Gleason equated the antimodern stance of the Catholic Church in the late nineteenth and early twentieth century with the Neo-Thomist movement; the conservative members of the Catholic Church who did not like the

---

56. Ibid., 130. The third visionary, Sister Lucia dos Santos, was there as well, as she was still alive at the time. (She died in 2005 at the age of ninety-seven.)

57. Ibid., 131.

58. Ibid., 133.

59. Ibid., 139.

60. Ibid., 140.

61. Ibid.

"liberal" changes brought on by Vatican II also clamored for a return to Thomism. Matter makes the link between those who are anti-Vatican II and those who support Marian apparitions.[62] She aptly summarizes this link between wishing for pre–Vatican II times while also facing apocalyptic fears:

> The particularly twentieth-century phenomenon of Marian apparitions is, therefore, a Janus-faced expression of Catholic identity. One side looks back, idealising a type of devotion more prominent before Vatican II and the modernising of the Church under Pope John XXIII and Paul VI. But the other face is set in dreadful anticipation towards the unfolding of the new millennium.[63]

This link between Mary and pre–Vatican II worldview made it hard for Mary to find a place amongst those who did not consider themselves "conservative" following Vatican II.

Mary in the Liturgy

As a result of the documents of Vatican II, the cult of Mary was "revised and reduced to its essential forms."[64] Accordingly, revisions were made to the liturgical calendar regarding Marian feasts, to the readings and offices that accompanied these feasts, and to other Marian prayers used throughout the liturgy.[65] Paul VI approved the changes to the liturgical calendar in 1969. In doing so, he tried to show that "there was no conflict" between the liturgical year and Marian feasts.[66] The number of Marian feasts in the new calendar had dropped, however, which did nothing to alleviate the fears of

62. Ibid., 141. Matter also makes the point that the changes in devotion to Mary brought on by Vatican II "caused great anxiety for many Catholics," perhaps further fueling the anger of the supporters of Marian apparitions toward Vatican II (ibid., 140).

63. Ibid., 141.

64. Pierre Jounel, "The Veneration of Mary," in *Liturgy and Time*, vol. 4 of *The Church at Prayer: An Introduction to the Liturgy*, ed. Aimé Georges Martimort (Collegeville, MN: Liturgical Press, 1986), 148.

65. Ibid.

66. ICEL, *Documents on the Liturgy*, 3880, as quoted in Thompson, "Vatican II and Beyond," 414–15.

226 Sing of Mary

those who were concerned that Mary would have less of a place in the liturgy following Vatican II's reforms.[67]

Jounel, however, claims that "little has been eliminated" and the only feasts that were removed were "the memorials of the Sorrows of Mary in Lent, the Holy Name of Mary, and Our Lady of Mercy."[68] In the new calendar, the three Marian solemnities included Mary Mother of God (January 1), the Assumption (August 15), and the Immaculate Conception (December 8). The two feasts of Mary in the new calendar were the Nativity of Mary (September 8) and the Visitation, which was moved from July 2 to May 31, "so that, in accordance with the narrative in St. Luke, it comes between the Annunciation of the Lord and the Nativity of John the Baptist." The four obligatory memorials include Our Lady of Sorrows (September 15), Our Lady of the Rosary (October 7), the Presentation of Mary in the Temple (November 11), and the Queenship of Mary (August 22), which was moved from May 31 to August 22 "where it functions as a kind of octave of the Assumption." Finally, there were the four optional memorials to Mary, which include the Immaculate Heart of Mary (moved from August 22 to the Saturday after the Second Sunday after Pentecost), Our Lady of Lourdes (February 11), Our Lady of Mount Carmel (July 16), and the Dedication of St. Mary Major (August 5). In addition to the changes made regarding which Marian feasts were celebrated and when, changes were also made to the readings for the feasts. There was also the addition of four Marian prefaces to the medieval preface already in existence.

In 1965, the year of the conclusion of Vatican II, Hilda Graef wrote that "Mariology follows the trend of theology as a whole,"[69] and this is certainly what is seen in the revisions to the liturgy that involve Mary, particularly in the calendar of Marian feasts. The readings for many of these feasts were changed, and the titles of many of the feasts were altered to highlight their christological character (such as the Presentation of Our Lord and the Annunciation of Our Lord). All this was done

---

67. Thompson, "Vatican II and Beyond," 415.

68. Jounel, "The Veneration of Mary," 148. All information in this paragraph is from Jounel, "The Veneration of Mary," 148–50.

69. Hilda Graef, *Mary: A History of Doctrine and Devotion; With a New Chapter Covering Vatican II and Beyond by Thomas A. Thompson* (Notre Dame, IN: Ave Maria Press, 2009), 400.

in order to create "a happy balance between levels of piety with regard to Christ and his mother."[70] In the past, many of these feasts were so focused on Mary that they almost obscured Christ. "The theological climate and the style of popular piety of a given historical moment affect how a Marian insight is liturgically appropriated by each age. . . . If the Marian theology is overdeveloped and too highly nuanced, this might be reflected in a liturgical proliferation which a later age will recognize as excessive."[71] It seems that over time, some had come to view Marian liturgy and devotion as "excessive," and as a result, the minimalist view of Mary won at Vatican II in regards to Mary's place in *Lumen Gentium*. This was further amplified by the call in *Sacrosanctum Concilium* (the Constitution on the Sacred Liturgy) to simplify the liturgy by removing accretions that had built up over time as well as anything deemed to be "out of harmony with the inner nature of the liturgy or has become less suitable" (SC 21).

One example of the attempt to appropriately integrate Mary into the liturgy according to the norms set out at Vatican II was the 1986 publication of the *Collection of Masses of the Blessed Virgin Mary*. These Masses were created "at the request of rectors of Marian shrines" in order to create "a set of votive Masses of the Blessed Virgin."[72] Pilgrimages to Marian shrines continued to be popular in the late twentieth century, particularly with the support of John Paul II, and these Masses, which are "arranged according to the seasons of the liturgical year," allow for those on pilgrimage at Marian shrines to integrate "Marian devotion into the various seasons of the liturgical year."[73]

Catholic Developments in the United States

The decisions made at Vatican II may be seen as a turning point in Mariology from a maximalist to a minimalist position. Lukas

---

70. Kilian McDonnell, "The Marian Liturgical Tradition," in *Between Memory and Hope: Readings on the Liturgical Year*, ed. Maxwell E. Johnson (Collegeville, MN: Liturgical Press, 2000), 395.

71. Ibid., 399–400. McDonnell points to the "catalog of about 940 universal and local feasts of Mary compiled by Holweck at the end of the nineteenth century" as "an expression of this."

72. Thompson, "Vatican II and Beyond," 429.

73. Ibid., 429–30.

Vischer further describes this change "not so much to the sphere of theology as to the sphere of meditation."[74] This change is a result of the "hierarchy of truths" which came out of the teachings of Vatican II.[75] As a result of this hierarchy, Mariology moved to a "subordinate place in theology. Statements about Mary must be strictly subordinated to those about Christ. Ultimately they are simply theological meditations intended to illustrate and clarify the central content of the Gospel. . . . Mariology is simply the foil of Christology."[76]

Vischer asks whether the "traditional images of Mary" make it impossible "to construct an image of Mary which would reflect this understanding of the Church," and this new understanding includes images such as the Church as a pilgrim people and servant community.[77] He proposes that the Catholic Church is today looking for new images of Mary, and that these "new pictures of Mary" have developed as a result of the decisions made at Vatican II.[78] The images that have developed are not of Mary as Queen, but Mary as an "ordinary woman" whose "poverty," "doubt," and "perplexity" in life has been emphasized.[79] These troubling images of Mary that focus on her passivity and unquestioning obedience can be seen in much contemporary theology, including that of Catholic theologian Hans Urs von Balthasar (1905–1988).[80] While von Balthasar offers many beautiful meditations on Mary and her faith, he also writes some problematic passages which seem to take Mary's faithfulness too far. In his attempt to bring us a picture in the work *Mary for Today*, he also paints a somewhat outdated version of Mary. He brings up the passage in Paul that discusses wives being subordinate to their husbands:

74. Lukas Vischer, "Mary—Symbol of the Church and Symbol of Humankind," *Mid-Stream* 17 (January 1978): 3.

75. Ibid., 3.

76. Ibid.

77. Ibid., 10.

78. Ibid.

79. Ibid.

80. See Hans Urs von Balthasar, *Mary for Today* (San Francisco, CA: Ignatius Press, 1987), esp. 56, 74; and Balthasar's "Commentary" in *Mary: God's Yes to Man*, esp. 178–79. Balthasar's views on Mary and women in general seem somewhat outdated, even for the time they were written (1980s).

But this mutual respect in love does not stop Mary, considering the dignity of her child, from complying with his wishes when she does not understand them. And here she fits herself into the Pauline picture of how a wife should behave toward her husband. We should not speak too easily of this view being sociologically outdated. Mary is not a feminist: she remains the "handmaid of the Lord," even when she can become the "all-powerful intercessor" with her son.[81]

This problematic quote suggests that we should hearken back to the days before the feminist movement when women "knew their place" and their lesser roles to their husbands.

Another problematic passage in *Mary for Today* is where von Balthasar says, "As a woman she has her heart where it ought to be and not in the brain; and she knows that even a God who thought woman up and created her can have his heart in no other place."[82] Here he is referencing the old idea that women are emotional while men are intellectual by saying Mary kept her place as a woman by using her heart and not her brain. The reuse of these outdated notions of women in relation to Mary is not helpful at all. As will be shown in the next chapter, there are new images of Mary, particularly found in hymns, which are both faithful to the Gospel and empowering to women.

Post–Vatican II Shift in Religious Worldview

In the introduction, it was noted how abruptly Marian devotions changed—seemingly almost overnight—in the wake of Vatican II. Noting this change, Robert Orsi described how "old devotions were derided as infantile, childish, or as exotic imports from Catholic Europe, alien and inappropriate in the American context."[83] These pre–Vatican II devotions, including Marian devotions, seemed to be at odds not only with the liturgical and theological changes of Vatican II but also with the ever-changing landscape of life for a US Catholic.

81. Balthasar, *Mary for Today*, 56.
82. Ibid., 74.
83. Robert A. Orsi, *Between Heaven and Earth: The Religious Worlds People Make and the Scholars Who Study Them* (Princeton, NJ: Oxford University Press, 2005), 56.

In chapter 5, the work of Ann Taves was drawn on to paint a picture of the religious worldview of US Catholics in the nineteenth century. She described the "affective bonds" (subjective) that were formed as a result of nineteenth-century devotions, which she saw as "encouraging the formation of emotionally-charged relationships between the believer and Jesus, Mary, and the saints."[84] However, the research of Elizabeth Johnson previously mentioned in chapter 6 revealed a shift at Vatican II from a subjective Marian devotion to an objective Marian devotion. Thus one aspect of pre–Vatican II Marian devotion did not fit into a post–Vatican II theological framework.

In chapter 4 it was discussed how ultramontanism, the centralization of devotions, and the use of indulgences attached to devotions played a major role in how the Catholic Church controlled how people prayed. As the Catholic Church has been forced to come to terms with an increasingly global church in the decades following Vatican II, and as the Church loses its Eurocentric grip on the Romanization of devotions, there seems to be more latitude for inculturation and the incorporation of local devotions. The increased allowance of the use of the vernacular allowed by *Sacrosanctum Concilium* (see SC 63) and the waning use of the Latin language has played a large role in this, as people are allowed to pray in their own languages instead of the Latin that was sent to them from Rome.

Paula Kane discusses the work of Rodney Stark in the "sociology of religious economies" as a possible reason for the decline in Marian devotions, especially those that were associated with rewards such as indulgences and the "treasury of merit." She writes that Stark's work theorizes "that people choose religions for rational reasons as the basis for the axiom that 'the more expensive (i.e., sacrifice-demanding) the religion, the better bargain it is (the greater the rewards).'"[85] Since Stark found that "the higher the costs, the greater the tendency to increase participation among joiners," he speculated that "when the costs of belonging to a religion diminish . . . so will

---

84. Ann Taves, *The Household of Faith: Roman Catholic Devotions in Mid-Nineteenth Century America* (Notre Dame, IN: University of Notre Dame Press, 1986), 81–82.

85. Kane, "Marian Devotion since 1940," 114.

the strength of the religion."[86] In fact, in *The Churching of America*, Stark and Roger Finke point to the decline of Catholicism following Vatican II as proof that their theory is correct.[87] Kane then applies their theory to Marian devotions, offering a key explanation for their post–Vatican II decline:

> it would follow that once the Church diminished its emphasis on the compensators and rewards associated with devotional practices, there was no compelling impetus for believers to continue to perform them. Of course irrational events such as sickness, catastrophe, and misfortune will always generate clients for supernatural patrons, but the heyday of devotionalism was effectively ended, according to Finke and Stark's model, by the liberalizing tendencies of Vatican II.[88]

Clearly, the pre–Vatican II religious worldview of the "household of faith" as described by Taves was radically dismantled following Vatican II. With the loss of indulgences, the "treasury of merit," and the "rewards" for devotions, people were less likely to perform the devotions since they "received" nothing in return.

Finke and Stark also point to the uniqueness of Catholicism's liturgy and devotions. This uniqueness was often used to demarcate boundaries between Catholics and Protestants. In the past Mary was used as a weapon against those deemed "evil" or "heretics," but this changed at Vatican II, as Mary was now seen as a bridge-builder and an instrument for ecumenism. Here is yet another instance where the pre–Vatican II associations with Mary did not fit into a post–Vatican II theological framework.

In addition to these theological shifts surrounding Mary, another important shift in the last half of the twentieth century can be seen in attitudes surrounding death. Philippe Ariès points out that with the medical advances of the twentieth century, society has entered a time of the "medicalization of death" in that doctors now had more

86. Ibid., 115.
87. Ibid. Kane describes "a process known as sect transformation or secularization" that was a result of "lift[ing] restrictions on behavior and soften[ing] doctrines that had formerly been countercultural."
88. Ibid.

control over when and how death occurred.[89] With the medical tools that give humans more control over how and when they die, some might see less of a need to pray to a higher force (e.g., Mary) for healing from illness and safety from death, choosing instead to put their trust in medicine and science.

In addition to secular shifts in death, there is also a theological shift surrounding death in the Catholic Church, particularly in the funeral rite. This rite was touched on in *Sacrosanctum Concilium*, where it says "funeral rites should express more clearly the paschal character of Christian death, and should correspond more closely to the circumstances and traditions of various regions. This applies also to the liturgical color to be used" (SC 81).[90] As a result of the directives of *Sacrosanctum Concilium*, the Congregation for Divine Worship published the funeral rite *Ordo Exsequiarum* on August 15, 1969.[91] The Latin text was translated into English by the International Commission on English in the Liturgy (ICEL) as the *Rite of Funerals* and took effect in the United States on June 1, 1970.[92]

In the introduction to the *Rite of Funerals*, the renewed emphasis on the "hope in eternal life (article 2)," the "paschal character of Christian death," and the "Christian hope of the people . . . in the future resurrection of the baptized with Christ" are clear.[93] This shift

89. Philippe Ariès, *The Hour of Our Death: The Classic History of Western Attitudes toward Death over the Last One Thousand Years*, trans. Helen Weaver (New York: Vintage Books, 1981), 583, 585.

90. As the penitential character of funerals became common in the medieval funeral liturgy, black vestments were worn, and this was the practice up until Vatican II. After Vatican II, white vestments were (normally) used to symbolize the hope of the resurrection and the white funeral pall recalled the deceased's baptismal garment. *Sacrosanctum Concilium* also goes on to call for the revision of the funeral rites for infants and the provision for a "special Mass for the occasion" (SC 82).

91. Richard Rutherford, *The Death of a Christian: The Order of Christian Funerals* (Collegeville, MN: Liturgical Press, 1990), 115.

92. For ICEL's part in the work of translating the *Ordo Exsequiarum*, see Michael Hodgetts, "Revising the Order of Christian Funerals" in *Shaping English Liturgy: Studies in Honor of Archbishop Denis Hurley*, ed. Peter C. Finn and James M. Schellman (Washington, DC: The Pastoral Press, 1990), 199–217.

93. Catholic Church, *Rite of Funerals: The Roman Ritual Revised by Decree of the Second Vatican Council and Published by Authority of Pope Paul VI. English Translation*

from a focus on the fear of death and the torments of hell to the hope of the resurrection can be seen further in the removal of the *Libera me/Dies Irae* from the funeral rite in 1969.[94] As seen throughout this study, Mary has often been associated with "the hour of death" and has been sought as an intercessor for the souls in purgatory. It is not surprising that a shift from the fear of death to the hope of the resurrection would correspond with a decline in the association of Mary with those themes, and a falling out of favor of Marian congregational songs containing those subjects.

In connection with changing views on death are perspectives regarding sin. One way of studying these shifts is through the practice of confession, especially where one confesses sins to a priest. James Carroll describes a pre–Vatican II worldview in which persons were very mindful of their sinfulness, beating their breasts during the liturgy and saying *Domine, non sum dignus*, "Lord, I am not worthy" three times.[95] The themes of unworthiness and sinfulness are often found in pre–Vatican II Marian congregational songs. Feelings of unworthiness can be seen in a corresponding regularity of the confession of one's sins. In his discussion of the shifts in confessional practices before and after Vatican II, James O'Toole writes that before Vatican II, "Churches everywhere reported that high percentages of parishioners were confessing as often as once a month."[96] The regularity with which Catholics confessed their sins was soon to change.

Approved by the National Conference of Catholic Bishops and Confirmed by the Apostolic See (New York: Catholic Book Publishing Co., 1971), 7, 11. In 1981 ICEL called for the revision of the funeral rites which resulted in the publication of the *Order of Christian Funerals* in 1989. See Rutherford, *The Death of a Christian*, 269–72.

94. The *Dies Irae* was the sequence used in the *Requiem* Mass up until 1969. This text asks "the Lord to deliver all the faithful departed from the pains of hell, from the deep pit, from the lion's mouth, and so on." Rutherford describes the 1969 shift as one of "the preference for *Alleluia* over *Dies Irae*." See Rutherford, *The Death of a Christian*, 59–60, 124.

95. James Carroll, *Practicing Catholic* (Boston: Houghton Mifflin Harcourt, 2009), 18.

96. James M. O'Toole, "In the Court of Conscience: American Catholics and Confession, 1900–1975," in *Habits of Devotion: Catholic Religious Practice in Twentieth-Century America*, ed. James M. O'Toole (Ithaca, NY: Cornell University Press, 2004), 134. O'Toole goes on to describe (135–36) how "confession was often connected to other religious practices, and this only swelled the already

Following Vatican II, there was a significant decline in the practice of confession. O'Toole observes, "almost overnight, a sacrament that had been at the center of American Catholic practice became rare."[97] In their study of US Catholic parishes, Jim Castelli and Joseph Gremillion came to a similar conclusion. While they found that "Confession remains a part of [the] Catholic identity for three-quarters of Core Catholics," they concluded that "it is clear that frequent Confession is no longer part of the religious consciousness of Core Catholics."[98] Even though there was little said about confession at Vatican II, following the council "the number of confessions had fallen off dramatically."[99]

Why then was there such a decline in confession? O'Toole offers a few possible explanations, including: "accumulated dissatisfactions with confession among the laity"; the notion that Vatican II "seemed to authorize the American Catholic laity to act on dissatisfactions"; allowing Masses on Saturday afternoon and evening, a "time traditionally given over to confession"; the "'psychologizing' of confession"; and the location of "forgiveness and reconciliation" within the Eucharist itself, not the confession required beforehand.[100] In addition to these and other factors, an important factor involving sin had to do with the Mass being said in the vernacular and the people being aware of what they were saying, specifically during

---

large numbers of penitents." These practices included "the popular 'First Friday' devotions to the Sacred Heart," the use of confession in parish missions, as well as preparation for the sacraments of marriage and Holy Communion.

97. Ibid., 168.

98. Jim Castelli and Joseph Gremillion, *The Emerging Parish: The Notre Dame Study of Catholic Life since Vatican II* (San Francisco, CA: Harper & Row, Publishers, 1987), 148. "Core Catholics" are described as "active parish members." Their study also found that confessional practices differ according to age: "Catholics over sixty are far more likely to go to Confession than are younger Catholics" (ibid., 4, 146).

99. O'Toole, "In the Court of Conscience," 168. O'Toole writes that the decline was seen especially in "college-age young adults," a trend that seems to correspond to the findings of Castelli and Gremillion (ibid., 170).

100. Ibid., 171–75, 181–82. O'Toole also points out that the rules concerning the need to go to confession before receiving the Eucharist were also loosened after Vatican II, and because people went to communion more frequently, they felt less of a need to go to confession.

the "confiteor," which asks for forgiveness and is followed by the priest's prayer of pardon.[101] There is the possibility that people began to consider this part of the Mass—whether consciously or not—as a replacement for regular confession.[102]

O'Toole points out two "especially significant" reasons for the decline in confession. The first is "the dramatic change in the American Catholic understanding of sin."[103] Before Vatican II, Catholics were taught to confess both mortal and venial sins, but after Vatican II, there seemed to be less of a stress on confessing venial sins and more on mortal sins.[104] The distinction between mortal and venial sins also began to fade away as people, priests included, began to wonder how anyone could really decide right from wrong,[105] perhaps in the spirit of freedom and the questioning of authority that was prominent in the US culture of the 1960s and 1970s. This questioning intensified when Paul VI wrote *Humanae Vitae* in 1968, condemning birth control. As O'Toole explains, many Catholics were upset with this, and because they disagreed with the teaching, they did not feel it was necessary to confess something they did not believe was a sin.[106] In addition to changing notions about what constituted a sin, O'Toole also suggests a shift in focus from individual sin to social/collective sins associated with "structural evils."[107]

With these changes in both the secular and religious culture around the notions of sinfulness, it makes sense that Marian congregational songs that embodied a strong notion of sinfulness and unworthiness would fall out of favor. Here again, many of the pre–Vatican II Marian congregational songs did not fit into a post–Vatican II theological framework, or, for that matter, the cultural framework of the time. Another cultural movement in the years following Vatican II, the feminist movement, also had a profound impact on Marian devotions and congregational song.

101. Ibid., 174.
102. Ibid.
103. Ibid., 177.
104. Ibid., 177–78. For O'Toole's discussion of venial versus mortal sins, see p. 147. Mortal sins are generally more serious than venial sins.
105. Ibid., 178.
106. Ibid., 179.
107. Ibid., 180.

The Influence of the Feminist Movement

Chapter 5 exposed evidence of a decline in Marian devotions prior to Vatican II, including the study done by Kelly and Kelly of the devotion to Our Lady of Perpetual Help in one Pennsylvania parish in the 1950s. Taves found that there were many more women involved in "devotional organizations" and that the obedience and dependence associated with these devotions "corresponds closely to the stereotypically 'feminine' role which nineteenth-century women were expected to assume in marriage"[108]—an observation also made by Barbara Welter in her work on "True Womanhood." It makes sense that if women made up the majority of those involved in Marian devotion, then a shift in their sense of self which led to their feeling oppressed by messages of obedience and subordination (often associated with Mary) would lead to their decision to stop participating in those devotions.

In 1949, Simone de Beauvoir (1908–86) wrote *The Second Sex*, which Miriam Schneir describes as "one of the most important books ever written about the oppression of women."[109] Against the previous Victorian notions that God made women subordinate to men in the "natural order" of the world, Schneir says Beauvoir argued that "womanhood as we know it is a social construct; that is, that the subordination of female to male does not represent an immutable state of nature, but is the result of various social forces. 'One is not born, but rather becomes, a woman.'"[110] This groundbreaking work allowed women the chance to think that they did not have to live second-class lives, subordinated as "the Other."[111]

Another important book was Betty Friedan's (1921–2006) *The Feminine Mystique*, written in 1963. Schneir writes that Friedan's book "connected with the important shift in women's behavior that had been developing, nearly unnoticed, for a decade and a half: the movement of women, especially older married women, into the labor force."[112]

---

108. Taves, *The Household of Faith*, 87.

109. Simon de Beauvoir, "Selection of *The Second Sex*," in *Feminism in Our Time*, ed. Miriam Schneir (New York: Vintage Books, 1994), 3.

110. Ibid.

111. Ibid., 4.

112. Betty Friedan, "Selections from *The Feminine Mystique*," in *Feminism in Our Time*, ed. Miriam Schneir (New York: Vintage Books, 1994), 48.

This was one of the factors Kelly and Kelly believed might have led to a drop in devotion to Our Lady of Perpetual Help. While speaking with her female friends from Smith College, Friedan realized that many of them were unhappy with their lives as housewives.[113] In trying to find the cause of their unhappiness, Friedan realized that there "was a concerted campaign waged since the end of World War II to convince American women they could achieve happiness in life only through marriage and motherhood—an ideology she labeled 'the feminine mystique.'"[114] Friedan's work allowed women to believe there was more to life than "my husband and my children and my home."[115]

Insights from the feminist movement were soon applied by theologians, particularly in the critique of the male-dominated Catholic Church by Mary Daly (1928–2010) in *The Church and the Second Sex*, first published in 1968. The works of Beauvoir and Friedan influenced Daly, and she refers to them throughout her book.[116] She writes of how women have been kept "on a pedestal at all costs" leading to the "paralyzing [of] her will to freedom and personhood."[117] Women have also been burdened with the notion of the "Eternal Woman," the idea that women are "said to have a vocation to surrender and hiddenness" in addition to the forgoing of "individual realization" for the "merely generic fulfillment in motherhood, physical or spiritual (the wife is always a 'mother to her husband' as well as to her children)."[118]

Daly also acknowledges the role Mary has played in the subordination of women, because Mary too has been put on a pedestal "without having any purpose of her own."[119] Daly critiques the notion of "Mary as the model of all women" because Marian devotion

---

113. Ibid.

114. Ibid., 48–49.

115. Ibid., 67.

116. Daly refers to Beauvoir's *The Second Sex* particularly in chapter 1 and Friedan's *The Feminine Mystique* in chapter 3.

117. Mary Daly, *The Church and the Second Sex* (Boston, MA: Beacon Press, 1985), 148.

118. Ibid., 149.

119. Ibid., 61, 161. Daly refers to how women are "transfigured and enslaved" by maternity, and "this enslavement was accomplished symbolically in the cult of the Virgin Mother of God, who is glorified only in accepting the subordinate role assigned to her."

is fostered by men who are celibate priests, giving them little to no understanding of what it means to have a family, sexual experiences, or simply some knowledge of the actual experiences of women.[120] Daly posits a correlation between a strong devotion to Mary with areas where clergy have the most power and women have the least social and legal standing.[121] Throughout her work, Daly makes a strong case for the Catholic Church to start incorporating women into leadership roles (i.e., ordaining them)[122] and to take Mary down from the pedestal where she is held up as an oppressive model for women.

What would happen to Mary now that the devotions and theology surrounding her were being critiqued so strongly? Matter points out that in Marina Warner's 1976 study of Mary, *Alone of All Her Sex*, Warner ends her work "with a lament for the inability of the Virgin Mary to fill the needs of contemporary women, to be a model for the New Woman."[123] Historian Jay Dolan echoes the lament of Warner as he describes how older devotions to Mary were not speaking to younger generations: "The old devotional rituals with their traditional model of femininity have lost their appeal to women who came of age in the post-1960 era. Their search for holiness takes them along paths different from those of their grandmothers."[124]

As put forward in chapter 4, one major stumbling block in Marian devotion (and congregational song) is that Mary is both virgin and mother, and because of this, Mary is "an icon impossible for ordinary women to follow."[125] Rosemary Radford Ruether, a feminist

---

120. Ibid., 160.

121. Ibid., 161.

122. Ibid., 196–97.

123. Matter, "Apparitions of the Virgin Mary in the Late Twentieth Century," 126. Matter quotes Warner directly: "As an acknowledged creation of Christian mythology, the Virgin's legend will endure in its splendor and lyricism, but it will be emptied of moral significance, and thus lose some of its present and real powers to heal and to harm." See Marina Warner, *Alone of All Her Sex: The Myth and the Cult of the Virgin Mary* (New York: Random House, 1976), 339.

124. Jay P. Dolan, *In Search of American Catholicism: A History of Religion and Culture in Tension* (Oxford: Oxford University Press, 2002), 241.

125. Mary Grey, "Europe as a Sexist Myth," in *The Power of Naming: A Concilium Reader in Feminist Liberation Theology*, ed. Elisabeth Schüssler Fiorenza (Maryknoll, NY/London: Orbis Books/SCM Press, 1996), 245.

theologian, supports this view, calling the "Marian ideal of virgin motherhood . . . both masochistic and impossible for any woman to exemplify."[126] Despite these negative associations, Ruether admits, there were "many Catholic women" who "continued to feel an attachment to Mary and some wished to reclaim her image for a more liberated way of being women or inclusively human."[127] Ruether points to Catharina Halkes, a Dutch theologian, who "sums up the twofold motivations of reclaiming Mary for liberated women: to liberate Mary herself from the projections attached to her by a male clergy and to liberate women from images of Mary that limit their full potential."[128]

How were people to go about liberating Mary so as to help her to become a positive role model? Theologian Patrick Cheng (b. 1968) offers one possibility, describing a movement away from putting Mary on a pedestal and emphasizing her as virgin and mother and instead focusing on her "as a symbol of fertility and motherhood."[129] This would signal a shift in veneration from "the 'quiet, weak, perpetual virgin'" to "instead the 'awesome, powerful, beautiful, and fertile Queen of Heaven.'"[130] With all of these factors swirling around in the wake of Vatican II, what was to be done about Marian devotion?

The Piety Void

The great outpouring of Marian congregational song following the promulgation of the dogma of the Immaculate Conception in 1854 began to see a decline in the years just before Vatican II. Following Vatican II, there seems to be a great diminution in both the music and devotion to Mary. The void was so perceptible that Thomas Thompson writes "the term 'Marian silence' is sometimes used to describe the

---

126. Rosemary Radford Ruether, "Mary in US Catholic Culture: Two Theologies Represent Deep Divisions," *National Catholic Reporter* (February 10, 1995): 16. The article begins by noting that Ruether was to give this article as a paper at a conference in Rome, but she was later banned from the conference by the Congregation for the Doctrine of Faith.

127. Ibid.

128. Ibid.

129. Patrick S. Cheng, *Radical Love: An Introduction to Queer Theology* (New York: Seabury Books, 2011), 91.

130. Ibid.

years immediately following the council."[131] Part of the reason is that pre–Vatican II Marian devotions did not fit into the post–Vatican II context which called for scriptural foundations with a "Christological and ecclesial dimension."[132] As seen in chapters 4 and 5, many Marian congregational songs reflect pre–Vatican II Marian devotion, which was not scriptural (rather it was often based on tradition or apocryphal sources) and often not christological (many of the Marian congregational songs make no mention of Christ whatsoever).

Cardinal Suenens, who was a supporter of Marian devotion, aptly summarizes the situation following Vatican II, describing it as "a time of considerable lessening of appreciation for Mary."[133] In addition to the call in *Lumen Gentium* that Marian devotions should be biblically based and christological, there was the directive in *Sacrosanctum Concilium*, that while devotions are "highly recommended" there is also a cautioning that "such devotions should be drawn up that they harmonize with the liturgical seasons, accord with the sacred liturgy, are in some way derived from it, and lead the people to it, since in fact the liturgy by its very nature is far superior to any of them" (SC 13). This harkens back to the critiques made by those in the liturgical movement who argued that many Marian devotions did not encourage corporate worship and/or obscured the liturgical year.

Thompson writes that because of these directives, some "displayed a condescending attitude toward popular devotion" while those who supported popular devotions were uncertain "how to undertake the reform called for by the council," leading them to stand against any changes to devotions.[134] As a result of this tension between those for and against devotions, Thompson believes the downplaying of devotions "was perhaps more responsible for the 'Marian crisis' in parish life" than the debate over whether Mary should have her own document at Vatican II or be included in *Lumen Gentium*.[135] What did this "Marian crisis" look like? James White describes a "significant slackening in Marian devotions," including the

131. Thompson, "Vatican II and Beyond," 415.
132. Ibid.
133. Cardinal Suenens, as quoted in ibid.
134. Thompson, "Vatican II and Beyond," 426.
135. Ibid.

loss of the rosary and Marian congregational songs such as the *Salve Regina* amongst younger generations.[136] He also describes how other Marian-related devotions "evaporated almost overnight," including novenas and the Stations of the Cross.[137]

Dan Herr, a columnist for *The Critic*, sums up the tensions between devotions and liturgy and the resulting "piety void" in 1965. He writes that while the new liturgy seems to have been well-received, it "has not yet become sufficiently meaningful or satisfying to fill the void left by pious devotions," leaving Catholics to "feel a loss."[138] As observed earlier in this chapter, Paul VI seemed to notice this "piety void" as it affected Marian devotion, prompting him to write *Marialis Cultis* in 1974. One year before *Marialis Cultis*, the US Catholic bishops wrote a pastoral letter on Mary, "Behold Your Mother, Woman of Faith," which Thompson describes as "an acknowledgment and response to the 'crisis'" surrounding Marian devotion.[139]

In "Behold Your Mother, Woman of Faith," the bishops admit that "the Church is suffering a malaise with respect to the commemoration of Mary" and as a result offers a "middle way" with regard to Marian devotion, "between the extremes of too much and too little."[140] In order to walk the "middle way" between what might have been seen as excessive devotion to Mary before Vatican II in contrast to almost no devotion to Mary following Vatican II, the bishops point out that the revised liturgy, calendar, and Lectionary offer many opportunities for prayer to Mary. The bishops also uplift "extra-liturgical devotional forms" such as the rosary.[141] In regard

---

136. James F. White, *Roman Catholic Worship: Trent to Today*, 2nd ed. (Collegeville, MN: Pueblo/Liturgical Press, 2003), 137.

137. Ibid., 137–38.

138. Dan Herr, "Stop Pushing," *The Critic* 24, no. 2 (October–November 1965): 4, 6, as quoted in Joseph P. Chinnici and Angelyn Dries, eds., *Prayer and Practice in the American Catholic Community*, ed. Christopher J. Kauffman, American Catholic Identities: A Documentary History (Maryknoll, NY: Orbis Books, 2000), 253.

139. Thompson, "Vatican II and Beyond," 416.

140. National Conference of Catholic Bishops, *Behold Your Mother: Woman of Faith. A Pastoral Letter on the Blessed Virgin Mary*, 21 November 1973 (Washington, DC: Publications Office, United States Catholic Conference, 1973), 34.

141. Ibid., 35–37.

to Marian devotion, "great inventiveness" was called for, leading to a desire to "revitalize old forms and devise new devotions corresponding to current needs and desires."[142] Was this call heard and responded to? Sociological studies done in the US Catholic Church following Vatican II can gauge the popularity of devotions.

In its exploration of "Devotions Past and Present," *The Notre Dame Study of Catholic Life Since Vatican II* (begun in 1982) admits that there are many Catholics who find pre–Vatican II devotions to be "outmoded relics from the church's past."[143] As a result, there has been a decrease in the practice of these devotions. In the table "Frequency of Core Catholic Devotions and Confession," both the public rosary and novena ranked as the top two devotions that Core Catholics never participated in (61 percent and 76 percent, respectively).[144] In addition to these startling findings, the authors of the study point out that "older women" are the group that is "far more likely to be involved in Novenas, Stations, and public praying of the Rosary" as compared to men.[145] On top of the gender differences, the study also found "major differences" according to age groups. At least half and up to 85 percent of Catholic youths "rarely or never participate in Stations, Novenas, public Rosaries or Benedictions."[146] It is not until the age of sixty that they found participation in these devotions. As a result, their data shows that pre–Vatican II devotions "have simply not persisted among post–Vatican II Catholics."[147] Was this the case? A more recent study specifically explored the religious experiences of young adult Catholics to see if the "piety void" had been filled by the end of the twentieth century.

The authors of the book *Young Adult Catholics: Religion in the Culture of Choice* undertook their study in the late 1990s "to gather reliable information on how young adult Catholics, both European-American

---

142. Ibid., 37.

143. Castelli and Gremillion, *The Emerging Parish*, 144–45.

144. See table 16 in ibid., 145.

145. Ibid.

146. Ibid.

147. Ibid. They did remark, however, that there was the possibility that "more young Catholics will adopt some of these [pre–Vatican II] practices as they grow older" (ibid.).

and Latino, live their Catholicism."[148] In their survey of young adult Catholics (all of whom were confirmed Catholics), they found that in the past two years: 29 percent of non-Latinos had "made the Stations of the Cross" as compared to 44 percent of Latinos; 46 percent of non-Latinos had "said the rosary" as compared to 64 percent of Latinos; and 51 percent of non-Latinos had "worn medals, crucifixes, scapulars, or rosaries" as compared to 70 percent of Latinos.[149] They also found that in the past two years, only 6 percent of non-Latinos had "attended Novenas" as compared to 19 percent of Latinos.[150]

In addition to confirming that "Latinos are higher in devotional practices than others," the study also found that young adults sometimes "noted that the most influential norm of spirituality in their life was a grandparent rather than a parent," showing that "some young adult Catholics today need to look back to a time before the Council (or to an immigrant expression of Catholicism) to find inspiring models of commitment to the gospel of Christ."[151] This finding seems to show that new forms of Marian devotion have not sprung up following Vatican II, but rather, the younger generations have looked to those who experienced Marian devotion before Vatican II to fulfill their own spiritual practices. The study also indicated that "the Virgin Mary endures as a cultural icon of Catholic identity"; in a list of "nineteen elements: how essential," "devotion to Mary the Mother of God" ranked fourth, with 53 percent finding it "essential to faith," 33 percent finding it "important but not essential," 7 percent finding it "not important to faith," and 4 percent finding it as something they are "unaware is part of [their] faith."[152]

Despite these results, the study concluded that Mary's "utility in the actual construction and expression of young adult Catholic

---

148. Dean R. Hoge, William D. Dinges, Mary Johnson and Juan L. Gonzales Jr., *Young Adult Catholics: Religion in the Culture of Choice* (Notre Dame, IN: University of Notre Dame Press, 2001), 1. The authors note (p. 3) that the data was mostly collected in 1997.

149. See table 7.3 "Current Catholics: Personal Religious Practices (*in percents*)" in ibid., 158–59.

150. See table 7.2 "Current Catholics: Participation in Groups (*in percents*)" in ibid., 156.

151. Ibid., 157, 159.

152. Ibid., 167, 200–201.

spirituality is limited," but this conclusion is less true, however, for "Latino Catholics for whom the cult of the Virgin Mary, such as Our Lady of Guadalupe, serves as a symbol both of religious and cultural identity and of liberation from unjust social structures."[153] Perhaps this conclusion is related to the lack of Marian devotions that spoke to young adult non-Latino Catholics at the end of the twentieth century. How has this "piety void" affected Marian congregational song?

Musical Developments

Musical and Liturgical Documents

Sacrosanctum Concilium *(1963) and* Musicam Sacram *(1967)*

Continuing in the vein of the liturgical movement and its desire for the laity to be able to participate in and understand the Mass, *Sacrosanctum Concilium* called for "full, conscious, and active participation" of the faithful, citing 1 Peter 2:9, 4-5 when it described the laity's mandate to participation as "a right and obligation by reason of their baptism" (SC 14). One way to aid in this fuller understanding and participation is through the increased allowance of the vernacular in the liturgy (SC 36). Another is through singing. Chapter 6 of *Sacrosanctum Concilium*, "Sacred Music," calls for "religious singing by the faithful" that is "intelligently fostered so that in devotions and sacred exercises as well as in liturgical services, the voices of the faithful may be heard, in conformity with the norms and requirements of the rubrics" (SC 118).

Chapter 6 of *Sacrosanctum Concilium* also offers a few suggestions about the type of sacred music that should be used. First of all, sacred music is designed for "the glory of God and the sanctification of the faithful" (SC 112). *Sacrosanctum Concilium* speaks of the need to care for the "treasury of sacred music," and Gregorian chant, which is "specially suited to the Roman liturgy" (SC 114), and is to "be given pride of place in liturgical services" (SC 116).[154] In a nod to incultura-

---

153. Ibid., 167.

154. *Sacrosanctum Concilium* also mentions "other kinds of sacred music, especially polyphony," as being suited for the liturgy (SC 116).

tion, there is also mention of music in "mission lands," which calls for placing their music in "proper esteem" while giving it "a suitable place" (SC 119). Regarding musical instruments in worship, while "the pipe organ is to be held in high esteem in the Latin Church," there is also allowance for "other instruments" as long as they are "suitable," in "accord with the dignity of the temple, and that they truly contribute to the edification of the faithful" (SC 120). Finally, composers are called on to "cultivate sacred music and increase its store of treasures" as long as their music increases active participation and the texts are "in conformity with the Catholic doctrine," i.e., "they should be drawn chiefly from the sacred scripture and from liturgical sources" (SC 121).

Yet *Sacrosanctum Concilium* "does not so much offer clear guidelines and definitions as a set of convictions regarding the employment of traditional music in the renewed liturgy."[155] In 1967, *Musicam Sacram* (the Instruction on Music in the Liturgy) was delivered by the Congregation of Sacred Rites and the Consilium "to offer guidance on the various questions and difficulties raised by the implementation of SC."[156] As Anthony Ruff notes, "tensions in the area of worship music"[157] are raised when *Musicam Sacram* expresses hope that pastors, musicians, and the faithful "will gladly accept these norms and put them into practice" (MS 4).[158] In *Musicam Sacram* the concept of "progressive solemnity" is articulated, which helps to direct musicians as to what parts of the Mass should be sung, meaning one should begin "with the singing of the most central elements and adding other elements progressively."[159] *Musicam Sacram* also emphasizes the notion of "full, conscious, and active participation"—both interior

---

155. Anthony Ruff, *Sacred Music and Liturgical Reform: Treasures and Transformations* (Chicago/Mundelein, IL: Hillenbrand Books, 2007), 338.

156. Ibid., 339. Ruff describes the Consilium as "the body set up by Pope Paul VI to implement the liturgical reform called for by the Second Vatican Council" (*Sacred Music and Liturgical Reform*, 339).

157. Ibid., 342. Those with more traditional views were fearful of a loss of music in Latin and Gregorian chant (ibid., 342n13).

158. Sacred Congregation of Rites, *Musicam Sacram* (Instruction on Music in the Liturgy) March 5, 1967, Adoremus Society for the Renewal of the Sacred Liturgy, http://www.adoremus.org/MusicamSacram.html, accessed June 2014.

159. Ruff, *Sacred Music and Liturgical Reform*, 344. (See MS 7).

and exterior—that was introduced in *Sacrosanctum Concilium*.[160] Ruff concludes that *Musicam Sacram* "succeeds in affirming both liturgical reform and inherited musical repertoires and that it offers guidance in finding compromises that are faithful to all the various and sometimes conflicting requirements of the liturgy."[161]

Music in Catholic Worship *(1972),* Liturgical Music Today *(1982), and* Sing to the Lord *(2007)*

The US Catholic bishops also offered documents to help guide the implementation of the musical changes brought on by the documents of Vatican II. The first of these was *Music in Catholic Worship* in 1972. There are two main sections of this document, the first of which is the "exposition of the three critical judgments" used to determine "the value of a given musical element in the liturgy."[162] These three judgments—musical, liturgical, and pastoral—would become cornerstones of the musical documents of the US bishops following Vatican II. The second section of *Music in Catholic Worship* delves into the theology of both "celebration" and "music in worship."[163]

Edward Foley notes that *Music in Catholic Worship* does not focus much on music outside of the Eucharist, and that *Liturgical Music Today*, released in 1982, tries to remedy this omission, serving as a "companion" to *Music in Catholic Worship*.[164] *Liturgical Music Today* also addresses new issues, such as "technology and musical worship," the "principle of progressive solemnity" that was outlined in *Musicam Sacram*, as well as the place of music in the Liturgy of the Hours and other sacraments.[165] Foley concludes, however, that this

160. Ibid., 347.

161. Ibid., 352.

162. Edward Foley, "Overview of *Music in Catholic Worship* and *Liturgical Music Today*" in *The Liturgy Documents: A Parish Resource*, ed. Elizabeth Hoffman, 3rd ed. (Collegeville, MN: Liturgical Press, 1991), 1:270. The complete texts of both *Music in Catholic Worship* and *Liturgical Music Today* can be found in this source.

163. Ibid., 271.

164. Ibid., 271–72.

165. Ibid.

document "does a better job of raising issues than of offering strong principles."[166]

Finally, in 2007 the US bishops published *Sing to the Lord*.[167] Foley observes that *Sing to the Lord*, while drawing heavily from *Music in Catholic Worship* and *Liturgical Music Today*, is much larger than its predecessors, making it "the most comprehensive music document the US bishop have ever issued."[168] *Sing to the Lord* retains the three musical judgments from *Music in Catholic Worship* while offering further explanations of each of the judgments and adding that "the three judgments are but aspects of one evaluation (STTL 26)."[169] This document also offers a "theological reflection . . . on 'why we sing.'"[170] Considering the viciousness of the worship wars in US Catholic churches following Vatican II—specifically regarding what music to use—many had hoped these documents would end the debate between "traditional" and "contemporary" music, yet these documents were not extremely helpful in directing parishes on *what* music to use in worship as opposed to *how* to go about choosing it.

The Effect of Official Documents on Hymnals

Many of the hymnals surveyed in this study reflect the changes brought about by the official Catholic documents, particularly *Sacrosanctum Concilium*. For instance, the 1964 *People's Mass Book: Hymns, Psalms, Masses, and Bible Services for Participation of the Faithful at Mass and*

---

166. Ibid., 272.

167. United States Conference of Catholic Bishops, *Sing to the Lord: Music in Divine Worship* 14 November 2007, The Catholic Church in Southwestern Indiana, http://www.evansville-diocese.org/worship/SingToTheLord.pdf, accessed June 2014.

168. Edward Foley, *A Lyrical Vision: The Music Documents of the US Bishops*, American Essays in Liturgy (Collegeville, MN: Liturgical Press, 2009), 57.

169. Ibid., 62–68. *Sing to the Lord* also rearranges the three judgments, putting the liturgical judgment first whereas in *Music in Catholic Worship* the musical judgment was listed first. Foley had previously criticized *Music in Catholic Worship* for seeming to place hierarchically the pastoral judgment above the musical judgment. See Foley, "Overview of *Music in Catholic Worship* and *Liturgical Music Today*," 273.

170. Ibid., 72.

Other Services According to the Second Vatican Council's Constitution on the Sacred Liturgy not only mentions *Sacrosanctum Concilium* in its title but also offers a discussion of "The Value of Active Participation."[171] The *Adoremus Hymnal* (1997), a more "traditional" post–Vatican II hymnal, in addition to referring to Pius X's *motu proprio*, also quotes *Sacrosanctum Concilium* and *Musicam Sacram*, noting that "from its inception, Adoremus has been dedicated to authentic implementation of the liturgical reforms initiated by the Second Vatican Council."[172] Reflecting the tensions between liturgy and devotions that are expressed in *Sacrosanctum Concilium, Cantate et Iubilate Deo* (1999) is a hymnal that attempts to address the need for balance between the devotional and liturgical:

> In the post-conciliar period the debate was not resolved: in many places devotions were sharply curtailed in order to give a greater prominence to [the] official liturgy of the church. In recent years, however, the pendulum seems to be swinging less violently from one extreme to the other, and a new equilibrium seems to be manifesting itself. The faithful need, desire, and take delight in both the liturgy and a great variety of devotions. The two different expressions of prayer are intimately related (however complex that relation may sometimes be) and interdependent.[173]

In addition to the tension between liturgy and devotions, the hymnals also had to address what style of music to use. Frank Quinn contends that although "metrical hymns" are scarcely mentioned in the documents discussed above, they have largely become the norm in US Catholic worship. Immediately following Vatican II, many of these "metrical hymns" were borrowed from Protestant

---

171. People's Mass Book Committee, ed., *People's Mass Book: Hymns, Psalms, Masses, and Bible Services for Participation of the Faithful at Mass and Other Services According to the Second Vatican Council's Constitution on the Sacred Liturgy. Voice Book*, 2nd ed. (Cincinnati, OH: World Library of Sacred Music, 1964), 7.

172. Adoremus Society for the Renewal of the Sacred Liturgy, ed., *The Adoremus Hymnal: A Congregational Missal/Hymnal for the Celebration of Sung Mass in the Roman Rite* (San Francisco, CA: Ignatius Press, 1997), 9.

173. James Socias and Christian F. Stepansky, eds., *Cantate et Iubilate Deo: A Devotional and Liturgical Hymnal* (Princeton, NJ: Scepter Publishers, 1999), xi. This hymnal references many documents in this study, including *Music in Catholic Worship, Mediator Dei, Musicam Sacram,* and *Sacrosanctum Concilium.*

traditions.[174] Some of these Protestant songs were "regarded suspiciously by Catholics with a limited ecumenical sense and to many, in the mood of the sixties, represented an anachronistic archaism that had no relevance in the contemporary Church."[175] Perhaps this "suspicion" is one reason why Catholic "folk" or "contemporary" music seems to have become common in the 1970s, particularly in the extremely popular *Glory & Praise* hymnals. Now, a closer look at how Marian congregational song has been affected by the liturgical and musical changes following Vatican II.

Post–Vatican II Marian Congregational Song

"The Council documents, liturgical changes affecting all of the sacraments, and the permission for Mass to be celebrated in the evening and in the vernacular all proved to be blows to Marian devotional practices."[176] While these practices had previously been in the vernacular and "provided rare outlets for lay participation and leadership,"[177] with the liturgical changes brought by Vatican II, the laity now had the opportunity both to exercise leadership roles and to pray and sing in the vernacular all within the context of the Mass. Many pre–Vatican II Marian congregational songs were associated with such "devotional practices" as the May devotions, novenas, and Benediction. As the popularity of these services waned after Vatican II, so did interest in the Marian congregational songs that accompanied them.

One of the directives from Vatican II is the "return to Scriptures."[178] As recognized in chapter 1, Mary does not figure prominently in the

---

174. Frank C. Quinn, "Liturgical Music as Corporate Song 2: Problems of Hymnody in Catholic Worship," in *Liturgy and Music: Lifetime Learning*, ed. Robin A. Leaver and Joyce Ann Zimmerman (Collegeville, MN: Liturgical Press, 1998), 316–17.

175. Michael James Molloy, "Liturgical Music as Corporate Song 3: Opportunities for Hymnody in Catholic Worship," in *Liturgy and Music: Lifetime Learning*, ed. Robin A. Leaver and Joyce Ann Zimmerman (Collegeville, MN: Liturgical Press, 1998), 332.

176. Kane, "Marian Devotion since 1940," 118.

177. Ibid.

178. Ibid.

Scriptures, and many of the pre–Vatican II Marian congregational songs do not rely on the Scriptures for their texts. One Marian scriptural passage that did seem to be popular after Vatican II is the *Magnificat*. This is particularly the case for more "contemporary" hymnals; in fact, it is often the case that the *Magnificat* is the only Marian congregational song in many of these hymnals that contain mostly "contemporary" congregational songs.[179]

Sacrosanctum Concilium and Marialis Cultis did encourage the writing of new congregational songs with Marian themes and the development of new Marian devotions, but it seems that many attempts at writing new Marian congregational songs were unsuccessful—there have not been a great deal of new songs with strong Marian themes written after Vatican II that have really caught on with the faithful. Many translations and paraphrases were written after Vatican II, yet there have been few Marian congregational songs written after Vatican II that are not a compilation of multiple texts and tunes that have gained widespread popularity (as the *Magnificat* is). Thomas Thompson discusses six Marian congregational songs that were written before Vatican II and "provided a basis for a repertoire of Marian hymns," as well as those that appear in the revised *Liturgy of the Hours* (1975), but even he admits that there is a question about how well "known and accepted" these are.[180]

179. See for example *Hymnal for Young Christians: A Supplement to Adult Hymnals. Designed for Use in Church and School. Melody Edition for Congregational Singing* (Chicago: F.E.L. Publications, 1966); The Word of God Music, ed., *Songs of Praise: Combined Edition* (Ann Arbor, MI: Servant Music Publications, 1982); and Thomas N. Tomaszek and Rick Modlin, eds., *Spirit & Song: A Seeker's Guide for Liturgy and Prayer*, Assembly/Guitar ed. (Portland, OR: Oregon Catholic Press, 1999).

180. Thomas A. Thompson, "The Popular Marian Hymn in Devotion and Liturgy," *Marian Studies* 45 (1994): 136, 140–41, 144. The six pre–Vatican II hymns he refers to are: "Mary, the Dawn," "O Mary of All Women," "Star upon the Ocean, Maria," "Virgin Born We Bow before Thee," "Sing of Mary," and "Praise to Mary, Heaven's Gate." The hymns from the *Liturgy of the Hours* he refers to are: "Mary Crowned with Living Light," "Mary, the Dawn," "Mary Immaculate Star of the Morning," "Mother of Christ, Our Hope, Our Patroness," "O Mary, of All Women," "Sing of Mary," and "Virgin Born, We Bow before You" as well as the following canticles of Lucien Deiss: "Joy to You, O Virgin Mary," " Rejoice, O Virgin Mary," and "Mother of Holy Hope." Thompson posits that "because of copyright restrictions, these hymns probably cannot be gathered together in

"Hail Mary: Gentle Woman," is one of the few post–Vatican II Marian congregational songs to gain widespread popularity.[181] The text and music were written in 1975 by Carey Landry (b. 1944), who is known for music that is "characterized by simplicity and assembly-friendly melodies."[182] The music is similar to many of the ballad-like Marian congregational songs from the late nineteenth century and earlier twentieth century in that the accompaniment, best suited for the piano, consists of arpeggios.[183]

The text, based on Luke 1:28, begins with the Hail Mary, and then moves into the refrain and verses:

Introduction: Hail Mary, full of grace,
the Lord is with you.
Blessed are you among women
and blest is the fruit of your womb, Jesus.
Holy Mary, Mother of God,
pray for us sinners now and at the hour of our death.
Amen.

Refrain: Gentle woman, quiet light,
morning star, so strong and bright,
gentle Mother, peaceful dove,
teach us wisdom; teach us love.

---

one source." While that might be part of the issue, I also have to wonder how much demand there actually is for many of these hymns. They are not well-known, and the content of Catholic hymnals in the United States is very much based on demand since there is no "official" hymnal. Rather there are multiple hymnals printed by multiple publishing companies.

181. In my quantitative study of Marian congregational songs, this was the only post–Vatican II song to appear on the "List of the Thirty Most Commonly Found Marian Congregational Songs." It came in at #22. Stephanie A. Budwey, "Mary, Star of Hope: Marian Congregational Song as an Expression of Devotion to the Blessed Virgin Mary in the United States from 1854 to 2010," *The Hymn* 63, no. 2 (Spring 2012): 11–12.

182. Donald Boccardi, *The History of American Catholic Hymnals Since Vatican II* (Chicago: GIA Publications, 2001), 35.

183. These types of accompaniments are often found in the early editions of the *St. Basil's Hymnal*.

1. You were chosen by the Father;
   You were chosen for the Son.
   You were chosen from all women
   and for woman, shining one. **R.**

2. Blessed are you among women,
   blest in turn all women, too.
   Blessed they with peaceful spirits.
   Blessed they with gentle hearts. **R.**[184]

In speaking of how the medieval music of "liturgy and courtly song" later blended into love poetry in the fourteenth century, Miri Rubin points out how the "lady" addressed in one of the poems "could be Mary or another beloved."[185] It seems very possible that "Hail Mary: Gentle Woman" could have a similar reinterpretation. When this song is sung in churches, the beginning "Hail Mary" section is often omitted, and instead the song is begun at the refrain of "Gentle woman," and this is the part that people know better than the two stanzas which speak more directly to Mary as being "chosen by the Father" and "Blessed . . . among women." As a result, this song is often chosen at funerals because it seems that the line has been blurred as to whether this "Gentle woman" is Mary or a deceased female/mother figure.

In the wake of Vatican II, several authors produced new Marian congregational songs utilizing the style of lyric then popular. The change in "style of discourse" from Culture Two to Culture Three—as described by John O'Malley and discussed earlier in chapter 6—is also noticed in a change in register of language following Vatican II, as is noted by Robin Knowles Wallace in her study of recent hymnody. She points out the shift in "language base of the church" from the King James to the RSV (1946, 1952) to the NRSV (1989) as well as a shift in linguistic register, which she defines as "a situation-based variety of language that shows a correlation between linguistic features and

184. #481 in Eric Schumock and Randall Keith DeBruyn, eds., *Journeysongs*, 3rd ed. (Portland, OR: OCP Publications, 2012). © 1975, 1978, Carey Landry and OCP. All rights reserved. Reproduced by permission.

185. Miri Rubin, *Mother of God: A History of the Virgin Mary* (New Haven, CT: Yale University Press, 2009), 195–96.

a situation."[186] Using Martin Joos's categories from his *The Five Clocks* (1967) this shift in linguistic register could be described as one from the *frozen, formal* side to the more *casual* and *intimate* side.[187]

Wallace describes *formal* as a style without participation because "the task is to inform, and form becomes the dominant character of discourse." Best described by words such as "detachment" and "cohesion," this style is often found in worship with such sentences as "Let us pray." Moving past *formal* is *frozen*, another style without participation but also without intonation. This style can be described as "being 'set in stone'" and Wallace describes hymns as falling "between formal and frozen."[188] Moving to the complete opposite side of the spectrum is *intimate*, which is "marked by extraction and jargon." Just before that is *casual*, which is "marked by ellipsis, slang, and formulas." While *formal* and *frozen* do not invite participation, *intimate* and *casual* do.

In the preface to volume one of the *Hymnal for Young Christians*, the editors of the hymnal state their goal: "The compilers of this collection have taken up the challenge of Vatican II to search for meaningful and new modes of expressing man's love of God and of neighbor."[189] Keeping this shift in register in mind, Ray Silvia's Advent text "Lullaby of the Spirit," published in the *Hymnal for Young Christians: Volume Three* (1973),[190] speaks to Catholics in a more colloquial manner, in the style of *casual* or *intimate*: "Hush! Shyly, I have

186. Robin Knowles Wallace, *Moving Toward Emancipatory Language: A Study of Recent Hymns*, Drew University Studies in Liturgy Series 8, ed. Kenneth E. Rowe and Robin A. Leaver (Lanham, MD, and London: The Scarecrow Press, 1999), 37, 47.

187. Ibid., 38–39. The following information on Wallace's description of Joos's five styles of language is all taken from these pages. The five styles, from one end of the spectrum to another, are: *frozen, formal, consultative, casual,* and *intimate*.

188. Because Joos says the frozen style offers "rereading and refeeling, that together can lead to wisdom," Wallace writes that hymns can be seen as "formal in their usage and can be studied because they are frozen" (see ibid.).

189. *Hymnal for Young Christians*, ii.

190. Ray Silvia, "Lullaby of the Spirit" in Roger D. Nachtwey, ed., *Hymnal for Young Christians: Volume Three; Accompaniment Edition for Chanter, Choir, and Guitarist* (Los Angeles, CA: F.E.L. Publications, 1973), 26–28.

this feeling. Hush! Shyly, Like a baby dreamin' Inside of me."[191] The first stanza even uses what might be described as intimate language, referring to Mary as "babe":

> The angel said to Mary: "Hey, babe, today's your lucky day!
> The Lord has given you his Baby; In you he'll grow and pray."
> But Mary felt frightened, was about to turn around and go,
> When a tiny voice whispered in her soul.[192]

The second stanza also refers to a common colloquial phrase of the 1970s, "keep on truckin'" when it refers to Jesus who "whistled as he trucked on down the road."[193] The third stanza makes reference to the scriptural image of Mary found in Revelation: "In the sun I saw a Woman With her Child standin' on the moon."[194] One could argue that this text is as culturally tied to its times as the Marian congregational songs from the pre–Vatican II era.

Why have there not been more Marian congregational songs from the post–Vatican II period examined here? The reason is that there are so few Marian congregational songs from this period as compared to before Vatican II. This leads to the question of whether or not there is a correlation between the apparent decline in Marian devotion following Vatican II and the decline in Marian congregational songs. The author believes that the answer is yes, since in a separate quantitative study, the data shows an 18.65 percent drop in the percentage of Marian congregational songs in a hymnal following Vatican II.[195] There are many factors that may have contributed to the decline of Marian devotion and the congregational songs that reflect Marian devotion, including the directive of *Sacrosanctum Concilium* that all devotions should lead up to the liturgy or flow from it.[196]

---

191. Ibid. It should be noted that the author's original text was "I got this feeling" but the publishers altered his text. Catherine Silvia, e-mail message to the author, January 30, 2014.

192. Nachtwey, *Hymnal for Young Christians: Volume Three*, 26–27.

193. Ibid., 27–28.

194. Ibid., 28.

195. Budwey, "Mary, Star of Hope," 9.

196. *Sacrosanctum Concilium* states: "Popular devotions of the Christian people, provided they conform to the laws and norms of the Church, are to be highly

> A style of piety [following the directives of *Sacrosanctum Concilium*] was fostered based more directly on biblical sources and on the public liturgy of the Church, to replace the so-called "devotionalism" and the paraliturgical practices that had characterized the Middle Ages and had showed great vitality in the 19th and early 20th centuries.[197]

As noted in chapter 4, many of the popular Marian congregational songs were tied to what John O'Malley has termed "paraliturgical practices," so it is natural that these songs would fall out of favor following the liturgical actions with which they were associated, such as "novena services, Benediction, parish missions, Stations of the Cross, and May crownings."[198] In addition to downplaying devotions, Vatican II lessened the emphasis on the "rewards" associated with these devotions, including indulgences.[199] This movement away from devotions can also be traced back to highlighted concerns of the liturgical movement.[200]

Another important factor from Vatican II was the decision to place Mary within the context of *Lumen Gentium* (the Dogmatic Constitution on the Church) rather than to create a separate document on Mary. As noted in chapter 6, the vote on whether or not to have a completely separate document on Mary or to include her in the document on the Church was the closest vote—and one of the most

---

recommended, especially where they are ordered by the Apostolic See. . . . But such devotions should be so drawn up that they harmonize with the liturgical seasons, accord with the sacred liturgy, are in some way derived from it, and lead the people to it, since in fact the liturgy by its very nature is far superior to any of them" (SC 13).

197. John W. O'Malley, *Tradition and Transition: Historical Perspectives on Vatican II* (Wilmington, DE: Michael Glazier, 1989), 18.

198. Boccardi, *The History of American Catholic Hymnals Since Vatican II*, 7. He notes that it was at these "paraliturgical" services where "most devout Catholics knew singing and vernacular hymns."

199. Kane, "Marian Devotion Since 1940," 115. See also her discussion of the loss of the "treasury of merit" and a vivid connection with Mary and the communion of saints (pp. 89–93), which was explored in chap. 5.

200. See Keith Pecklers, *The Unread Vision: The Liturgical Movement in the United States of America: 1926–1955* (Collegeville, MN: Liturgical Press, 1998).

debated—of the entire council.[201] Chapter 8 of *Lumen Gentium* is solely devoted to Mary and puts forth more of a minimalist view of Marian devotion, as opposed to the maximalist view (high Mariology) that had been supported by the Catholic Church for quite some time. Part of the reason for wanting to downplay a high Mariology was that many of the documents from Vatican II were devoted to fostering ecumenism. Much attention was given to the ecumenical consequences of any further declarations on Mary (especially following the promulgation of her Assumption in 1950), as she was now being hailed as the "Promoter of Christian union."[202]

Another factor in the decline of Marian devotion following Vatican II could be the rise of the feminist movement. Throughout history, Mary, the "Virgin most pure," was upheld as a model of faith and "perfect humanity."[203] She was pure, chaste, obedient, passive, lowly, meek, and mild. These descriptions of Mary are found in many pre–Vatican II Marian congregational songs, along with the description of Mary as both virgin and mother.[204]

This chapter attests to how many feminists came to view these descriptions highlighting Mary's submissive nature and virginity as oppressive. They also pointed out the impossibility for any other woman to be both virgin and mother. Mary Daly was one who challenged the placing of Mary on an unattainable pedestal when she questioned the phenomenon of "Mary as the model of all women."[205] As the feminist movement created an environment where people could challenge the image of the "pure virgin" as a model for all women to strive toward, many of the pre–Vatican II Marian congregational songs that espoused these virtues may have sounded outdated and thus fell out of favor, creating the need for new images of Mary.

201. See Xavier Rynne, *Vatican Council II* (Maryknoll, NY: Orbis Books, 1993), 212.

202. See Giuseppe Alberigo, ed., *History of Vatican II*, English version ed. Joseph A. Komonchak, 4 vols. (Maryknoll, NY: Orbis; Leuven: Peeters, 1995–2003), 1:260.

203. Warner, *Alone of All Her Sex*, xxiii.

204. See examples from chap. 4 of this work such as "How pure and frail and white" and "Ave Maria! Thou Virgin and Mother."

205. Daly, *The Church and the Second Sex*, 157. See especially her chapter "The Pedestal Peddlers."

As Eamon Duffy attests, "the conventional forms of Marian devotion . . . were often pressed into service to endorse social and political attitudes, and modes of self-perception and self-evaluation, which now seem alien and distasteful to many Christians."[206] Duffy's observation includes the social attitudes espoused in the Victorian notion of "True Womanhood" and its "four cardinal virtues" of "piety, purity, submissiveness and domesticity,"[207] which were often associated with Mary and found in pre–Vatican II Marian congregational songs.

One final factor to consider is that those supporting "traditional" music often closely follow official documents from the Catholic Church regarding liturgical practices, including music. Many of the titles of the "traditional" hymnals note their desire to adhere to Pope Pius X's *motu proprio* of 1903,[208] which clearly called for sacred music over secular. Much of the music found in the pre–Vatican II Marian congregational songs was based on secular or "contemporary" styles of music, so some deemed them inappropriate for "traditional" hymnals.

The shift away from music and texts often described as "sentimental" was seen in the 1958 edition of *The New St. Basil Hymnal*. The previous edition, the *St. Basil Hymnal* of 1935, was filled with many of these "sentimental" congregational songs, especially those devoted to Mary. It seems the editors of the *New St. Basil Hymnal* decided to discard many of the "good, old hymns" in place of *"better, and in some cases older* hymns of genuine piety and dignity."[209] From this decision can be seen the workings of the liturgical movement, which called for a focus on corporate worship rather than on

206. Eamon Duffy, *Faith of Our Fathers: Reflections on Catholic Tradition* (London & New York: Continuum, 2004), 34–35.

207. Barbara Welter, "The Cult of True Womanhood: 1820–1860," *American Quarterly* 18, no. 2 (Summer, 1966): 152.

208. 208. E.g., the reference to the *motu proprio* in the title: Marist Brothers, ed., *American Catholic Hymnal: An Extensive Collection of Hymns, Latin Chants and Sacred Songs for Church, School and Home, Including Gregorian Masses, Vesper Psalms, Litanies, Motets for Benediction of the Blessed Sacrament, Etc., According to the Motu Proprio of His Holiness Pope Pius X* (New York: P. J. Kenedy and Sons, 1921).

209. The Basilian Fathers, ed., *The New St. Basil Hymnal* (Cincinnati, OH: Ralph Jusko Publications / Willis Music Company, 1958), v (emphasis Basilian Fathers).

individual, private devotions, many of which were Marian.[210] Also, following Vatican II, many of the Marian congregational songs in the Victorian musical style fell out of use in favor of a new style of "contemporary song" that was based on the type of folk music that became popular during the 1960s and 1970s.

It is also interesting to note that after Vatican II, many "contemporary" hymnals have fewer Marian congregational songs than their "traditional" counterparts.[211] First, two definitions: "traditional" is defined to mean (mostly) four-part, homophonic music, often considered a "hymn." "Contemporary" is defined to mean a style that sometimes borrows from secular music, often considered a "song."[212] This relates to the discussion earlier in this chapter regarding what Ann Matter said about conservatives leaning toward pre–Vatican II Marian devotions as well as supporting Marian apparitions following Vatican II. It seems that this may also include a penchant for traditional Marian hymnody.

The period immediately preceding Vatican II could be described as one of a high Mariology (maximalist view) and a low Christology (minimalist view). During this period, Mary is seen as a mediator, someone to speak to in order to reach Jesus. The idea that no son (Jesus) can deny his mother (Mary), and that any petition brought to Mary will be heard (found in the *Memorare* of St. Bernard) is found in many Marian congregational songs before Vatican II.[213] Following

---

210. This includes the common occurrence of the recitation of the rosary during Mass. See Pecklers, *The Unread Vision*, 39.

211. For a more in-depth look at the quantitative analysis that undergirds this conclusion, see Stephanie A. Budwey, "Mary, Star of Hope: Devotion to the Blessed Virgin Mary in the United States from 1854 to 2010, as Seen through the Lens of Roman Catholic Marian Congregational Song" (ThD diss., Boston University, 2012), 288–91.

212. For instance, in the nineteenth century, what is considered "contemporary" music would be in the Victorian style of the time, often with a more piano-like accompaniment. Post–Vatican II "contemporary" music was often written in a folk-style form, with the accompaniment often for piano and/or guitar. So a "traditional" hymnal contains mostly "traditional" music (often written for the organ) while a "contemporary" hymnal contains mostly "contemporary" music.

213. See stanza 2 of #113, "O Mother Blest," in *St. Basil's Hymnal: An Extensive Collection of English and Latin Hymns for Church, School and Home. Arranged for Feasts and Seasons of the Ecclesiastical Year. Gregorian Masses, Vespers, Motets for*

Vatican II and the minimalist movement to control Marian devotion, the roles of Mary and Jesus seem to reverse: there is a low Mariology (minimalist view) and a high Christology (maximalist view). Jesus becomes more personal, so there is less need to have Mary as a mediator in order to reach Jesus. This leads to more congregational songs that focus on personal relationships with Jesus, rather than Mary. In each of these periods before and after Vatican II, the "contemporary" songs seem to correlate to the maximalist views; that is, a high Mariology before Vatican II and a high Christology after Vatican II. These songs tend to be more individualistic, and they focus on personal relationships with Mary and with Jesus.[214]

Supporters of "traditional" hymnals after Vatican II often disapprove of "contemporary" songs not only for their texts but also for their style of music.[215] Many who supported "traditional" music (e.g., Gregorian chant) before Vatican II, such as those in the liturgical movement, seemed to ascribe to Philip Gleason's notion of the "Mythic Middle Ages." Those who have supported "traditional"

Benediction, Litanies, Etc., ed. the Basilian Fathers, 39th ed. (Detroit, MI: Basilian Press, 1935), 98. See also the refrain of "Wilt thou look upon me Mother" #44 in *Laudate Pueri! A Collection of Catholic Hymns with an Appendix of Prayers*, ed. Sisters of Notre Dame (Cleveland), 3rd ed. (Cleveland, OH: The Ohio Printing Co., 1903), 338–39.

214. Also, in his introduction to *For the Beauty of the Church*, Taylor mentions that "a minimalist rather than a maximalist aesthetic will usually be seen as more representative of the 'pure gospel.'" W. David O. Taylor, ed., *For the Beauty of the Church: Casting a Vision for the Arts* (Grand Rapids, MI: Baker Books, 2010), 20. This quote may help explain why before Vatican II the more "traditional" hymnals did not include some of the more "contemporary" songs, as they were often more devotional and not always biblically based. The post–Vatican II "traditional" hymnals, while not necessarily having what might be called a "maximalist" view of Mary, did keep many "traditional" Marian congregational songs because these belong to the "golden age" of pre–Vatican II.

215. See, for instance, the Preface of *The Adoremus Hymnal* which explains the great lengths they went to in choosing the "best of English and Latin hymnody ever composed" as well as their emphasis on Gregorian chant. Adoremus Society for the Renewal of the Sacred Liturgy, ed., *The Adoremus Hymnal: A Congregational Missal/Hymnal for the Celebration of Sung Mass in the Roman Rite* (San Francisco, CA: Ignatius Press, 1997), 7–9. Note that the preface was written on the Feast of the Assumption of the Blessed Virgin Mary, August 15, 1997.

music after Vatican II also seem to lean toward upholding the past, particularly Gregorian chant.

This study has revealed significant information about Marian theology and devotion through the lens of song, exposing a considerable decline following Vatican II. What can be gleaned from this study, and what might these findings mean for the future of Marian theology, devotion, and congregational song?

Chapter Eight

Come, Join in Mary's Prophet-Song

Come, join in Mary's prophet-song
of justice for the earth,
for right outgrows the fiercest wrong,
revealing human worth—
bound not within the wealth we crave
or in the arms we bear,
but in the holy sign God gave:
the image that we share.[1]

—Adam M. L. Tice,
"Come, join in Mary's prophet-song"

Introduction

So Adam Tice (b. 1979), a Mennonite pastor and hymn writer, begins his hymn with echoes of Mary's *Magnificat*, a clarion call to

1. Stanza 1 of "Come, join in Mary's prophet-song," by Adam M. L. Tice, *Woven Into Harmony: 50 Hymn Texts* (Chicago: GIA Publications, 2009), 28–29. Reproduced by permission from GIA Publications © 2009. The text is set to the tune KINGSFOLD with SALVATION and RESIGNATION listed as alternate tunes (ibid., 28).

261

justice, peace, and the end of war. Tice remarks that he was "inspired by Fred Kaan's interpretations of the Magnificat," which will be examined later in this chapter.[2] It is fitting to end this study by looking through the lens of Mary's song, the *Magnificat*. By singing the *Magnificat*, we let it be known that the God we believe in "has respect for the Marys of Nazareth, for vulnerable, pregnant, unmarried women"; we let it be known that this God is "a God who rummages through the dump with the hungry; a God who cries when children are killed and women are raped; a God who sees visions with poor farmers and plants roses on their hillsides."[3]

By reflecting on what has been learned at the conclusion of this exploration of Marian theology and devotion through the lens of song, it is possible to see how these findings may hint at the future of Marian theology, devotion, and congregational song. The first consideration is what might be needed to reinvigorate Marian devotion and congregational song, given the decline in some areas following Vatican II. Might Marian theology, devotion, and congregational song shed its former associations as a weapon against Communism and other "evils" and "heresies" (including the modern world), and as an aid in relegating women to a second-class status? How can Marian congregational song speak to the twenty-first century, both inside and outside of the Catholic Church? Next is an exploration of where Marian devotion is flourishing—particularly Latino cultures—as well as some contemplation on what gifts from those contexts might reinvigorate Marian devotion and congregational song in the United States among non-Latino communities (this is particularly pertinent as the current pope hails from South America). Finally, the opportunity will be taken to envision what Marian theology, devotion, and congregational song might look like in the future. What qualities

2. Ibid. According to Tice, Kaan's interpretations of the *Magnificat* that have inspired him to include "Sing we a song of high revolt" and "Come! Sing and live a world Magnificat." Adam Tice, conversation with author, March 19, 2014. In his notes to "Come, join in Mary's prophet-song," Tice also notes that he "wrote this hymn text just before Christmas in 2005, as four Christian Peacemaker Team members were held hostage in Iraq." Tice, *Woven Into Harmony*, 28.

3. Bonnie Jensen, "We Sing Mary's Song," in *American Magnificat: Protestants on Mary of Guadalupe*, ed. Maxwell E. Johnson (Collegeville, MN: Liturgical Press, 2010), 169.

would help proclaim Mary's prophetic—and dangerous—message that calls for a world turned upside down?[4]

"The Maiden Mary, Not So Mild"[5]

Eamon Duffy writes that "one of the most striking developments in post-Conciliar Catholicism has been the way in which Marian piety has simply ceased to feature as a vital dimension of their faith for a growing number of people."[6] This loss of Marian piety is reflected in the post–Vatican II drop in Marian congregational songs in Catholic hymnals in the United States, which is detailed elsewhere.[7] In chapter 6 it was shown that there was an attempt to correct what was seen as excessive devotion to Mary (a maximalist view) and replace it with a more "appropriate," biblical, Christocentric Mariology (a minimalist view). However, "corrective reactions have a habit of swinging to opposite extremes,"[8] leaving Catholics with the "piety void" explored in chapter 7 that was seen numerically in the analysis of Marian congregational songs in my article "Mary, Star of Hope." With the dramatic drop in the number of Marian congregational songs in most contemporary hymnals, the Catholic Church seemed to experience what Duffy describes as "an exegetical failure, confusion and uncertainty about how to 'place' Mary within a more self-consciously scriptural Christianity."[9]

---

4. Acts 17:6.

5. Stanza 2 of "Come, join in Mary's prophet-song" from Tice, *Woven Into Harmony*, 28–29.

6. Eamon Duffy, *Faith of Our Fathers: Reflections on Catholic Tradition* (New York: Continuum, 2004), 29.

7. Stephanie A. Budwey, "Mary, Star of Hope: Marian Congregational Song as an Expression of Devotion to the Blessed Virgin Mary in the United States from 1854 to 2010," *The Hymn* 63, no. 2 (Spring 2012): 7–17. The main finding of this study is that from 1854 to 1963 the average percentage of Marian congregational songs in a hymnal is 24.85 percent, while the average from 1964 to 2010 is 6.20 percent, for a difference of 18.65 percent.

8. Duffy, *Faith of Our Fathers*, 26.

9. Ibid., 30.

While Mary's uniqueness was seen "exclusively" before Vatican II, Duffy reflects on the changes in Marian devotion that came after Vatican II to render her uniqueness as "inclusive":

> Where post-medieval Mariology often emphasized Mary's difference from every other Christian, her purity contrasting with our filth, her powerful intercession contrasting with our helplessness, the Council, following the mainstream of patristic and early medieval exegesis, emphasized her role as type and model for the Church, and each of its members.[10]

Duffy attributes this change to "an exegetical shift from the Gospel of St John to that of St Luke."[11] While the Mary of Cana and the cross in John's gospel is *different from* and *over against* others, the Mary of the annunciation in Luke's gospel is "a light to guide" and the "model of every believer's response to the call of God."[12] This perspective offers a positive way to look at Mary, as opposed to the interpretation in prose and poetry from before Vatican II in which Mary is "different from" and "over against" others and is portrayed as an unattainable model—the "pure" and "spotless" woman who is simultaneously virgin and mother. If, however, the emphasis is on Mary as a model of one who answered God's call,[13] then that focus can be more realistically striven toward, particularly in the call of the *Magnificat* to help those who are poor and oppressed.

Duffy claims that in order to overcome the "discomfort" with some of these earlier associations, "any new and healthy Marian piety will need to reorient itself in order to free itself from this particular cultural, political and psychological heritage."[14] He points to the work of liturgical reformer Louis Bouyer (1913–2004), who, in his book *Life and Liturgy* (1956), "warned against simply jettisoning the devotional developments of the medieval and Baroque period," and instead sug-

10. Ibid., 35.
11. Ibid.
12. Ibid. (emphasis Duffy).
13. This notion has ecumenical implications, as it is a theme that plays a large part in Luther's sermon on the *Magnificat*. Thanks to Dr. Francine Cardman for making this connection.
14. Ibid.

gested that "if they were unliturgical or anti-liturgical, they should be reformed and reintegrated into a liturgical framework."[15] Bouyer's comments can be interpreted as a call to reform and reintegrate Marian devotion and congregational song in a manner that fits into a post–Vatican II theological framework.

There is a need for new Marian congregational songs that incorporate "new and creative understandings" of what Mary means to people today. Joyce Ann Zimmerman, in her analysis of the section on Marian devotion in the Catholic Church's *Directory on Popular Piety and the Liturgy* (2001), echoes the need for new Marian congregational songs: "one challenge is for hymnwriters and composers to produce new hymns that are inspired by recent gains in Mariology and could be used in the liturgy, particularly for Marian festivals or feastdays."[16] She asserts that many of the Marian congregational songs in the "Catholic treasury of songs" are "devotional in nature and therefore are not appropriate for liturgical use" and any that are "theologically suspect" should not even be kept for devotional use.[17] Many of the pre–Vatican II Marian congregational songs certainly fit this description. So who will write new Marian congregational songs "encourag[ing] us to live as faithful disciples and to make God's reign present in our contemporary world?"[18]

Adam Tice's text masterfully engages the problems and injustices in our world today, and reimagines Mary as the maiden who is "not so mild" in stanzas 2 and 3 of "Come, join in Mary's prophet-song":

2. The "Peace on earth" which shepherds heard
    is not some fantasy.
The angels sang to greet the Word,
    whose birth is victory.

15. Ibid., 26.

16. Joyce Ann Zimmerman, "Veneration of the Holy Mother of God," in *Directory on Popular Piety and the Liturgy: Principles and Guidelines. A Commentary*, ed. Peter C. Phan (Collegeville, MN: Liturgical Press, 2005), 111.

17. Ibid., 110 and 110n8.

18. Ibid., 112.

The maiden Mary, not so mild,
    borne into death's domain
true God, and yet an infant child,
    Who over death would reign.

3. Emmanuel, God-with-us here,
    grows peace where we would dare
to act despite our trembling fear
    and bring God's holy care.
The image God made "Us" to be
    is also borne on "Them."
Christ bids us join our enemy
    to sing war's requiem.[19]

Alan Hommerding, Senior Liturgy Publications Editor at World Library Publications, also has composed some new, excellent Marian texts.[20] In "We sing with holy Mary," Hommerding focuses on "sharing in what God called her to do: bear the Word in the witness of our flesh and to be filled with God's grace":

We sing with holy Mary in spirit, heart, and voice,
Your Word incarnate bearing, in you our souls rejoice!
You chose her for your mother and named her "favored one"
For Christ, our Lord and brother, your own beloved Son.
Grace us to live her story: to serve you as we ought;
To sing in endless glory our own Magnificat![21]

19. "Come, join in Mary's prophet-song" from Tice, *Woven Into Harmony*, 28–29.

20. Thanks to Alan Hommerding for graciously sharing his Marian texts. All texts and notes on texts are taken from Alan Hommerding, e-mail message to author, January 9, 2009. Many of Hommerding's texts can be found in hymnals published by World Library Publications/J. S. Paluch Company. "Sing 'Ave!'" and "Come, sing a home and family" can be found in *Song of the Spirit*, a collection of Alan J. Hommerding hymn texts published by World Library Publications, 2002.

21. Second stanza of "We sing with Holy Mary" by Alan Hommerding, set to the tune THAXTED. Reproduced by permission from World Library Publications © 2004.

Another text by Hommerding that combines Mary and the call to service is "By God kept pure: Hymn to the Immaculate Heart of Mary," where in the third stanza he is able to link powerful images of Mary at Pentecost with the Church's mission:

> Mary, steadfast, grace-filled woman, waiting in the upper room
> For the power of the Spirit that had once flowed in your womb;
> Then that Spirit's flaming whirlwind launched the Church
>   that shall endure,
> Sent us out, on fire for mission with one heart, alive and pure.[22]

"Sing 'Ave!'" beautifully reflects on the mysteries of the rosary, including the new Luminous Mysteries. Hommerding skillfully wrote this text "for a Marian conference" where he was asked to "write a text based on the mysteries of the rosary with a post–Vatican II theology of Mary, ecumenically sensitive, and in a meter which could be sung to a variety of commonly-known tunes." Hommerding shows that it is possible to write about Mary in a post–Vatican II world, while also allowing Mary to speak to those outside the Catholic faith:

> Through each life's unfolding mysteries,
>   God's redemption weaves its course;
> Holy Mary, God's great Mother,
>   Lead us to redemption's source.
> As we follow Christ in mission,
>   Full of Grace, you guide our way:
> Joyful, light-filled, sorrowing, glorious,
>   One in faith, we sing "Ave!"[23]

Hommerding also has the ability to articulate Mary's role as mother in a way that speaks to those who may fall outside of what is considered a "family" by the Catholic Church in "Come, sing a home

---

22. This text is set to the tune Mundo Corde, also composed by Hommerding. Reproduced by permission from World Library Publications © 2007.

23. Stanza 1 of "Sing 'Ave'!" by Alan Hommerding. The suggested tune for this text is In Babilone or Pleading Savior. Reproduced by permission from World Library Publications © 2000, 2009.

and family": "this text was written in response to a sad story told to me by a single mother who had attended Mass with her boys on the feast of the Holy Family; the pastor requested that single-parent households not stand up to receive the 'special family' blessing at the end of Mass." In the fourth and final stanza of "Come, sing a home and family," Hommerding not only refers to Mary as the "maiden bold," but also speaks to the single mother and to all those who may not be part of what is considered a "traditional family":

> Whatever form our family takes
>   The gospel way we seek:
> To feed the hungry, tend the sick,
>   Raise up the poor and weak.
> In daily life and simple tasks
>   The song must never cease
> Of dreaming worker, maiden bold
>   And child of lasting peace.[24]

Patrick Cheng offers a similar reflection on Mary, taken from the perspective of queer theology. He sees Mary as the "bearer of radical love because her very existence dissolves traditional boundaries about family life as well as gender."[25] In fact, Cheng describes Mary, a "pregnant woman who was not yet married" as the

> antithesis of "family values" insofar as she erases the boundaries between the traditional family categories of parent, spouse, and child. This is significant because we can understand Mary as deconstructing gender and family roles, as opposed to merely reinforcing them as the Roman Catholic church and fundamentalist Christians would have us believe.[26]

---

24. Stanza 4 of "Come, sing a home and family" by Alan Hommerding. The suggested tune for this text is MOZART. Reproduced by permission from World Library Publications © 1994. This text is also set to the tune CAROL at #439 in *Worship*, 4th ed., ed. Kelly Dobbs-Mickus (Chicago: GIA Publications, 2011).

25. Patrick S. Cheng, *Radical Love: An Introduction to Queer Theology* (New York: Seabury Books, 2011), 87.

26. Ibid., 87, 89.

This view of Mary offers hope and consolation to the mother in Hommerding's story and to all those who do not fit into society's norm of what constitutes a "traditional family." In addition, this unmarried, pregnant woman—a sexual outcast—also offers hope to those in the LGBT community. Cheng quotes queer theologian and former Catholic (Jesuit) priest John McNeill, who writes that "Mary is the ideal person to intercede for those of us who are her 'special children'—'all of us queers, fags, dykes, fems, fairies, fruits, transvestites, transsexuals, and all sexual exiles.'"[27]

Clearly, Mary can be reimagined in ways that are powerful and speak to a broad range of people, particularly those who may not fit into the box of what the Catholic Church—or society in general—deems as "acceptable." Edith Sinclair Downing (b. 1922), in "We remember Mary," speaks to Mary's ability to transcend boundaries:

> We remember Mary,
> sister who transcends
> every class and culture,
> and God's power extends.
> Mary, model, mentor,
> may we learn from you
> how to live God's promise,
> witness faith anew.[28]

"Sing We a Song of High Revolt"

> 1. Sing we a song of high revolt;
>   make great the Lord, his name exalt!
>   Sing we the song that Mary sang
>   of God at war with human wrong.

---

27. John J. McNeill, *Taking a Chance on God: Liberating Theology for Gays, Lesbians, and Their Lovers, Families, and Friends* (Boston: Beacon Press, 1996), 143, as quoted in Cheng, *Radical Love*, 89.

28. Stanza 5 of "We remember Mary." Reproduced courtesy of Edith Sinclair Downing, *Sing Praise for Faithful Women*, ed. Lucia Sullivan (Colfax, NC: Wayne Leupold Editions, 2009), 34–35. © 2009 Wayne Leupold Editions. The suggested tunes are Au Clair De La Lune and King's Weston.

2. Sing we of him who deeply cares
and still with us our burden bears.
He who with strength the proud disowns,
brings down the mighty from their thrones.

3. By him the poor are lifted up;
he satisfies with bread and cup
the hungry ones of many lands;
the rich must go with empty hands.

4. He calls us to revolt and fight
with him for what is just and right,
to sing and live Magnificat
in crowded street and council flat.[29]

Fred Kaan's paraphrase of the *Magnificat* compellingly tells of a God who lifts up the poor, leaving the rich "with empty hands" while crying out to us to join in the struggle for justice. This is a text about action; the title of this hymn, "Magnificat now!" expresses Kaan's passionate desire to "bring the song of Mary into the present world."[30] In fact, the hymn was even seen to be controversial, and in 1972 it was discussed in Parliament because of its presence in *New Life*, a school hymnal.[31] It is not uncommon, however, for Kaan's texts to challenge those who sing them; he not only looks at the

29. Fred Kaan, "Sing we a song of high revolt (Magnificat now!)," Hope Publishing Company, http://www.hopepublishing.com/html/main.isx?sitesec =40.2.1.0&hymnID=5225, accessed March 22, 2014. Reproduced by permission from Hope Publishing Company © 1968. This text has been set to multiple tunes, including the well-known tune Truro. Carl Daw points out that "the very British idiom 'council flat' (i.e., subsidized housing) did not resonate with North Americans and kept the text from catching hold here." Carl P. Daw, Jr., e-mail message to author, February 13, 2012. As a result, some American hymnals changed the text to "walk-up flat." Alan Luff, "Sing we a song of high revolt," The Canterbury Dictionary of Hymnology, http://www.hymnology.co.uk/s /sing-we-a-song-of-high-revolt, accessed March 2014. In fact, the last line is completely altered in Nicholas T. Freund and Betty Zins Reiber, eds., *Rejoice: Songs of Praise and Thanksgiving* (Schiller Park, IL: J. S. Paluch Company, 1989). The hymn appears at #228 and the last line reads "To ease his people's sorry lot."
30. Luff, "Sing we a song of high revolt."
31. Ibid.

effects of worship on the lives of Christians outside of church but also "challenges complacency and the failure of Christians to be as alert in their Christian lives as they are in other aspects of living. He expects Christians to take risks."[32] Perhaps there is no one who has taken the *Magnificat* as Kaan has and translated it into such a passionate call to action. No wonder he had Parliament worried.

Kaan's text was published in 1968, the same year as the Latin American Episcopal Conference (CELAM) in Medellín, Colombia, which was highly influential in the history of liberation theology and the development of the notion of the preferential option for the poor. A diocesan priest from the *Colegio Máximo* where Pope Francis has served as rector highlights the importance of the popular devotions to those living in the slums of Argentina when he says "to disregard popular faith . . . is, in a way, to disregard the option for the poor."[33] The Latino churches, both in North and South America, are one example where Mary is flourishing in a positive way. For many in this culture, she is seen as an empowering, liberating figure that encourages resistance to oppression.[34] The history of the Conquista must be kept in mind, however, where soldiers arrived fighting with Mary on their banners as her devotion was violently forced on people.[35] In addition, Marian devotion was used specifically to oppress women and to teach them to be resigned and passive to their captors who often performed unspeakable acts on them.[36]

In their chapter on "Mary and God's Wonders among the Poor," Ivone Gebara and Maria Clara Bingemar speak highly of Mary, because, "in Latin America one cannot speak about the church of the poor or of pastoral work among the popular classes without dealing with the figure of this woman who carried the Liberator of the poor

---

32. Alan Luff, "Frederik Kaan," The Canterbury Dictionary of Hymnology, http://www.hymnology.co.uk/f/frederik-kaan, accessed March 2014.

33. Paul Vallely, *Pope Francis: Untying the Knots* (London: Bloomsbury, 2013), 137.

34. Mark R. Francis, "Liturgy and Popular Piety in a Historical Perspective," in *Directory on Popular Piety and the Liturgy: Principles and Guidelines. A Commentary*, ed. Peter C. Phan (Collegeville, MN: Liturgical Press, 2002), 35.

35. Marcella Althaus-Reid, *From Feminist Theology to Indecent Theology* (London: SCM Press, 2004), 38.

36. Althaus-Reid, *From Feminist Theology to Indecent Theology*, 31, 38–42.

in her womb and gave birth to him."[37] Mary, herself "a poor woman and socially insignificant" is "a symbol of hope that nourishes the poor along the way."[38] Because Mary journeys with those who are suffering, she is known as "Mother of the Oppressed," "Our Lady of Latin America," and "Mother of the Forgotten."[39]

Gebara and Bingemar describe the *Magnificat* not only as Mary's Song but also as the "Song of the People," which they see as "fundamental for a better understanding of Marian piety in Latin America."[40] While many speak of Mary's *fiat* or assent to God at the annunciation, Gebara and Bingemar write that Mary is "the channel both of God's 'yes' to the people and of God's 'no' to the forces that hinder the same people from living the covenant with their God."[41] The *Magnificat* offers the assurance that God will say "no" "to any kind of sin that impedes or blocks the Kingdom of justice and freedom from arriving."[42] In addition to Mary's saying " 'yes' to God and God's plan," there is also the side of Mary that says " 'no' to injustice and to the state of things with which there can be no compromise. This is Mary's 'no' to the sin of alienation, to what is not done when others are being victimized and are suffering."[43]

What does all this mean for the Church? Gebara and Bingemar say that "it will mean evaluating itself on its commitment to announcing the good news to the poor and denouncing anything that prevents this good news from becoming a reality."[44] This is not

---

37. Ivone Gebara and Maria Clara Bingemar, *Mary: Mother of God, Mother of the Poor*, trans. Phillip Berryman (Maryknoll, NY: Orbis Book, 1989), 159. Althaus-Reid critiques the work of Gebara and Bingemar for, among other reasons, their tendency to essentialize the "women" they are speaking of in their book as only being peasant women (in rural situations), rather than also speaking to poor women in urban situations. Marcella Althaus-Reid, *Indecent Theology: Theological Perversions in Sex, Gender and Politics* (London and New York: Routledge, 2000), 64. For her extended critique, see ibid., 40–46.

38. Ibid., 161–62.

39. Ibid., 163.

40. Ibid., 164.

41. Ibid., 165.

42. Ibid., 169.

43. Ibid., 170.

44. Ibid.

always a welcome message to those in political and/or religious power. In fact, in the words of Johann Baptist Metz, it can be seen as a "dangerous memory" in that "the definite memory of suffering . . . is dangerous in its capacities both (1) to render a critique of the evolutionary world view and (2) to stimulate human imagination for social-political action."[45] The ability of the *Magnificat* to stir people to social action is so profound, and the "message is so subversive that for a period during the 1980s the government of Guatemala banned its public recitation."[46] Liberation theologian Gustavo Gutiérrez echoes the notion that the revolutionary force of Mary's song cannot be contained: "Any exegesis is fruitless that attempts to tone down what Mary's song tells us about preferential love of God for the lowly and the abused, and about the transformation of history that God's loving will implies."[47]

Bonnie Jensen, in her meditation "We Sing Mary's Song," refers to Luther's commentary on the *Magnificat* when she says "each time we sing the *Magnificat*, we proclaim to each other what sort of God we believe in and especially, as Luther says, how God deals with those of low and high degree. Luther says we sing it for three reasons: (1) to strengthen our faith, (2) to comfort the lowly, and (3) to terrify the mighty."[48] In referring to how singing the *Magnificat* can comfort the lowly, Jensen adds "we sing to put ourselves in solidarity with the lowly and those who suffer. We sing in order to bring in the reign and community of our Lord Jesus Christ."[49] This is important in that *Magnificat* not only brings comfort to those who are suffering

45. Bruce T. Morrill, *Anamnesis as Dangerous Memory: Political and Liturgical Theology in Dialogue* (Collegeville, MN: Liturgical Press, Pueblo, 2000), 30. Morrill states that Metz sees these narratives of suffering as irreducible because they "neither allow themselves to be abridged nor allow their hearers to continue with their lives or arguments (reason) unaffected." In fact, they goad those who hear them to the praxis of the *imitatio Christi*. See Morrill, *Anamnesis as Dangerous Memory*, 46, 34.

46. Elizabeth Johnson, *Truly Our Sister: A Theology of Mary in the Communion of the Saints* (New York: Continuum, 2003), 269.

47. Gustavo Gutiérrez, *The God of Life*, trans. Matthew O'Connell (Maryknoll, NY: Orbis, 1991), 185, as quoted in Johnson, *Truly Our Sister*, 269.

48. Jensen, "We Sing Mary's Song," 167.

49. Ibid., 169.

but also allows those who may not be suffering but are striving for justice to be in solidarity with their sisters and brothers who are in need. In both cases, those who are suffering and those in solidarity are both singing for the coming of justice and freedom that Gebara and Bingemar refer to.

The *Magnificat* terrifies the mighty because it challenges their power. This speaks to the situation where liberation theology and its "dangerous memory" make those in position of power, both religious and political, very uneasy. Jensen describes how Luther delivered a very disruptive message to the mighty: "Luther said, 'The mightier you are, the more you must fear' when you sing the *Magnificat*. We fear because we *sing in faith*, believing God does bring down the mighty."[50] This is why the *Magnificat* is so powerful, and as seen above, so dangerous that the government in Guatemala would not allow it to be recited. We also "take the risk" of singing the *Magnificat*, "knowing that fear can lead us to repentance, and repentance prepares us for the coming reign of God."[51] How can we put the *Magnificat* into action, heeding Kaan's plea of "Magnificat now!" as we help bring about God's kingdom here and now?

"And the World Is about to Turn!"

In Rory Cooney's (b. 1952) paraphrase of the *Magnificat*, the "Canticle of the Turning," the refrain speaks of a world that is on the verge of change:

> My heart shall sing of the day you bring.
>   Let the fires of your justice burn.
> Wipe away all tears, for the dawn draws near,
>   And the world is about to turn![52]

50. Ibid., 168 (emphasis Jensen).
51. Ibid.
52. Rory Cooney's paraphrase of the *Magnificat*, "Canticle of the Turning," set to the tune STAR OF THE COUNTY DOWN, #624 in *Worship*, 4th ed. Reproduced by permission from GIA Publications © 1990.

A similar view is present in the *Magnificat*-based poem "Our Lady" by Mary Coleridge (1861–1907). In discussing the poem, Nancy de Flon comments: "in Mary Coleridge's hands the *Magnificat* becomes the song of reversal as we interpret it in our own age—a hymn to the God who turns the world upside down by liberating the oppressed, with Mary, God's mother, leading us in that song."[53] How can Marian congregational song help people want to turn toward their neighbor and take up the action called for in the *Magnificat*? Four qualities should be included in future Marian congregational songs in order to encourage Christians to engage in Mary's call to turn the world upside down, a world where

> The mighty have been vanquished,
>   the lowly lifted up.
> The hungry find abundance;
>   the rich, an empty cup.[54]

The first quality that future Marian congregational songs should possess is a strong biblical foundation. Vatican II emphasized the biblical nature of Marian devotions not only to control their excesses, but also to address ecumenical concerns. Max Thurian explores the ecumenical aspects of Mary's role and vocation in *Mary, Mother of all Christians*, writing that "instead of being a cause of division amongst us, Christian reflection on the role of the Virgin Mary should be a cause of rejoicing and a source of prayer."[55] In certain biblical

53. Nancy de Flon, "Mary in Nineteenth-Century English and American Poetry," in *Mary: The Complete Resource*, ed. Sarah Jane Boss (Oxford: Oxford University Press, 2007), 519.

54. Stanza 3 of "My soul proclaims with wonder," set to the tune St. Theodulph at #15 in Carl P. Daw, Jr., *To Sing God's Praise: 18 Metrical Canticles* (Carol Stream, IL: Hope Publishing Company, 1992). Reproduced by permission from Hope Publishing Company © 1989. As mentioned in the introduction, this study has primarily focused on the texts of Marian congregational songs. The four qualities put forward will continue in this vein by looking at issues in the texts, not music, of future Marian congregational songs.

55. Max Thurian, *Mary, Mother of all Christians*, trans. Neville B. Cryer (New York: Herder and Herder, 1964), 7. Thurian also points out that in addition to being wary of excess in Marian devotion, we also "must not give way to a silence and avoidance of Mary in the Christian conscience which would be equally unfaithful to the Gospel of Christ" (ibid., 183).

passages, Mary is mentioned with implications that speak to Christians today.

One such story from Scripture is the threat from Herod and the subsequent flight into Egypt (Matt 2:13-23).[56] Carl P. Daw, Jr. (b. 1944), points out the importance of looking at this passage in connection with the *Magnificat*'s call to put down the mighty and lift up the lowly. Here Mary thwarts Herod's plan "by active avoidance rather than by confrontation . . . one way to weaken the mighty is to remove oneself from their area of influence."[57] Perhaps this is why in his own hymn on this text, "Gentle Joseph heard a warning," Daw writes in stanza 1 of "Gentle Joseph" and "valiant Mary," writing that "the epithets for Joseph and Mary are intentionally reversed from the usual gender stereotypes."[58] Mary takes an active role in the *Magnificat*'s call in this biblical example. She also experiences what it is like to be an exile in a foreign land: "Through her journey into a foreign land, Mary takes her place among the refugees of the world, deepening and enlarging her identification with the oppressed and voiceless."[59]

Delores Dufner, OSB (b. 1939) reflects on this aspect of Mary's life in "Mary, first among believers." In the second stanza, Dufner writes how Mary's experience as an exile helps her identify with those who are displaced just as she was:

> Mary, first among the exiles,
>   Seeking refuge in the night,
> You left home with spouse and Infant,
>   Fleeing Herod's sword in fright.
> Mother now of all the exiles,
>   Give them sleep without alarm;

56. As noted in chap. 7, this passage is cited in Pope Paul VI, *Marialis Cultis* (For the Right Ordering and Development of Devotion to the Blessed Virgin Mary), February 2, 1974, 37, Papal Encyclicals Online, http://www.papalencyclicals.net/Paul06/p6marial.htm, accessed June 2014.

57. Carl P. Daw, Jr., e-mail message to author, February 13, 2012.

58. Carl P. Daw, Jr., *A Year of Grace: Hymns for the Church Year* (Carol Stream, IL: Hope Publishing Company, 1990), 38–39.

59. Ibid.

> Give them clothing, food, and shelter;
>> Keep them safe and free from harm.[60]

Thurian comments how Mary is "deeply touched by this tragedy [the killing of infants as ordered by Herod] from which she escapes."[61] In the process, Mary herself becomes "an exile, a refugee."[62] Daw reflects on this notion in the third and final stanza of "Gentle Joseph heard a warning" where he calls us to see Joseph, Mary, and Jesus in the face of all refugees we meet:

> Give us, God, such faith and courage
>> when we move from place to place,
> and to those who come among us,
>> make us channels of your grace.
> Let us see in every stranger
>> refugees from Bethlehem,
> help us offer each one welcome
>> and receive the Christ in them.[63]

Another biblical passage that could be used in Marian congregational songs is the scene at the foot of the cross, particularly in the Gospel of John (John 19:25-27). Thurian describes how this passage shows that Mary is "the type of the Church and of every Christian who, persecuted or on the very edge of distress, believes and hopes against all hope."[64] Mary's sufferings at the cross also allow her to participate in "the human sorrow of a woman who sees her only Son die" as well as "the spiritual grief of a believer who sees hope die."[65]

---

60. Stanza 2 of "Mary, first among believers," set to the tune Pleading Savior at #897 in *Worship*, 4th ed. Reproduced by permission from GIA Publications © 2011.

61. Thurian, *Mary, Mother of all Christians*, 112.

62. Ibid.

63. Daw, Jr., *A Year of Grace*, 38–39. The suggested tune for this text is either Pleading Savior or In Babilone. Reproduced by permission from Hope Publishing Company © 1990.

64. Thurian, *Mary, Mother of All Christians*, 115.

65. Ibid., 161. Thurian writes that Mary "will suffer more than any other Christian, since the object of her faith, He who is exposed to the world's prosecution,

In stanza 4 of "Mary, first among believers," Dufner picks up on the theme of Mary's suffering:

> Mary, first among the suff'ring,
>   Standing bowed beneath the cross,
> You knew all the pain and anguish
>   Of oppression, grief, and loss.
> Mother now of all the suff'ring,
>   May we show Compassion's face;
> May the victims of injustice
>   Know, through us, God's love and grace.[66]

Mary's suffering has led her to become the Mother of all those that suffer today. It compels us to show compassion to those who are suffering, allowing God's love and grace to shine through us.

Both of these biblical passages have shown how stories from the Bible can still have implications for our present situations. This leads to the second quality that future Marian congregational songs should possess: the ability to speak to the problems of today. As seen throughout this chapter, many new paraphrases of the *Magnificat* do speak to the plight of the poor and oppressed in our world today. But what about other issues, such as the oppression of people based on their race, class, gender, sexual orientation, and/or gender identity? Thurian emphasizes the need to be relevant, saying that "we no longer have the right to produce theology which is irrelevant to contemporary needs."[67] Liberation theologian Leonardo Boff (b. 1938), speaks specifically to the need of theology to be relevant in issues of gender:

> Is it not a sign for Western culture that Pope John Paul I could state, in public audience, that while God is indeed our Father, God is our Mother even more? Theology, like any science or discipline, must examine the relevant themes of its time. . . . But it depends for its subject matter on culture, society, and historical situations. These,

---

is at the same time the Son to whom she has given birth and whom she loves as a human mother" (ibid., 107).

66. "Mary, first among believers" is #897 in *Worship*, 4th ed.

67. Thurian, *Mary, Mother of all Christians*, 9.

after all, are what challenge it, thereby imposing a direction on its reflections.[68]

Boff goes on to say that because societal norms surrounding gender are changing, this leads to "an invitation to revitalize and recast traditional perspectives of faith on Mary. If theologians will not assume this task, who will?"[69] We have already seen how many hymn writers have refused to go along with the "normative" notion of Mary as a meek and mild woman, while also breaking open notions of how she can lead us to wider understandings of who "counts" as family and who is "included" in God's love.

Theologians and hymn writers must also examine and critique the structures that are leading to oppression, creating cries for the poor and lowly to be raised up. In addition, they must recognize that there are often multiple oppressions occurring at the same time. Cheng points out that "many progressive theologies—including early liberation theologies—are actually monochromatic theologies. That is, monochromatic theologies focus primarily on liberation from a singular oppression, as opposed to challenging the interplay of multiple oppressions."[70] The world is not simply black and white anymore; Cheng calls for a "rainbow theology" which takes into account multiplicity, which he defines as "a state of having multiple coexisting and overlapping identities, as opposed to a singular dominant identity."[71] For instance, when considering "the complexities of the category of 'gay'" one must also consider "the multiple intersecting identities such as race, ethnicity and class."[72]

One theologian who takes the notion of multiplicity into account in considering how Mary has been used as an oppressive figure is Marcella Althaus-Reid (1952–2009). Born in Argentina, she explores her notion of "indecent theology" which she describes as a

---

68. Leonardo Boff, *The Maternal Face of God: The Feminine and Its Religious Expression*, trans. Robert R. Barr and John W. Diercksmeier (San Francisco, CA: Harper & Row Publishers, 1987), 3.

69. Ibid., 5.

70. Patrick S. Cheng, *Rainbow Theology: Bridging Race, Sexuality, and Spirit* (New York: Seabury Books, 2013), xviii.

71. Ibid., 89.

72. Ibid., 94.

"theology which problematises and undresses the mythical layers of multiple oppression in Latin America," drawing from Liberation Theology and Queer Thinking as she examines both economic and theological forms of oppression.[73] Mary is often wrapped up in the structures of oppression; in fact, Althaus-Reid claims that "in Latin America the whole social structure of patriarchalism rests upon the pillars of Mariology," leading to the oppression and domestication of women as they internalize the stereotypes of what it means to be a Latin American woman through the figure of Mary.[74] Althaus-Reid critiques the "heterosexual matrices" of theology and society—both arenas where Mary and Mariology play strong roles—because these matrices lead to oppression based on gender, sexuality, race, and class among other attributes.[75] Theologians and hymn writers must take up the task of calling attention to how Mary is complicit in structures of oppression around the world and help her to become a symbol of hope, rather than oppression, to all those who are cast aside as "other" or "less than" in society.

If the oppressive social structures that Mary has helped to support are critiqued and fall by the wayside, new ways to speak about Mary can emerge. In his article on "Liturgical Language in a Socio-linguistic Perspective," David Crystal writes that "language rarely changes of its own volition (though it used to be thought that this was so). Language changes because society changes—not only in the obvious sense that new concepts give rise to new vocabulary, but more fundamentally, in that new social structures generate new linguistic identities."[76] What new linguistic identities can be given to Mary in congregational song and theology? This leads to the third quality that future Marian congregational songs should possess: the avoidance of past and present associations with Mary that are nega-

---

73. Althaus-Reid, *Indecent Theology*, 2.

74. Althaus-Reid, *From Feminist Theology to Indecent Theology*, 31. Althaus-Reid wonders if "a serious criticism of Mariology has not started, perhaps because Mariology fulfils such a crucial role in the patriarchal order of our society, much more than Christology" (ibid., 39).

75. Althaus-Reid, *Indecent Theology*, 82–83.

76. David Crystal, "Liturgical Language in a Sociolinguistic Perspective," in *Language and the Worship of the Church*, ed. David Jasper and R.C.D. Jasper (New York: St. Martin's Press, 1990), 145.

tive and oppressive while also looking for new and creative ways to speak about Mary.

Mary Frances Fleischaker's (b. 1945) text, "Mary, woman of the promise," is one of the few texts written after Vatican II that is not a paraphrase of the *Magnificat* yet still has something new and powerful to say about Mary. It was written in 1988 for a Marian Hymn Contest sponsored by the Huron Valley Chapter of the Hymn Society and the Liturgical Commission of the Diocese of Lansing.[77] This beautiful text "reflects on the role of Mary in the gospel stories and offers new and creative understandings of this woman of faith."[78] Over the course of five stanzas, Mary is referred to as: "woman of the promise"; "song of holy wisdom"; "morning star of justice"; "model of compassion"; and "woman of the Gospel." The text refers to Mary's predestination ("Sung before the world began"), the familiar notion from earlier texts of Mary as "a beacon for our sight," Mary as one who suffered at the foot of the cross ("Wounded by your offspring's pain"), and, in the final stanza, Mary as a model for discipleship.

Fleischaker has managed to join older images of Mary (articulated in a new way) with newer images of Mary to create a text that speaks to Mary today. The emphasis on Marian biblical sources as seen in chapter 6—part of Vatican II's push to downplay the excessive nature of some Marian devotion (LG 67)[79]—has had a profound impact on Marian congregational song following Vatican II and has led to a call for "new and creative understandings" of Mary, a call that Fleischaker has skillfully answered.

---

77. This text was the winning entry in the Marian Hymn Contest for the Huron Valley Chapter of the Hymn Society and the Liturgical Commission of the Diocese of Lansing. A second contest to write the accompanying tune was won by Alfred V. Fedak for his tune Gratia Plena. See Hymn Society of the United States and Canada, "New Hymn and Tune," *The Hymn* 41, no. 1 (January 1990): 36.

78. Kristen L. Forman, ed., *The New Century Hymnal Companion: A Guide to the Hymns* (Cleveland, OH: Pilgrim Press, 1998), 273.

79. Here there is a warning against "false exaggeration" in Marian devotion. See also John O'Malley, *What Happened at Vatican II* (Cambridge, MA: The Belknap Press of Harvard University Press, 2008), 188.

1. Mary, woman of the promise;
     Vessel of your people's dreams,
   Through your open, willing spirit
     Waters of God's goodness streamed.

2. Mary, song of holy wisdom,
     Sung before the world began,
   Faithful to the Word within, you
     Carried out God's wondrous plan.

3. Mary, morning star of justice;
     Mirror of the radiant light,
   In the shadows of life's journey,
     Be a beacon for our sight.

4. Mary, model of compassion;
     Wounded by your offspring's pain,
   When our hearts are torn by sorrow,
     Teach us how to love again.

5. Mary, woman of the Gospel;
     Humble home for treasured seed,
   Help us to be true disciples
     Bearing fruit in word and deed.[80]

While Barbara Pope points out that liberation theologians and feminists have tried to "redefine Mary's role in the church," it seems that most progressive Catholics "are at present more committed to redefining living women's roles than to rehabilitating a symbol weighed down by a heritage of defensive conservatism and male projection."[81] Future Marian congregational song has the potential

80. "Mary, woman of the promise," #477 in *Journeysongs*, ed. Eric Schumock and Randall Keith DeBruyn, 3rd ed. (Portland, OR: OCP Publications, 2012). © 1998, Mary Frances Fleischaker. All rights reserved. Reproduced with permission of Selah Publishing Co., exclusive agent. In *Journeysongs* the text is set to the tune Drakes Broughton, elsewhere it is set to Quem Pastores and Stuttgart. Fleischaker's preference is that the text be set to Stuttgart. Mary Frances Fleischaker, e-mail message to author, January 28, 2014.

81. Barbara Corrado Pope, "Immaculate and Powerful: The Marian Revival in the Nineteenth Century," in *Immaculate & Powerful: The Female in Sacred Image and*

to lead the way in theology, in an attempt to shed both past and present negative associations with Mary as well as the use of Mary as a weapon against certain groups of people. By doing so, perhaps these future texts will lead to a shift from "as the Church goes, so goes Mary" to the return of "as Mary goes, so goes the Church."[82]

The fourth and final quality that future Marian congregational songs should possess is a move from the previous passive, spiritual understanding of Mary's message in the *Magnificat* to an active turn toward actual works of social justice and love of neighbor. Duffy notes a shift after Vatican II from the Mary of John's gospel to the Mary of Luke's gospel. He writes how the "promises" made in the *Magnificat* would have been "spiritualized" in nineteenth-century Mariology (and arguably in Mariology up until Vatican II), as "the text was emphatically not read as having a bearing on social justice more generally, and in a Mariology which endorsed right-wing regimes so long as they were Catholic, the text could be recited by stony-faced *generalissimos* without a qualm."[83] After Vatican II, however, liberation theology helped the *Magnificat* to not "be spiritualized into harmlessness" as "Mary's song becomes a manifesto for the justice already erupting into the present world order . . . and Mary herself becomes a representative figure, a source of hope and strength for all who struggle for freedom from oppression."[84]

Duffy also makes an important point about how the *Magnificat* is used liturgically: "Because it is recited so often, daily in the divine office, it is a text whose implications often pass unnoticed. Its rhetoric is that of the world turned upside down—the hungry fed, the rich sent empty away, the kings dethroned, the poor and oppressed raised up."[85] The *Magnificat*—particularly before Vatican II—was most likely used during the Divine Office, particularly at Sunday Vespers, which was quite popular in the late nineteenth and early twentieth centuries.[86]

Social Reality, ed. Clarissa W. Atkinson, Constance H. Buchanan and Margaret R. Miles (Boston, MA: Beacon Press, 1985), 196.

82. Ibid.

83. Duffy, *Faith of Our Fathers*, 36–37.

84. Ibid.

85. Ibid., 36.

86. See Thomas E. Wangler, "Catholic Religious Life in Boston in the Era of Cardinal O'Connell," in *Catholic Boston: Studies in Religion and Community,*

After Vatican II and *Sacrosanctum Concilium*, which described the liturgy as fount and summit (SC 10), the focus seems to have been on the Mass and reception of the Eucharist. Focus on the laity's participation in the Liturgy of the Hours seems to have waned.[87] This most likely means that the *Magnificat* in English, while often being placed in sections of hymnals devoted to Evening Prayer, is presumably being sung at a Mass, particularly Masses celebrated on Marian feasts. While in the years immediately after Vatican II the *Magnificat* may have been kept because it was biblical and because people were unsure about how to go writing new congregational songs about Mary that reflected their current context, the *Magnificat* seems to continue to thrive today.

With the distinct possibility that the only time a normal Sunday morning (or Saturday evening) churchgoer would hear the *Magnificat* is in the context of the Eucharist, perhaps this context can be used to capitalize on the "unread vision" of the liturgical movement—as described by Keith Pecklers—in the joining of liturgy and the issues of social justice that Duffy speaks to. Zimmerman calls for new Marian congregational songs. She also appeals for Marian devotion that leads "beyond individual piety and affective satisfaction to public witness to the gospel and to the social dimension of Christian life and prayer," so that devotions not only "lead to and from the liturgy but also must bring us to and from care and concern for others."[88]

In his discussion of the *Magnificat*, Thurian writes that

> for the Virgin the signs of the mercy of the Lord are the putting down of the proud and the powerful and the exalting of those of low degree, the sending away empty of the rich, so that the hungry might be filled with good things. She could have enumerated other signs but these two are sufficient to reveal that the love of God takes a concrete human social form and is not simply an interior spiritual consolation.[89]

1870–1970, ed. Robert E. Sullivan and James M. O'Toole (Boston MA: Roman Catholic Archbishop of Boston, 1985), 239–72.

87. See Robert Taft, *The Liturgy of the Hours in the East and West: The Origins of the Divine Office and its Meaning for Today*, 2nd rev. ed. (Collegeville, MN: Liturgical Press, 1993), 317.

88. Zimmerman, "Veneration of the Holy Mother of God," 110.

89. Thurian, *Mary, Mother of all Christians*, 93.

Here Thurian is moving away from "an interior spiritual consolation" to the active, exterior signs of exalting those of low degree and filling the hungry with good things. Black liberation theologian James Cone (b. 1938) similarly warns against spiritualizing the cross in *The Cross and the Lynching Tree*. Just as the *Magnificat* is a call to action to help the poor and the oppressed, the cross is not simply for "contemplation and adoration"; rather, the cross challenges us to take concrete action, or in the words of "Latin American liberation theologian Jon Sobrino . . . 'to take the crucified down from the cross.' "[90]

Perhaps Mary, her *Magnificat,* and future Marian congregational song can lead us to turn "towards, not away from, engagement with and commitment to practical attempts to order the 'earthly and temporal city.' "[91] Perhaps in singing the *Magnificat*, the joining of the power of music from Culture Four, the "Artistic Culture," with Culture One, the "Prophetic Culture," which counts among its ranks such visionaries as Martin Luther King, Jr., will be the forces necessary to "shock us out of our complacency"[92] to help our sisters and brothers in need. Many of the hymn writers quoted in this chapter are not Catholic.[93] Perhaps this is a sign that Mary—and her *Magnificat*—can truly be the "Promoter of Christian union" that Vatican II hoped for, leading all denominations to engage not only with each other but also with those in the world who most desperately need our compassion and love, leading us, in the words of the great civil rights leader and theologian Howard Thurman (1900–81) to be "apostles of sensitiveness" who in loving "make of one's heart a swinging door."[94]

90. Jon Sobrino, *No Salvation outside the Poor: Prophetic-Utopian Essays* (Maryknoll, NY: Orbis Books, 2008), 1–17, as quoted in James H. Cone, *The Cross and the Lynching Tree* (Maryknoll, NY: Orbis Books, 2011), 161.

91. Duffy, *Faith of Our Fathers*, 37–38.

92. John O'Malley, *Four Cultures of the West* (Cambridge, MA: The Belknap Press of Harvard University Press, 2004), 74.

93. Carl Daw is an Episcopalian, Edith Sinclair Downing is a member of the Presbyterian Church (USA), Fred Kaan is a member of the United Reformed Church in the United Kingdom, and Adam Tice is a Mennonite.

94. Howard Thurman, *A Strange Freedom: The Best of Howard Thurman on Religious Experience and Public Life*, ed. Walter Earl Fluker and Catherine Tumber (Boston, MA: Beacon Press, 1998), 12, 184.

One man who has regularly employed these four qualities and has turned the world upside down is Pope Francis. He has done this by following the example of his namesake, St. Francis of Assisi, proclaiming that he wants a "Church which practices what it preaches," thus following the saying attributed to St. Francis, "You must preach the gospel at all times, and if necessary use words."[95] Pope Francis not only tells people they should care for the poor and oppressed, but he also sets an example for all to follow by living a simple life, embracing and caring for the sick, and serving those less fortunate—perhaps even sneaking out of the Vatican at night to do so.[96]

Here is someone who is not spiritualizing the message of the *Magnificat*, but rather is putting it into action by lifting up the lowly and feeding the hungry. Francis further translates this message for the entire Church, saying that it should not be turned in on itself, but rather, it should be turned outward, or as he likes to say, "[a] Church that stays in the sacristy too long gets sick."[97] He brought this up during the conclave where he was eventually elected pope when he reminded those present that

> the Church is supposed to be the *mysterium lunae*—the mystery of the moon is that it has no light but simply reflects the light of the sun. The Church must not fool itself that is has light of its own; if it does that it falls into what Henri De Lubac in *The Splendour of the Church* called the greatest of evils—spiritual worldliness. That is what happens with a self-referential Church, which refuses to go beyond itself.[98]

This "Pope for the Poor"[99] has made it clear that he follows Mary's call to lift up the lowly and fill the hungry with good things. Throughout his life he has spoken up for the poor and cared for them, calling

95. Vallely, *Pope Francis*, 195–96.

96. "Is Pope Francis Leaving Vatican at Night to Minister to Homeless?" (December 2, 2013), The Huffington Post, http://www.huffingtonpost .com/2013/12/02/pope-francis-homeless_n_4373884.html, accessed January 13, 2014.

97. Vallely, *Pope Francis*, 106.

98. Ibid., 155.

99. Ibid., 127.

them "the treasure of the Church" while also saying that "our true power must be service."[100] In looking at the plight of the poor, Francis calls for "solutions of justice and not just philanthropy" because "extreme poverty and unjust economic structures are 'violations of human rights.'"[101] This focus on action and addressing the structures which oppress the poor has continued into his pontificate, as the first major papal document to be written solely in his hand—*Lumen Fidei* having been mostly written by Benedict XVI before he resigned—is *Evangelii Gaudium*, a strongly worded condemnation of capitalism, which he calls the "new tyranny" as he also attacks the "idolatry of money."[102] The pope not only calls for care for the poor but he also criticizes the structures that bring about such gross injustice and inequality.[103] Francis writes that until the "structural causes of inequality" are dealt with, "no solution will be found for the world's problems or, for that matter, to any problems. Inequality is the root of social ills."[104]

Later in *Evangelii Gaudium* Francis describes the Church's work of evangelization as having a "Marian 'style.'"[105] He says that by looking to the model of Mary, "we come to believe once again in the revolutionary nature of love and tenderness." Throughout the Bible, we see patterns in Mary of the "interplay of justice and tenderness, of contemplation and concern for others." This makes her a "model of evangelization" and is why she is referred to as "The Star of the new evangelization," because just as she has been referred to a star

---

100. Jorge Mario Bergoglio and Abraham Skorka, *On Heaven and Earth: Pope Francis on Faith, Family, and the Church in the Twenty-First Century*, trans. Alejandro Bermudez and Howard Goodman, ed. Diego F. Rosemberg (New York: Image, 2013), 173.

101. Vallely, *Pope Francis*, 195.

102. Francis, *Evangelii Gaudium* (On the Proclamation of the Gospel in Today's World), November 24, 2013, 55–56, The Holy See, http://w2.vatican.va/content /francesco/en/apost_exhortations/documents/papa-francesco_esortazione-ap _20131124_evangelii-gaudium.html, accessed June 2014.

103. Ibid., 53–54.

104. Ibid., 202.

105. Ibid., 288. All quotations from *Evangelii Gaudium* in this paragraph are from para. 288.

leading us throughout the centuries, now she is a model for the new evangelization espoused by the pope.

In Francis, the world has an example of someone who has taken the biblical message of the *Magnificat*, made it relevant for today, added new and creative understandings of Mary, and put the words of the *Magnificat* into concrete action. In doing so, he has injected new life into the Church, inspiring millions around the world—both those inside and outside of the Catholic Church. Francis ends *Evangelii Gaudium* with a beautiful prayer to Mary, asking her to

> help us to bear radiant witness to communion,
> service, ardent and generous faith,
> justice and love of the poor,
> that the joy of the Gospel
> may reach to the ends of the earth,
> illuminating even the fringes of our world.[106]

And the world is about to turn.

106. Ibid., 288.

Bibliography

Primary Sources

Apocryphal Literature

"The Protoevangelium of James," in *The Apocryphal New Testament: A Collection of Apocryphal Christian Literature in an English Translation*, edited by James Keith Elliott, 48–65. Oxford: Clarendon Press, 1993.

Catholic Documents (Official)

Directory on Popular Piety and the Liturgy: Principles and Guidelines. December 17, 2001. The Holy See. http://www.vatican.va/roman_curia/congregations/ccdds/documents/rc_con_ccdds_doc_20020513_vers-direttorio_en.html (accessed June 2014).

National Conference of Catholic Bishops. *Behold Your Mother: Woman of Faith. A Pastoral Letter on the Blessed Virgin Mary*, November 21, 1973. Washington, DC: Publications Office United States Catholic Conference.

———. *Order of Crowning an Image of the Blessed Virgin Mary*. New Jersey: Catholic Book Publishing Corp., 2005.

Rite of Funerals: The Roman Ritual Revised by Decree of the Second Vatican Council. Published by authority of Pope Paul VI. English translation approved by the National Conference of Catholic Bishops and confirmed by the Apostolic See. New York: Catholic Book Publishing Co., 1971.

Sacred Congregation of Rites. *Musicam Sacram* (Instruction on Music in the Liturgy), March 5, 1967. Adoremus Society for the Renewal of the Sacred Liturgy. http://www.adoremus.org/MusicamSacram.html (accessed June 2014).

Catholic Experiences/Narratives

Carroll, James. *Practicing Catholic*. Boston: Houghton Mifflin Harcourt, 2009.

Rivers, Caryl. *Aphrodite at Mid-Century: Growing Up Catholic and Female in Post-War America*. Garden City, NY: Doubleday, 1973.

Sumrall, Amber Coverdale, and Patrice Vecchione, eds. *Bless Me, Father: Stories of Catholic Childhood*. New York: Plume, 1994.

———. *Catholic Girls: Stories, Poems and Memoirs by Louise Erdrich, Mary Gordon, Audre Lorde, Mary McCarthy, Francine Prose, and 47 Others*. New York: Plume, 1992.

Catholic Liturgical Books

Book of Mary: Prayers in Honor of the Blessed Virgin Mary/Secretariat, Bishops' Committee on the Liturgy, National Conference of Catholic Bishops. Washington, DC: Office of Publishing and Promotion Services, US Catholic Conference, 1987.

Catholic Liturgical Documents

The Canons and Decrees of the Council of Trent. Translated by H. J. Schroeder, Rockford, IL: Tan Books and Publishers, 1978.

Hoffman, Elizabeth, ed. *The Liturgy Documents: A Parish Resource*. 3rd ed. Vol. 1. Collegeville, MN: Liturgical Press, 1991.

Society of St. Gregory of America. "The Black List: Disapproved Music." Musica Sacra Church, Music Association of America, http://www.musicasacra.com/pdf/blacklist.pdf (accessed June 2014).

United States Conference of Catholic Bishops. *Sing to the Lord: Music in Divine Worship*, November 14, 2007. The Catholic Church in Southwestern Indiana. http://www.evansville-diocese.org/worship/SingTo TheLord.pdf (accessed June 2014).

Hymnals

Adoremus Society for the Renewal of the Sacred Liturgy, ed. *The Adoremus Hymnal: A Congregational Missal/Hymnal for the Celebration of Sung Mass in the Roman Rite*. San Francisco, CA: Ignatius Press, 1997.

The Basilian Fathers, ed. *The New Saint Basil Hymnal*. Cincinnati, OH: Ralph Jusko Publications / Willis Music Company, 1958.

———. *St. Basil's Hymnal: Containing Music for Vespers of All the Sundays and Festivals of the Year. Three Masses and over Two Hundred Hymns*. Toronto: St. Michael's College, 1891.

———. *St. Basil's Hymnal: Containing Music for Vespers of All the Sundays and Festivals of the Year. Three Masses and over Two Hundred Hymns, Together with Litanies, Daily Prayers, Prayers at Mass, Preparation and Prayers for Confession and Communion, and the Office and Rules for Sodalities of the Blessed Virgin Mary.* 10th ed. Toronto, and Medina, NY: St. Basil's Novitiate and James Brennan, 1906.

———. *St. Basil's Hymnal: An Extensive Collection of English and Latin Hymns for Church, School and Home. Arranged for Feasts and Seasons of the Ecclesiastical Year: Gregorian Masses, Vespers, Motets for Benediction, Litanies, Etc.* Chicago: John P. Daleiden Co., 1918.

———. *St. Basil's Hymnal: An Extensive Collection of English and Latin Hymns for Church, School and Home. Arranged for Feasts and Seasons of the Ecclesiastical Year; Gregorian Masses, Vespers, Motets for Benedictions, Litanies, Etc.* 35th ed. Los Angeles, CA: C.F. Horan Co., 1925.

———. *St. Basil's Hymnal: An Extensive Collection of English and Latin Hymns for Church, School and Home. Arranged for Feasts and Seasons of the Ecclesiastical Year. Gregorian Masses, Vespers, Motets for Benediction, Litanies, Etc.* 39th ed. Detroit, MI: Basilian Press, 1935.

Blue, Robert, et al., eds. *Hymnal for Young Christians, Volume Two: Accompaniment Edition for Chanter, Choir, and Guitarist.* Los Angeles, CA: F.E.L. Publications, 1970.

Bonvin, Ludwig, ed. *"Hosanna" Catholic Hymn Book: With an Appendix of Prayers and Devotions.* 4th ed. St. Louis, MO: B. Herder, 1914.

Christian Brothers, ed. *The Catholic Youth's Hymn Book: Containing the Hymns of the Seasons and Festivals of the Year, and an Extensive Collection of Sacred Melodies. To which are Added an Easy Mass, Vespers, and Motets.* New York: P. O'Shea, 1871.

———. *The De La Salle Hymnal for Catholic Schools and Choirs.* New York: La Salle Bureau, 1913.

De Brant, Cyr, ed. *Mediator Dei Hymnal: For Unison Choirs and Congregations.* Toledo, OH: Gregorian Institute of America, 1955.

Episcopal Church. *The Hymnal 1982: According to the Use of the Episcopal Church.* New York: Church Hymnal Corp., 1985.

Freund, Nicholas T., and Betty Zins Reiber, eds. *Rejoice: Songs of Praise and Thanksgiving.* Schiller Park, IL: J. S. Paluch Company, 1989.

Glory & Praise: Classic Edition. Phoenix, AZ: North American Liturgy Resources, 1990.

Glory & Praise: Parish Music Program. Phoenix, AZ: North American Liturgy Resources, 1984.

Hurlbut, Sidney S., ed. *A Treasury of Catholic Song: Comprising Some Two Hundred Hymns from Catholic Sources Old and New. Gathered, Edited and Allotted to Fitting Tunes for Congregational Use.* New York, NY: J. Fischer and Bro., Publishers, 1915.

Hymnal for Young Christians: A Supplement to Adult Hymnals. Designed for Use in Church and School. Melody Edition for Congregational Singing. Chicago: F.E.L. Publications, 1966.

Marier, Theodore, ed. *Hymns, Psalms and Spiritual Canticles: A Parish Music Manual.* Belmont, MA: BACS Publishing Co., 1983.

Marist Brothers, ed. *American Catholic Hymnal: An Extensive Collection of Hymns, Latin Chants, and Sacred Songs for Church, School, and Home, Including Gregorian Masses, Vesper Psalms, Litanies.* New York: P.J. Kenedy and Sons, 1913.

Montani, Nicola A., ed. *The St. Gregory Hymnal and Catholic Choir Book: A Complete Collection of Approved English and Latin Hymns, Liturgical Motets, and Appropriate Devotional Music for the Various Seasons of the Liturgical Year. Particularly Adapted to the Requirements of Choirs, Schools, Academies, Seminaries, Convents, Sodalities and Sunday Schools.* Philadelphia: St. Gregory Guild, 1920.

Nachtwey, Roger D., ed. *Hymnal for Young Christians, Volume Three: Accompaniment Edition for Chanter, Choir, and Guitarist.* Los Angeles, CA: F.E.L. Publications, 1973.

Never Too Young: Spirit & Song for Young People; A Music Resource for Prayer, Worship & Classroom. Portland, OR: spiritandsong.com, 2007.

Our Parish Prays and Sings: Dialog Mass, Hymns, Chants. Collegeville, MN: Liturgical Press, 1959.

The People's Hymnal Committee, ed. *The People's Hymnal: Voice Book.* 2nd ed. Cincinnati, OH: World Library of Sacred Music, 1961.

People's Mass Book Committee, ed. *People's Mass Book: Hymns, Psalms, Masses, and Bible Services for Participation of the Faithful at Mass and Other Services According to the Second Vatican Council's Constitution on the Sacred Liturgy; Voice Book.* 2nd ed. Cincinnati, OH: World Library of Sacred Music, 1964.

Pius Tenth School of Liturgical Music, ed. *The Pius X Hymnal: For Unison, Two Equal, or Four Mixed Voices.* Boston, MA: McLaughlin and Reilly Co., 1953; reprint, 1956.

Reilly, James A., ed. *The Standard Catholic Hymnal: Complete Edition.* Boston, MA: McLaughlin and Reilly Co., 1921.

Rice, Richard, ed. *The Parish Book of Chant: A Manual of Gregorian Chant and a Liturgical Resource for Scholas and Congregations; Including Order of Sung Mass for both Ordinary and Extraordinary Forms of the Roman Rite with a Complete Kyriale, along with Chants and Hymns for Occasional and Seasonal Use and Their Literal English Translations.* 2nd exp. ed. The Church Music Association of America, 2012. http://media.musicasacra.com/books/pbc_2nd.pdf (accessed April 2014).

Roesler, Alexander, ed. *Psallite: Catholic English Hymns; With an Appendix of Prayers and Devotions*. 8th ed. St. Louis, MO: B. Herder Book Company, 1918.

Schumock, Eric, and Randall Keith DeBruyn, eds. *Journeysongs*. 3rd ed. Portland, OR: OCP Publications, 2012.

Sisters of Notre Dame, ed. *Sunday School Hymn Book*. Boston: Oliver Ditson Company, 1907; reprint, Philadelphia, PA: Oliver Ditson Company; Theodore Presser Co., Distributors, 1915.

―――. *Wreath of Mary: Companion to the May Chimes. A Collection of Hymns to the Blessed Virgin*. Boston, MA: Oliver Ditson and Co., 1883.

Sisters of Notre Dame, Cincinnati, ed. *May Chimes: A Collection of Hymns to the Blessed Virgin*. Boston, MA: Oliver Ditson Co., 1871.

Sisters of Notre Dame, Cleveland, ed. *Laudate Pueri! A Collection of Catholic Hymns with an Appendix of Prayers*. 3rd ed. Cleveland, OH: The Ohio Printing Co., 1903.

Socias, James, and Christian F. Stepansky, eds. *Cantate et Iubilate Deo: A Devotional and Liturgical Hymnal*. Princeton, NJ: Scepter Publishers, 1999.

Theological College (Washington, DC), ed. *The People's Hymnal*. Cincinnati, OH: World Library of Sacred Music, 1955.

Tomaszek, Thomas N., and Rick Modlin, eds. *Spirit & Song: A Seeker's Guide for Liturgy and Prayer*. Assembly/Guitar ed. Portland, OR: Oregon Catholic Press, 1999.

Tozer, A. Edmonds. *Catholic Church Hymnal with Music*. New York: J. Fischer and Bro., 1905.

Tozer, A. Edmonds, ed. *Catholic Hymns, Original and Translated: With Accompanying Tunes*. New and enlarged ed. London and Boston, USA: Cary and Co. and Oliver Ditson Co., 1898.

The Word of God Music, ed. *Songs of Praise: Combined Edition*. Ann Arbor, MI: Servant Music Publications, 1982.

Young, Alfred, ed. *The Catholic Hymnal: Containing Hymns for Congregational and Home Use, and the Vesper Psalms, the Office of Compline, the Litanies, Hymns at Benediction, Etc.; The Tunes by Rev. Alfred Young, Priest of the Congregation of St. Paul the Apostle; The Words Original and Selected*. New York: Catholic Publication Society Co, 1884.

Young, J. B., ed. *The Roman Hymnal: A Complete Manual of English Hymns & Latin Chants for the Use of Congregations, Schools, Colleges and Choirs*. 16th ed. New York and Cincinnati: Fr. Pustet and Co., 1897.

Papal Declarations/Encyclicals

Francis. *Evangelii Gaudium*, On the Proclamation of the Gospel in Today's World, November 24, 2013. The Holy See. http://w2.vatican.va /content/francesco/en/apost_exhortations/documents/papa -francesco_esortazione-ap_20131124_evangelii-gaudium.html (accessed June 2014).

John Paul II. *Mary: God's Yes to Man—Pope John Paul II's Encyclical* Redemptoris Mater. Introduction by Joseph Cardinal Ratzinger and Commentary by Hans Urs von Balthasar. San Francisco, CA: Ignatius Press, 1988.

Leo XIII. *Aeterni Patris*, On the Restoration of Christian Philosophy, August 4, 1879. Papal Encyclicals Online. http://www.papalencyclicals.net /Leo13/l13cph.htm (accessed June 2014).

———. *The Rosary of Mary: Translations of the Encyclical and Apostolic Letters of Pope Leo XIII*, edited by William Raymond Lawler. Paterson, NJ: St. Anthony Guild Press, 1944.

The Papal Encyclicals. Vol. 2, 1878–1903, edited by Claudia Carlen. Ann Arbor, MI: The Pierian Press, 1990.

Paul VI. *Marialis Cultis*, For the Right Ordering and Development of Devotion to the Blessed Virgin Mary. February 2, 1974. Papal Encyclicals Online. http://www.papalencyclicals.net/Paul06/p6marial.htm (accessed June 2014).

Pius IX. *Ineffabilis Deus*, the Immaculate Conception, December 8, 1854. Papal Encyclicals Online. http://www.papalencyclicals.net/Pius09 /p9ineff.htm (accessed June 2014).

———. *Ubi Primum*, On the Immaculate Conception, February 2, 1849. Eternal World Television Network. http://www.ewtn.com/library /encyc/p9ubipr2.htm (accessed June 2014).

Pius X. *Ad Diem Illum Laetissimum*, On the Immaculate Conception, February 2, 1904. Papal Encyclicals Online. http://www.papalencyclicals .net/Pius10/p10imcon.htm (accessed June 2014).

———. *Tra le Sollecitudini*, Instruction on Sacred Music, November 22, 1903. Adoremus Society for the Renewal of the Sacred Liturgy. http://www .adoremus.org/MotuProprio.html (accessed June 2014).

Pius XI. *Ingravescentibus Malis*, On the Rosary, September 29, 1937. Papal Encyclicals Online. http://www.papalencyclicals.net/Pius11/P11GRAVE .HTM (accessed June 2014).

Pius XII. *Ad Caeli Reginam*, Proclaiming the Queenship of Mary, October 11, 1954. Papal Encyclicals Online. http://www.papalencyclicals.net /Pius12/P12CAELI.HTM (accessed June 2014).

————. *Munificentissimus Deus*, On the Assumption of the Blessed Virgin Mary, November 1, 1950. Eternal World Television Network. http://www .ewtn.com/library/PAPALDOC/P12MUNIF.HTM (accessed June 2014).

Secondary Sources

Aesthetics

Balthasar, Hans Urs von. *The Glory of the Lord: A Theological Aesthetics*. Vol. 1: *Seeing the Form*. Edited by Joseph Fessio and John Riches. Translated by Erasmo Leiva-Merikakis. San Francisco, CA: Ignatius Press, 1982.

Catholic Church/History

Bergoglio, Jorge Mario, and Abraham Skorka. *On Heaven and Earth: Pope Francis on Faith, Family, and the Church in the Twenty-First Century*. Translated by Alejandro Bermudez and Howard Goodman. Edited by Diego F. Rosemberg. New York: Image, 2013.

Kelly, J. N. D. *The Oxford Dictionary of Popes*. Oxford: Oxford University Press, 2006.

Kertzer, David I. *Prisoner of the Vatican: The Popes' Secret Plot to Capture Rome from the New Italian State*. Boston, MA: Houghton Mifflin Company, 2004.

Kiser, John W. *The Monks of Tibhirine: Faith, Love, and Terror in Algeria*. New York: St. Martin's Griffin, 2002.

O'Malley, John W. *Four Cultures of the West*. Cambridge, MA: The Belknap Press of Harvard University Press, 2004.

Prior, Joseph G. *The Historical Critical Method in Catholic Exegesis*. Rome: Pontifica Università Greogriana, 1999.

Vallely, Paul. *Pope Francis: Untying the Knots*. London: Bloomsbury, 2013.

Wessels, Helmut. *Neuss and St. Quirin on Foot*. Translated by John Sykes. Cologne: J.P. Bachem Verlag, 2005.

White, James F. *Roman Catholic Worship: Trent to Today*. 2nd ed. Collegeville, MN: A Pueblo Book/Liturgical Press, 2003.

Yallop, David. *In God's Name: An Investigation into the Murder of Pope John Paul I*. New ed. New York: Basic Books, 2007.

Catholic History in the United States

Chinnici, Joseph P., and Angelyn Dries, eds. *Prayer and Practice in the American Catholic Community*. American Catholic Identities: A Documentary

History. Edited by Christopher J. Kauffman. Maryknoll, NY: Orbis Books, 2000.

Dolan, Jay P. *In Search of American Catholicism: A History of Religion and Culture in Tension.* Oxford: Oxford University Press, 2002.

Gleason, Philip. *Keeping the Faith: American Catholicism Past and Present.* Notre Dame, IN: University of Notre Dame Press, 1987.

Guilday, Peter. *A History of the Councils of Baltimore 1791–1884.* New York: MacMillan Co., 1932.

Hennesey, James J. *American Catholics: A History of the Roman Catholic Community in the United States.* New York: Oxford University Press, 1981.

Orsi, Robert A. *Between Heaven and Earth: The Religious Worlds People Make and the Scholars Who Study Them.* Princeton, NJ and Oxford: Oxford University Press, 2005.

———. *The Madonna of 115th Street: Faith and Community in Italian Harlem, 1880–1950.* New Haven, CT: Yale University Press, 1985.

———. *Thank You, St. Jude: Women's Devotion to the Patron Saint of Hopeless Causes.* New Haven, CT: Yale University Press, 1996.

O'Toole, James M. "In the Court of Conscience: American Catholics and Confession, 1900–1975." In *Habits of Devotion: Catholic Religious Practice in Twentieth-Century America,* edited by James M. O'Toole, 131–85. Ithaca, NY: Cornell University Press, 2004.

Taves, Ann. *The Household of Faith: Roman Catholic Devotions in Mid-Nineteenth Century America.* Notre Dame, IN: University of Notre Dame Press, 1986.

Wangler, Thomas E. "Catholic Religious Life in Boston in the Era of Cardinal O'Connell." In *Catholic Boston: Studies in Religion and Community, 1870–1970,* edited by Robert E. Sullivan and James M. O'Toole, 239–72. Boston, MA: Roman Catholic Archbishop of Boston, 1985.

Winters, Michael Sean. "Marian Spirituality in Early America." In *American Catholic Preaching and Piety in the Time of John Carroll,* edited by Raymond J. Kupke, 87–103. Lanham, MD: University Press of America, 1991.

Church Music History/Studies

Foley, Edward. *A Lyrical Vision: The Music Documents of the US Bishops.* American Essays in Liturgy. Collegeville, MN: Liturgical Press, 2009.

———, ed. *Worship Music: A Concise Dictionary.* Collegeville, MN: A Michael Glazier Book/Liturgical Press, 2000.

Hildegard of Bingen. *Symphonia: A Critical Edition of the* Symphonia armonie celestium revelationum *[Symphony of the Harmony of Celestial Revela-*

tions]. Introduction, translations, and commentary by Barbara Newman. 2nd ed. Ithaca and London: Cornell University Press, 1998.

Lentini, Anselmo. *Te decet hymnus: l'innario della "Liturgia horarum."* Città del Vaticano: Typis Polyglottis Vaticanis, 1984.

Molloy, Michael James. "Liturgical Music as Corporate Song 3: Opportunities for Hymnody in Catholic Worship." In *Liturgy and Music: Lifetime Learning,* edited by Robin A. Leaver and Joyce Ann Zimmerman, 324–39. Collegeville, MN: Liturgical Press, 1998.

Quinn, Frank C. "Liturgical Music as Corporate Song 2: Problems of Hymnody in Catholic Worship." In *Liturgy and Music: Lifetime Learning,* edited by Robin A. Leaver and Joyce Ann Zimmerman, 308–23. Collegeville, MN: Liturgical Press, 1998.

Ruff, Anthony. *Sacred Music and Liturgical Reform: Treasures and Transformations.* Mundelein, IL: Hillenbrand Books, 2007.

Feminist and Queer Studies/Theologies

Althaus-Reid, Marcella. *From Feminist Theology to Indecent Theology.* London: SCM Press, 2004.

———. *Indecent Theology: Theological Perversions in Sex, Gender, and Politics.* London and New York: Routledge, 2000.

Beauvoir, Simone de. "Selection of *The Second Sex.*" In *Feminism in Our Time,* edited by Miriam Schneir, 3–20. New York: Vintage Books, 1994.

Boff, Leonardo. *The Maternal Face of God: The Feminine and Its Religious Expressions.* Translated by Robert R. Barr and John W. Diercksmeier. San Francisco, CA: Harper and Row, Publishers, 1987.

Cheng, Patrick S. *Radical Love: An Introduction to Queer Theology.* New York: Seabury Books, 2011.

———. *Rainbow Theology: Bridging Race, Sexuality, and Spirit.* New York: Seabury Books, 2013.

Daly, Mary. *The Church and the Second Sex: With the Feminist Postchristian Introduction and New Archaic Afterwords by the Author.* Boston, MA: Beacon Press, 1985.

Epstein, Heidi. *Melting the Venusberg: A Feminist Theology of Music.* New York: Continuum, 2004.

Friedan, Betty. "Selections from *The Feminine Mystique.*" In *Feminism in Our Time,* edited by Miriam Schneir, 48–67. New York: Vintage Books, 1994.

Gebara, Ivone, and Maria Clara Bingemar. *Mary: Mother of God, Mother of the Poor.* Translated by Phillip Berryman. Maryknoll, NY: Orbis Books, 1989.

Grey, Mary. "Europe as a Sexist Myth." In *The Power of Naming: A Concilium Reader in Feminist Liberation Theology*, edited by Elisabeth Schüssler Fiorenza, 242–49. Maryknoll, NY/London: Orbis Books/SCM Press, 1996.

Warner, Marina. *Alone of All Her Sex: The Myth and the Cult of the Virgin Mary*. New York: Random House, 1976.

Welter, Barbara. "The Cult of True Womanhood: 1820–1860." *American Quarterly* 18, no. 2 (Summer, 1966): 151–74.

Hymn Collections and Hymnal Companions/Resources/Hymnology

Boccardi, Donald. *The History of American Catholic Hymnals since Vatican II*. Chicago: GIA Publications, 2001.

Bradley, Ian. *Abide with Me: The World of Victorian Hymns*. Chicago: GIA Publications, 1997.

Budwey, Stephanie A. "Mary, Star of Hope: Marian Congregational Song as an Expression of Devotion to the Blessed Virgin Mary in the United States from 1854 to 2010." *The Hymn* 63, no. 2 (Spring 2012): 7–17.

Daw, Jr., Carl P. *To Sing God's Praise: 18 Metrical Canticles*. Carol Stream, IL: Hope Publishing Company, 1992.

———. *A Year of Grace: Hymns for the Church Year*. Carol Stream, IL: Hope Publishing Company, 1990.

Dobbs-Mickus, Kelly, ed. *Worship*, 4th ed. Chicago: GIA Publications, 2011.

Downing, Edith Sinclair. *Sing Praise for Faithful Women*. Edited by Lucia Sullivan. Colfax, NC: Wayne Leupold Editions, 2009.

Forman, Kristen L., ed. *The New Century Hymnal Companion: A Guide to the Hymns*. Cleveland, OH: Pilgrim Press, 1998.

Glover, Raymond F., ed. *The Hymnal 1982 Companion*. 3 vols. New York: The Church Hymnal Corporation, 1990–94.

Graham, Fred. *"With One Heart and One Voice": A Core Repertory of Hymn Tunes Published for Use in the Methodist Episcopal Church in the United States, 1808–1878*. Lanham, MD: Scarecrow Press, 2004.

Higginson, J. Vincent. *Handbook for American Catholic Hymnals*. New York: The Hymn Society of America, 1976.

———. *History of American Catholic Hymnals*. Springfield, OH: The Hymn Society of America, 1982.

Hommerding, Alan J. *Song of the Spirit*. Schiller Park, IL: World Library Publications, 2002.

Hymn Society of the United States and Canada. "New Hymn and Tune." *The Hymn* 41, no. 1 (January 1990): 36.

Lenti, Vincent A. "The Face That Most Resembles Christ." *The Hymn* 45, no. 2 (April 1994): 18–22.

Stulken, Marilyn Kay, and Catherine Salika. *Hymnal Companion to Worship.* 3rd ed. Chicago: GIA Publications, 1998.

Thompson, Thomas A. "The Popular Marian Hymn in Devotion and Liturgy." *Marian Studies* XLV (1994): 121–51.

Tice, Adam M. L. *Woven into Harmony: 50 Hymn Texts.* Chicago: GIA Publications, 2009.

Wallace, Robin Knowles. *Moving Toward Emancipatory Language: A Study of Recent Hymns.* Drew University Studies in Liturgy Series 8, edited by Kenneth E. Rowe and Robin A. Leaver. Lanham, MD, and London: The Scarecrow Press, 1999.

Watson, J. R., and Emma Hornby, eds. *The Canterbury Dictionary of Hymnology.* http://www.hymnology.co.uk/.

Hymnody in the United States

Hobbs, June Hadden. *"I Sing for I Cannot Be Silent": The Feminization of American Hymnody, 1870–1920.* Pittsburgh, PA: University of Pittsburgh Press, 1997.

Marini, Stephen A. *Sacred Song in America: Religion, Music, and Public Culture.* Urbana, IL: University of Illinois Press, 2003.

Stowe, David W. *How Sweet the Sound: Music in the Lives of Spiritual Americans.* Cambridge, MA: Harvard University Press, 2004.

Liturgical History/Studies

Baldovin, John F. *Bread of Life, Cup of Salvation: Understanding the Mass.* Lanham, MD: A Sheed and Ward Book/Rowman and Littlefield Publishers, 2003.

———. *The Urban Character of Christian Worship: The Origins, Development, and Meaning of Stational Liturgy.* Rome: Pont. Institutum Studiorum Orientalium, 1987.

Bishop, Edmund. "The Genius of the Roman Rite." Chap. 1 (pp. 1–19). In *Liturgica Historica: Papers on the Liturgy and Religious Life of the Western Church.* Oxford: Clarendon Press, 1962.

Bradshaw, Paul F. *The Search for the Origins of Christian Worship: Sources and Methods for the Study of Early Liturgy.* New York: Oxford University Press, 2002.

Bradshaw, Paul F., and Maxwell E. Johnson. *The Origins of Feasts, Fasts, and Seasons in Early Christianity.* London and Collegeville, MN: SPCK and Liturgical Press, 2011.

Brennan, R. E. "The Leonine Prayers." *American Ecclesiastical Review* 125 (1951): 85–94.

Bugnini, Annibale. *The Reform of the Liturgy 1948–1975*. Translated by Matthew J. O'Connell. Collegeville, MN: Liturgical Press, 1990.

Crystal, David. "Liturgical Language in a Sociolinguistic Perspective." In *Language and the Worship of the Church*, edited by David Jasper and R. C. D. Jasper, 120–46. New York: St. Martin's Press, 1990.

Duffy, Eamon. *The Stripping of the Altars: Traditional Religion in England 1400–1580*. New Haven, CT: Yale University Press, 2005.

Francis, Mark R. "Liturgy and Popular Piety in a Historical Perspective." In *Directory on Popular Piety and the Liturgy: Principles and Guidelines. A Commentary*, edited by Peter C. Phan, 19–43. Collegeville, MN: Liturgical Press, 2002.

Harper, John. *The Forms and Orders of Western Liturgy from the Tenth to the Eighteenth Century: A Historical Introduction and Guide for Students and Musicians*. Oxford: Clarendon Press, 1991.

Jungmann, Joseph A. *Christian Prayer through the Centuries*. Translated by John Coyne. New York: Paulist Press, 1978.

———. *The Mass of the Roman Rite: Its Origins and Development (Missarum Sollemnia)*. Translated by Francis A. Brunner. 2 vols. Westminster, MD: Christian Classics, 1986.

Mitchell, Nathan D. "Theological Principles for an Evaluation and Renewal of Popular Piety." In *Directory on Popular Piety and the Liturgy: Principles and Guidelines; A Commentary*, edited by Peter C. Phan, 59–76. Collegeville, MN: Liturgical Press, 2002.

Parker, Elizabeth C. "Architecture as Liturgical Setting." In *The Liturgy of the Medieval Church*, edited by Thomas J. Heffernan and E. Ann Matter, 273–326. Kalamazoo, MI: Medieval Institute Publications, 2001.

Rutherford, Richard. *The Death of a Christian: The Order of Christian Funerals*. Rev. ed. Collegeville, MN: Liturgical Press, 1990.

Taft, Robert. "How Liturgies Grow: The Evolution of the Byzantine 'Divine Liturgy.'" *Orientalia Christiana Periodica* 43 (1977): 8–30. http://jbburnett.com/resources/taft,%20evolution%20of%ltg.pdf (accessed August 2014).

Walsh, Christopher. "Stations of the Cross." In *The New Westminster Dictionary of Liturgy and Worship*, edited by Paul Bradshaw, 450. Louisville and London: Westminster John Knox Press, 2002.

Westerfield Tucker, Karen B. "Christian Rituals Surrounding Death." In *Life Cycles in Jewish and Christian Worship*, edited by Paul F. Bradshaw and Lawrence A. Hoffman, 196–213. Notre Dame, IN: University of Notre Dame Press, 1996.

White, James F. *Protestant Worship: Traditions in Transition*. Louisville, KY: Westminster/John Knox Press, 1989.

Liturgical Movement

Beauduin, Lambert. *Liturgy the Life of the Church*. Translated by Virgil Michel. Collegeville, MN: Liturgical Press, 1926.

Botte, Bernard. *From Silence to Participation: An Insider's View of Liturgical Renewal*. Translated by John Sullivan. Washington, DC: The Pastoral Press, 1988.

Michel, Virgil. "Liturgy as the Basis of Social Regeneration." *Orate Fratres* 9 (1935): 536–45.

Pecklers, Keith. *Dynamic Equivalence: The Living Language of Christian Worship*. Collegeville, MN: A Pueblo Book/Liturgical Press, 2003.

———. *The Unread Vision: The Liturgical Movement in the United States of America: 1926–1955*. Collegeville, MN: Liturgical Press, 1998.

Liturgical Theology

Hoffman, Lawrence A. *Beyond the Text: A Holistic Approach to Liturgy*. Bloomington, IN: Indiana University Press, 1987.

Kavanagh, Aidan. *On Liturgical Theology: The Hale Memorial Lectures of Seabury-Western Theological Seminary, 1981*. New York: Pueblo Pub. Co., 1984.

Morrill, Bruce T. *Anamnesis as Dangerous Memory: Political and Liturgical Theology in Dialogue*. Collegeville, MN: A Pueblo Book/Liturgical Press, 2000.

Zimmerman, Joyce Ann. *Liturgy and Hermeneutics*. American Essays in Liturgy, edited by Edward Foley. Collegeville, MN: Liturgical Press, 1999.

Marian Apparitions

Blackbourn, David. "Apparitions of the Virgin Mary in Nineteenth-Century Europe," in *Marpingen: Apparitions of the Virgin Mary in a Nineteenth-Century German Village*, 3–41. New York: Vintage Books, 1993.

Matter, E. Ann. "Apparitions of the Virgin Mary in the Late Twentieth Century: Apocalyptic, Representation, Politics." *Religion* 31 (2001): 125–53.

Marian Devotion (Catholic)

Agbasiere, Joseph Therese. "The Rosary: Its History and Relevance." *African Ecclesial Review (AFER)* 30 (August 1988): 242–54.

Boss, Sarah Jane. "Telling the Beads: The Practice and Symbolism of the Rosary." In *Popular Devotions*, edited by Lawrence S. Cunningham, 64–75. London: The Way Publications, 2001.

Buono, Anthony M. *The Greatest Marian Prayers: Their History, Meaning, and Usage*. New York: Alba House, 1999.

de Flon, Nancy. "Mary in Nineteenth-Century English and American Poetry." In *Mary: The Complete Resource*, edited by Sarah Jane Boss, 503–20. Oxford: Oxford University Press, 2007.

Duffy, Eamon. *Faith of Our Fathers: Reflections on Catholic Tradition*. London and New York: Continuum, 2004.

Fulton, Rachel. *From Judgment to Passion: Devotion to Christ and the Virgin Mary, 800–1200*. New York: Columbia University Press, 2002.

Kane, Paula M. "Marian Devotion since 1940: Continuity or Casualty?" In *Habits of Devotion: Catholic Religious Practice in Twentieth-Century America*, edited by James M. O'Toole, 88–129. Ithaca, NY: Cornell University Press, 2004.

Kelly, Timothy, and Joseph Kelly. "Our Lady of Perpetual Help, Gender Roles, and the Decline of Devotional Catholicism." *Journal of Social History* 32, no. 1 (Fall 1998): 5–24.

O'Sullivan, Daniel. *Marian Devotion in Thirteenth-Century French Lyric*. Toronto: University of Toronto Press, 2005.

Pope, Barbara Corrado. "Immaculate and Powerful: The Marian Revival in the Nineteenth Century." In *Immaculate & Powerful: The Female in Sacred Image and Social Reality*, edited by Clarissa W. Atkinson, Constance H. Buchanan, and Margaret R. Miles, 173–200. Boston, MA: Beacon Press, 1985.

Rothenberg, David J. "The Marian Symbolism of Spring, ca. 1200–ca. 1500: Two Case Studies." *Journal of the American Musicological Society* 59, no. 2 (Summer 2006): 319–98.

Ruether, Rosemary Radford. "Mary in US Catholic Culture: Two Theologies Represent Deep Divisions." *National Catholic Reporter* (February 10, 1995): 15–17.

Saylors, Darris Catherine. "The Virgin Mary: A Paradoxical Model for Roman Catholic Immigrant Women of the Nineteenth Century." *Journal of the National Collegiate Honors Council*, Spring/Summer (2007): 109–44.

Zimmerman, Joyce Ann. "Veneration of the Holy Mother of God." In *Directory on Popular Piety and the Liturgy: Principles and Guidelines. A Commentary*, edited by Peter C. Phan, 101–12. Collegeville, MN: Liturgical Press, 2005.

Marian Liturgical Studies

Calabuig, Ignazio M. "The Liturgical Cult of Mary in the East and West." In *Liturgical Time and Space*. Vol. 5 of *Handbook for Liturgical Studies*, edited by Anscar J. Chupungco, 219–97. Collegeville, MN: Liturgical Press, 2000.

Johnson, Maxwell E. "*Sub Tuum Praesidium*: The *Theotokos* in Christian Life and Worship before Ephesus." In *The Place of Christ in Liturgical Prayer: Trinity, Christology, and Liturgical Theology*, edited by Bryan D. Spinks, 243–67. Collegeville, MN: A Pueblo Book/Liturgical Press, 2008.

Jounel, Pierre. "The Veneration of Mary." In *Liturgy and Time*. Vol. 4 of *The Church at Prayer: An Introduction to the Liturgy*, edited by Aimé Georges Martimort, 130–50. Collegeville, MN: Liturgical Press, 1986.

McDonnell, Kilian. "The Marian Liturgical Tradition." In *Between Memory and Hope: Readings on the Liturgical Year*, edited by Maxwell E. Johnson, 385–400. Collegeville, MN: Liturgical Press, 2000.

O'Donnell, Christopher. *At Worship with Mary: A Pastoral and Theological Study*. Wilmington, DE: Michael Glazier, 1988.

Mariology

von Balthasar, Hans Urs. *Mary for Today*. San Francisco, CA: Ignatius Press, 1987.

Boss, Sarah Jane. *Empress and Handmaid: On Nature and Gender in the Cult of the Virgin Mary*. London and New York: Cassell, 2000.

Brown, Raymond E., Karl P. Donfried, Joseph A. Fitzmyer, and John Reumann, eds. *Mary in the New Testament*. New York: Paulist Press, 1978.

Butler, Sara. "The Immaculate Conception: Why Was It Defined as a Dogma? And What Was Defined?" In *Studying Mary: The Virgin Mary in Anglican and Roman Catholic Theology & Devotion; The ARCIC Working Papers*, edited by Adelbert Denaux and Nicholas Sagovsky, 147–64. New York and London: T & T Clark, 2007.

Carroll, Michael P. *The Cult of the Virgin Mary: Psychological Origins*. Princeton, NJ: Princeton University Press, 1986.

Dodds, Monica, and Bill Dodds. *Encyclopedia of Mary*. Huntington, IN: Our Sunday Visitor, 2007.

Gambero, Luigi. *Mary and the Fathers of the Church: The Blessed Virgin Mary in Patristic Thought*. San Francisco, CA: Ignatius Press, 1999.

Graef, Hilda. *The Devotion to Our Lady*. New York, NY: Hawthorn Books, 1963.

———. *Mary: A History of Doctrine and Devotion; With a New Chapter Covering Vatican II and Beyond by Thomas A. Thompson*. Notre Dame, IN: Ave Maria Press, 2009.

Johnson, Elizabeth. *Truly Our Sister: A Theology of Mary in the Communion of the Saints*. New York: Continuum, 2003.

Miravalle, Mark, ed. *Coredemptrix, Mediatrix, Advocate: Theological Foundations; Towards a Papal Definition?* Santa Barbara, CA: Queenship Publishing, 1995.

O'Carroll, Michael. *Theotokos: A Theological Encyclopedia of the Blessed Virgin Mary*. Wilmington, DE: Michael Glazier, 1986.

Pelikan, Jaroslav. *Mary through the Centuries: Her Place in the History of Culture*. New Haven, CT: Yale University Press, 1996.

Rubin, Miri. *Mother of God: A History of the Virgin Mary*. New Haven, CT and London: Yale University Press, 2009.

Tavard, George. *The Thousand Faces of the Virgin Mary*. Collegeville, MN: Liturgical Press, 1996.

Thurian, Max. *Mary, Mother of all Christians*. Translated by Neville B. Cryer. New York: Herder and Herder, 1964.

Vischer, Lukas. "Mary—Symbol of the Church and Symbol of Humankind." *Mid-Stream* 17 (January 1978): 1–12.

Protestant Hymnody/Marian Devotion

Jensen, Bonnie. "We Sing Mary's Song." In *American Magnificat: Protestants on Mary of Guadalupe*, edited by Maxwell E. Johnson, 167–69. Collegeville, MN: Liturgical Press, 2010.

Mouw, Richard J., and Mark A. Noll, eds. *Wonderful Words of Life: Hymns in American Protestant History and Theology*. The Calvin Institute of Christian Worship Liturgical Studies Series, edited by John D. Witvliet. Grand Rapids, MI: Eerdmans Publishing Company, 2004.

Sociological Studies

Ariès, Philippe. *The Hour of Our Death: The Classic History of Western Attitudes toward Death over the Last One Thousand Years*. Translated by Helen Weaver. New York: Vintage Books, 1981.

Castelli, Jim, and Joseph Gremillion. *The Emerging Parish: The Notre Dame Study of Catholic Life since Vatican II*. San Francisco, CA: Harper and Row, Publishers, 1987.

Heriveu-Léger, Danièle. *Religion as a Chain of Memory*. Translated by Simon Lee. New Brunswick, NJ: Rutgers University Press, 2000.

Hoge, Dean R., William D. Dinges, Mary Johnson, and Juan L. Gonzales Jr. *Young Adult Catholics: Religion in the Culture of Choice*. Notre Dame, IN: University of Notre Dame Press, 2001.

Theology of Music

Blackwell, Albert L. *The Sacred in Music*. Louisville, KY: Westminster John Knox Press, 1999.

Milwaukee Symposia for Church Composers. "The Milwaukee Symposia for Church Composers: A Ten-Year Report (July 9, 1992)." Archdiocese of Milwaukee. http://www.archmil.org/ArchMil/Resources/The MilwaukeeStatement.pdf (accessed June 2014).

Taylor, W. David O., ed. *For the Beauty of the Church: Casting a Vision for the Arts*. Grand Rapids, MI: Baker Books, 2010.

US Historical/Religious History and Theology

Cone, James H. *The Cross and the Lynching Tree*. Maryknoll, NY: Orbis Books, 2011.

Shilts, Randy. *And the Band Played On: Politics, People, and the AIDS Epidemic*. New York: St. Martin's Griffin, 1987.

Thurman, Howard. *A Strange Freedom: The Best of Howard Thurman on Religious Experience and Public Life*. Edited by Walter Earl Fluker and Catherine Tumber. Boston, MA: Beacon Press, 1998.

Vatican II and Ecumenism

Alberigo, Giuseppe, ed. *History of Vatican II*. English version edited by Joseph A. Komonchak. 4 vols. Maryknoll, NY: Orbis; Leuven: Peeters, 1995–2003.

Flannery, Austin, ed. *Vatican Council II: The Conciliar and Postconciliar Documents*. Collegeville, MN: Liturgical Press, 2014.

McDannell, Colleen. *The Spirit of Vatican II: A History of Catholic Reform in America*. New York: Basic Books, A Member of the Perseus Books Group, 2011.

O'Malley, John W. "Introduction." In *Vatican II: Did Anything Happen?*, edited by David G. Schultenover, 1–23. New York: Continuum, 2007.

———. *Tradition and Transition: Historical Perspectives on Vatican II*. Wilmington, DE: Michael Glazier, 1989.

———. "Vatican II: Did Anything Happen?" In *Vatican II: Did Anything Happen?*, edited by David G. Schultenover, 52–91. New York: Continuum, 2007.

———. *What Happened at Vatican II*. Cambridge, MA: The Belknap Press of Harvard University Press, 2008.

Rynne, Xavier. *Vatican Council II*. Maryknoll, NY: Orbis Books, 1993.

General Index

Index of Hymn Authors, Composers, Texts, Tunes, and Hymnals

Hymn Tunes

Hymnals